International Securitisation

Zoë Shaw is Director, Corporate Finance at WestLB UK Ltd where she is responsible for arranging and distributing asset-backed securities. She has recently concluded the first securitisation of an unsecured personal loan portfolio in the UK. In her previous role as a vice president at Bank of America International, she concluded a number of mortgage-backed transactions for the subsidiaries of life companies and other specialised lenders. She is the Course Director for Euromoney's teaching seminar on securitisation and has published several articles on the subject as well as being a regular conference speaker. She is a graduate of Cambridge University.

International Securitisation

The scope, development and future outlook for asset-backed finance

Editor: **Zoë Shaw**

M
stockton
press

Published in the United States and Canada by
STOCKTON PRESS, 1991
257 Park Avenue South,
New York, N.Y. 10010, USA

ISBN 1-56159-025-8

First published in the United Kingdom by
MACMILLAN PUBLISHERS LTD, 1991
Distributed by Globe Book Services Ltd
Brunel Road, Houndmills
Basingstoke, Hants RG21 2XS, England

ISBN 0-333-55923-1

A catalogue record for this book
is available from The British Library.

Typeset by Wyvern Typesetting Limited, Bristol BS4 3EH
Printed in Great Britain by Antony Rowe Ltd

Contents

Contributors

Steve Almond is a group partner in the financial institutions' practice of Touche Ross, London. His current client list contains a wide range of banks, corporate financiers and centralised mortgage lenders.

His experience includes working as group head of the financial division of JP Morgan Securities and a two-year secondment to the banking supervision division of the Bank of England where his principal function was to undertake risk management reviews of banks operating in London.

Theodore V. Buerger, a founding principal of Financial Security Assurance (FSA), directs the company's international operations from FSA's London representative office. He serves as FSA's treasurer and is a member of the company's management committee. Prior to taking charge of FSA's international activities, he headed FSA's program development group, which devises new financial guaranty products.

Previously he was senior vice president and general partner of S&B Insurance Services Company and treasurer of Hanover Capital Corporation. He began his career as a certified public accountant with Price Waterhouse & Company.

Jeff Connor is a manager at Bankers Trust Australia Limited (BTAL), Sydney, Australia. On joining BTAL he worked on fixed interest analysis and advisory work on public sector fund raising and liability management. His subsequent involvement in structuring capital market products has culminated in responsibility for BTAL's securitisation initiatives. He is a chief tutor for the Institute of Actuaries of Australia's professional examinations for finance and investment.

Julie Craik is a director of Bankers Trustee Company Limited, London, and product manager of asset-backed trustee products. Bankers Trustee Company is part of Bankers Trust Company.

Anthony Cutcliffe is a vice president at Citicorp Investment Bank, London. He joined Citicorp in 1987 and works in the asset securitisation department. As well as structuring the Chariots transaction, he has worked on several UK mortgage transactions and arranged the first autoloan securitisation in Spain, which was completed in November 1990.

Peter L. R. Deckers is a partner in Slaughter and May's Paris office. He has a general commercial and banking practice in English and French law, including joint ventures, corporate investment and divestment, securitisation and other funds, project, multiple option and other financings and privatisations. He produced most of the documentation and was adviser to the joint venture company which was responsible for the creation of the first securitisation fund to be listed in France.

Thomas Federspiel is a partner in Gorrissen & Federspiel, Copenhagen, Denmark. He has worked with a French group of companies in Paris and Senegal, with law firms in Copenhagen, London and New York.

Fiona Ferguson is a partner in Slaughter and May, London specialising in corporate tax.

Eilís Ferran is a lecturer in company law, corporate finance law and securities regulation at Cambridge University, and a solicitor. She is a consultant to Slaughter and May.

Mark F. Fisher is an assistant director in the capital markets group at Samuel Montagu & Co. Ltd, London, where he is involved in structured finance for UK and European clients through both the public and private markets.

Prior to this he worked in swaps and derivatives where he gained extensive experience in issue-related transactions and the creation of repackaged assets for investors.

Ruth Fox is a partner in Slaughter and May, London. She works in the firm's Company Commercial department, dealing principally with banking and capital markets transactions.

Bruce Gaitskell is director and head of the asset-backed group at UBS Phillips & Drew, London. He is responsible for origination of asset-backed securities and provision of credit enhancement in Europe.

As the former chief executive of the CIBC-owned Mortgages plc, he was involved in the first mortgage-backed securities issue using Eurocommercial paper and the first arrears bond. He has also worked for National Home Loans Corporation. A widely travelled consultant, he is a regular conference speaker and contributor to books on securitisation.

Marc van der Haegen is a partner in Liederkerke Wolters Waelbroeck & Kirkpatrick, Brussels, Belgium. His field of activities includes corporate law, banking law, commercial and financial transactions.

Candy Helman is a vice president at JP Morgan Securities, London, responsible for the bank's European asset-backed financing activities.

Prior to this she was a banking officer at Morgan Guaranty Trust Company of New York covering UK-centralised mortgage lenders and gained extensive experience of the UK mortgage-backed securities markets. She worked on a number of innovative transactions, including the first senior-subordinated UK mortgage-backed Floating Rate Note, the first fixed-rate UK mortgage-backed bond and the first publicly rated asset-backed Eurocommercial paper programme.

Patrick Hunerwadel is an associate of the law firm Lenz & Staehelin, Zurich, Switzerland. He is an attorney at law and a lecturer on Swiss Corporation law and Code of Obligations at the university of St. Gall.

Jonathan E. Keighley is the managing director of Gracebury Securitisation Ltd., an associated company of Chartered WestLB Ltd., the international merchant bank owned jointly by Standard Chartered PLC and Westdeutsche Landesbank Girozentrale. With a background in leasing, corporate finance and capital markets he now specialises in arranging asset-backed securitisations.

Nigel King is a vice president in the Real Estate Finance Group of Salomon Brothers International Limited, London. He is primarily involved with global capital raising for securitised debt and equity for major European properties.

Prior to joining the Real Estate Finance Group, he managed a fixed-income research group which advised the trading desks and clients of Salomon Brothers on fixed-income portfolios and interest rate risk management using options and futures.

Mark Lewis is an assistant vice president and deputy head of the asset-backed group at UBS Phillips & Drew, London. His responsibilities include originating, structuring, and providing AAA-rated credit enhancement and bank funding facilities to support the issuance of asset-backed financings in both the securities and banking markets.

Lionel J. Marsland-Shaw is a vice president at Standard & Poor's London office where he is directly involved in the rating of international asset-backed financings.

A specialist in credit analysis, he spent many years with a merchant bank in the City of London and then with a merchant bank and management company in the Caribbean. On returning to the UK, he worked for the leasing company of a major international bank before taking up his present role.

Dr Otto Ortner is a partner in Ortner Poch Foramitti, Vienna, Austria. He is general counsel to Oesterreichische Kontrollbank Aktiengesellschaft and mainly advises corporate clients in Austria and abroad on all aspects of commercial law. He has published various legal articles and *Sonnenaufgang uber Osterreich* (1989).

Stephen Powell is an assistant solicitor with Slaughter and May, London. His work has particularly involved the fields of banking, capital markets and derivative products.

Blaine Roberts is a senior managing director of Bear Stearns and Co., Inc., New York. He is in charge of the financial analytics and structured transactions department.

Prior to joining Bear Stearns, he was vice president and director of mortgage-backed securities research for Merril Lynch and has been an expert consultant to the Federal Home Loan Bank Board in Washington, D.C.

Simon Robinson is a company and commercial partner in Slaughter and May, London. He advises UK and overseas clients on a wide range of banking, securities, investment management and natural resources transactions and has been involved in securitisation work since the earliest transactions were undertaken in the UK.

Donald E. Selzer is an assistant vice president at Moody's Investors Service. He is the manager of Moody's London structured finance group which is responsible for rating all securitisation transactions in the UK and providing support for the analysis of continental securitised transations.

Prior to joining Moody's London office, he was a part of the mortgage pass-through and collateralised mortgage obligations team in its New York structured finance group.

Stephen L. Wenman is chairman of the Special Risk Services group of companies, the only Lloyd's insurance brokers to focus exclusively on serving the financial sector. He has been an insurance broker continually since leaving school 24 years ago.

Simon White is assistant treasurer of Halifax Building Society, Yorkshire. He is responsible for capital markets activities, including the raising of medium- and long-term wholesale funds.

Prior to joining the Halifax in 1988, he worked as an investment banker in London. He is a member of the UK Council of Mortgage Lenders' Secondary Markets Sub-Committee.

1: Introduction and Overview

Zoë Shaw, WestLB UK Limited

Although many sections of the financial community are now broadly acquainted with the concept of securitisation it nonetheless remains a complex subject which may appear confusing or mysterious to those who have not been actively involved in structuring transactions. In order to avoid compounding these confusions we should proceed with a definition at the outset. The term 'securitisation', as described in this book, involves the packaging of designated pools of loans and receivables (with appropriate credit support) and the underwriting and sale of these packages to investors in the form of securities which are collateralised by the underlying assets and their associated income stream. Despite the manifest differences in the legal and regulatory environment in which securitisation may take place these basic principles remain more or less unchanged. Securitisation as defined here is therefore a process through which illiquid assets can be transformed into a more liquid, manageable form and distributed to a broad range of investors through the medium of the international capital markets. Since the packaging process typically involves the transfer of the underlying assets to an investment vehicle on a non-recourse basis, the sponsoring institution (the 'originator') will usually seek to account for the transaction as a sale.

The purpose of this book is to provide a comprehensive discussion of the development of securitisation outside the USA. It attempts to provide an up-to-date summary of the key legal, regulatory and structural issues in each of the major markets in which securitisation has taken root and to draw some conclusions (albeit tentative) about its future scope for development. The book is aimed at anyone interested in this new and complex area of finance, including corporate treasurers, bankers and those with a more academic interest in the development of financing techniques in the capital markets. With this audience in mind, the contributors have been drawn from highly diverse backgrounds and they each bring with them a different perspective on the issues involved. It is hoped that the breadth of topics covered will help readers to come away with a clearer understanding of the rationale for securitisation and the practical steps required to implement a programme.

Before embarking on the individual chapters it would perhaps be useful to recap on the background and development of securitisation as a source of finance. This may serve as a useful background to the chapters which follow and provide an indication of the key factors which will influence the future growth of the markets.

The logical starting point in the analysis of any market is the motivation of the major players. It will become rapidly apparent from the sections which follow that securitisation is both time-consuming and expensive. Participants will readily attest to the complexity of the issues involved. Transactions typically take many months to complete and require input from a large number of interested parties. So why bother?

Securitisation provides lenders with an alternative to traditional on-balance-sheet lending. It allows lenders to monetise previously illiquid assets, recycle cash to be invested in further receivables and to expand the volume of their business without a corresponding increase in equity capital. This process generates off-balance-sheet income since the originator retains part of the net margin on the securitised assets in the form of servicing fees which boost overall profitability and increases return on equity. Securitisation is therefore an important tool in controlling capital usage and should appeal to a wide range of institutions, including corporates managing the growth of their captive finance subsidiaries and financial institutions constrained by prudential capital ratios.

Indeed, it is the continued pressure on bank capital which is likely to provide the most important stimulus for growth in the securitised markets in the 1990s. Following the moves towards common capital standards driven by the Bank for International Settlements (BIS), banks are under greater pressure to raise new capital. However, equity investors, influenced by erratic bank earnings and the on-going effects of the LDC debt crisis, remain unreceptive and many institutions may be unable to raise new equity on acceptable terms. The structure of asset-backed securities, using thinly capitalised vehicle companies and third-party credit enhancement, allows banks to 'rent' capital from other sectors which are able, for regulatory or other reasons, to provide this support on more favourable terms. Securitisation is therefore an important tool for banks in managing their balance sheet growth and one which, in the long term, few will be able to ignore.

As securitisation gathers pace it will inevitably bring about changes in the way in which banks conduct their business. It will encourage them to move away from their traditional role of direct lender towards that of an originator or arranger, sourcing an increasing volume of business from their client base, repackaging the underlying credit and interest rate risk with appropriate enhancement techniques, and selling these restructured assets into the most efficient investor base.

It is clear that the process has advantages for issuers. However, growth of the market on an international scale requires the participation of a large number of investors.

Investors benefit from the process in a number of ways:

- A broader range of investment opportunities. This is most typically seen in the development of collateralised mortgage obligations (CMOs) in the US, where asset pools are divided into separate tranches with specific duration and maturity profiles and then sold to different categories of investors whose criteria vary.
- Asset-backed securities typically offer a yield premium over conventional debt instruments with comparable rating.
- Asset-backed securities usually offer a greater level of protection from event risk and rating downgrade due to their multiple layers of credit enhancement.
- The packaging process facilitates access to retail assets. It provides investors with the opportunity to participate in a particular market (for example the UK mortgage market) without creating a large infrastructure to lend directly to individual borrowers.

Does this process also benefit the man in the street whose loan is being securitised? In the long term, the answer is probably yes. By promoting greater efficiency in the financial system and reducing the concentration of credit and other risks in a lender's portfolio (and hence the excess equity cushion these concentrations produce), securitisation should lead to tangible cost savings in the provision of financial services which can be passed on to the consumer. These benefits have been estimated at approximately 100 basis points in the fixed rate US mortgage markets.

Securitisation as a technique has been imported from the US where, in the course of the last 20 years, the markets have grown at a rapid pace. In the US the range of assets securitised has expanded from mortgages to include credit card receivables, auto-loans, boat loans, recreational vehicle loans, corporate loans and LBO debt. Securitised debt is now available to US investors in a variety of forms allowing them to select instruments which meet specific risk and maturity preferences. The total amount of outstanding securitised mortgages as at year end 1989 stood at $904bn. Moreover $37bn of non-mortgage assets (auto receivables, credit cards) were originated in 1990 alone.

A number of key factors contributed to the successful development of this market. First, securitisation played an important role in rebalancing the mismatch in the supply of funds between the East and West Coast. Second, the existence of government agencies which sponsored the development of the market by providing a guarantee of outstanding mortgages was of considerable importance. Third, the size of the outstanding balances in the US undoubtedly permitted originators to reap economies of scale which justified the initial set-up costs involved. We shall return to this discussion later in this chapter to establish the extent to which the forces which drove the expansion of the US market are evident in Europe.

The nascent asset-backed markets outside the US appear to be poised for expansion. Perhaps the major beneficiary of US technology to date (albeit with significant adaptation) has been the UK mortgage sector. Although the first mortgage-backed transaction was issued in 1985 for a vehicle company called MINI, securitising a pool of mortgages originated by Bank of America, the market took off in earnest in 1987 when National Home Loans Corporation PLC (NHL) issued a £50m FRN (National Home Loan First Funding PLC). The champions of this new technology were the so-called centralised lenders. These companies entered the UK mortgage market in the mid 1980s with the objective of challenging the existing building society cartel through the provision of a more streamlined service and an innovative set of products. Since these companies were often operating on a smaller capital base without any access to retail deposits, securitisation fitted well into their overall strategy and allowed them to build market share rapidly.

Nearly all outstanding securitised issues in the sterling market have been floating rate notes (FRN) issued by special purpose vehicle companies (SPV). The FRNs are secured on an underlying mortgage pool and have the following characteristics: a typical stated maturity of 27–42 years; an estimated average life typically in the region of four to eight years; coupons linked to quarterly LIBOR; and the provision to redeem substantially all of the outstanding note principal prior to the final redemption date.

Each issue incorporates additional credit enhancement to provide protection against specific structural risks which arise in the packaging process, namely credit, liquidity, reinvestment and basis risk. The removal or reduction of these risks is essential in obtaining an appropriate rating, in achieving off-balance-sheet status for statutory and prudential accounting purposes and in demonstrating the integrity of the overall structure to investors. Perhaps the most important of these is credit risk, i.e. the possibility that borrowers in the underlying pool may default on their payments, leading to shortfalls in scheduled payments of principal and interest to investors. In UK mortgage-backed FRNs this risk has typically been addressed through the purchase of pool insurance or the issue of a privately placed note whose principal and interest payments are subordinated to those of senior noteholders.

All of the public securities issues in sterling have received a rating from Standard & Poor's and/or Moody's which have each established rigorous guidelines for the ratings of UK mortgage-backed transactions. The role of the rating agencies in structuring asset-backed issues is discussed below in chapters 16 and 17.

The structure of mortgage-backed FRNs clearly reflects the characteristics of the underlying UK mortgage product on which they are secured. As this pattern of retail product origination has changed, these developments have been reflected in the structure of mortgage transactions. In 1987, when the first asset-backed FRNs were issued, the pools were composed almost exclusively of 'standard' 25–30 year floating rate endowment or pension loans. The composition of collateral pools has changed significantly since the beginning of 1989. There are two main reasons for this. First, the dramatic rise in sterling mortgage rates has led to an increase in deferred interest and fixed-rate products which allow mortgagors to mitigate the effects of high short-term rates. Second, the specialised lenders have typically been innovative in offering clients more flexible products, such as self-certification loans; since these companies are still largely reliant on the wholesale markets they have been compelled to include these in securitised pools. Nearly all issues made in 1989 and 1990 incorporated a proportion of 'non-standard' products of this type.

The inclusion of these products in mortgage pools required approval from the rating agencies, credit enhancers and, in many cases, some additional financial engineering to manage a more complex cash-flow profile. In general, mortgage originators have been successful in securitising these new products without incurring significant extra cost. In chapter 6 Candy Helman describes the development of structural innovations in sterling asset-backed securities.

The investor base for sterling mortgage-backed FRNs has expanded dramatically since the initial transactions were issued in 1987 and now embraces UK, European and Far Eastern investors, including banks, corporates and fund managers. Since August 1988 building societies have been permitted to invest in sterling mortgage-backed FRNs. However, these holdings constitute 'class 3' or long-term assets for prudential purposes and were excluded from the Building Society Commissioner's Consultation paper on liquid asset regulations published at the end of 1990. This has acted as a disincentive to investment since current yields are unlikely to provide a sufficiently high return for class 3 assets.

However, concerted lobbying may produce a change in sentiment and enable building societies to recategorise mortgage-backed securities as liquid assets. The Bank of England currently allows institutions authorised under the Banking Act to apply a 50 per cent weighting to mortgage-backed securities but after 1992, when convergence occurs under BIS, this is likely to be changed to 100 per cent.

As the market has developed it has become possible to identify specific maturity preferences among investors. For example, the increase in corporate liquidity has drawn in a large number of corporate treasuries which are primarily interested in a short-term money-market security with good liquidity and a transparent credit rating. Commercial bank investors, on the other hand, are generally prepared to accept a less liquid security with a longer average life and a better return. These investor preferences have been one factor in the development of so-called 'fast-pay, slow-pay' structures where repayments from the pool are used to pay down each tranche in turn, creating securities with radically different expected average lives. This process was facilitated by the change in the Bank of England's rule concerning the issue of securities of less than five years maturity. There have been six such issues, three by the National Home Loans vehicles, Collateralised Mortgage Securities (No. 1) PLC, (No. 7) PLC and (No. 9) PLC, TMC PIMBS Third Financing PLC, MFC4 and Temple Court No. 2.

Despite the significant expansion of the investor base for mortgage-backed FRNs, secondary market liquidity remains limited. At the time of writing there are 16 major market-makers in building society FRNs whereas there are only six banks actively quoting prices for mortgage-backed notes. The bid-offer spread for mortgage-backed FRNs is correspondingly higher than that quoted for building society paper (typically 15 basis points for amounts of £0.5m compared to an average spread of 5 basis points on £5m transactions for building society debt). In addition, rated, secured mortgage-backed notes have consistently traded at higher yields than unsecured and unrated or lowly rated building society FRNs. Poor liquidity is largely explained by the structural complexity of asset-backed issues: in particular, the uncertain redemption profile.

The expansion of the investor base since 1987 has produced positive effects. For example, there has been a progressive increase in the size of new issues as the product has achieved wider acceptance. This trend is demonstrated by the TMC Programme for Issuance of Mortgage Backed Securities (PIMBS) which aimed at minimising up-front expenses by incorporating a number of different structures within one set of pre-agreed documentation and, more recently, by the £2bn STARS programme originated by Citibank Trust Ltd.

Despite the greater level of investor awareness, the all-in cost of mortgage-backed FRNs still remains relatively high given their excellent credit quality. The initial transactions were not well received by investors and were issued at progressively higher margins, culminating in Mortgage Funding Corporation No. 1 PLC which was launched at an all-in cost of LIBOR plus 0.54 per cent in February 1988. Discounted margins then fell progressively as investors became more comfortable with the instrument and this trend culminated in a number of issues in the autumn of 1989 with discounted margins of 0.22 per cent. More recently, new issue terms have deteriorated substantially and at the time of writing the most recent issue (STARS 1 referred to above) was launched at a discounted margin of 0.42 per cent. It could be argued that the major weakness of the sterling asset-backed market is its almost complete reliance upon the FRN market as a funding vehicle. Since the FRN investor base is still composed of a significant proportion of banks looking for a spread over their cost of funds this may place a floor on the levels at which sterling mortgage-backed FRNs may trade.

The desire to seek a broader institutional investor base led the Household Mortgage Corporation (HMC) to issue three fixed-rate mortgage-backed bonds, HMC Mortgage Notes 101 PLC, HMC Mortgage Notes 102 PLC, and 103 PLC which were issued in October 1988, February 1989 and May 1991.

National Home Loans also issued a fixed rate transaction, CMS No. 10, also in May 1991. These issues were designed to broaden distribution away from the traditional FRN base towards domestic and foreign institutions. Despite the poor reception given to HMC No. 102, which was issued on tight terms in a falling market, the transactions were successful in reaching a new group of investors including insurance companies and domestic and off-shore money funds. In addition, the structure relied upon a put option to finance the purchase of the fixed rate bonds at maturity. Since writers of such put options (typically AAA entities) are relatively uncommon, it is unlikely that this or a similar structure could become a standard feature of the market.

Bear Stearns Mortgage Securities No. 1 PLC represented the first attempt to fund a fixed rate 25-year mortgage portfolio by issuing a long-term fixed-rate instrument targeted at institutional investors. This transaction was similar to the US fixed-rate 'pass-through' structure in which principal redemptions on the underlying fixed rate mortgages are applied in redeeming notes on each monthly interest payment date; investors are therefore exposed to considerable risk if the average life proves shorter than the estimated figure of ten years. The issue was priced at a yield of 150 basis points over the 9 per cent of 2008 gilt and was mainly targeted at UK and European institutional investors. However, there was considerable resistance to the concept and it is not certain whether this market could be developed further without considerably more effort to educate institutional investors about this type of instrument and the associated risks. The absence of a developed sterling fixed-rate mortgage market makes this task more difficult, since statistics on prepayment rates are not readily available and it is difficult to project the average life of such transactions with any degree of accuracy.

There have been well over 50 public mortgage-backed issues in the sterling market and outstanding securitised debt exceeds £10bn. However, the composition of the originators of this debt is perhaps less encouraging. Issuance in the public market has been confined almost exclusively to the centralised lenders and foreign banks. Only two UK banks have issued (Barclays and TSB); one insurance company has issued twice (Legal & General); and no building societies have entered the FRN market (the Leamington Spa accessed the commercial paper market, although the transaction was subsequently unwound). These figures are even more interesting when one considers the breakdown of market share in the UK with the building societies and banks accounting for approximately 90 per cent of mortgage lending. The attitude of the banks and building societies to securitisation are investigated in more detail in chapters 3 and 5 respectively. Until these important lenders can be induced to enter the market its scope for further development may be limited.

The opportunity for the securitisation of non-mortgage assets in the UK has been given a considerable fillip by the successful launch of the first issue backed by a pool of car loans (Cardiff Automobile Receivable Securitisation (UK) PLC) in July 1990. (A detailed description of this transaction is included in chapter 7.) This has spawned the hope of further issues, possibly by banks, since the assets have a 100 per cent weighting under the Bank of England guidelines and are therefore more attractive than mortgages since the amount of capital released by their sale is significantly greater.

More recently the first issue of a sterling security backed by a portfolio of commercial properties was launched (BHH International Finance PLC). The transaction was structured as a £90m FRN guaranteed by an FSA surety bond. The transaction may prove to be an important landmark in establishing a blueprint for the pooling of commercial properties (see chap. 8). This structure is likely to be of interest to numerous institutions seeking to expand the opportunities for the funding of property portfolios through the capital markets.

Although the UK asset-backed market is currently the most developed European sector, the technology has begun to spread to other areas. In France, for example, a legal framework was established in 1988 which laid the foundations for a broad market in asset-backed securities ('Titrisation'). Securitisation takes place through investment funds (*Fonds Communs de Créances* or FCCs) which hold the loans and fund them through the issue of units. The FCC is established jointly by a management company and a depositary which holds the loans and the accounts of the FCC. The FCCs cannot be used for any purpose other than the purchase of the loans and issuance of the units and cannot file for bankruptcy.

In addition, there are a number of other guidelines which must be adhered to. Assets securitised must, for example, have a minimum original maturity of two years and no substitution is permitted. This stipulation originally precluded the possibility of securitising credit card or trade receivables, although the Commission Bancaire is now reviewing this situation with a view to relaxing its regulations to accommodate transactions of this kind. The resulting issue must have a credit rating and an appropriate form of credit enhancement.

Unlike the UK, however, mortgages were not the most immediate candidate for securitisation, largely because of the structure of the mortgage market, with asset yields below the level necessary to cover the costs of securitisation. Indeed, the first French securitisation took place at the end of 1989 and involved the repackaging of 22 loans to French stock brokerage firms.

Since that date there have been a further 13 transactions (including one offshore issue backed by auto loans) and the estimated outstandings now exceed Ffr 19bn. The full impact of this new financing opportunity and the legal and regulatory framework in France are discussed in chapter 9.

In Italy, the first lira-denominated transaction was completed in 1990 (Chariots No. 1 Ltd) in which Citicorp sub-participated a pool of L222bn auto-loans generated by its Italian subsidiary, Citicorp Finanziaria SpA (Citifin). In general, the prospects for future growth of the Lira market are perceived to be favourable. Moody's estimates that Italian automobile loan originations, for example, total L4,600bn (£2.1bn) annually. Certainly a number of the major Italian banks were rumoured to be looking carefully at the concept of securitisation, notably Istituto San Paolo di Torino through its collaboration with Salomon Brothers. (For more on the Italian market see chapter 10.)

The Scandinavian market is also an area of considerable potential. The first securitisation of a portfolio of Swedish mortgages (and the first Continental European mortgage securitisation) was completed in November 1990 (Osprey Mortgage Securities (No. 1) Ltd). The transaction securitised a portfolio of Skr1bn fixed-rate mortgages secured on single family houses in Sweden through a US dollar FRN. The Swedish krona mortgage market has estimated outstanding balances of approximately Skr600bn (£60bn) and the prospects for future issues are therefore very favourable (see chap. 18).

Other issuers have accessed the fixed-rate US dollar sector to fund pools of foreign currency denominated assets. In 1989, for example, there were two fixed-rate issues (GMBS nos. 1 and 3), which were backed by pools of New Zealand and Australian dollar mortgages respectively. Both transactions were issued with a guarantee from Financial Security Assurance and included currency swaps to generate funding in the originator's domestic currency. (The background of these transactions is discussed in chapter 11.) In certain circumstances this route may provide originators with a more liquid marketplace for securitised debt than their domestic sector, providing the additional structural complexities can be overcome at reasonable cost. This is particularly the case in New Zealand dollars, for example, where the domestic capital market is relatively small and lacking in sophistication. It is less so in Australia, however, where there is a relatively well developed asset-backed sector with outstandings of approximately US$4bn.

The market for asset-backed US-dollar-denominated Eurobonds has expanded significantly throughout the last year. To a large extent this has been driven by the global issues of credit-card-backed debt launched by the US banks (in particular by Citicorp). These transactions involved the securitisation of US dollar credit card debt originated by Citicorp in the US. Nonetheless, the significant increase in volume has led to a deterioration in pricing and it remains to be seen whether this sector will be capable of absorbing large volumes of new paper.

Other countries, too, are currently examining the potential for development of an asset-backed sector, notably Spain, Germany and Japan. The extent to which the technology takes root in these markets will depend upon a number of factors, including the financial circumstances of the potential users (commercial banks, corporates, finance companies), the legal framework and regulatory environment. In Germany, for example, the sale of assets is viewed in an extremely negative light by the major commercial banks and it is not clear whether there is sufficient scope for development outside of the banking community, although a number of the major corporates, including Volkswagen, are known to have been contemplating it. In Germany the two transactions arranged to date are KKB's DM 230 million Schuldschein issue supported by a letter of credit from WestLB and a private transaction to fund equipment lease receivables funded using USCP. In Spain Citifin Espana issued a PTS 7 billion unrated private placement to fund fixed-rate auto loans supported by a partial guarantee from UBS. This transaction is discussed in more detail by Mark Lewis in Chapter 13.

The preceding discussion has provided an indication of the overall size and scope of securitisation outside the US. The technology has begun to pervade a number of quite diverse markets and, although it is still largely in the development stage, it would appear that there is ample scope for growth in the next few years as information becomes more widely disseminated among both issuers and investors. Nonetheless, it is all too easy to exaggerate the ease with which the international securitisation markets can develop. There are many outstanding obstacles which are unlikely to be removed in the short term and due weight must be given to these if we are to arrive at a balanced assessment of the market's potential.

It might be useful at this point to make a general comparison with the US. It is undoubtedly true that the success of securitisation in the US was fostered, in part, by the enormous size of the domestic credit markets; the homogeneity of the underlying assets; the development of a consistent approach in the legal, accounting and regulatory treatment of securitisation; and a deep and relatively sophisticated capital market. It might be argued that securitisation will become truly viable only if Europe develops a single market and common currency which would allow institutions to originate assets across borders and benefit from much greater economies of scale. This point can be illustrated by consideration of a number of areas which influence the structure and timing of transactions.

Regulatory environment

The Bank of England has ventured forth with a paper (*Loan Transfers and Securitisation*) which outlines its basic approach to asset sales by banks governed by it. This paper has undoubtedly influenced other central banks in their approach to securitisation and has been largely incorporated by the Accounting Standards Committee in the UK in the detailed provisions relating to securitised mortgages in Exposure Drafts 49 and 50. The French authorities have, as we have seen, introduced specific legislation dealing with securitisation which sets out guidelines for the structure of transactions. As yet, however, there are no generally applied rules as there are for bank capital ratios. Indeed, the inconsistencies between regulators are apparent. The Commission Bancaire has recently stated its intention to modify existing legislation to permit the securitisation of credit cards. The Bank of England, however, appears to be opposed to credit card securitisation on the grounds that the issuing vehicle and the originator should be entirely separate and that this is more difficult to accommodate in the securitisation of revolving credits. If the securitised markets continue to grow, regulators may be forced to consider the introduction of general standards applicable to all banks. However, this appears to be a remote possibility at present.

Legal and tax issues
Legal and tax issues are clearly a major consideration in structuring particular transactions. Some of the key issues in different markets will be discussed in greater detail in chapters 18 and 19. However, it is clear that individual legal systems have an individual approach to the transfer of assets and there may be considerable obstacles to securitisation arising from different legal or tax treatment. The difficulties inherent in accommodating legal differences even within national boundaries can be demonstrated by the problems experienced in the UK in securitising Scottish mortgages. It is also important to note that the French had to introduce specific legislation to facilitate securitisation. Due consideration must also be given to the introduction of European Community legislation such as the Seventh EC Directive, which was incorporated into the Companies Act 1989 in the UK.

Accounting treatment
The impact of accounting treatment is discussed in chapter 20. In the UK, for example, there are still significant differences within the accounting professions as to the correct approach to the treatment of off-balance-sheet finance. Confusion over future accounting treatment is a major difficulty facing UK originators in considering the securitisation of assets as a means of balance sheet management. These difficulties will be resolved when the profession adopts a consistent attitude to off-balance-sheet finance.

Cost of securitisation
The cost of securitisation is considerable. The process requires large amounts of development work in advance of an issue and large up-front expenses. Securitisation is generally appropriate only where the originator can recover its investment costs through a continuous programme of issues over a long period. However, individual European credit markets are frequently small and there is often inadequate scope for repeat issues.

There are notable exceptions to this, such as the UK mortgage market (outstanding balances of £290bn), but in many cases the existing balances are too small to justify securitisation. This situation contrasts dramatically with the US market, where total mortgage debt, for example, (securitised and non-securitised) totalled US$2.4 trillion at year end 1989.

Arbitrage opportunities
Another important factor which has contributed to the growth of the US market is the possibility which securitisation presents to certain categories of US issuers to obtain significant cost savings by repackaging assets. For example, a single-A-rated corporation may be able to obtain a net saving (after all additional costs are taken into account) by repackaging high quality receivables in the form of a AAA security. This is largely because the cost differential between issues with different ratings (i.e. AAA, AA, etc.) tends to be very wide and this in turn creates a favourable arbitrage. As things currently stand in the European markets these substantial savings are not yet available to issuers since the cost differential between a triple-A asset-backed security issued in the euromarkets and the equivalent cost of on-balance-sheet medium-term funding can be negative. However, as the costs of on-balance-sheet funding rise as they have done so recently, this differential will narrow markedly.

Relative capital requirements
It is clear that one of the major forces driving the securitisation of assets in the US was the relatively weak capital ratios of the thrifts and, more recently, of many of the major US banks. To some extent, as we have indicated, there is a capital shortage among many European banks. However, given the diversity of individual markets and different access to capital, the requirements of particular institutions will vary considerably. For example, the French and Italian banking sectors are relatively undercapitalised, while German banks and some of the UK banks are comfortably above minimum BIS capital ratios. This may be a factor which retards the growth of individual markets where domestic financial institutions are not constrained by balance sheet considerations.

1990 and 1991 have been years of considerable progress in the development of European securitisation. In the sterling market, despite the difficulties experienced by the UK housing market and the resulting downturn in new issue volume, there have been pioneering transactions in the commercial property and auto-loan sectors. 1990 has also seen the first securitised transactions in Sweden, Italy, Germany and Spain. These are clear indications that the technology has become widely understood in Europe and other issuers are likely to follow suit.

Notwithstanding these positive signs, we have also seen that the process of packaging and selling assets is not without its complexities. This will undoubtedly influence the pace at which the securitised markets develop. Most notable among these problems are the relatively high costs of issue (including considerable development costs); differences in regulatory and accounting treatment; and the fragmented nature of the individual currency sectors in Europe which reduce economies of scale.

Although these represent significant short-term obstacles to growth, there are other forces at work which will be favourable for securitisation. Perhaps the most important of these is the trend towards convergence of capital adequacy standards under the influence of the BIS guidelines. This will be a major factor in encouraging banks to manage asset growth and securitisation is a natural solution to these balance sheet constraints. As more issues are launched in a range of currency markets investors will become increasingly aware of the advantages offered by asset-backed securities and, as the international investor base expands, costs should fall in the longer term.

The forces underpinning the expansion of the market are therefore very strong and its advantages to issuers and investors are likely to be too great to be ignored. Securitisation will almost certainly become a permanent feature of the financial scene throughout the 1990s.

2: The Risks of Asset-Backed Securities: Lessons from History

Theodore V. Buerger, Financial Security Assurance

Asset-backed securities (ABS) form one of the safest classes of investments. They have far lower default than unsecured corporate bonds, less exposure to LBO event risk and far better recoveries in the rare instances of default. This is not to say, however, that asset-backed securities are risk-free. Despite the high quality of ABS, default is not impossible, and downgrade, which can have serious negative consequences for trading value, is a constant concern.

First of all, ABS depend on the cash flows and, sometimes, liquidation values of discrete pools of assets. The investor must be assured of the quality of the assets today and of adequate protection against deterioration of asset quality tomorrow. This is the 'asset quality risk'.

Potentially more treacherous, and certainly less well understood by many investors, is 'securitisation risk', which arises from the complex structured nature of these financings. The buyer of an asset-backed security invests only indirectly in the underlying assets but invests directly in the structure that repackages the assets. Thus, even if assets perform as expected, the investment is at risk in terms of its technical framework and the various participants in the securitisation structure.

The consequences of a structural failure can be far more severe than those related to asset quality. An asset quality problem can lead to a lowered rating and, in extreme circumstances, insufficient cash flows, but a problem with the securitisation structure can lead to a loss of rating, a complete interruption of payments or even the invalidity of the securities themselves.

Not only do securitisation risks have severe potential consequences; they can also be difficult to identify, especially because of the complexity of asset-backed financings. Simply put, the more things that have to go right at the same time, the more likely it will be that something will go wrong.

Moreover, even superficially similar transactions can vary greatly. As Fitch Investors Service, Inc. pointed out, writing of credit card securitisations:

> Various forms of credit enhancement techniques combined with innovative legal and financial structures have been used to substantially mitigate or eliminate credit

> concerns. Nevertheless, in Fitch's view there are clear quality gradations of credit strength and payment structures among these highly rated securities.[1]

This chapter examines both categories of risk in light of the admittedly short history of the asset-backed securities market. Most of the examples provided come from the US market, where the technology of structured finance has been tested for the longest time. In a few cases, where relevant, precedents are cited from outside the asset-backed market.[2]

2.1 ASSET RISK

Of the two types of risk—asset risk and securitisation risk—the former is the more straightforward to evaluate. Nevertheless, investors must guard against a false sense of security. Asset analysis is not an exact science.

The layman's instinct is first to make a reasonable estimate of losses over the life of the security, based primarily on historical losses reported in a prospectus. A multiple of these levels might then seem to determine the amount of overcollateralisation or other forms of first-loss protection that is needed to absorb defaults in the underlying portfolio under worst-case conditions.

Unfortunately, statistical analysis of historical data is insufficient to determine the required level of loss protection. Ultimately there is no substitute for informed judgement. To give some examples:

1. *Underwriting inconsistency*—The portfolio being securitised may not reflect the same origination standards, procedures and/or quality as the portfolio on which the historical data is based.
2. *Favourable historical factors*—A favourable historical environment may mask underwriting weaknesses. For example, rising real estate values may have avoided losses on foreclosure; furthermore, the number of defaults may also have been artificially reduced as troubled borrowers chose to sell their homes at rising prices.
3. *Negative selection*—It is important that the assets be randomly selected from the originator's portfolio. Even then, the portfolio may itself become the victim of negative selection—for example, poor-quality credit card borrowers often increase their borrowing until their line is exhausted; because their balances are greater than those of the average credit card user, the loss rate on the portfolio can suddenly become very large due to defaults by a small percentage of credit card users.
4. *Credit cliffs*—Portfolio quality can sometimes fall off a 'credit cliff' due to converging negative factors. This is most often apparent when new lending activities are curtailed or a changed economic environment (such as recession) puts new stresses on the portfolio.

The resulting volatility of future portfolio losses requires insightful analysis: portfolio and standards review, loss development analysis, statistical testing, meetings with management and staff, discussions with competitors and consumers, search for hidden correlations, and, ultimately, informed judgement about the economic factors and actions of the various parties. Only then can one gain the best possible understanding of the loss volatility embedded in the transaction.

This uncertainty as to future portfolio performance is not a criticism of asset-backed securities as compared to unsecured corporate bonds. A clearer understanding can be gained concerning the forces affecting a given pool of assets than can be gleaned about a corporation, which is subject to many more external factors affecting sales and expenses, as well as to changing internal judgements. And because of the 'built-in capital' in asset-backed issues, recoveries in the unlikely event of default are generally expected to be a very high percentage of par, not the 15 to 40 per cent recoveries typical of unsecured corporate bonds.

However, unlike other durable triple-A obligations sought by investors as a safe haven, asset-backed issues have a reliance on underlying portfolio performance than can lead to problems long before default, because of the risk of downgrade.

One of the profound lessons of the mortgage-backed market in the US has been that deteriorating asset quality can burn far enough through the first-loss protection that rating agencies feel compelled to downgrade the issue. One such case involved ComFed Savings Bank Mortgage Pass-Through issues. During a period of strong real estate values in the New England area in the mid-1980s, Boston-based ComFed reportedly took a high-volume approach (which it later abandoned) to mortgage lending on houses and condominiums. Some of its adjustable-rate loans had negative amortisation and were issued under limited documentation underwriting policies. These and other loans were securitised in senior/subordinated issues, which were originally rated Aa/AA by Moody's Investors Service, Inc. and Standard & Poor's Corporation. Sizing the subordination for such a specialised pool would have been difficult even with perfect foresight about the New England economy. In fact, to the surprise of many observers, regional real estate values weakened dramatically, and a number of ComFed pass-throughs were downgraded by both rating agencies.[3]

The ComFed downgrades demonstrated one inherent weakness in issues based on the senior/subordinated structure. Asset-backed securities that rely on any form of partial (i.e. less than 100 per cent) credit enhancement—whether senior/subordinated structuring, overcollateralisation, third-party first-loss facilities or recourse to the seller—have some measure of asset risk.

Among the many other examples of asset-related downgrades is one by Moody's in 1990 that affected $548m of secured notes backed by the 53-storey office building at 55 Water Street, near Wall Street in New York. Because Moody's judged that weak local real estate markets and reduced space requirements of financial service firms would be likely to prevail through a period of significant leasing exposure for the building (17 per cent vacancy rate), Moody's downgraded the issue three rating refinements from Aa1 to A1.[4]

Note that collateral may deteriorate for reasons other than unanticipated economic conditions. For example, $800m of GMAC auto receivable-backed issues were placed on rating agency review for weaker than anticipated collateral performance; ratings were confirmed following removal of a class of higher risk receivables.[5] Similarly, a $1bn auto loan-backed issue experienced poor collateral performance because of errors in computer procedures and faulty inclusion of higher-risk/first-time-buyer loans in the underlying portfolio. Loss-to-principal liquidation ratios were in excess of 6.2 per cent, putting pressure on the 7.5 per cent partial enhancement. In this case the partial enhancer, a bank, agreed to increase its letter of credit to 9.5 per cent of outstandings, averting a downgrade.[6] But investors cannot automatically count on such voluntary corrective action. Indeed, such action may not be possible in other cases, for it may threaten a 'true sale' accounting opinion that is essential to the securitisation structure.

Physical collateral is also subject to normal property and casualty risks as well as special hazards such as earthquakes and hurricanes. Although these risks can generally be addressed through special hazard insurance policies and adequate diversification, no amount of analysis can fully anticipate the effects of 'acts of God'. Recognising this, in the wake of the 1989 San Francisco earthquake, Standard & Poor's reviewed property damage reports from the issuers of more than $12bn of mortgage-backed securities.[7] Although in this instance no securities were downgraded, Standard & Poor's noted that the 'substantial appreciation in property values in most of these areas served as a cushion to absorb losses that may have otherwise resulted in special hazard claims had the earthquake occurred in a more depressed economic area'.[8]

Poor disclosure of deteriorating asset performance is an additional concern. In 1990 Moody's withdrew its rating from $150m of commercial mortgage-backed securities issued by Realty Frends-I, citing 'lack of financial information on the underlying collateral'. The Baa3-rated issue had been under review primarily because of the deteriorating regional real estate market.[9]

The ultimate asset risk is default, of course, and it is not unknown. Several mortgage-backed securities issued in the early 1980s have defaulted due to deteriorated asset quality. A number of municipal leases have also defaulted.

2.2 SECURITISATION RISK

Although asset and economic risk cannot be ignored, the methods of containing it—statistical analysis and first-loss protection—are reasonably straightforward and familiar to investors. Securitisation risk, on the other hand, presents entirely different challenges, stemming from the complex, often innovative and sometimes fragile arrangements and numerous parties to structured transactions.

2.2.1 Bankruptcy consolidation risk

It is imperative in asset-backed securities that collateral not be disturbed in the event of the bankruptcy of the asset seller (or, for that matter, any other party to the transaction). Without appropriate legal structuring, securitised assets might become part of the estate of a debtor in bankruptcy. The consequences of such a consolidation will vary from jurisdiction to jurisdiction. In the US access to the collateral could be interrupted by the automatic stay during bankruptcy proceedings, the lien on the collateral could be subordinated to new indebtedness ('primed'), or collateral could be substituted for the collateral initially provided. To cite one example, the judge in the Continental Airlines bankruptcy replaced with airplanes the short-term receivables collateralising certain creditors.

Moreover, as *The Economist* noted in February 1990:

> Bankruptcy's international fragmentation poses difficulties for businesses that are rapidly going global ... National bankruptcy systems have a wide variety of standards of openness to [foreign creditors]. ... Under British law a French creditor of a bust British company would usually have the same rights as a British one, though the French taxman would rank below Britain's. Swiss law gives preference to Swiss creditors.[10]

The threats to bankruptcy-remoteness can be subtle. In 1988 Moody's placed on watchlist $861m of collateralised mortgage obligations (CMOs) issued by Ryland Acceptance Corporation Four (RAC Four). The rating agency was concerned because some RAC Four CMOs were backed by mortgage securities issued or guaranteed by US government agencies while others were backed by whole loans with credit enhancement from a private mortgage insurer. Moody's feared that if a whole-loan backed CMO were to default, holders of that CMO could petition RAC Four into bankruptcy, thereby jeopardising full and timely payment to the holders of agency-backed issues. RAC Four responded by placing the collateral of the watchlisted series into separate trusts. This resulted in the upgrading of some maturity classes but the downgrading of $416.1m of other classes, because the trusts were to terminate before the stated maturity of many of the classes. Upon termination of a trust, the collateral would revert to holders of residual class bonds—described by Moody's as likely to be low-rated thrifts or real estate investment trusts—from whose potential insolvency the holders of the longer maturity classes would no longer be insulated. To reverse the downgrades, RAC Four had to undertake a second restructuring.[11]

Even in the relatively well-developed US market, uncertainty exists under certain conditions with respect to the structures intended to achieve bankruptcy-remoteness. In 1990 Fitch Investors Service Inc. downgraded $1bn of senior/subordinated securities backed by Sears, Roebuck & Co. credit cards, reasoning that 'since Sears' corporate family retains the risk of loss, via the retention of the subordinate certificates, a Sears bankruptcy might lead to a legal argument that could disrupt the flow of funds to investors'.[12] Specifically, Sears' creditors could argue that the transfer of the credit card collateral to the issuing trust was not a 'true sale' but merely a pledge, because the seller retained default risk in excess of the historic default rate of the collateral. Because Fitch felt that in the unlikely event of bankruptcy (Sears was AA) and treatment as a pledge, investors would be secured by the assets and, therefore, not suffer any ultimate loss, the asset-backed issue's rating should remain higher than Sears' own. But Fitch considered the risk sufficient to downgrade the issues to AA in tandem with a downgrade of Sears to A.[13]

As a general rule, therefore, the asset-backed investor will wish to consider not just the likelihood of bankruptcy but the security position in the event that an unanticipated bankruptcy does occur.

2.2.2 Legal and regulatory uncertainty

The legal framework for asset-backed securities varies from country to country. In the USA, where the technology first developed, and in a number of other countries, asset securitisations rest to a large extent on legal assumptions derived from case precedents and from laws conceived before asset-backed securities existed. Such assumptions are customarily assessed in legal opinions rendered by independent or internal counsel.

Among the most important concerns addressed by these legal opinions are the questions of true sale and bankruptcy remoteness. Other opinions address such concerns as the validity of security interests, the validity of various obligations, tax treatment and the implications of specific matters raised by relevant securities laws.

Although legal opinions are intended to reassure investors about various securitisation risks, sophisticated investors understand the lawyers' adage that 'a legal opinion is only an opinion'. The comfort obtained from any legal opinion depends on a number of factors, including:

1. The calibre of the counsel rendering the opinion. The investor must ascertain whether the counsel is independent and of sound reputation.
2. The legal profession's concurrence with the opinion. Is it one that other law firms would be willing to give.
3. The scope of the opinion. Does the opinion address not just some, but *all* aspects of a particular risk?
4. The factual assumptions upon which the opinion is based. The reasonableness and accuracy of such factual assumptions must be evaluated.
5. Whether the opinion is a 'clean' opinion, stating a legal view conclusively, or a 'reasoned' opinion, stating a legal view that is reasoned and defensible, but not free from doubt.

These caveats apply even more strongly to 'legal letters', which are less conclusive than opinions but have provided essential support for billions of dollars of structured financings, including many asset-backed issues. One such letter, for example, was written by the then general counsel of the US Federal Home Loan Bank Board (FHLBB) to address the 'enforceability of [transaction] provisions requiring the liquidation of collateral' in the event of the insolvency of a thrift institution whose deposits were insured by the Federal Savings and Loan Insurance Corporation (FSLIC). Many transactions have relied on this letter, despite its opening statement that the FSLIC 'will not provide commitments as to what it, in its capacity as receiver, would do in hypothetical situations with respect to receiverships of FSLIC-insured institutions'.[14]

Furthermore, new legislation can render both opinions and letters meaningless. In fact, as a result of legislation passed in 1989, the FHLBB's responsibilities with respect to conservatorships and receiverships were assumed by the Resolution Trust Corporation (RTC), which shortly thereafter brought regulatory risk into vivid focus. The RTC asserted that once a bank or thrift had been placed under a conservator or receiver, the RTC had the power to disallow the payment of interest that subsequently accrues on secured obligations of the insolvent institution. This contradicted legal correspondence from the FHLBB and threw into question the ratings of as much as $26bn of collateralised notes and mortgage-backed bonds.[15] The RTC resolved the problem by stating that, as a matter of *policy*, it would not exercise its authority to withhold post-insolvency interest from adequately secured investors, but it has not relinquished its *authority* to do so. At the time of this writing, uncertainty still hovers over treatment in conservatorship/receivership of bank and thrift obligations originally sold at discounts.

Even without a change in law, legal opinions may be withdrawn. For example, investors saw the rating removed and the market value of a $200m county bond issue decline in 1987 when, as reported in *The American Lawyer*, a Pittsburgh law firm 'withdrew its legal opinion ... after learning that funds to cover the bonds were not on deposit at Mellon [Bank] when the deal closed'.[16]

Finally, a legal opinion that correctly reflects case history cannot anticipate changes in interpretation of law or regulation. Indeed, different courts may hand down contradictory rulings. The questionable 'Twist Cap' ruling, for example, surprised many observers. In the case of Twist Cap, a bank had issued letters of credit to a bond trustee for a debtor's account and received a secured reimbursement obligation from the debtor. The bankruptcy trustee succeeded in obtaining a preliminary injunction against the bank's payment under the letters of credit based on the theory that the letter of credit draw would subject the debtor's estate to the bank's secured claim rather than the previously existing unsecured claim of the bondholders. The court reasoned that the unsecured bondholders would receive preferential treatment relative to the debtor's other unsecured creditors.[17]

Similar concerns were recently raised when a bankruptcy court issued a preliminary injunction against the disbursement by a bond trustee of funds received from draws under letters of credit upon the bankruptcy of the debtor. The court subsequently ordered return of the funds to the letter of credit banks and reinstated the letters of credit.[18]

Another example of an unanticipated judicial decision occurred in the UK in 1990, when as reported in the *Financial Times*:

> The House of Lords ruled that all local authority interest rate swap deals are illegal. The decision could cost the [counterparty] banks up to £750m and, additionally, they will have to pay millions of pounds in legal fees if they want to force any compensation at all.

The invalidation of any security is possible as a result of a subsequent legal or regulatory ruling, but this risk is greatest when there is little legal precedent for the opinions to rest on. This is often the case with asset-backed securities, for which legal principles must be applied to facts the law does not specifically address. While an argument could be made that invalidation of an asset-backed security could threaten the payment obligations, more likely effects would be to undercut the value of collateral or the priority of the lien.

If an important transaction document is found to be invalid, the mechanics of a structured transaction may cease to function and the issuer may not have the necessary funds to make payments on its securities. The US market was stunned in the early 1980s by the suspension of payments on some $2.25bn of securities issued to finance two nuclear generating units of the Washington Public Power Supply System (WPPSS). Take-or-pay contracts covering debt service on the bonds 'whether or not any of the Projects are completed, operable or operating' were declared void by the Washington State Supreme

Court.[20] Only the bond holders with 100 per cent third-party credit enhancement, in the form of a surety bond or 100 per cent letter of credit, continued to receive full bond payments.

The pursuit of legal remedies after a securitisation fails is likely to absorb inordinate time and expense because of the complex transaction structure. Indeed, the structure may be confusing to some judges and most juries, no matter how well originally understood by the transaction parties, and aggressive attorneys may exploit seemingly minor ambiguities in the documentation to call into question investors' legal protections.

Moreover, the conflicting interests of aggrieved creditors can hamper coordination of legal and workout strategies, even in private transactions with only a few major investors. In public issues, involving thousands of bondholders, the ability to take decisive action and to compromise is even more limited. Consider one meeting of the creditors and bondholders of the failed WPPSS nuclear projects. The meeting was so large that it was held in the 5,000-seat Felt Forum at New York's Madison Square Garden.

Conflicting investor interests are inherent in structured transactions that have multiple investor classes with differing levels of seniority in terms of payment. Unless all classes can agree on an 'equitable' workout strategy, extended litigation may be unavoidable.

Ultimately, although an investor in a failed transaction can personally control his own actions in pursuing his legal rights, he cannot control the actions taken by other investors, other transaction parties or the courts. Each investor can count on being just one voice in what is often a large crowd.

2.2.3 Reliance on representations, warranties and other assurances

There is no mathematical formula for analysing and reducing securitisation risks. Instead, investors are provided with legal opinions (discussed above) and an amalgam of representations, warranties, indemnities, due diligence investigations, comfort letters and the like to provide reassurance about the accuracy of critical facts and assumptions. These assurances cannot be taken at face value; they must be carefully examined.

Representations, warranties and indemnities

In every transaction, assumptions must be made about the accuracy and reliability of essential, underlying information. The investor must rely on various representations, warranties and indemnities to identify and confirm the major applicable assumptions. The quality of such assurances varies. At a minimum, the investor must ask:

1. How much recourse is available from the maker of each representation,

warranty or indemnity? Although the provision may be broad, the damages payable upon a breach may be limited to a specific dollar amount or specific assets, or the recourse may expire after some limited time period.
2. How creditworthy is the maker of the representation, warranty or indemnity? Triple-A securities often rely to some degree on key warranties made by entities that are less than triple-A, and sometimes even less than investment grade.
3. To what extent are representations and warranties made on a 'best of our knowledge' basis. This qualification places the risk of the unknown and the uncertain on the security holders.

Due diligence investigations

Customarily a number of parties to an asset-backed transaction will conduct due diligence investigations, which address both asset and securitisation risks. With regard to the securitisation risks, the purpose of these investigations is to verify that the risks associated with the securities, including those related to the strength of the asset seller, have been properly disclosed in the offering materials. In the case of publicly offered US securities, this type of an investigation may also provide the underwriter with a 'due diligence' defence to strict liability for damages under the US Securities Act of 1933. Although due diligence investigations are standard procedure, investors will want to determine:

1. Whether sufficient time has been devoted to the investigation.
2. The scope of the investigation.
3. The experience of the investment bankers or attorneys performing the investigation.

Accountants' Comfort Letters and Certificates

Certain financial aspects of asset securitisations are typically addressed by comfort letters and certificates of independent accountants. Regrettably, time and cost constraints often limit the scope of review actually performed by these accountants. In some instances, investors have questioned the degree of comfort actually provided by such letters, since accountants' reviews often rely on financial and other information prepared by the issuer.

2.2.4 Risk of fraud

The potential for fraud exists in every financial transaction, but it grows as the number of participants in the complexity of a financing increase. Since asset-backed securities tend to involve many parties and complex structures, they demand heightened vigilance against fraud.

Fraud can arise in conjunction with any aspect of a financing, from the securitised financial assets to the underlying opinions. The assets were the subject of fraud in the OPM Leasing Services case, in which OPM's management successfully 'conned 19 banks, insurance companies, and pension funds', according to the *Wall Street Journal,* in what had been described as a secured lease-backed financing.[21] As reported in the *Legal Times,*

> Using forged or altered documents and in many cases referring to equipment that did not exist, OPM defrauded [these] lenders into forwarding more than $200 million to finance the purchase of computer equipment leased by OPM to Rockwell International Corp.[22]

In the case of Spangler Group Inc. in 1986, according to the *Wall Street Journal*, the Securities and Exchange Commission alleged that Mark E. Spangler, head of a firm that managed a total of $25m for approximately 150 clients, 'gave potential clients a copy of a fabricated opinion letter concerning Spangler Group's performance that was typed on Arthur Young & Co. letterhead'. Spangler was barred from 'ever working for an investment advisor, brokerage firm or investment company', noted the *Journal.* 'Spangler settled the SEC's administrative proceedings against him, without admitting or denying guilt, by agreeing to the sanction.'[23]

Even more alarming than these cases are those of fraud or alleged fraud involving the investors' primary line of defence against such actions—the 'experts' (accountants, attorneys and investment bankers) involved in a transaction. An example occurred in 1987 in the US tax-exempt structured finance market. According to the *Wall Street Journal*, 'About $1 billion of tax-exempt bonds underwritten by New York based Matthews & Wright in 1985 and 1986 is under scrutiny amid allegations involving fraud and possible illegal payments to public officials.' The article noted that Moody's 'withdrew ratings' on eight issues after a legal opinion was 'reported withdrawn amid inquiries by the Federal Bureau of Investigation and several US attorneys' offices'.[24] In 1989, under the settlement terms of an SEC complaint, reported in the *New York Times*, 'Matthews & Wright agreed to allow the S.E.C. to revoke its broker-dealer license.'[25]

Although fraud, when discovered, may not be made public, professionals who structure and monitor ABS do know of specific instances where fraud or knowing misrepresentation has occurred in asset-backed issues, and there are cases of fraudulent activities affecting types of loans that are only now being considered for securitisation. Clearly, in these and other cases, representations and warranties, due diligence investigations, legal opinions, accountants' comfort letters and the like all proved inadequate to contain the risk of fraud. As the US National Commission on Fraudulent Financial Reporting, whose mission was limited to the study of only one of the many types of fraud, reported:

> No company, regardless of size or business, is immune from the possibility that fraudulent financial reporting will occur. That possibility is inherent in doing business.[26]

The Commission's statement might well have been applied to all types of fraud possible in asset securitisations.

2.2.5 Third-party and seller/servicer risk

Asset-backed securities typically involve numerous parties in addition to the asset seller. Depending on the transaction, these 'third parties' provide a variety of essential services, including:

- trustee services
- primary and backup loan servicing
- first loss coverage (e.g. pool mortgage insurance or first-loss letters of credit)
- investing cash flow prior to distribution dates (usually at a guaranteed rate of return)
- advances against delinquencies
- advances against prepayment shortfalls
- repurchases of assets not meeting contracted standards (such as assets whose origination standards do not conform to representations or warranties)
- repurchases of assets subject to other repurchase obligations (such as loans that must be repurchased if they are converted from floating rate to fixed rate or from one rate to another)
- interest rate swaps
- currency swaps
- primary mortgage insurance or mortgage indemnity guarantees
- special hazard and other insurance
- taking deposits for reserve, spread or other types of accounts
- monitoring and surveillance
- leasing (both lessors and lessees)
- portfolio management
- withholding tax indemnities

Because performance failures in any of these functions can cause serious problems, rating agencies often base their ratings on what may be called the 'weakest link' theory. The agency will analyse the transaction to determine which services are essential and potentially irreplaceable and then assign the same rating as that of the lowest-rated party providing any of those services. The investor should be aware, however, that the rating agencies do not consider, for rating purposes, the likelihood of a performance failure by certain parties. For example, Standard & Poor's wrote in 1986 that 'the risk of non-performance by a trustee or other agent of its fiduciary responsibilities should be taken into account by a bondholder' and cautioned investors that a rating by S&P 'does not make an assessment of the probability that a particular trustee will misinterpret the legal provisions or ignore them in managing the financing'.[27]

Trustee risk

Although trustee performance does not directly influence the cash generated by a pool of underlying receivables, it does affect the security of this cash once it is collected and the timeliness with which it is passed through to investors. Strict transaction provisions attempt to control this risk, but they cannot completely prevent mismanagement. In 1987, for example, The Citizens & Southern Corporation (C&S) settled a $32.6m class action suit brought by trust fund customers who charged that the Citizens and Southern National Bank, a C&S unit, 'mismanaged an income fund designed for conservative investors'. In this case, the investors received some compensation; however, it came nearly three years after the initial filing of the case and several weeks into the actual trial.[28]

Servicer risk

The servicer is the investor's chief defence against a deterioration of the asset pool. In a receivable-backed financing, for example, the servicer is the one party in a position to directly influence payment behaviour on the underlying contracts. An interruption in the servicing process may not only result in payment delays to investors, but may also lead to a permanent diminution in overall credit quality. When receivable-backed transactions are structured, certain assumptions about delinquencies, defaults and recoveries are made based on historical experience. To the extent that this experience was a function of the servicing process, the structure of a transaction may indirectly rely not only on the quality of servicing but also on a particular servicer.

For example, many servicers of automobile contracts have extensive dealer arrangements that are fundamental to their servicing records, but which may not be easily transferable to a successor servicer. Even when dealer arrangements take the form of formal contractual agreements, it may still be very difficult for replacement servicers to enforce them. Other servicers, which are also manufacturers, may provide warranties on their products. The existence of such warranties can be a key factor in resale values and therefore liquidation proceeds. If this type of servicer becomes insolvent, overall portfolio cash flow may be significantly reduced because recovery rates can be a prime determinant of aggregate portfolio losses. Even when the insolvent entity fully intends to honour its warranty commitments, significant buyer uncertainty will probably remain—witness the depressed resale market for

Chrysler automobiles during that company's near financial collapse in the early 1980s.

If the asset seller or originator provides servicing (or any other essential ongoing function), there is the risk that, because of a high correlation between the servicer's overall business and the collateral pool in a specific securitisation, the servicer may be weakened at precisely the time that a given issue's collateral is underperforming.

The downgrade of a servicer or a guarantor of servicing obligations can threaten the rating of an asset-backed security. In December 1987 Moody's placed on its watchlist $120m of Kidder, Peabody Acceptance Corporation Series 1987–1 mortgage-backed securities because Shearson Lehman Brothers Holdings, Inc., which had provided a performance guaranty for master servicing obligations in the transaction, had been placed under review (and later downgraded to A3) as a result of Shearson's acquisition of the E.F. Hutton Group Inc. The issue's Aa2 rating was not confirmed until the following August, when an Aaa-rated bank issued an irrevocable letter of credit to support the servicing obligations.[29]

Swap counterparty risk

A number of downgrades and rating agency reviews have been related to currency or interest rate swaps, which are a part of many asset-backed transactions. One example was the 1987 downgrade of a mortgage-backed Euroyen issue (Great American First Bank Savings Euroyen Notes), which resulted from the downgrade of a Japanese bank that had provided a currency swap. The issue was backed by GNMA, FNMA and FHLMC collateral—considered the most secure mortgage collateral in the US because of government agency guarantees—but the quality of the collateral could not prevent the downgrade, illustrating the importance of considering securitisation risk no matter how minimal the asset risk.[30]

Sovereign risk

International issues that depend on currency convertibility can be adversely affected by changes in country debt ratings. For example, $300m of preferred stock of the First Australian Prime Income Fund, Inc., a leveraged income fund consisting of Australian government and semi-government bonds, was downgraded when Moody's downgraded Australia's sovereign rating in 1989.[31]

GIC provider risk

The cash flows in asset-backed transactions must be accumulated in accounts for a variety of reasons, including the proper timing of payments to investors and creation of reserve funds to protect investors. To minimise interest rate risk, investment agreements, or guaranteed investment contracts (GICs), are made intrinsic to the transaction structures. These agreements may be crucial to proper functioning of the transaction. In the case of Domus Mortgage Finance No.1 PLC, a UK mortgage-backed floating rate note (FRN) issue, the bank providing the issue's interest rate maintenance agreement was downgraded, first from Aa3 to A1 in 1989 and then to A2 in 1990. Each time, the Domus issue was also downgraded.[32]

The potential effects of such downgrades are large. In 1990 more than $900m of US public housing agency issues were placed under review because they involved investment agreements with a single money-centre bank that had been downgraded.[33] In 1988 a triple-A-rated CMO was placed under review pending the review of its guaranteed reinvestment agreement counterparty, a triple-A-rated bank. The same bank's guaranteed investment contracts were part of the reason for a simultaneous review of more than $5bn of auto receivable-backed issues.[34]

Lessee risk
Some transactions depend on the ability of third parties to sustain cash flow in the collateral. In 1990 a commercial mortgage-backed issue was downgraded after the real estate lessee was downgraded.[35] Similarly, equipment trust issues in which American Airlines is the lessee were downgraded when the airline was downgraded.

2.3 RISK REDUCTION THROUGH CREDIT ENHANCEMENT

The purpose of credit enhancement is to reduce the risk in asset-backed securities. It may take the form of overcollateralisation, senior/subordinated structuring, recourse to the seller, reserve funds that build up over time in a transaction, or full or partial guarantees provided by sellers, their affiliates, banks, insurance companies or other third parties.

Seller recourse
When the seller or one of its affiliates provides recourse or a guarantee, the quality of the asset-backed issue is not completely separated from that of the seller. In the period from January 1987 through April 1990, more than $11bn of structured financings were placed on watch list or downgraded by Moody's because of downgrades or reviews for possible downgrade of sellers or affiliates that had provided credit enhancement for those issues.

Third-party credit enhancement
By the same token, when a third-party guarantor provides credit enhancement, the issue's quality becomes linked to that of the credit enhancer. In the same January 1987 to April 1990 period, more than $8bn of structured issues

supported by first-loss letters of credit from banks were downgraded or placed on Moody's watchlist because of changes or potential changes in the credit quality of the letter-of-credit banks.

Subordination

The risks inherent in linkage to a seller or third-party guarantor's credit quality have been a selling point for senior/subordinated issues, which, in theory, have no seller or third-party risk. In practice, however, senior/subordinated structures are subject to all the third-party risks described earlier in this chapter, for they have trustees, servicers (who are often the asset sellers and therefore likely to have unwanted risk correlations with the securitised assets), GIC providers, advance providers, swap counterparties, property/casualty insurers and repurchase obligors. Even the quality and role of the subordinated debt holder must be examined, as in the Sears credit card issues mentioned above, which were downgraded by Fitch.

In credit card issues and other transactions where the collateral pool may be replenished during an issue's lifetime, maintenance of credit standards is critical. If the subordinated debt-holder also provides origination and servicing, it has control of the transaction. If its financial condition deteriorates, questions may arise to threaten the trading value of the senior tranche. Conversely, if the originator sells its subordinated interest, it may be reducing its incentive to maintain monitoring and servicing at previous levels.

It should be noted that senior/subordinated structuring provides only first-loss protection and therefore protects only against asset risk and only up to a specific percentage of a portfolio. Securitisation risks are addressed through care in structuring, documentation, legal opinions, 'reps and warranties' and so forth, making each transaction unique in terms of its demands on the investor's resources. This imposes considerable burdens in terms of time and expense, both before the transaction and throughout its life. Investors are showing increasing concern about this as more asset-backed issues involve unfamiliar assets, often in distant locations, and employ complicated structures that require constant monitoring until maturity. According to *Global Asset Backed Monitor*, for example, 'investors seem to have been suspicious of the lack of third party surveillance' in a 1990 senior/sub Euro-issue allowing reinvestments in new underlying loans for seven years.[36] The presence of a third-party partial guarantor provides some relief for a portion of the asset risk through its independent due diligence and monitoring, though it provides no coverage against risks stemming from other third parties, legal or regulatory uncertainties, fraud or structural malfunction.

100 per cent Coverage

Complete coverage against both asset and securitisation risk is available when 100 per cent of principal and interest is guaranteed. This type of coverage is generally available for asset-backed securities only from a monoline financial guaranty insurance company, which will 'wrap' its 100 per cent guaranty around a transaction that already contains one or more forms of first-loss credit enhancement. Monoline insurers require that these underlying enhancements provide for investment-grade credit quality *before* application of the 100 per cent guaranty. While this greatly simplifies the investor's research, the investor should nevertheless examine the ability of the guarantor to pay its claims, the nature of the guarantor's obligation (e.g. Is the guaranty unconditional? Irrevocable? Does it waive fraud as a defence?) and the secondary market liquidity of transactions the guarantor has insured.

2.4 CONCLUSION

Risk is an unavoidable element of any investment. Asset-backed securities are safer in many ways than most alternative types of investments. They are structured to be exceptionally dependable in recessionary environments and to provide for high recovery rates even in worst-case default scenarios. But due to the sheer complexity of asset securitisation, every transaction, no matter how well structured, thoroughly researched and precisely documented, will still present some risks. Investors must therefore identify these risks, analyse their magnitude, examine the ways they have been reduced and assess the effectiveness of such risk reduction devices. In this way they can discriminate among issues of differing quality and determine whether the yield of a given issue is appropriate to its risk.

The trend in ABS is toward more complexity and risk, as Moody's pointed out in its January 1990 *Structured Finance Annual Report*:

> More structured transactions during 1989 involved complex or unusual risks, including swapped and unswapped interest-rate risk in CBOs; complicated hedging instruments; new kinds of collateral, notably home equity loans; limited-documentation loans backing mortgage pass-throughs; credit card receivables of lower-rated retail companies; a greater variety of lower-rated tranches in some structures; and market value structured securities using assets traded in still-developing secondary markets.
>
> Other trends in structured finance have also increased credit risk and continue to receive close attention from Moody's. Most important is heightened competition among transaction participants, including underwriters, trustees, lawyers, and accountants, and collateral credit enhancers. The potential pressure on credit standards is obvious.[37]

Though the *magnitude* of asset risk is usually limited in ABS, the *diversity* of securitisation risks complicates the investor's analysis of these securities. This may be the reason why asset-backed securities often offer higher yields than other securities with comparable ratings. In fact they offer some of the highest returns for top-rated investments available in the market. These yields are a worthwhile reward for the investor who makes the effort to understand the risks in ABS and the means of controlling them.

Alternatively, for those who wish to avoid the multiplicity of downgrade risks in ABS while earning higher yields than government, sovereign or government agency issues, fully guaranteed ABS may be more suitable.

1 *Special Report: Credit Card Deals Aren't Equal,* Fitch Investors Service, Inc., 10 April, 1990, p. 2.
2 Some material in this chapter is adapted from a chapter written by Theodore V. Buerger and Linda S. Iseley for *The Asset Securitization Handbook,* ed. Philip L. Zweig (Dow-Jones Irwin, 1989).
3 *Mortgage-Backed Securities Letter,* 30 October 1989. *Moody's Structured Finance,* August 1990, November 1989.
4 *Moody's Structured Finance,* July 1990, p. 49.
5 *Moody's Structured Finance,* March 1989, p. 35.
6 *Moody's Structured Finance,* May 1989, p. 27.
7 *Standard & Poor's CreditWeek,* 1 January 1990.
8 *Standard & Poor's CreditWeek,* 16 April 1990.
9 *Moody's Investor's Service, Inc.,* press release, 28 September, 1990.
10 *The Economist,* 24 February, 1990, p. 78.
11 *Moody's Structured Finance,* May 1988, pp. 40–44; July 1988, pp. 34–5.
12 *Special Report: Credit Card Deals Aren't Equal,* Fitch Investors Service, Inc., 10 April, 1990.
13 *Ibid.*
14 FSLIC ratings criteria, *Standard & Poor's CreditWeek,* 2 April, 1984, p. 1926. The author and Linda S. Iseley warned of this risk in 1988 in Zweig, *op. cit.*
15 *Standard & Poor's CreditWeek,* 26 March, 1990, p. 23; 9 April, 1990, p. 26. *Moody's Structured Finance,* April 1990, p. 50.
16 'Buchanan's Negative Rainmaking', *American Lawyer,* October 1987.
17 See In Re Prime Motor Inns, Inc. et al. (Bkcy, S.D. Fla, No. 90-0504, 30 October, 1990).
18 *Financial Times,* 5 November, 1990.
19 See Twist Cap, Inc. v. Southeast Bank of Tampa, 1 B.R. 284 (1979).
20 'What Went Wrong with WPPSS', *Municipal Finance Journal,* Winter 1984, p. 81.
21 'O.P.M. Fraud Raises Questions About Role of a Criminal's Lawyer', *Wall Street Journal,* 31 December, 1982, p. 1.
22 'Trustee's Criticism of Lawyers in O.P.M. Imbroglio', *Legal Times,* 2 May, 1983, pp. 20–23.
23 'SEC Bars Spangler From Work As Investment Adviser', *Wall Street Journal,* 19 June, 1986, p. 8.
24 'Rating of Five Bonds Issued in Pennsylvania Restored by Moody's', *Wall Street Journal,* 20 August, 1987, p. 33.
25 'S.E.C. Complaint is Settled by Bond Dealer', *New York Times,* 28 April, 1989, p. D5.
26 'Exposure Draft', The National Commission on Fraudulent Financial Reporting, April 1987, p. 5.
27 'Trustee's Role in Structured Financings', *Standard & Poor's CreditWeek,* 21 April, 1986.
28 'C&S Settles Suit, to Pay Up to $32.6 Million', *American Banker,* 6 August, 1987, p. 2.
29 *Moody's Structured Finance,* September 1988, p. 33.
30 *Moody's Structured Finance: Annual Report,* March 1988, p. 19.

31 *Moody's Structured Finance: Annual Report,* January 1990, pp. 5, 34.
32 *Moody's Structured Finance,* November 1989, p. 61.; May 1990, p. 47.
33 *Standard & Poor's CreditWeek,* 7 May, 1990, p. 24.
34 *Moody's Structured Finance: Annual Report,* March 1989, pp. 35, 36.
35 *Moody's Structured Finance,* April 1990, p. 54.
36 *Global Asset Back Monitor,* 25 May, 1990.
37 *Moody's Structured Finance: Annual Report,* January 1990, pp. 5, 6.

The Market in the United Kingdom

3: The UK Banks' Perspective

Mark F. Fisher, Samuel Montagu & Co. Ltd

This chapter looks at the sterling asset-backed markets from the perspective of the major UK commercial banks. The definition of 'commercial banks' is nowadays somewhat more difficult than it was formerly as more and more entities are seeking banking status. For the purposes of this discussion we shall define them as the London and Scottish clearing banks and other banks with a sizeable market presence, conducting lending business with a broad range of personal and corporate customers. While theory suggests that commercial banks should be among the most active players in this sector, they have to date largely ignored the market. This chapter attempts to provide an explanation for this apparent contradiction. It is divided into three broad parts: section 3.1 examines the objectives of commercial banks in raising funding through securitisation and explores the UK asset-backed sector in the light of this; section 3.2 discusses in detail some of the practical hurdles they must overcome in constructing transactions which meet relatively strict regulatory and accounting guidelines; finally, in section 3.3 we shall attempt to draw some tentative conclusions about the future growth of the sterling asset-backed market and the role of banks within it.

This chapter will not deal in any great detail with the objectives of other players—the UK building societies or the centralised lenders for example—since these institutions are covered in detail in other chapters. In addition, we shall not restrict the discussion to mortgage-backed issues since, as we shall see below, mortgages are in many respects the least attractive candidate for securitisation from the perspective of a commercial bank.

3.1 THE UK BANKS AND SECURITISATION

3.1.1 Background

The UK commercial banks are well positioned to take advantage of the techniques of asset securitisation. Those assets suitable for repackaging typically meet the following criteria:

- large volume of homogeneous assets to facilitate statistical analysis of prepayment and default;
- geographic and socio-economic diversification to minimise the risk of borrower concentration and associated credit risk;
- assets must meet a basic credit quality (third-party credit enhancers will not typically underwrite risks that originators themselves find unacceptable).

It is clear from the above that many of the assets which meet these criteria in the UK are concentrated in the hands of commercial banks or their subsidiaries and will include (among others) residential mortgages, hire purchase and lease receivables and credit card debts. The UK commercial banks have a strong presence in each of these sectors and have sufficiently large balances to contemplate a continuous programme of issues with attendant cost savings. This contrasts with many of their competitors, such as the finance subsidiaries of corporates, which account for a much smaller percentage of overall lending. The size of the individual portfolios held by these institutions may render securitisation impractical. For example, the sterling credit card market is dominated by the four major clearers. Of the total outstanding balances of credit and store card debt in 1989 Barclays, NatWest, Lloyds and Midland accounted for approximately 60 per cent between them.

Banks not only have the opportunity to benefit from securitisation by virtue of this concentration, but now also have the motivation to manage their balance sheets more aggressively. The major impetus for change has resulted from the capital adequacy guidelines laid down by the Cooke Committee of the Bank for International Settlements (BIS) in 1988 which take legal effect in the European Community from 1991. These guidelines set down a strict definition of bank capital, a minimum capital ratio and a framework for risk weighting of assets. Capital is divided into Tier I, consisting of equity (including non-cumulative irredeemable preference shares) and disclosed reserves, and Tier II, which comprises reserves, hybrid instruments and term-subordinated debt. Although the BIS guidelines set a minimum capital ratio of 8 per cent (of which Tier I should constitute at least 4 per cent) most banks will wish (or will be obliged by their central banks) to exceed this minimum.

At a time when banks are facing growing regulatory pressure, the opportunities to raise new capital, particularly Tier I equity, are more limited. The well-publicised difficulties arising from various bad debt crises and the general underperformance of bank stocks have led to increasing investor disenchantment and the possibility of raising new equity on acceptable terms is diminished. In the extreme case the equity markets may periodically be closed to banks.

The equity markets are also making greater demands on banks to improve their performance and focus increasingly on return on equity as a measure of relative success. Given the recent volatility of returns on bank stocks, investors are no longer inclined to regard banking as a stable low-risk business. This means that investors will be more likely to require a higher benchmark return on equity for bank stocks, reflecting a greater risk premium. As a consequence, banks are being forced to scrutinise their component businesses more closely with a view to generating an acceptable return from scarce capital. Failure to produce a coherent strategy backed-up by strong performance from individual businesses will feed back directly into impaired market valuation.

It is more difficult for banks to meet more stringent return on equity targets since asset margins are under pressure from increased competition. For example, increasing competition is particularly evident in the UK retail sector, where in recent years a variety of new players have entered the market attracted by historically high returns: the centralised mortgage lenders, building societies converting to bank status and corporates offering banking services. Moreover, these competitive pressures will increase with the breakdown of separate national markets and the provision of cross-border services through the introduction of European Community Banking Directives.

3.1.2 The rationale for securitisation

Asset securitisation may be a useful tool in allowing banks to enhance their overall profitability in an environment of increasing competitive pressure. The business case for securitisation can be summarised as follows:

- By freeing-up capital, securitisation allows the originating bank to expand its business volume without a corresponding increase in its capital base.
- This, in turn, allows the bank to increase asset turnover and to increase its market share in sectors which might not otherwise provide an acceptable return on equity.
- Since the originating bank may increase the turnover of its business while at the same time retaining a portion of the net spread in the form of off-balance-sheet fee income, this will increase overall return on equity and, all things being equal, should lead to improved market valuation of the group's shares.

Securitisation also produces other benefits which are important but not of prime significance, namely:

- It may allow banks to match fund assets and hence reduce balance sheet mismatches.
- Investors purchasing the resulting securities are not looking to the origin-

ator's credit for repayment of principal and interest. This allows banks to issue a continuous programme of securities without any negative impact on their name.

We have looked at the advantages of securitisation, but what of its cost? It is regrettably true that securitisation is in current market conditions a relatively expensive means of finance. A number of factors are relevant in evaluating the total cost of a securitisation project.

- The *all-in cost of the resulting security* (whether fixed or floating) expressed as a spread to LIBOR.
- Due consideration must be paid to the *associated costs* of a public issue, including trustee, paying agency and audit fees.
- There is the *additional cost* of credit enhancement and liquidity support. This will reflect a number of factors including the type of assets securitised and the overall quality of the pool.
- Securitisation entails large *development costs* in advance of an issue, in particular adjustment to the originator's data processing systems to facilitate identification and monitoring of the securitised assets and significant legal expenses. If a bank wishes to securitise non-mortgage assets where there is no established technology these development costs may be very substantial.
- The amount of *management time* required to co-ordinate a securitisation project successfully must also be evaluated. Unlike other forms of finance, securitisation requires input from a large number of departments: finance, systems, marketing and capital markets. These costs will inevitably be very high for an initial issue since management will be required to adapt existing procedures and controls to accommodate the requirements of a securitisation progamme.
- Securitisation may also involve *additional penalties* which cannot be easily quantified and which are not, therefore, evident in the all-in costs of a transaction. For example, mortgage securitisation may require modification to existing or future mortgage documentation to cover matters such as borrower consent, the Data Protection Act and the Statement of Practice. This may have a negative impact on the bank's marketing strategy and will be discussed in more detail below.
- Although securitisation releases capital, UK banks regulated by the Bank of England are nonetheless required to make certain *deductions from their capital base* in respect of any capital support provided to the vehicle company. This support typically takes the form of first loss provisions or subordinated facilities to fund up-front fees and expenses and ways must be found of minimising such deductions.

It is clear from this that the total cost of an initial issue of a sterling asset-backed security is likely to be substantially above LIBOR. This compares unfavourably to alternative on-balance-sheet funding sources available to commercial banks. It should also be recognised that although securitisation can improve profitability (measured by return on equity) this is at the expense of total profit since the repackaging process entails significant incremental costs and the net margin available as a servicing fee after sale may be very narrow. However, these figures must be balanced against the equivalent cost of raising new equity to support asset growth, if indeed this option is available in the short term.

This raises two key questions. First, which assets should a commercial banks seek to securitise? Second, in which circumstances is securitisation an appropriate strategy?

The answer to the first question is relatively simple: assets with a 100 per cent weighting under the BIS guidelines and a margin below the group's target return on equity but above the total cost of securitisation. Clearly there are a number of assets which would satisfy the former criterion but not the latter. Although banks might consider securitising some of their higher-quality corporate loan assets, the general erosion of margins in this sector means that there would probably not be adequate yield to cover securitisation costs.

The answer to the second question depends upon the particular circumstances of the originating bank. For institutions subject to capital constraints it can be an important means of raising new capital without recourse to the equity markets. In France, for example, where the banking sector is relatively undercapitalised, the process has been deliberately encouraged by the French regulatory authorities in order to allow banks to meet BIS requirements. Notwithstanding this, securitisation is not necessarily appropriate where a bank has adequate capital and can generate an appropriate return on equity on new business opportunities. In these circumstances it is perhaps better to keep assets on balance sheet and thus increase total profit.

Securitisation can also be seen as a positive tool in increasing market share in key strategic businesses where competitive pressures are driving down returns. In these circumstances, where a continuing presence in a market sector is regarded as essential, the bank may choose to maintain its role as an originator and servicer of assets, benefiting from the fee income derived from these activities, while funding the assets off balance sheet through the capital markets. However, if the business is not of strategic importance to the group a simpler alternative is to sell the whole subsidiary. Sale of the whole business will generally produce a greater impact on capital ratios within a much shorter timeframe. Securitisation, as we have seen, involves a considerable lead time to develop. Moreover, a single securitisation issue of, say, £250m is likely to have only a limited impact on a bank's total capital position once deductions for any capital support have been made.

3.1.3 Why UK banks have been slow to issue

This analysis has important implications for the UK asset-backed market. It explains why the UK clearing banks have not been active players in this market to date and permits us to make some predictions about their likely future activity in this sector.

The sterling asset-backed market which has emerged over the last three years has largely been driven by the requirements of the centralised lenders. These entities were established with the specific intention of securitising mortgage assets and in most cases had a relatively small capital base on which to build new business. The sterling asset-backed sector looks less attractive from a commercial bank's perspective. All the issues to date (with the exception of one transaction for Standard Chartered Bank and a commercial property transaction for BHH) have been backed by mortgages. Loans secured by residential mortgages still carry a 50 per cent weighting under the most recent European Community guidelines (although mortgage-backed securities may attract a 100 per cent weighting from January 1993) and their sale therefore releases relatively little capital. Mortgages have also typically constituted a 'core' relationship product for UK banks, which frequently opens the door for incremental fee-related business such as insurance. This is precisely the kind of income which banks should be seeking to improve their earnings. Under the Department of Environment's Statement of Practice mortgage lenders are required to notify borrowers if they intend to transfer the assets and this may undermine the relationship between lender and client and diminish the prospects for new business from the same account.

We have already seen that securitisation is a relatively expensive form of finance which compares unfavourably with funding available to commercial banks through on-balance-sheet finance. When one considers the fiercely competitive environment in which new mortgage business is written and the consequent reduction of the differential between the mortgage rate and LIBOR, it is critical that an analysis is made of the vehicle company's ability to service the coupon and other annual costs from its expected future income. Given the significant expenses involved in structuring transactions, the economics of a residential mortgage securitisation are likely to be very finely balanced.

On this basis it is easy to see why the UK banks have been reluctant to enter the market. To date only Barclays and TSB have been tempted to securitise mortgages, and neither have issued repeat transactions. It is also worth noting that Barclays did not securitise its existing branch-held mortgage portfolio but rather a special group of loans held by Barclays Direct Mortgage Service and generated by *third-party* institutions and estate agents.

It is clear that the securitisation of mortgage assets is a relatively unattractive proposition for UK banks, but what of the opportunities to securitise other assets such as credit cards or hire purchase receivables? In principle, these assets are more interesting for a number of reasons. First, these assets are 100 per cent weighted and therefore have a higher capital usage. Second, the competitive pressures described above will undoubtedly continue to place pressure on margins in a number of business sectors and make these assets less attractive if held on balance sheet. Finally, the sale of these assets may be less emotive than mortgages since the opportunities for cross-selling of other products are not present to the same extent.

However, the costs involved in securitisation remain a major obstacle in the short run. As we have seen, the development costs involved in structuring asset-backed transactions are significant and are greatly multiplied where the originator is pioneering new techniques. Although consumer receivables typically possess high margins, these margins naturally reflect increased credit risk. For example, there is a significant difference in securitising high-quality, secured mortgage assets compared to unsecured credit card debt. Sale of unsecured assets increases both the amount and cost of credit enhancement and requires greater support from the originator in the form of a first-loss provision and/or spread account. The impact of these costs and the implications for capital release must be carefully evaluated in determining the overall viability of the project.

These costs would be more acceptable if it could be demonstrated that the resulting security could be sold on terms which fully reflected its rating and that the repackaging process therefore generated new cost savings. This is not the case however. Despite several years of intensive marketing by underwriters, discounted margins on new asset-backed FRNs remain obstinately high. Indeed, over the course of the last two years discounted margins on new issues have widened from a low-point of 0.22 per cent in September 1989 to levels in excess of LIBOR plus 0.70 per cent and have now fallen back to approximately 0.55–0.60 per cent. It is particularly galling when one considers that unrated, unsecured building society debt consistently trades on tighter terms than triple-A rated, secured mortgage-backed FRNs. Furthermore, this situation contrasts very unfavourably with the US market, where the cost savings from securitisation are often of a much greater magnitude. For example, relatively low-rated US borrowers may obtain substantial cost savings by repackaging assets in triple-A form. No such arbitrage is currently possible for a UK originator securitising sterling-denominated assets through the euromarkets.

3.1.4 Inhibiting factors in reducing the cost of asset-backed securities

Securitisation involves the unbundling of an asset margin into component parts. Some of the margin is absorbed by legal and set-up costs; a portion is paid to credit enhancers to induce them to assume capital risk; an element is paid to investors in the security; and the remaining portion is extracted by the originator as servicing fees. Of these elements, the most significant variable is the cost of the security. This inevitably leads us to question why sterling asset-backed debt has persistently traded at a premium above comparable corporate and sovereign risks and what the prospects are for an improvement in trading levels in the short term.

This premium does not appear to be related to any investor perception of credit or structural risk. Asset-backed securities are, without exception, highly-rated instruments. 47 of the 54 public sterling mortgage-backed issues have achieved triple-A ratings. The assumptions used by the rating agencies to established levels of credit enhancement are highly conservative and are designed to ensure the integrity of the structure under the most extreme economic circumstances. This is borne out by the experience of the UK mortgage-backed market, where, despite extremely difficult conditions in the housing market over the last two years, there have been no recorded claims under pool insurance policies supporting the securities. Asset-backed securities also provide investors with additional protection against event risk since they are supported by a number of components (the credit enhancer, liquidity provider, GIC provider, servicer and swap counterparty), and the risk of downgrade is therefore effectively spread across several parties.

Three factors are critical in explaining relatively high yields on these transactions. Firstly, asset-backed securities represent a *new phenomenon* for euromarket investors. Although the technology and risks are well understood in the US it should not be forgotten that it has taken nearly 20 years for the US market to reach its current level of sophistication. It is therefore to be expected that there will be a period of education during which investors will wish to familiarise themselves with these structures and establish a track record for specific asset types.

A second, and more fundamental reason, is the *technical complexity* of these transactions and, in particular, prepayment risk. This factor distinguishes asset-backed transactions from mainstream euromarket issues with bullet maturities. Let us take a familiar example. The UK mortgage-backed sector has been largely built upon the FRN market, precisely because the instrument lends itself more readily to uncertain principal repayment. Many investors are commercial banks able to match fund through the interbank market and reduce their funding in line with prepayment. The difficulties involved in marketing these transactions to institutional investors were clearly demonstrated by the recent issue for Bear Stearns Mortgage Securities No. 1 PLC which proved notably less successful. Investors resisted the concept of monthly 'pass-through' of principal and interest and an estimated average life based upon sparse (mainly US) statistical data. To an extent, investor resistance to amortising fixed rate issues with an uncertain cash-flow profile is quite understandable, since they entail significant reinvestment risk. In the US, where there is an abundance of statistical data and elaborate analytical material, it is easier for investors to price these risks more exactly.

This fundamental difficulty leads to the third problem—*illiquidity*. Most asset-backed securities issued to date in the euromarkets have limited secondary market liquidity. Lack of liquidity is closely related to prepayment risk and structural complexity. In the sterling mortgage-backed market, for example, a number of the early issues have prepaid far more rapidly than anticipated. This was largely due to the inability of servicers to provide substitute assets which met the relatively restrictive substitution criteria established when the transactions were originally launched. This has resulted in much shorter average lives than estimated at the time of issue. Many of these issues are completely illiquid and trading in these securities has virtually ceased. The uncertainty over the reliability of estimated average lives has influenced secondary market prices and many investors are reluctant to purchase securities above par since an acceleration in prepayments will reduce their yield.

The solution to these problems might be thought to lie in the creation of asset-backed stuctures which fall within the mainstream eurobond markets. In reality, this means meeting wherever possible eurobond investors' long-standing preference for bullet repayment, large size and broad distribution. Progress has been made in this direction. In the sterling market, the issues for HMC 101, 102 and 103 and CMS 10 eliminated the structural uncertainties inherent in the traditional FRN and created a fixed rate bond with a bullet maturity. The reward for the issuer was clear: significantly better terms than those available through the FRN route and access to a broader institutional investor base. A similar process has taken place in the US dollar sector, where Citicorp's recent spate of credit-card securities (Euro Credit Card Trust) have gone some way towards transforming the cash flows from a complex portfolio into a manageable bullet maturity bond. The relative simplicity of this structure allowed Citicorp to target the bond at a broad investor base and benefit from significant economies of scale.

In reality, it is not always possible to eliminate all structural risks arising in asset-backed securities. There are clear regulatory barriers to the creation of bullet maturities. The Bank of England's guidelines on asset transfer expressly forbid anything which remotely resembles a commitment to repurchase the underlying assets (except where the pool has fallen to less than 10 per cent of its original value). Success often depends upon the capacity of the insurance market to underwrite these risks through, for example, the provision of put options or buyback facilities which permit assets to be sold with a guaranteed maturity. Nor is it always feasible, as we have seen, to maintain the outstanding principal balance through substitution of new assets. It is interesting that the recent dollar-denominated credit card transactions referred to above do not provide complete certainty on the timing of cash flows. These transactions typically contain an early redemption clause triggered by a deterioration of portfolio quality and allow for principal repayments beyond the target maturity date if cash flows from the pool are insufficient fully to repay the bonds.

3.2 KEY ISSUES IN SECURITISATION

We have established that securitisation should have an important role to play in managing commercial bank portfolios and that their interest is not likely to be restricted to mortgages. However, commercial banks generally face greater regulatory hurdles in securitising assets than their non-bank counterparts. Once a decision has been made to proceed with a particular project the practical difficulties involved in implementing the strategy remain severe. This section looks in more detail at some of these issues. This will inevitably be a somewhat selective discussion. There are a number of problems arising at all parts of the process and it would not be possible to do justice to each of these here.

3.2.1 Bank of England

One of the major hurdles facing commercial banks is the requirement to meet the Bank of England's guidelines on asset transfer. The Bank of England's notice, *Loan Transfers and Securitisation*, outlines the requirements for the exclusion of assets from the risk asset ratios of banks supervised by the Bank of England. The requirements imposed on banks are relatively strict and can be summarised as follows:

- A bank originator (the 'originator') may not hold any shares in the SPV and the board of the SPV must be independent of it (although the originator may have one director representing it).
- Funding and credit support provided to the vehicle company ('SPV') is extremely limited. The originator may not bear any recurring expenses but can make a one-off contribution on establishment of the transaction. It is also permitted to make a long-term subordinated loan to the SPV to fund its initial expenses, but this is only repayable on winding-up of the

scheme. Any such contribution or loan will be deducted from the bank's regulatory capital.

- Originators may not provide a liquidity facility to fund temporary delays in the SPV's receipts.
- Originators are permitted to enter into interest rate swaps with the vehicle 'at market prices' and it appears from subsequent discussion that the Bank of England will permit banks to make net payments through the swap. (It should be noted that the tax position of interest rate swaps as a means of profit extraction is currently under attack).
- The notice places a great deal of emphasis on the 'moral' risks involved in securitisation and the Bank of England suggests originators publicly disassociate themselves from any losses which the SPV may incur following sale, and make statements to this effect in the offer document.
- The originator cannot enter into an arrangement to repurchase mortgages except where a breach of warranties has occurred. However, the Bank will permit originators to retain an option to purchase mortgages if less than 10 per cent of the pool remains outstanding. This option only applies to fully performing loans.
- The originator must have evidence available from its auditors and legal advisers that the terms of the scheme protect it from any liability to investors.

It is important to recognise that the Bank of England's paper only represents a series of guidelines. While it sets out the Bank's basic approach to risk transfer in securitisation it does not cover all possible eventualities and many issues will inevitably require detailed negotiation. For example, it is clear that the paper does not provide much guidance on the sale of revolving assets such as credit cards, where it is more difficult to completely isolate the originator from the on-going funding of the pool. This particular issue appears to create considerable philosophical difficulties for the Bank.

As interest in securitisation grows and structures become more sophisticated, it is likely that the Bank of England will be confronted by increasingly complex issues. It is essential that the Bank maintains a flexible and constructive approach to resolving structural difficulties if UK banks are not to face a competitive disadvantage in raising capital through securitisation.

3.2.2 Off-balance-sheet treatment

The long-standing confusion over the achievement of off-balance-sheet status for statutory accounting purposes has been a major impediment in developing transparent guidelines for asset securitisation.

The Companies Act 1989 embodies a new and stricter definition of a 'subsidiary' which will influence the way in which transactions are structured and will require consolidation of many existing off-balance-sheet vehicles as a matter of law. A number of structures have been used in the UK mortgage market which may fall within the category of 'controlled non-subsidiaries' and, as a result, these vehicles may now be consolidated with the originator's accounts. The new act also specifically implements the Seventh EC Company Law Directive, which itself was designed to eliminate irregularities in the presentation of consolidated accounts within the European Community.

The Accounting Standards Committee produced in May 1990 a revised Exposure Draft (*Reflecting the Substance of Transactions in Assets and Liabilities*, ED49) and ED50 covering consolidated accounting in June 1990, and it is hoped that this will remove some of the uncertainties which have persisted since the publication of Exposure Draft 42 (ED42) in 1988 and will create clear and precise guidelines. ED49 and ED50 are expected to be issued in Financial Reporting Statement (FRS) form at the end of 1991 or beginning of 1992.

The revised Exposure Draft, ED49, follows the approach adopted in ED42 and focuses on the substance of individual transactions. It also includes a new section on the identification of control (in light of the Companies Act 1989) and detailed application notes dealing with specific forms of off-balance-sheet finance, including securitised mortgages (which are addressed in Application Note D). Application Note D is strongly influenced by the Bank of England's paper (*Loan Transfers and Securitisation*).

The revised Exposure Draft sets out a series of tests which must be satisfied if the transaction is to be treated as an effective sale for accounting purposes and the assets are to be excluded from the originator's individual or consolidated balance sheet. These tests address 'standard' residual risks such as interest rate exposure, repurchase obligations and liquidity support. There is also a specific test related to control by the originator of the SPV which incorporates both the legal definition of subsidiary and the accounting definition of 'quasi-subsidiaries' (i.e. 'entities which are not subsidiary undertakings but which are subject to a similar level of control by the reporting company').

If the originator meets the provisions set out in the application notes, disclosure is still required through notes to the accounts to explain the originator's interest in the SPV and any income it derives from it. The minimum suggested disclosure is a summary balance sheet of the SPV at the originator's balance-sheet date and a summary profit and loss for the period covered by the originator's accounts with the income recognised from the transaction in that period. The accounts of two or more SPVs may be combined and disclosure should include an estimation of the approximate periods for which income from the SPV will continue.

Although the passing of the Companies Act 1989 and the publication of

ED49 may adversely affect some existing issues it is anticipated that carefully structured transactions will still permit originators fully to remove assets from their balance sheet. However, some members of the accountancy profession have expressed the view that Application Note D, while dealing with the removal of risk from the vendor, does not address the subject of rewards and may therefore be regarded as inconsistent with the overall thrust of ED49. Hence there is some uncertainty at the time of writing as to whether ED49 (and Application Note D) will survive in this form or will be finally cast in a less favourable way.

3.2.3 Asset transfer

Asset transfer is a significant issue facing a commercial bank in structuring a securitised transaction. While the exact method of transfer (legal or equitable assignment, sub-participation etc.) is largely a technical matter requiring detailed legal and tax advice, there are nonetheless a number of important commercial considerations which must first be addressed.

One issue which requires attention is the question of customer consent to any transfer. In the case of mortgages, the Department of Environment has published a Statement of Practice (the 'Statement') to which the major lenders have subscribed. This is not a legal document but is concerned with customer protection and the maintenance of uniform standards amongst lenders. Nevertheless the adoption of the Statement can have legal implications. In particular there is a concern that its adoption (and publication or notification of the fact of adoption) could constitute a legally binding representation by a lender to a potential borrower or alternatively could result in the Statement becoming incorporated into the terms of the lender's contract with his borrower. The Statement sets out procedures which lenders must follow if they intend to transfer mortgages outside their company group. The Statement also outlines two types of consent. Where a borrower continues to administer arrears and set the mortgage rate after sale a general consent in required. General consent is obtained on existing loans through individual approaches in which borrowers must be given a reasonable opportunity to decline. Specific consent must be obtained where the lender gives up these two functions. In these circumstances the lender is required to obtain a formal written consent from the customer to the transfer. In most securitisations, of course, the originator continues to service the accounts after sale through a management contract with the vehicle company. It is therefore to be expected that in most cases a general consent is sufficient.

The key point, however, is that mortgage customers will inevitably need to be informed about the bank's intentions. This may, of course, have a negative impact on marketing strategy. Although the transfer of the beneficial interest to a special purpose company is, in reality, merely a financing arrangement involving no substantive change in the customer–bank relationship, it may give rise to confusion among customers who are unfamiliar with the concept. Since mortgages have constituted a central product for the UK banks which cements a long-term relationship and may generate further fee income, the decision to securitise is in itself a major strategic issue. While the question of customer consent has been historically a contentious question, most of the major UK banks have now included clauses permitting future securitisation in new mortgage documentation. However, they are likely to remain reluctant to approach existing mortgagors to obtain their general consent.

As far as other assets are concerned there is, as yet, nothing corresponding to the Statement of Practice. As such, lenders are not obliged to seek formal consent to transfer. In most cases, documentation governing these assets does allow for transfer and, providing this can be effected through equitable assignment, this greatly simplifies matters since it is not usually necessary to enter into the expensive and time-consuming process of individual customer notification.

3.2.4 Systems development

We have already touched on the question of systems development above. As we have seen, certain data processing modification will be required to facilitate selection and monitoring of the pool assets. The extent of this work can be determined through detailed discussion with the lead manager and the rating agencies who will advise on the selection criteria for the pool and the reporting requirements resulting from the issue. It will usually take several months to implement these changes. These problems are not unique to commercial banks. All entities contemplating securitisation face precisely the same problem, although institutions establishing a new lending business with the specific intention of securitising assets may be less constrained by the limitations of existing systems which were not designed with this function in mind.

However, this does give rise to an important resource allocation question. Systems staff in a major bank will typically be faced with a number of competing projects, each requiring committed resources. The financial case for securitisation must therefore be clearly made if full-time development work is to be undertaken. Securitisation is not appropriate therefore where the existing asset portfolio is below a critical size (say £350m) or where new business originations are not projected to be significant. It is only truly effective where the initial development costs can be spread over a number of future issues.

3.3 OUTLOOK AND CONCLUSION

What is the likelihood of UK banks issuing more securitised debt in the short term? Despite our negative conclusions on the mortgage-backed sector the outlook for the supply of non-mortgage issues is not entirely unfavourable. The pressure on capital ratios, the high costs of raising new equity and increasing pressure on margins will force banks to scrutinise individual businesses and their capital requirements far more carefully. Securitisation can, as we have seen, play an important role in allowing banks to square the circle—that is generate a higher volume of lower-yielding assets in an environment of capital constraint. The resulting fee income will boost return on equity and increase market valuation of the group's share capital. The assets most likley to be sold are those with high capital weightings—especially credit cards (if the Bank of England can be made comfortable with the resulting structures), hire purchase and lease receivables. The sale of these assets is less emotive than mortgages since the opportunities for cross-selling are not present to the same extent.

However, the total costs of securitisation are significant. Because of this it is essential that it is viewed as a long-term project, the benefits of which will only be fully realised over a large number of issues. Because UK banks have large outstanding balances of assets they are well positioned to take advantage of securitisation as a financing tool and benefit from the economies of scale which make the process viable. As securitisation becomes more widely adopted, both in Europe as well as the UK, commercial banks will be tempted to understand and develop the technology, both for their own purposes and as a product to be marketed to their clients. Securitisation skills can be used to create further fee income either from advice on structuring securities or by using systems to administer third-party asset portfolios.

There will undoubtedly continue to be resistance to the process of securitisation. Costs remain an important issue and, without a significant improvement in new issue terms, will hamper the growth of the market in the short term. One of the main barriers to a reduction in costs is the reliance upon the sterling floating rate note market. While the willingness of FRN investors to accept the uncertain cash-flow profile resulting from these transactions has allowed the market to develop quickly, this has only been achieved at the cost of relatively high yields. The FRN market has never been capable of sustaining sub-LIBOR coupons in the longer term and this may create a floor on the levels at which asset-backed securities can be issued. The major challenge is to create a broader range of structures which will draw in fixed investors to the market, both in the medium and longer-term maturities. The danger is that the sterling asset-backed market will continue to be regarded as a specialised sector and important new entrants, the banks and building societies, will be discouraged from issuing. This in turn will damage the market's overall credibility and further impair liquidity.

In conclusion, it seems likely that overall capital pressures will continue to be brought to bear and that in the post-BIS environment banks will be forced to pay continuing attention to balance-sheet growth and to means of enhancing profitability. Securitisation can clearly assist in this process and will inevitably become more widely deployed in the financial markets of the 1990s.

4: The Securitisation Issuer's Perspective

Bruce Gaitskell, Union Bank of Switzerland

4.1 SECURITISATION BY CENTRALISED MORTGAGE LENDERS

4.1.1 The development of securitisation in the 1980s

In the early 1980s three North American Banks—Citibank, Bank of America and Chemical Bank—established centralised lending operations. In each case the long-term objectives was to establish a retail banking presence in the UK. Only Citibank achieved that objective. The other two operations, although they prospered during the first half of the decade, were eventually sold (to Bank of Ireland and BNP respectively). Each mortgage operation processed applications and administered loans centrally, had standardised lending terms and sourced a substantial volume of its total business through intermediaries.

The establishment of these three lenders proved that there was a place for centralised lenders in the UK despite the dominant position of the UK building societies as providers of residential mortgage finance. During the mid-1980s a positive spread emerged between mortgage rate and LIBOR which made it possible for new-start operations, funding solely from wholesale sources, to prosper. The first of these new entrants included National Home Loans, the Mortgage Corporation and CIBC Mortgages. Others quickly followed including Mortgage Funding Corporation, Household Mortgage Corporation and First Mortgage Securities. In 1987 the centralised lenders, together with the UK clearing banks, took over half the new mortgage loans granted in the UK.

Although centralised lenders made progressive use of securitisation as a funding source following the first UK securitisation by National Home Loans in 1987, they borrowed in excess of £3bn from the banking market in the period 1985–7.

The first centralised lender to sponsor a rated issue of mortgage-backed securities was National Home Loans (NHL) in early 1987. Although not under capital or gearing pressure at that time, NHL had borrowed extensively from the banking market and recognised the finite nature of that market.

NHL was soon followed by the Mortgage Corporation, a lender which had planned securitisation to be its major funding source as it grew. Others have followed, utilising a variety of different structures, although most have used similar technology. The main stimulus has been availability of funds, with the added advantage of funding to the maturity of the underlying asset. In most cases the all-in funding cost has been higher than that enjoyed by the originator for its on-balance-sheet funding programmes.

4.1.2 Concentration and economies of scale

Centralised lenders enjoyed strong growth, low loan losses and generally good profitability throughout the period to 1989. The slow-down in the housing market which commenced in early 1989, together with the spirited fight back by the building societies, has resulted in more difficult times for centralised lenders over the past few years. LIBOR funding has been expensive relative to retail, and societies have generally begun to offer similar products to those of the centralised lenders. It might reasonably be argued that only the stronger and larger centralised lenders will survive in their present form. The willingness of CIBC to sell its UK mortgage operation and the recent announcement of the closure of the TSB subsidiary Mortgage Express bear out the more difficult times faced by centralised lenders.

Some centralised lenders, most notably NHL, have sought to diversify, interestingly at a time when most societies are returning to a strategy of 'sticking to the knitting'. Only time will tell if one strategy is superior to the other. Certainly some of the new business areas are inherently more risky than residential mortgage lending as many societies have found to their cost.

Mortgage lenders have not been immune from economic recession. Many have announced substantial provisions for 1990. Together with the sharp reduction in house prices this has substantially reduced the availability of bank facilities to fund the new orgination of mortgage lenders. This factor, more than any other, will ensure a growing use of securitisation by centralised and other mortgage lenders.

4.2 WHY SECURITISE?

A vital starting point for a corporate or financial institution contemplating securitisation is to define clearly the objective or objectives of the process. While it can provide clear benefits, securitisation is an expensive and time-consuming process for a first-time issuer. Disappointment is likely to be the result in the absence of a clear understanding of what the organisation is trying to achieve through securitisation. The principal reasons for considering securitisation can be found in one or more of the objectives described below. A securitisation may be structured as an on-balance-sheet of off-balance-sheet transaction, depending on the objectives to be achieved.

4.2.1 Return on capital

For an institution which falls to be regulated by a central bank or other regulator (for example, in the case of a UK building society, the Building Societies Commission) securitisation through an off-balance-sheet structure achieves a reduction or the elimination of the requirement for capital to be held in respect of the securitised assets for regulatory purposes. If assets are removed from the balance sheet there may still be a requirement for some regulatory capital if the originator has given a partial guarantee or established a first-loss fund. Taking the example of a UK mortgage originator which securitises a pool of mortgages supported by a mortgage pool insurance policy, the terms of that insurance will usually oblige the originator to establish a reserve fund representing between 0.20 and 1.00 per cent of the issue size. The establishment of such a fund requires a capital to be utilised equal to the full amount of the fund. However this compares favourably with the 4 per cent requirement in respect of the entire pool of assets when they were on the originator's balance sheet prior to securitisation. It can be seen from the example that the capital requirement has been reduced by a factor of between 4 and 20. The gearing effect is increased in the case of other assets, which carry an 8 per cent capital requirement. Assuming the absolute profitability of the assets has not been significantly reduced by the process of securitisation, the return on capital to the originator (who effectively receives the net profit on the assets through fees, deferred consideration or some other profit extraction mechanism) is significantly increased. For an institution which regards return on capital as its primary measure of success securitisation is a powerful tool.

Turning to an unregulated institution, gearing constraints in its financing documentation or articles represent a constraint which is in practice similar to the capital adequacy requirements for regulated institutions. An off-balance-sheet securitisation removes the borrowing associated with the previously owned assets, and as a result reduces the company's gearing. Assuming that the company was subject to gearing constraints prior to securitisation the process of securitisation allows it to redeploy borrowings to acquire new assets and thereby generate additional profit without the need to raise additional equity. As a result return on capital is increased (i.e. higher earnings per share).

4.2.2 Funding to maturity

Organisations such as banks, mortgage lenders, leasing companies, finance companies and other financial institutions finance the assets which they generate through a combination of medium-term banking facilities and uncommitted short-term borrowings. Generally (and particularly in the case of mortgage portfolios) these facilities will be of shorter maturity than the underlying assets being financed, thereby leading to the necessity of refinancing before the maturity of the assets. The pricing of such refinancing cannot be known at the time the asset is created and, more seriously, the availability of finance in the quantity required by some of these types of institutions cannot by guaranteed in the tighter banking market which has emerged since late 1990. Securitisation matches the maturity of the funding to the maturity of the financed asset. Put simply, securitisation ensures that assets are financed through to their maturity with the added advantage that the funding cost is known at the outset. Refinancing risk is therefore eliminated.

4.2.3 Diversification of sources of funding

Many fast-growing companies, particularly mortgage lenders and leasing companies, have begun to exhaust their ability to raise significant incremental funding in the essentially domestic banking market. This is a result of lending limits applied by banks both to individual names and, to a lesser extent, whole sectors. The international capital markets represent an alternative source of funding which is broader and deeper than the banking market. However, only companies which have a prime credit rating are able to tap this market. Through securitisation, assets of companies which do not themselves have the necessary credit rating can be repackaged in such a way as to achieve the highest credit ratings and therefore find ready investor demand in the ratings-driven capital markets.

It is sometimes suggested that as banks are major buyers of long-term securities no diversification is really achieved. However, the main credit exposure which investors face in a securitisation transaction is not the performance of the underlying assets but that of the credit enhancements supporting the assets, which are usually in the form of insurance policies, letters of credit or other facilities issued by rated institutions. It can therefore be argued that a bank which is, for example, 'full' on UK property risk should still feel able to purchase mortgage-backed securities since it should have regard principally to its exposure to the providers of credit enhancements rather than the mortgage lender.

4.2.4 Funding cost

The first institutions outside the US to exploit securitisation techniques were UK mortgage lenders. A number were bank subsidiaries which enjoyed relatively cheap funding from the parent bank. The pressure to securitise in these cases came not from pricing pressures (securitisation for such institutions in fact generally involved a higher funding cost) but rather from the increasing demands which they placed on the parent's capital and/or a cap on the amount of intra-group funding available.

The majority of new entrants to the securitisation market over the next few years are likely to come from the corporate rather than banking sector. Corporates do not generally benefit from cheap intra-group funding and are likely to find the margins on bank facilities increasing as existing facilities mature. For many of them, particularly those that do not themselves have credit ratings, the cost of funding in an off-balance-sheet securitisation in the capital markets may well be less than the cost of incremental bank funding on-balance-sheet.

4.3 WHAT STRUCTURE?

Having established its objectives and made the decision to securitise, the company, working with its lead manager and legal advisers, will need to determine what structure best meets its objectives.

The first question to be addressed is whether the structure needs to achieve off-balance-sheet treatment for accounting and/or regulatory purposes. Where the asset originator is effectively subject to the BIS or similar capital adequacy requirements the answer will invariably be yes. In the case of a corporate originator the answer is less clear-cut. If the corporate's primary objective is diversity of funding, reduced cost of funds, funding to maturity or any combination of these, it might be possible to achieve these objectives through an on-balance-sheet transaction and therefore avoid the complexities involved in structuring to achieve off-balance-sheet treatment.

However, a reduction in the company's gearing might be the key objective. If this is so the nature of the gearing needs to be carefully analysed. Does it arise from the company's articles, its financial covenants to its bankers or how it is rated by equity investors and analysts? The most commonly encountered constraint is that which arises in a company's financing documents. It might be possible for such a company to securitise assets by financing them on non-recourse terms in a non-guaranteed subsidiary and persuade the company's bankers to disregard such assets and the associated financing (notwithstanding that being on-balance-sheet they are shown in the consolidated accounts) and thereby avoid the need to establish an off-balance-sheet structure. The basis on which such assets might be disregarded is that investors who provide the debt of the subsidiary have recourse only to the assets in that subsidiary and have no claim on the parent. In reality the originator/original owner of the assets will have usually provided some limited first-loss protection when selling the assets (by way of a cash deposit, limited recourse loan or continuing support obligation), but this will often be 1 per cent of the asset value or less whereas an asset held on the parent balance sheet would typically require 10 to 20 per cent 'loss cover' provided by way of the company's equity. Therefore, lending banks may require some reduction in the pre-securitisation gearing limit to the extent that of the first-loss protection or other support sold with the assets or provided directly to the securitisation issuer.

4.4 PREPARING TO SECURITISE

A would-be issuer needs to allow up to 18 months between commencing the activities described below as Phase One and actually making its first securitisation issue.

Phase One is essentially an internal preparatory process, lasting up to one year whereby an originator of assets gets to the stage where legal documentation for an issue can begin and, around six months later, actually issuing securities. Phase One involves the following basic steps:

1. Establish a securitisation committee.
2. Check that the asset documentation will meet requirements of the rating agencies.
3. Review lending terms, product types, internal administration procedures and authorisations.
4. Establish an audit function to check that assets are being properly created.
5. If appropriate establish an off-balance-sheet corporate structure.
6. Review data capture and management information systems.

Establish a securitisation committee

The securitisation process makes demands on a number of different operating units of any organisation. It is important to involve each of these units in the planning process so that if and when a securitisation issue takes place it has the full support and understanding of those units which are to be involved. The membership of such a committee will vary depending on the organisational structure of the company but will generally include senior representatives from:

- Treasury
- Finance
- Underwriting
- Loan administration
- Computing

Other individuals may be co-opted at a later stage in the process or invited to attend particular meetings. In Phase One such a committee would probably meet monthly.

Check asset documentation

If a securitisation is to take place in 12–18 months' time it is likely to be the assets which are being created today onwards which will form the underlying security for the issue. It is important to ensure that the documentation used in creating the assets (including in particular the loan conditions and associated security documents) is adequate for a securitisation and in particular, gives rise to assets which are enforceable and freely transferable. A relatively small amount of time and expense incurred at this stage in having documentation reviewed by a prospective lead manager and/or legal advisor experienced in securitisation can save a considerable amount of cost and trouble later. Indeed, there are originators which have had to abandon issues at a fairly late stage because their documentation turned out to be fundamentally flawed. In relation to mortgage assets it is also important to consider any relevant statement of practice on loan transfers such as those published by the Department of the Environment and the Building Societies Association.

Review lending terms, product types, internal procedures

When making decisions about the detailed lending terms, status requirements etc. which are to be applied in originating assets it is advisable to have securitisation in mind. Small changes which make little difference to the attractiveness or effectiveness of the product can lead to cost savings when and if the asset is securitised.

Establish an audit function

A first-time issuer will normally be required to carry out a 100 per cent external audit of loan files (or exceptionally a 100 per cent internal audit coupled with a statistically designed sample audit by external auditors). The external auditors would usually be the originator's own auditors. The purpose of the auditors is to check that the assets have been properly originated in accordance with the originator's standard documentation, lending guidelines and procedures. This process is made much easier and less costly if each loan file is audited immediately after completion of the loan. Errors found at this time are much easier to correct than those discovered when a loan is several years old. Such post-completion 'audits' are normally carried out by a combination of clerical/temporary staff and experienced personnel and do not generally involve qualified audit staff.

Establish an off-balance-sheet corporate structure
A series of off-balance-sheet companies is inexpensive to establish but can take a considerable time to put into place, particularly if Consumer Credit Act and MIRAS and other authorisations are required. In the case of MIRAS it is necessary to allow up to 12 months as MIRAS designation is given by statutory order and at present only two statutory orders are made each year.

Review data capture and management information systems
Before a securitisation takes place rating agencies will wish to analyse the asset portfolio in great detail. Where a large portfolio is involved (for example 4,000 mortgages or 30,000 consumer loans), such analysis can only be cost-effectively achieved if the necessary data about each asset is held on a computer system which has a good management information capability. Where this is not already the case a considerable lead-time is needed. The best time to capture required data is at the point of origination of the assets; this may necessitate changes to application forms and other documents used in the origination process as well as input procedures.

The Phase One groundwork can be carried out at modest cost since it would by undertaken using the company's own resources and personnel. Phase Two is more expensive since it involves the preparation of the legal documentation, the rating process and the final asset selection. Phase Two costs are reduced to the extent that Phase One has been properly carried out.

4.5 CREDIT ENHANCEMENTS

Credit enhancements are a key feature of each securitisation transaction. When combined with the raw assets and the structural features of the transaction they enable a portfolio of assets (or a stream of cashflows deriving from those assets) to achieve a prime credit rating.

There are a number of different credit enhancements needed for a typical securitisation. Some are most efficiently provided by banks, and others by insurance companies (including monoline insurers such as Financial Security Assurance (FSA), CapMac and FGIC). Other things being equal, the most cost-efficient provider of any particular credit enhancement will be that suitably rated entity which incurs the lowest capital requirement in providing the particular enhancement. Insurance company capital requirements are broadly premium-related (and hence risk-related), whereas capital requirement for banks is linear (i.e. in direct proportion to the size of the facility). Hence, as a general rule, large low-risk enhancements are more efficiently covered by insurers, whereas smaller, more concentrated enhancements are better provided by banks. Other factors which influence the choice of provider include the nature and frequency of payments to be made. A liquidity facility may be frequently drawn and repaid. This presents no problem to banks but might be administratively difficult for insurers, particularly where payments have to be available as same-day cleared funds.

4.6 CHOOSING A MANAGER

Securitisations outside the US have to date been arranged by a relatively small group of arrangers which have devised the structures for the transactions and gone on to lead-manage them. For a first-time issuer there is obvious merit in selecting a lead-manager which has signficant experience of this market. This applies just as much to the experience of the individuals involved as the bank which he or she represents. The same is true for the law firms selected. If the individuals forming the project group are experienced, the first-time issuer will make significantly quicker and easier progress in executing the transaction.

The manager needs to understand thoroughly both the nature of the particular assets to be securitised and the procedures operated by the originator since he will have to discuss and comfort the rating agencies with regard to particular issues arising in relation to those assets and the adequacy of the originator's administration procedures and identify the risks inherent to those particular assets.

The manager will also be responsible for arranging the provision of credit enhancements. Where the lead-manager has an AAA rating, those enhancements most appropriately provided by a bank will normally be provided in-house. Experienced lead managers with ratings below that of the transaction are generally able to arrange for the enhancements to be provided, perhaps at greater cost, by other banks which have the appropriate rating.

Increasingly, as banks withdraw from market-making in certain sectors, managers are unable to offer prospective issuers access to all relevant markets. Ideally managers should be capable of distribution in the sterling and US dollar FRN markets, as well as the long-term fixed market and the euro-commercial paper market. If this is not the case the would be securitiser may instead find the structure dictated by the manager's distribution capabilities rather than the asset characteristic suggesting the most appropriate market for the asset.

Securitisation is a difficult process for the first-time issuer. Generally the asset audit and rating process will show up deficiencies in the originator's procedures or record information systems; these problems have to be corrected before an issue can take place. Following an issue the complex requirements of the transaction documentation need to be translated into written operating procedures for the originator/administrator of the assets. An experienced lead-manager can do much to assist the smooth implementation of these new procedures and reporting requirements to ensure the proper administration of the assets and the issuer's corporate affairs after the issue has been closed.

4.7 THE RATING PROCESS

Securitisation transactions are acknowledged to be highly complex. Some of the most innovative transactions have taken a number of months to put together and yet would-be investors have hours, or at best a few days, to decide whether to purchase part of an issue of asset-backed notes during its primary distribution phase. It is not surprising therefore that issuers seeking investors in the public markets invariably seek and obtain credit ratings from one or both of the leading international rating agencies—Standard & Poor's and Moody's. Generally issuers have achieved the highest long-term ratings (AAA/Aaa). The external credit rating has, for most investors, become an important supplement to their internal credit review.

An intending issuer needs to take an early decision on which rating agency to approach as much is gained from having early discussions with the agencies before the documentation of the transaction. The lead-managers can assist issuers to structure the transaction to achieve the desired rating, which, as indicated above, is usually AAA/Aaa. Consideration needs to be given as to whether the higher coupon which would be demanded by investors for a lesser rating would be justified by the reduced costs of insurances and other enhancements. For a lower-rated transaction, these should not only be less expensive but also be available from a wider range of institutions. In the early development of the UK mortgage-backed securities market the economics of an AAA-rated transaction and one rated AA were similar. The coupon differential in 1987/8 was typically 0.0025 per cent. This widened to 0.0050 per cent in early 1989, and from that point on issuers have generally chosen to structure AAA-rated transactions. One has to wonder whether, in the present market climate, there would be investor demand for an AA-rated transaction following the 'flight to quality' which commenced in late 1988 and which continues. On the assumption there are always some investors at the right price one would be inclined to think that the spread differential between AAA- and AA-rated paper has moved out beyond 0.10 per cent.

A critical choice for the issuer is which of the major rating agencies to approach for a rating. The two major agencies, Standard & Poor's and Moody's, have a different approach and methodology.

Standard & Poor's have detailed published criteria for the rating of securitisations utilising most types of assets. Increasingly, published criteria are also available in respect of the major continental countries. The S&P approach has two main tenets: (1) that the rated securities have to continue to perform in a timely manner when stress-tested under a full-scale recession senario; (2) each link in the credit chain has to be an obligation of an institution rated at least as highly as the rating sought for securities to be issued (or represents a deposit of cash held at a suitably rated bank). There is little scope for flexibility in either area.

Moody's use a similar stress test approach and generally look for each credit enhancer to have the appropriate rating to support the transaction (although on occasions 'shadow' ratings are permitted). There is, however, a greater judgemental element involved in the Moody's process, involving the weighing up of the totality of the entire transaction and forming a subjective view of its quality. This can give an issuer greater flexibility in structuring a transaction and in the selection of credit enhancers. However, it also allows the agency to require additional enhancements or protections which are not identified as being necessary by cash-flow analysis or other quantitative techniques. Additionally, Moody's have required a rated stand-by administrator to be appointed in the case where the primary administrator is not a rated institution.

To the extent that each of the major agencies has a slightly different approach it is generally thought that investors should be more comforted by dual-rated issues than those with only one rating. While this is undoubtedly true, there is little evidence that issuers who have chosen a dual rating have gained in terms of tighter pricing of an issue. A dual rating involves considerable extra cost which arises from three sources; the additional rating fee (which may be as much as $100,000), the additional cost of a credit enhancement not required by one agency but demanded by the other and the additional legal costs incurred by the additional time spent accommodating the requirements of two agencies rather than one. (Generally the legal costs of a transaction are directly related to the length of time it takes to structure and document a transaction.) To date it has not been necessary to dual-rate securitisations which utilise the long-term capital markets. It is, however, customary to seek a dual rate for commercial paper programmes. Because of their short-term nature the requirements in order to achieve the highest ratings are less stringent than those applied to long-term issues and there is a justification for a dual rating both in terms of pricing and depth of distribution (i.e. the potential investor base is significantly widened by a dual rating).

4.8 ON-GOING ADMINISTRATION

Once an issue has closed, the originator/servicer is left to run the transaction in accordance with the inevitably complex transaction documentation. This can be a daunting task for the first-time issuer. However, two steps can be taken to reduce the difficulty of this task. First, the lead-manager can continue to be involved in ensuring that proper procedures and a detailed diary system are implemented to facilitate compliance with the documented requirements. Second, the servicer of the assets should establish detailed written procedures for all aspects of the administrative process. The writing of such manuals should take place during the latter stages of the securitisation process so that they are ready for use immediately after the securitisation transaction has closed. It is not unusual for the first interest period to be short (less than three months) and this first interest payment date needs to be carefully planned for. It is essential that regular reports are properly prepared and produced in a timely manner for the trustee to the issue, the rating agencies and the independent directors of the issuer.

4.9 REGULATORS

The principal regulators likely to be involved in the securitisation process are central banks (in the UK the Bank of England), the Building Societies Commission in respect of UK building societies, and in the case of UK insurance companies, the DTI (Department of Trade and Industry). I have confined my comments here to the Bank of England and the Building Societies Commission.

Following the early issues of mortgage-backed securities in 1987 the Bank of England acknowledged the need to develop a regulatory framework for such transactions and indeed loan transfers in general. The BIS guidelines had not included any recommendations on securitisation of assets and, as securitisation in the UK preceded that in other European countries it was necessary for the Bank of England to develop its own approach.

A consultation process commenced in December 1987 and resulted, in early 1989, in the issue of a notice to authorised institutions (BSD/1989/1: *Loan Transfers and Securitisation*). The notice seeks to cover all types of loan transfer—not simply mortgage loans—making a distinction between the transfer of portfolios of loans (which is described as 'securitisation') and the transfer of a single loan or commitment. Broadly, the notice sets out a list of conditions, each of which has to be met if the transfer is to result in the asset being disregarded for capital adequacy purposes. There is no concept of a reduced capital requirement for a partial sale or upon the satisfaction of some but not all of the conditions in the notice. The notice acknowledges that some risks might still exist after an asset has been transfered—in particular administration risk and moral risk (i.e. the risk that a bank, while it has no legal obligation to provide support, will feel obliged to rescue an off-balance-sheet company which it has effectively established for the purposes of a securitisation)—but the Bank has not laid down specific requirements for these risks, preferring to deal with each institution on an issue-by-issue basis.

The Building Societies Commission published its own notice *Capital Requirements for Off-Balance Sheet Mortgage Lending* (PN88/2) in early 1988. This incorporates all the features of the Bank of England notice but has some additional requirements which appear to reflect the special relationship which societies enjoy with their customers and therefore the particular sensitivity of a building society securitising its mortgage loans.

In both cases the rules present a challenge to those who wish to securitise, but they are broadly logical and, with care, can be fully complied with.

4.10 THE FUTURE

It is always dangerous to predict the future but it falls to me to attempt to do so. Writing at the beginning of April 1991, one can safely predict that the securitisation of mortgage assets by UK centralised lenders will continue for the reasons set out at the beginning of this chapter.

One of the big questions is whether, and if so when, a UK building society will undertake a securitisation transaction. I feel confident that this will eventually come, either towards the end of 1991 or early in 1992. A more important question is: when will securitisation become a regular funding technique for the majority of larger societies? Here one has to be more cautious. I do feel, however, that this will come in time, partly as a result of capital presures which are light at present but can only become more restrictive as time goes on and partly as a result of the increasing cost of bank funding and the raising of subordinate debt.

We have already seen one consumer loan securitisation in the UK (the CARS UK transaction) and no doubt more will follow. The technology is similar to a mortgage securitisation, but the resultant capital saving for a regulated institution is at present twice as large. The same is true for most other bank lending to individuals.

Leasing companies have found it increasingly difficult to raise the substantial additional funding required each year and there is a powerful incentive to use securitisation. There are problems in the area of stamp duty (to be abolished in April 1992), retention of capital allowances in the main leasing company and the rating agency view on residual values, but each of these problems can be overcome. Lease receivables are generally considered to be the most difficult domestic assets to securitise but nevertheless the difficulties will be overcome in the next year or so.

Another possible area is credit card receivables. The techniques developed in the US are broadly applicable in the UK. The constraint to date has been that the majority of credit card balances are held by clearing banks, which have not yet felt the necessity to securitise.

Turning to Europe, it is interesting to note that a mortgage securitisation was carried out in late 1990 using Swedish five-year mortgages. More issues can be expected during 1991 from Scandinavian countries.

In France the enabling legislation has turned out to be cumbersome, and has resulted in securitisation being prohibitively expensive. Some changes to the primary legislation will be necessary before French securitisation becomes an active market.

The lifting of certain restrictions on raising debt in foreign markets by Spanish-based companies should accelerate the development of securitisation in Spain.

Much interest has been shown by Australian, New Zealand and South African corporates and banks in the securitisation process. The 'English Law' and Bank of England style regulatory environment make it likely that UK securitisation technology will be applied in these countries.

Despite the shaky start that securitisation has had outside the US, the adoption of the BIS regulations around the world and the tightening of global banking markets has set the conditions which will lead to a sharp increase in the use of securitisation in the 1990s.

5: The Building Societies' Perspective

Simon White, Halifax Building Society

Building societies have historically been the predominant residential mortgage lending institutions in the United Kingdom. Until the beginning of the 1980s their dominance was almost absolute. Following the entry into the market of the UK clearing banks, foreign banks and the centralised lenders and the conversion of Abbey National from a building society to a bank, the building societies still accounted for 61 per cent of all outstanding residential mortgages in the UK at the end of 1990 and during the last quarter of 1990 took a market share of 76 per cent of new loans. Yet, apart from a single aborted scheme, no building society has originated an issue of mortgage-backed securities to date. This chapter analyses why this should be the case and assesses the likelihood of building societies securitising in the future. It also chronicles the activities of societies as purchasers of mortgage-backed securities and their involvement to date in other areas of the secondary market for mortgages.

Three factors that dominate any study of this subject are discussed in detail: the pricing of mortgages and of funding alternatives, the availability of capital and the regulatory environment. It is aspects of these three factors that have contrived to keep building societies from securitising to date. At times in the past when securitisation has been feasible for pricing reasons, capital pressures have not been strong and regulation has not permitted societies to securitise. Now that regulation allows for securitisation, albeit retaining some disincentives and with a few loose ends yet to be tidied up, the pricing of securitisation has rarely been more unattractive and there remain no strong pressures on capital.

5.1 PRICING

From the late 1970s onwards there was a marked increase in competition between banks and building societies for both mortgage business and retail funds. The election of the Conservative government in 1979 had a hand in this, as the encouragement of home ownership, deregulation and increased competition were all fundamental tenets of its policies. Government encouragement of wider share ownership fostered a further source of competition for retail funds, especially from unit trusts and the privatisation of various state-owned industries.

Competition from external sources led to different reactions from societies, resulting in the break-up of the cartel that had established mortgage rates in the UK since 1939. The existence of the cartel had engendered particularly stable mortgage rates that bore little relation to the more volatile money market rates of interest. In fact, for significant periods during the 1970s the mortgage rate was either more than 3 per cent higher or lower than three-month LIBOR, the benchmark money market rate of interest, with the difference on occasions being as great as 5 per cent. By the mid-1980s, increased competition had forced societies to react promptly to changes in market rates in order to retain retail investors when rates increased and mortgage borrowers when they fell.

From 1983 until the end of 1988, the mortgage rate was consistently at a premium that averaged more than one full percentage point over three-month LIBOR. This interest rate environment was particularly favourable for wholesale funded mortgage lending, as the vast majority of mortgage lending in the UK was, and remains, on a variable interest rate basis. It led directly to the establishment of the centralised, wholesale funded lenders, the most notable of which are Household Mortgage Corporation, The Mortgage Corporation and National Home Loans. While they were developing and adapting to the UK market the securitisation techniques that were widely used in the United States, the centralised lenders funded their rapidly growing mortgage portfolios through bank borrowings. The volume of business was such that this source was quickly exhausted and in 1987 they commenced the regular and large scale origination of mortgage backed securities. The status of London as the centre of the Eurobond markets and ever finer spreads a feature of the sterling floating rate note sector, helped to ensure that the new market got off to a healthy start.

Although not having the powers to issue mortgage-backed securities when the UK market was created in 1987, building societies had by this time benefited from considerable deregulation of their wholesale funding activities. In 1983 they became able to pay interest gross on certificates of deposit and time deposits, which effectively opened up these two markets for the first time. In the same year borrowing from banks also became feasible. In 1985 societies were permitted to issue Eurobonds in the form of sterling floating rate notes and in 1986, when the power was granted to transact interest rate swaps, this was extended to sterling fixed rate issues. Finally, from the beginning of 1987 the power was granted to transact currency swaps, thereby opening up the opportunity of issuance of bonds in other currencies. Since then many new markets have been accessed and products utilised such as the domestic United States commercial paper market, non-sterling certificates of deposit and Euro medium term note programmes.

Not all societies have access to all sectors of the wholesale markets and many products, such as US commercial paper and non-sterling eurobonds, are only available to the largest societies. However, as the top 15 represent over 90 per cent of all building society assets, the ability to tap these markets is of great significance. The price that the larger societies pay for their medium-term wholesale funds has always been considerably less than the cost of issuing mortgage-backed securities, despite the fact that the societies' credit ratings are generally in the double-A band, whereas most issues of mortgage-backed securities have been rated triple-A. This is because societies are more understandable credits than highly structured mortgage-backed securities and most importantly because cash flows are certain, whereas those on mortgage-backed issues are subject to prepayment of the underlying mortgages and therefore uncertain. Issues of securities by building societies also have the benefit of a tax gross-up provision which is not acceptable to the agencies that rate mortgage-backed issues and, for those investors that are subject to capital backing requirements, a lower risk asset weighting.

Building societies are subject to a limit imposed by the Building Societies Act 1986 on the amount of wholesale funds they may raise. This is expressed as 40 per cent of total share, deposit and loan liabilities. At the end of 1990, the weighted average level of wholesale funding of the largest 15 societies was 19.3 per cent. Given that to reach the limit these societies would have to raise wholesale funds of almost £40bn without increasing retail funds, it is unrealistic to suggest that this 40 per cent limit represents a general constraint that could lead the building society movement to securitise its mortgage assets in the foreseeable future.

Since the stock market crash of 1987, retail funds that had been channelled previously into equities were reclaimed by the building societies to a considerable degree. Recent government measures have also helped to stimulate retail inflow. These are the abolition of composite rate tax on retail deposits, the ability of societies to pay interest gross to registered non-taxpayers and the creation of tax-exempt special savings accounts (TESSAs), whereby taxpayers can also be paid interest gross on specified maximum amounts and subject to certain other conditions. While many societies pay rates of interest well over LIBOR for some retail accounts, this is only at the margin in the context of their total retail funds. Average costs are generally at levels substantially below LIBOR.

In conclusion, there is currently no incentive for the building society movement as a whole to seek to securitise its mortgage assets for reasons related to either the price or availability of either wholesale or retail funds. Following the entry of sterling into the exchange rate mechanism of the European

Monetary System, longer-term expectations are for lower and more stable rates of interest and inflation. This is likely to increase further the competition for retail funds and could well force small societies to consider securitisation as an alternative funding source. It is unlikely to have the same effect on the larger societies, which enjoy considerable economies of scale and far greater access to the wholesale markets.

5.2 CAPITAL

It has already been mentioned that building societies' capital bases have not been and are not under any strong pressures. The weighted average of the core capital-to-risk-assets ratio of the eight largest commercial banks in the UK is estimated at 6.0 per cent, whereas that for the eight largest building societies is estimated at 9.3 per cent. Analysis of all societies would probably reveal a slightly higher figure as smaller societies tend to be better capitalised.

Capital for most societies is not a scarce resource, but why should this be so, particularly at a time when banks world-wide are struggling to meet ratio requirements? First, societies have been very restricted in the past as to the nature and levels of lending that they may engage in, other than traditional residential mortgage lending. The latter has proved a particularly safe class of assets, thus provisioning for future losses and actual write-offs have been historically at minimal levels. Second, being mutually owned organisations they do not of course pay dividends and thus a greater part, if not all, of net profit after tax is added to reserves.

Societies are currently required to keep at least 80 per cent of their total commercial assets in the form of loans to individuals that are fully secured by mortgage on land which is for their residential use, known as class 1 assets. Class 2 assets are other loans secured on land and class 3 assets include other loans and investments in subsidiary and associated companies. Class 1 assets attract the lowest capital backing requirements and class 3 assets the highest. The minimum level for class 1 assets will be reduced to 75 per cent in January 1993 but current legislation does not contemplate or permit any further reduction. Thus the fundamental nature of societies' lending activities will not change in the near future.

It is true that many of the new areas of business that societies have entered into during the past five years have resulted in greater provisioning and losses than societies had previously experienced in respect of their core mortgage business. However, it must be remembered that many of these areas such as estate agency, commercial mortgage lending, credit cards and unsecured personal lending are all adjuncts to or defensive of the core business of taking retail deposits and lending on residential mortgages. Teething problems (which are perhaps inevitable) are unlikely to be either repeated or tolerated if they persist. Some new areas of business, such as estate agency, will provide benefits to a society, such as introducing new mortgage business and generating insurance commissions, that are not identifiable in published accounts.

A number of well documented factors, most notable among them being the UK's high interest rates since late 1988, have resulted in significantly increased provisioning by building societies of late in respect of their core mortgage lending business. Given the nature of the institutions, this provisioning is likely to have been conservative in amount and many salutary lessons will have been learned. Any losses are unlikely to have a materially adverse effect on the overall capital position of the industry, and although of the greatest concern to societies, the amounts involved are insignificant in the context of the provisioning and losses of UK and other major banks around the world.

In addition to the ability to create tier 1 capital through retaining earnings, regulations are to be enacted during 1991 that will give societies the ability to issue tier 1 capital in the form of Permanent Interest Bearing Shares (PIBS). These are similar to non-cumulative preference shares issued by banks. It will be legally possible to sell PIBS through branches to retail customers, but several problems are likely to preclude this. In practical terms it is thought that PIBS will be bought only by domestic UK institutions, thereby restricting the size of the market and in all likelihood restricting access to it to only a handful of the larger societies.

Societies are also able to raise tier 2 capital in the form of subordinated debt, but regulations have yet to be announced that will distinguish between upper tier 2 undated capital and lower tier 2 dated capital. The largest group of lenders of subordinated debt has been Japanese leasing companies, but since early 1990 they have suffered reduced access to and increases in the cost of their own funding and have significantly reduced their activities after lending heavily to building societies in 1988 and 1989. Societies do not, however, enjoy uniform access to subordinated debt. The Halifax with dated subordinated debt ratings of Aa3 has issued, and remains capable of issuing, 25-year fixed-rate public subordinated debt. The remaining top 15 societies are currently unlikely to be able to raise dated subordinated debt for more than ten years and those outside the top 15 have never been able to raise subordinated debt without having to abide by over-restrictive covenants.

In conclusion, there are currently no pressures on building societies' capital that would precipitate a need to securitise mortgages in order to maintain the current volume of business. The competitive nature of the mortgage market is such that it is doubtful if societies would significantly increase market share, no matter how much capital they had. Residential mortgages attract low capital weighting and represent an efficient and profitable use of balance sheet resources for building societies. It is therefore unlikely that in its present shape the industry will need to securitise in the future for lack of capital.

5.3 REGULATION

Under the Building Societies Act 1962, societies did not have the power to securitise. Its successor, the Building Societies Act 1986 (the '86 Act') was many years in the drafting and when the main provisions came into force on 1 January 1987 they did not, naturally enough, contemplate securitisation. Building societies' powers are derived exclusively from the 86 Act, which broadly speaking means that they may only engage in activities that are expressly permitted by the 86 Act or other activities that are ancillary to those expressly permitted.

The 86 Act is a long and complex document, dealing with all aspects of societies and their activities. It contains 126 sections and 21 schedules, many of which provide for delegated legislation. Copious use has been made of these provisions by the Building Societies Commission, the regulatory authority established under the 86 Act, with 25 statutory instruments being made in 1987 alone. It is not, therefore, proposed to trace in detail the history of building society legislation as it relates to securitisation, although it is worth recording that the various aspects of securitisation have been dealt with at different times and in different ways and that societies do not enjoy the luxury of a single section or instrument that covers securitisation.

There is no doubt that building societies now have the powers to securitise both new and existing mortgage assets. There are, however, a number of impediments to doing so in a manner that will ensure off-balance sheet status for such mortgages. Most of these impediments are derived from Prudential Note 1988/2 entitled *Capital Requirements for Off-Balance Sheet Mortgage Lending*, issued by the Building Societies Commission. It is these and other aspects of the current regulatory environment that the remainder of this section seeks to address.

Perhaps the first hurdle for a building society stems from the first paragraph of the Prudential Note which reads as follows:

> In order to satisfy the Commission that no capital need be held for a particular group of loans, a society needs to demonstrate that for all practical purposes it is absolved from any continuing credit or interest rate risk, and that it will not, in practice, feel compelled to support the off-balance sheet arrangement if difficulties arise: for example, it might feel obliged to do so in the case of a special purpose mortgage finance vehicle set up by the society and publicly identified with it.

The issues raised by this paragraph might not be of concern to a centralised mortgage lender that generates business through intermediaries and is somewhat detached from its customers. For a building society with a major and visible presence in the high streets and a reputation for stewardship built up over perhaps more than a hundred years it is a major consideration.

The Prudential Note defines several characteristics that a 'mortgage finance vehicle' must have and a number of conditions that must be satisfied in order for the vehicle to be considered fully distanced from a society and therefore be treated as being off-balance sheet. Most of these do not present a problem, but four do, two of which are connected. These are that the vehicle is financed independently from the society and that it 'bears all its expenses' (i.e. they are not borne by the society). In this respect societies are at a disadvantage to banks, which are permitted to make one-off contributions and long-term subordinated loans to vehicles under the terms of the Bank of England's Notice on Loan Transfers and Securitisation BSD/1989/1. In order to provide credit enhancement and liquidity a vehicle established by a building society would have to utilise pool insurance and any subordinated funding or liquidity facility would have to be provided by third parties. An alternative would be to establish the vehicle as a subsidiary (an 'appropriate mortgage company', as described at the end of this section) and finance it on-balance-sheet prior to selling it or its assets.

A further condition is that a society's auditors must approve the arrangements as being off-balance sheet for accounting purposes. However, it is not entirely certain that they would be able to do so without qualification prior to the adoption of the accounting standards contemplated by Exposure Draft 49 entitled *Reflecting the Substance of Transactions in Assets and Liabilities*. As at May 1991 this is still under discussion and there are a number of aspects with which both building societies and banks are not satisfied.

The fourth condition that presents a problem is that societies are not permitted to engage in swaps with mortgage finance vehicles which precludes one of the means of profit extraction. Even if this were permitted, societies do not currently have the power to enter into swaps for such purposes. There are a number of alternative means of profit extraction, all with their own tax problems and other complications, including deferred payment for mortgages and investment in mortgage-backed securities (defined under the 86 Act as 'mortgage finance rights') on a subordinated basis with a variable but hopefully artificially high return. How the first securitised issue originated by a building society will deal with this will be closely analysed by many interested market practitioners.

Other regulatory anomalies that exist but are surmountable include a requirement of the Prudential Note that transfers of mortgages by a society must be outright legal assignments rather than the assignment of the equitable interests in the loans and mortgages. This takes more time, costs more and generally increases the administrative burden. The same effect is caused by the need for a society to obtain the specific consent of the borrower before transferring a mortgage; other institutions may rely on general consents given at the time that mortgage loans are made.

A consultation draft of a revised Prudential Note on capital requirements for off-balance sheet mortgage lending was issued by the Building Societies Commission at the end of August 1991. If it is adopted as drafted, societies will become permitted to make contributions to the up-front expenses of mortgage finance vehicles and also to make subordinated loans to them, putting societies on an equal footing in these respects with UK banks. Among other proposed changes, the transfer of mortgages by equitable assignment will also be permitted, subject to certain conditions.

Great care must be taken in respect of membership rights of a society. A code of practice accepted by all major building societies requires that the implications of a transfer of his mortgage must be made clear to a borrowing member even if the transfer is only to an associated body of the society. There is a similar requirement of an associated body of a society that lends on mortgage to make clear to borrowers that they have no membership rights of the parent society, that it is a separate legal entity and that the mortgage may be transferred (if such is the case). Societies will also need to comply with the terms of the Department of the Environment/HM Treasury Statement of Practice on the Transfer of Mortgages, which is believed to have been accepted by all mortgage lending institutions in the UK.

Brief mention should be made of 'appropriate mortgage companies' (AMCs), which have already been referred to in this chapter and will be mentioned again. When the 86 Act came into force it did not permit a society to acquire mortgage loans from any institution in any manner other than from another building society under the somewhat cumbersome transfer of engagements provisions of the 86 Act. Under a statutory instrument that came into force in August 1988, societies became able to establish AMCs, which are permitted to grant, acquire, dispose of and securitise mortgage loans. Mortgage assets held by AMCs are subject to the same capital backing requirements as those held on a society's main balance sheet subject to an aggregate maximum of 15 per cent of class 1 assets. Any excess would be considered class 3 assets. This is intended to preserve the fundamental nature of societies and to prevent them from simply becoming holding companies for AMCs. Any securitisation activity by an AMC is likely to be limited to its being used as a vehicle to build up a mortgage pool that is subsequently sold. An AMC would not be considered to be off-balance sheet and would attract full capital backing if it were simply to securitise its own assets.

5.4 INTERNAL CONSIDERATIONS

Since pushing hard for the powers to securitise, which were largely obtained during 1987 and the first half of 1988, the absence of any economic benefit in securitising has led to the great majority of societies losing the impetus to take the matter any further. The next step of preparing the organisation for securitisation has been taken by only a few societies and only one, the Skipton, is publicly known to be geared up to securitise more or less immediately upon it becoming economically attractive.

The resources required to prepare a building society to a state of readiness for securitisation should not be underestimated. Systems have to be able to select, analyse, administer and separately account for each mortgage pool. This capability will certainly extend beyond that normally required for building society systems. Staff training will extend far beyond basic product education. Forms and marketing literature will have to be redesigned, product procedure manuals rewritten, the quality of systems input will have to be increased and, of course, staff associations and/or unions will be involved. Securitisation is thus not merely a funding decision for the treasurer, but a major strategic objective that will require considerable investment and will impact on all staff levels and many different departments, and will thus require their support.

Other factors that require detailed consideration include the desirability and possible consequences of interest rate and arrears policies for securitised issues differing from those adopted by a society for its on-balance sheet mortgage book. Interest rates may have to be higher than on the main book to enable a vehicle company to honour its obligations. Rating agencies, credit enhancers and insurers will require pre-agreed arrears procedures to be followed, whereas branch managers may have considerable discretion to practice forbearance under general guidelines. The marketing of such potentially very different mortgage products will also need to be particularly carefully planned in order to avoid bewilderment among customers.

5.5 INVESTMENT IN MORTGAGE-BACKED SECURITIES

Societies obtained the power to invest in mortgage-backed securities in August 1988 but the statutory instrument granting the power requires that they are class 3 assets. A consultation paper on proposed new liquid asset regulations was issued in December 1990 by the Building Societies Commission which states that it is not intended to reclassify mortgage-backed securities as liquid assets. There has been intense lobbying by societies, the

Building Societies Association, the Council of Mortgage Lenders and by many investment banking institutions for this to be reversed, but as at May 1991 the outcome is not known.

As a more general matter, the investment by societies in mortgage-backed securities be they classified as liquid assets or not, makes a great deal of sense as the credit risks could not be better understood. For those societies that are carrying surplus capital, both senior and subordinated notes would seem to be natural investment instruments.

5.6 THE SECONDARY MORTGAGE MARKET

The only society to have originated mortgage-backed securities in any form is the Leamington Spa, which is now to merge with the Bradford and Bingley. In 1988 it established an off-balance sheet vehicle which was to finance a mortgage pool in the initial stages by issuing US dollar mortgage-backed euro-commercial paper swapped into sterling and backed by an underwritten note issuance facility. The intention was then to refinance this through a long term issue of mortgage-backed securities when the mortgage pool had reached a sufficient size. In the event, the downturn in the housing market in 1989 led to lower than expected volumes of new business and although small amounts of the euro-commercial paper were issued, volumes were insufficient to justify the continuance of the scheme and the vehicle company was taken on to the society's balance sheet as an AMC.

The secondary mortgage market in the UK is not confined to issuance of and investment in mortgage-backed securities. Since 1988, five societies are known to have been actively engaged in agency lending involving the origination of mortgage loans onto the balance sheet of another organisation, usually a foreign bank. Dutch, German, Swiss, French and Japanese banks are among the recipients of these loans, although activity is understood to have declined as the downturn in the UK housing market became more severe during 1990.

Many societies have purchased mortgage pools, through AMCs, from other organisations, most notably the staff mortgage books of foreign banks operating in the UK, insurance companies and some corporates. The advantages for the vendor are the freeing up of balance sheet capacity and less administration. The advantages for the purchasing society are principally that such transactions are discreet and that the assets acquired will be class 1 assets rather than, in the case of purchasing mortgage backed securities, class 3 assets. During 1989 and 1990 such purchases provided societies with particularly high quality assets that might otherwise have been hard to come by at a time when new business activity in the mortgage market was subdued.

Mortgage administration has also developed into a business in its own right, with a number of organisations, including building societies, offering this service for both securitised and non-securitised mortgage pools. The Skipton is the most prominent society in this market, having set up its own subsidiary and subsequently purchased one of its competitor mortgage administration companies.

The Prudential Note makes reference to both agency lending and mortgage administration and requires, quite reasonably, that arrangements are structured so that a society does not bear any credit or interest rate risk if it wishes to avoid capital backing. It goes on, however, to state that 'if a society undertakes a significant amount of off-balance sheet business, the Commission may wish to discuss subjective adjustments to the society's desired level of capital to reflect the increased operational risks, which may come to be disproportionate to the society's balance sheet size.'

5.7 THE FUTURE

It has already been concluded that the building society movement as a whole is unlikely in the foreseeable future to seek to securitise its mortgage assets for reasons related to the pricing or availability of wholesale or retail funds, or for lack of capital. There will, of course, be exceptions to this generality and in a healthy mortgage market it is not difficult to envisage a few societies becoming active in the origination of mortgage-backed securities. However, the great strength of building societies has been, and remains, their ability to hold mortgages on their balance sheets and it is therefore currently unrealistic to expect that the movement as a whole will securitise any substantial part of its mortgage assets.

6: Developments in Financing Techniques

Candy Helman, JP Morgan Securities

The decade of the 1980s saw the introduction of asset-backed securities to Europe and a number of borrowers took advantage of this new type of finance. The early asset-backed issuers made great strides in solving the tax, legal, accounting and regulatory problems related to securitising their assets but they were significantly less creative in the structuring of their securities. Innovation focused on devising off-balance-sheet company structures and on extracting profits efficiently—two areas where issuers had great interest. When confronted with the decision of what type of debt to issue, most borrowers chose the familiar floating rate note (FRN) even when this structure did not match their assets. Because of the large up-front costs of securitising assets, few borrowers wished to be pioneers. Also, many bankers argued that uniformity was a key factor in the development of an asset-backed market, so that investors could choose from a large pool of virtually identical bond issues.

By contrast, the 1990s are likely to see greater innovation by issuers in the engineering of their securities as the market enters the second stage of its development. Particularly in the current environment, where there is likely to be greater competition among borrowers for a smaller pool of funds, borrowers will have more incentive to design issuing structures that appeal to investors. However, as attention shifts from borrower to lender, it is important not to lose sight of the issuers' objectives and there will be a challenge for bankers to create structures that are attractive to investors and meet the needs of issuers.

6.1 FINANCIAL ENGINEERING IN THE ASSET-BACKED MARKETS

There are a number of reasons why financial engineering is likely to play a more important role in the asset-backed markets in the future. The first is that as the attractions of asset-backed bonds—a premium return for a high-quality risk—have become known in Europe and the Far East, the universe of investors interested in buying asset-backed securities has grown. However, many of these investors have limited access to foreign currency funding, while others may have negative views of a particular currency. Therefore, their interest in buying sterling- or dollar-denominated asset-backed paper will be affected by currency factors totally unrelated to the underlying value of the security. Similarly, different investors will have differing preferences for fixed- or floating-rate investments. Through financial engineering, an issuer can structure a security with a rate basis and currency different from that of the underlying assets, and by doing so can reach a wider investor base.

Although US investors are familiar with the unpredictable cash flows of US mortgage-backed securities and, in fact, welcome the trading opportunities that arise from these uncertainties, European and Far Eastern investors are much less willing to accept the interest rate risks that random prepayments create. These investors prefer bullet maturity securities and again there is a role for financial engineering to smooth out the cash flows of an asset pool in order to create a security that will appeal to the widest possible investor base.

The lukewarm response of European investors to the few euroasset-backed transactions that have passed the prepayment risk to noteholders is proof of investors' unwillingness to accept interest rate risk. Nor will euromarket investors accept currency risk arising from prepayments.

The final reason for interest in financial engineering is the concern shown by issuers and investors alike that traditional markets may not be able to absorb the high volume of debt planned by issuers in the coming years. In the UK mortgage-backed market, for example, the amounts available for investment in floating-rate sterling-denominated debt may not be sufficient to accommodate the high volume of asset-backed issues planned by borrowers. However, through financial engineering, UK mortgage originators can reach new types of investors who buy only, for example, fixed-rate or yen-denominated debt.

The European asset-backed markets have seen some early attempts by issuers to use financial engineering to create new types of instruments. For example, CIBC Mortgages PLC, the mortgage subsidiary of the Canadian Imperial Bank of Commerce, established a highly successful UK mortgage-backed Euro Commercial Paper (ECP) programme under the name of MAES ECP PLC. In this case, the financing is provided by short-term US-dollar-denominated Euro Commercial Paper, while investors' security is a pool of 25-year sterling-denominated residential mortgages. Another specialist mortgage lender in the UK, Household Mortgage Corporation PLC, has issued several five-year fixed-rate sterling bonds, again backed by pools of long-term variable-rate mortgages. Although these borrowers faced high research and development costs in designing new structures, both the ECP programme and the fixed-rate bonds proved to be very attractive sources of funds and I expect others to follow their leads. Even within the familiar FRN structure various issuers have introduced structural innovations in an attempt better to address the needs of particular investors. For example, the National Home Loans Group has issued several FRNs under the Collateralised Mortgage Securities' name which have been divided into a series of tranches each with a different expected average life. A number of US asset-backed issuers, the most prominent among them being Citibank, have created bonds that resemble bullet maturity corporate debt despite being secured against a pool of assets with uncertain cash flows. The Citibank issues have proved popular with euromarket investors and I expect European asset-backed issuers to copy their example.

All of the examples mentioned above rely on financial engineering to transform the cash flows of an asset pool with a particular profile into a different form which is more attractive to potential investors. Some of these financial engineering techniques, such as interest rate and currency swaps, are familiar to most corporate treasurers in their everyday business. Others, such as Guaranteed Investment Contracts, are less well known and their application to asset-backed securities is specialised. Many of these techniques have been imported from the US where asset-backed technology is most advanced and it is often the US issuers such as Citibank that have introduced them to the Euromarkets.

In this chapter I will discuss a number of different financial engineering techniques and their applicability to the asset-backed markets. My focus will be on the ways in which an issuer can transform the cash flows of his assets to suit his investors' preferences and I will concentrate on three specific areas: structuring a bond in a currency or rate basis different from that of the underlying assets; smoothing out the cash flows of an asset pool to create a known repayment schedule; and assuring a more certain final maturity for a transaction. Finally, I will describe how a Euro Commercial Paper programme can be used to provide attractive non-recourse asset-backed finance.

6.2 CREATING FIXED-RATE AND FOREIGN CURRENCY BONDS

6.2.1 Basis risk: changing between floating- and fixed-rate cash flows

Interest rate swaps can be used in asset-backed securities to transform a cash flow linked to a variable-rate asset into a fixed cash flow and, by creating a fixed rate instrument, an issuer can reach a large body of investors who have appetite for asset-backed risk but do not buy FRNs. This was the aim of Household Mortgage Corporation in structuring the fixed rate UK mortgage-backed bonds, HMC Mortgage Notes 101, 102 and 103. This objective was largely successful as a high proportion of the fixed rate bonds were placed with UK insurance companies and pension funds that had not previously purchased mortgage-backed FRNs.

Alternatively, if an issuer and his lead-manager determine that, due to market conditions, there is likely to be greater demand or a better reception for a FRN than for a fixed bond, swaps can also be used to hedge fixed assets and create a FRN backed by fixed interest assets. This was the case for the CARS (UK) transaction, an FRN backed by fixed-rate hire purchase receivables. Another recent transaction, Osprey Mortgage Securities (No. 1), which was backed by fixed-rate Swedish krona-denominated residential mortgages, employed a cross-currrency fixed-floating-rate swap to allow the issuer to tap the dollar FRN market.

Because of the nature of asset-backed securities, the use of swaps to hedge asset-backed cash flows does present some difficulties. A major complication arises from the repayment profile of the underlying asset pool. Swap counterparties, similarly to investors, will not wish to bear the interest rate risks that arise from an uncertain repayment schedule. This means that asset-backed issuers that wish to incorporate swaps into their bonds must present potential swap counterparties with either a certain amortisation schedule or, preferably, with a non-amortising fixed principal value. The solution to this problem is to engineer predictable cash flows on the bond; the following section describes various techniques which an issuer can use to achieve this.

Because of the difficulty of engineering a predictable cash flow for an asset-backed bond, some issuers may prefer to use amortising swaps to provide a hedge. A randomly amortising swap, were it to be available in the market, would be extremely expensive. Therefore, when an issuer uses an amortising swap, it is normally on the basis that the originator of the assets writes an offsetting swap with the rated counterparty. This transfers the interest rate risk of prepayments from the counterparty to the originator so that the swap counterparty retains only the issuer's and the originator's credit risks. Although that is an acceptable structure from the point of view of the investors and the rating agencies, many originators feel uncomfortable retaining some element of prepayment risk. Auditors and regulatory authorities may also be reluctant to allow off-balance-sheet treatment of the asset-backed debt if the originator is retaining significant risks.

The second area of difficulty arising from the use of swaps in asset-backed securities is related to tax issues. In order to avoid suffering adverse economic consequences, it is important for an issuer to ensure that the tax treatment of the swap flows is symmetrical. It is not necessarily a problem if the payments that the issuer receives are subject to tax, provided that he can benefit from an offsetting deduction on the payments he makes. The risk of asymmetrical tax treatment is particularly serious for a foreign currency bond issued in the UK. This is because the UK tax authorities require tax to be paid on currency gains realised on assets (the swap) while they do not allow deductions on currency losses on liabilities (the bond issue), despite the fact that the economic gains and losses are fully offsetting. In order to avoid an unfavourable tax position, a UK asset-backed issuer wishing to tap the foreign currency markets must issue the bond from an offshore vehicle located in a jurisdiction that treats the currency gains and losses identically. While it is relatively easy to establish an offshore vehicle, issuing from another legal jurisdiction may introduce other problems. For instance, in the case of a transaction backed by UK mortgages, the assets must be owned by a UK-domiciled company in order to qualify for the MIRAS tax deduction at source.

Withholding tax issues can also present potential problems to asset-backed issuers who undertake swaps. Although swap payments made to bank counterparties are not subject to withholding tax in most countries, there is nonetheless a risk that withholding tax will be imposed in the future. This risk becomes even greater if various tax jurisdictions are involved, as they will be if the issuing vehicle is located offshore. Corporate borrowers normally provide a swap counterparty with an indemnity obliging them to gross up swap payments in the event of the imposition of a withholding tax. However, an asset-backed issuing vehicle has limited resources and the rating agencies will not take a view on the ability of a special-purpose company to satisfy a future liability such as a tax gross-up that cannot by quantified. Therefore, the rating agencies will not rate an asset-backed issue if the vehicle gives investors a withholding tax indemnity. In the past issuers have solved this problem by arranging for a third party with an adequate rating to provide this indemnity. In the case of the HMC 101 issue, that indemnity was provided as part of the interest rate swap itself. Alternatively, an issue may carry a mandatory call option in the event of the imposition of a withholding tax provided it is supported by an assured source of refinancing from an institution of adequate credit quality.

Not surprisingly, the rating agencies will expect to review the documentation of any swap that is incorporated into the structure of an asset-backed issue. Past issuers have used the International Swap Dealers Association master agreement to form the basis of the swap documentation but it is necessary to make some substantial amendments to the terms. For example, certain standard clauses, such as a Credit Event Upon Merger, will not be acceptable to the rating agencies because they provide for the termination of the swap. The concerns of the agencies in reviewing the documentation will be to ensure that neither counterparty can terminate the swap unless and until a noteholder Event of Default has occurred.

6.2.2 Managing cash flows: creating a predictable payment profile

Many assets, such as credit card receivables, can be repaid by the obligor at will and this creates potential problems for an asset-backed issuer. The simplest way for an issuer to handle the repayments it receives from borrowers is to pass them on to noteholders on a monthly or quarterly basis. Many sophisticated investors are willing to accept uncertain repayments, provided that their bonds carry a floating rate of interest and repayments do not expose them to reinvestment risk. However, other investors will not buy amortising instruments at all and the universe of investors in Europe that purchase fixed-rate amortising bonds is very small.

Fortunately, there are a number of ways to engineer uncertain cash flows in order to provide investors with predictable bond payments. The simplest way to smooth out uneven cash flows is through substitution, that is the replacement of those assets that repay before the maturity of the bond with new assets of a similar type. In fact, it is uneconomic to securitise assets with very short maturities, such as credit card receivables, without substitution because the up-front costs of structuring the transaction must be amortised over a very short period. For this reason, originators in France, where the securitisation legislation prohibits substitution, are reluctant to consider issuing credit-card-backed debt despite a strong desire to remove those types of assets from their balance sheets.

Although substitution answers investors' concerns about repayments and allows an issuer to create a bullet maturity bond, the inclusion of new assets in a security pool raises various credit issues. Unless investors have some assurance that the substitute assets will be of at least as good quality as those in the original pool, the credit quality of the bond could be reduced by the inclusion of new, riskier assets. This is a major concern of the rating agencies when they review a transaction that includes a substitution option and normally it is addressed by allowing the issuer to include only assets originated under the same lending criteria as the original portfolio. In addition, the issuer must ensure that the overall profile of the pool (loan to value ratios, seasoning, geographic distribution, etc.) remains largely unchanged following substitution.

Although in practice an issuer can use substitution to create a non-amortising bond, the rating agencies will have concerns that the originator may not have sufficient substitute assets available to replace those that repay. Therefore, they will require an issuer to have some form of 'backstop' investment available to it in the event that it does not have replacement assets for substitution.

An issuer can address the rating agencies' concerns by arranging a Guaranteed Investment Contract (GIC) with a AAA-rated party. This contract must be for the life of the borrowing and it must guarantee a minimum rate to be paid on deposits of excess cash placed with the GIC provider. In the case of floating-rate assets, the guaranteed rate is usually on the order of LIBOR – 0.50 per cent p.a. For a fixed-rate pool, the guaranteed rate must be set at a margin over the fixed rate on the borrowing. Whether or not an issuer will require the GIC to bear a fixed or floating rate of interest depends on the structure of the bond. For example, a floating-rate GIC may be acceptable even for a fixed-rate transaction if a swap is in place for the full value of the borrowing. In this case the issuer's obligation would be to pay floating-rate interest to the swap counterparty in return for receiving from the counterparty the fixed interest payments due to noteholders.

6.2.3 Hard bullets: using put options and maturity guarantees

Although investors have bought amortising asset-backed bonds with 30- or 40-year final maturities, investors generally have a preference for both shorter transactions and known maturities. Therefore, one way to increase investor interest in asset-backed securities is to create instruments with short- or medium-term assured maturities.

The difficulty for an issuer in creating a bond of a particular maturity is that the term of his assets may not match that of the borrowing. This is a particular problem with long-term assets such as mortgages, which may not mature until long after the desired term of a bond. Some maturity mismatches will occur even in transactions backed by very short-term assets such as credit card receivables. Although substitution can be used to keep a bond outstanding for a particular period, it is difficult if not impossible for an originator to time the maturities of his assets to coincide exactly with the bond maturity. In fact, substitution can compound the maturity mismatch problem by lengthening the average term of the assets in a pool.

In order to address investors' preferences for short-term bullet maturity securities, many asset-backed issuers have turned to a number of financial tools such as put options and so-called soft bullet or hard bullet maturity guarantees. In the case of very long-term assets such as mortgages, the investors' maturity can be assured by a put option provided to the issuer by an appropriately rated institution. The terms of the option allow the issuer to sell his assets or a note backed by his assets to the provider on a single day in the future that coincides with the bond maturity at a price of par. In the event that the issuer is unable to refinance his assets at maturity, he can exercise the put option, using the proceeds of the sale of his assets to the put provider to repay noteholders. This was the structure used in the HMC Mortgage Notes 101 and 102 issues mentioned previously and in another more recent issue, Collateralised Mortgage Securities No. 10. The put provider in this case agreed to buy a mortgage-backed note from the issuing vehicle on the bond's fifth anniversary. Although the mortgage-backed note has a 32-year final maturity, the fixed bondholders can look to the put option to assure their repayment in year five.

In the case of transactions backed by very short-term assets such as credit card receivables, it is usual for the issuer's substitution rights to end six to twelve months prior to the expected maturity in order to allow the assets to partially or fully repay. During this period, the issuing vehicle will be accumulating cash and must have the benefit of a GIC in order to ensure that the investment return earned on its funds is sufficient to allow the issuer to service its debt.

The length of the accumulation period that is required will depend on assumptions as to the likely repayment rate of the assets. Although experienced originators are probably able to predict their repayment rates fairly accurately, many issuers choose to give investors greater certainty of repayment by providing a maturity guarantee. The terms of each maturity guarantee will differ from transaction to transaction. For a so-called soft bullet, the repayment assumptions will be based on a rate close to the originator's actual experience, while in the case of the hard bullet, the issuer will conservatively assume a slower repayment rate. Naturally, the larger the value of the guarantee, the more certainty investors will have of timely redemption. In the case of most transactions that utilise an accumulation period and a maturity guarantee, in the unlikely event that repayments received by the issuer and calls under the maturity guarantee are insufficient to repay the bond in full on maturity, investors receive a *pro rata* share of collections as they are received on a monthly or quarterly basis. Any debt that remains outstanding would bear a floating rate of interest.

Some issuers in the UK mortgage-backed market have attempted to address investors' varying maturity preferences by dividing their debt into a series of tranches each with a differing expected average life. These issues are based on a popular US development, the Collateralised Mortgage Obligation (CMO). Although the holders of the various tranches of a CMO are secured against a single pool of mortgages, loan repayments are passed through first to holders of the short or 'fast-pay' tranche. Holders of the latter 'medium-pay' or 'slow-pay' tranches do not begin to receive repayments of principal until the previous tranches are fully retired. By adjusting the size and number of different tranches an issuer can create the most attractive range of maturities for investors given market conditions at the time of launch.

These tranched issues have been most successful when they have targeted the requirements of a particular investor group. For example, the fast-pay tranche of the recent Collateralised Mortgage Securities No. 7 issue was particularly attractive to Bank of England regulated investors because it is expected to mature prior to the 1992 date when the Bank is scheduled to change the capital weighting for mortgage-backed securities from 50 to 100 per cent in accordance with its acceptance of the EC Banking Directive.

The drawback for an issuer of launching a CMO-style bond is that he may have to forego the option to substitute new assets for those that repay in order to create a very short maturity for the first tranche. Although the option to substitute is very valuable, a CMO can be economic particularly for an experienced issuer with minimal up-front structuring costs. The documentation and rating of a multi-tranche CMO introduces few complications and I believe this structure is a useful alternative for issuers to have in certain market conditions.

6.3 STRUCTURING AN ASSET-BACKED EURO COMMERCIAL PAPER PROGRAMME

Another way to address investors' objections to the uncertain cash flows and long-term maturities that typify many asset-backed bonds is to structure the borrowing as a Euro Commercial Paper (ECP) programme rather than as a bond issue. Although only a small number of asset-backed ECP programmes have been established to date, this form of financing can be attractive to issuer and investor alike. From the borrower's point of view, issuing ECP will allow him to reach a new investor base as well as give him greater flexibility in managing his borrowings. Because ECP can be issued in a series of tranches with differing maturities from one to three months or more, a borrower can adjust the outstanding amount of his debt almost daily, passing repayments through to investors very quickly after they are received and thus significantly reducing reinvestment risk. The US dollar ECP market is a deep one and even issuers with non-dollar assets can access this large market without facing some of the problems of a longer-term foreign currency issue. This is because the short-term nature of the ECP notes allows a borrower to hedge in the more liquid foreign exchange market rather than the cross-currency swap market. From an investor's point of view, asset-backed ECP represents a good quality alternative to sovereign or corporate debt. Certainly, asset-backed ECP programmes, such as the MAES ECP No. 1 programme, backed by UK residential mortgages, have found favour with investors and this has resulted in a very competitive cost of funds for the borrower.

Although an ECP programme suits short-term assets well, in the case of other assets, such as residential mortgages, there will be a maturity mismatch between the very short term of the notes and the much longer term of the assets. Any potential refinancing risk that exists in an ECP programme must be addressed in the structure. Although it is expected that the borrower will refinance outstanding notes by issuing a new tranche of debt to the same or different investors, the rating agencies will not rely on a borrower's ability to issue new ECP. Therefore, to satisfy their concerns, the programme must have a committed source of refinancing and this is commonly provided by a backstop facility from a group of banks. This transfers the risk that the assets cannot be refinanced at maturity of the notes to the lenders, but banks are better able to evaluate and accept this risk than ECP holders.

Although banks are generally comfortable lending against pools of good assets, the documentation of an asset-backed ECP backstop will be unfamiliar to them and this may cause them to seek a higher-than-usual return on their commitments. In reviewing the facility agreement, the rating agencies will seek to ensure that the backstop banks cannot cancel their commitments while notes are outstanding unless the issuer has defaulted on a payment due. This means that many of the standard loan documentation clauses such as breach of warranty cannot be events of default. The backstop facility agreement must strike a fine balance between providing the bank lenders with protection without prejudicing the position of the ECP noteholders.

If a borrower holding non-dollar assets wishes to issue dollar-denominated ECP (and the dollar sector of the market is by far the largest), he will have to hedge his liabilities in the foreign exchange market. The rating agencies will require the issuer to be fully hedged at all times and will wish to see the terms of the issuer's foreign exchange trades with bank counterparties documented. Again, this will be unusual for banks, which normally document foreign exchange transactions with only a confirmation telex. The foreign exchange agreements will set out the procedures for settling outstanding foreign exchange trades in an event of default and the rating agencies will be particularly concerned that counterparties are prohibited from netting their exposures. Again, this will run counter to usual market procedures, so that banks providing foreign exchange lines may seek some additional compensation to cover these small but unfamiliar risks.

Although an asset-backed ECP programme can be complex and therefore more costly to establish than a familiar fixed- or floating-rate bond, it can be an extremely competitive source of funds on a running cost basis. The MAES UK mortgage-backed ECP programme regularly achieves a rate of LIMEAN on its notes. In addition to this, it must pay commitment fees to the banks providing the backstop facility. However, even after doing so, it achieves an all-in cost of around LIBOR plus $\frac{1}{8}$ per cent. This compares very favourably with the cost of a mortgage-backed FRN in today's market of LIBOR plus 0.40 per cent or more.

As the universe of both asset-backed investors and issuers grows, the markets are likely to see greater innovation in the structuring of asset-backed securities. Investors will demand new structures and issuers will accommodate them in an attempt to find the widest possible placement for their debt. Already we have seen the first examples of financial engineering in the form of fixed-rate bullet maturity asset-backed bonds and asset-backed ECP programmes and I am confident that the coming years will see more of these structures. The task in the 1990s for bankers and issuers in the asset-backed markets will be to refine and improve these structures.

7: Securitisation of Automobile Receivables: The Experience of CARS (UK)

Jonathan E. Keighley, Gracebury Securitisation Ltd

7.1 TRANSACTION HISTORY

In July 1988 the Basle Committee on Banking Regulations and Supervisory Practices published its report on the *International Convergence of Capital Measurement and Capital Standards*. This caused banks worldwide to focus increasingly on their balance sheets, capital structures and return on capital employed. Standard Chartered PLC was no exception. Chartered Trust plc, its consumer credit subsidiary in the UK whose principle business was the provision of hire purchase finance for motor vehicles, was growing vigorously. Securitisation was considered to be an innovative way by which Chartered Trust could continue its growth without further calls on the capital resources of its parent. At the same time the transaction was regarded as an attractive way in which the capital ratios of both Standard Chartered and Chartered Trust could be improved, since it removed assets from the balance sheet, releasing capital for alternative use, while at the same time retaining a substantial proportion of the profits earned from those assets.

Whilst the securitisation of mortgage assets was becoming fairly commonplace in the UK, no one had yet successfully securitised hire purchase receivables. Indeed, there were many people who said that the legal, taxation and accounting problems were such that it would be impossible to do so.

During October 1988 Standard Chartered Merchant Bank Ltd, the UK merchant banking arm of Standard Chartered (which was to become Chartered WestLB Limited following the sale of 50 per cent of the company to Westdeutsche Landesbank Girozentrale in January 1990), approached several investment banks with experience of securitising consumer credit in the US environment. Goldman Sachs International Ltd. immediately agreed to devote research effort towards assisting Chartered WestLB to examine the feasibility of, and subsequently to realise the project. By January 1989, in the light of the initial research, the chief executive of Standard Chartered had authorised serious development work to commence.

Early in 1989 various events were also taking place on the regulatory front which were to have a significant bearing on the transaction: the Companies Bill 1989 was published; the Bank of England abolished the five-year rule for sterling securities; and in February 1989 the Bank of England published the regulatory framework for securitisation entitled *Loan Transfers and Securitisation.* As regards UK accounting standards, ED42, *Accounting for Special Purpose Transactions,* had appeared in 1988, and was to be replaced by ED49, *Reflecting the Substance of Transactions in Assets and Liabilities,* which appeared in May 1990, just prior to the launch of the transaction.

The two rating agencies, Standard & Poor's and Moody's, visited Chartered Trust. The quality of Chartered Trust's computer systems enabled the production and analysis of various credit-related statistics so that an early provisional view could be formed of the viability of the project. The production and analysis of this historical and current data required by the rating agencies can often prove a major stumbling block for securitisation.

It is often easier to justify securitisation in a large group of companies at parent company level than at subsidiary level. At subsidiary level, a major securitisation involves a significant diversion of scarce management resources. The balance sheet size of the subsidiary company is likely to be fairly dramatically reduced, as will the absolute level of profit (especially if the subsidiary is to bear the full costs of the exercise). If it is intended that some or all of the capital released by securitisation is returned to the parent company, the subsidiary may feel its access to capital for future expansion is potentially threatened. Furthermore, delicate issues such as the cost of equity and term debt being supplied from the parent company to the subsidiary have to be re-examined carefully. How such issues are resolved can affect the entire economics of the transaction when looked at uniquely from the perspective of the subsidiary. All these issues had to be discussed in detail with Chartered Trust.

By September 1989 the board of Chartered Trust had approved the transaction, and the real work began in earnest to structure the transaction in a manner which was satisfactory from both a legal and a fiscal standpoint. At the same time it was necessary to embark on the task of modifying Chartered Trust's computer systems to cope with the practical aspects of initially undertaking and subsequently managing the securitisation.

It was not until July 1990, some 18 months after the initial work on the project had begun, that the issue of the Cardiff Automobile Receivables Securitisation (UK) PLC £328m Floating Rate Notes due 1995 was launched. It was the first securitisation of non-mortgage assets in the UK and the largest securitisation of automobile receivables to have taken place in Europe.

7.2 THE TRANSACTION

Pioneering the securitisation of automobile receivables in the UK involved high initial costs. It was therefore necessary to ensure that the transaction was of sufficient size and had a reasonable maturity so as to spread these costs. Since the underlying hire purchase loans had rather short average lives, it was desirable that the initial pool of receivables should be capable of being topped up so that the financing would have a reasonable maturity. While a syndicated bank-loan-financed securitisation was also considered and would have had similar costs, Standard Chartered had a marginal preference for accessing the international capital markets.

To give the transaction good investor appeal Chartered WestLB and Goldman Sachs decided that an issue of asset-backed securities needed to carry the AAA rating of both rating agencies. Since the underlying assets were consumer credit loans, to acquire AAA status would require some form of credit enhancement. Credit insurance from various insurance companies was considered but rejected as being relatively costly, leaving partial credit enhancement from a bank or a senior subordinated structure as the two viable alternatives. Partial credit support from an AAA-rated bank appeared at the time to be the most attractive solution for credit enhancement, because it was inevitably going to be necessary for a bank also to provide a liquidity facility to the special-purpose company. Furthermore, at the time this decision had to be taken problems were beginning to be encountered in the junk bond market in the US and it was felt that difficulties might later have been encountered in placing the subordinated tranche if a senior/subordinated structure had been chosen. After discussions with several AAA rated banks, Union Bank of Switzerland was selected for the credit enhancement role.

Since the market for asset-backed securities in Europe was still relatively undeveloped, and European investors unaccustomed to assessing securities backed by any assets other than mortgages, it was decided that the issue should be targeted at only the most sophisticated investors. The obvious choice for a public issue targeted at such institutional investors was to launch a sizeable AAA rated FRN.

7.3 DEAL STRUCTURE

Stripped to its principal elements the transaction structure is portrayed in figure 7.1. The essential ingredients of the structure for the securitisation consisted of the establishment of a bankruptcy-remote special purpose company, Cardiff Automobile Receivables Securitisation (UK) plc (appropriately

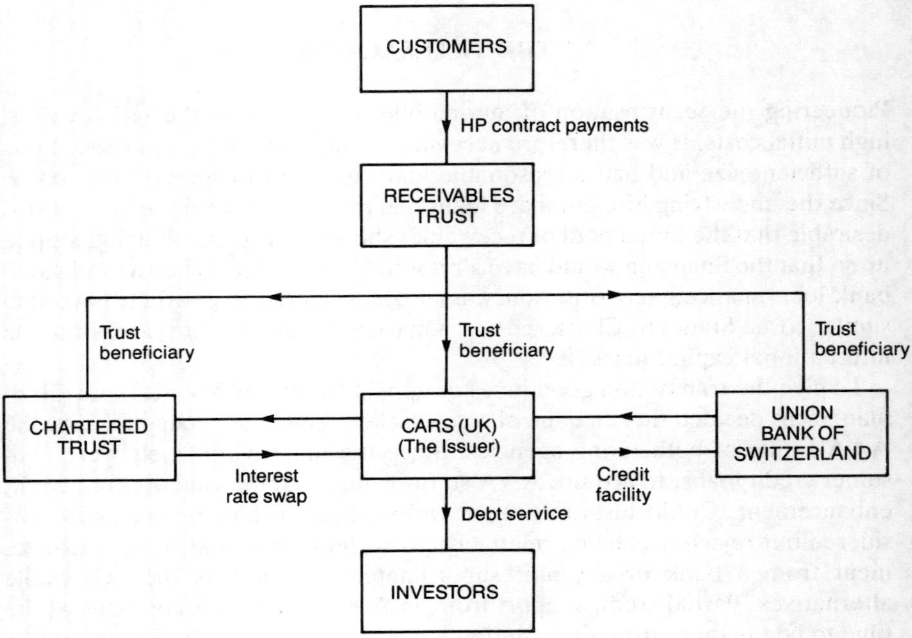

Figure 7.1.

referred to by its acronym, CARS (UK)), which became the issuer of the securities, and its associated Receivables Trust managed by CARS Trustee (UK) Ltd, the function of which is described below. CARS (UK) acquired the securitised hire purchase contracts from Chartered Trust, financing their acquisition by an issue of FRNs to investors. UBS provided credit enhancement to CARS (UK) by means of a credit facility for 15 per cent of the principal value of the FRNs. CARS (UK) entered into an interest rate swap with Chartered Trust to insulate itself from the interest rate exposure of having fixed rate income from the hire purchase receivables and floating rate liabilities. Income from the securitised hire purchase contracts arrived in the Receivables Trust from hirers and was distributed by the Receivables Trust according to a set of predetermined rules between CARS (UK), UBS and Chartered Trust. The structure, its constituent parts and their operation are described in greater detail below.

The discretionary trust arrangements adopted in most UK mortgage-backed securitisations was followed for the corporate ownership of the securitisation special purpose company and the Receivables Trust. The organisational structure is shown in figure 7.2.

The Securitisation Trust, a discretionary trust with charitable objectives, was established to be the ultimate owner of the special purpose companies required for the securitisation. The Eagle Star Trust Company (now renamed LDC Trustees Ltd) held all the shares in this company on a discretionary trust with charitable objectives and provided two of the three directors for each of the operating companies. The INSEAD Trust for Management Education was nominated as a suitable charity to be the principal beneficiary of the trust. The Securitisation Trust held all the shares in a holding company, Securitisation Holdings Ltd., which in turn held all the equity of two operating companies, Cardiff Automobile Receivables Securitisation (UK) plc, the issuer of the FRNs, and CARS Trustee (UK) Ltd, the trustee of the Receivables Trust. The trustee for the noteholders was the Law Debenture Corporation plc.

The principal problem in structuring any securitisation is ensuring that some of the cash flow from the underlying assets can be passed from the securitised special purpose company back to the origination company without incurring additional taxation over and above that which would have been paid had the assets remained on the originator's balance sheet. A novel feature incorporated in the structure for obtaining this result was the use of the Receivables Trust.

In the CARS (UK) transaction the concept used followed the principle of a legal technique known as partial equitable assignment. The idea was to assign to CARS (UK) the whole of the capital element of each receivable from the underlying hire purchase contracts, but only sufficient of the income element as would exactly match the expenditure of CARS (UK) in any given accounting period, effectively retaining any remaining cash flow within Chartered Trust. Each receivable from the hire purchase contracts consisted of a capital element, which was used to pay off the principal amount advanced for the purchase of the goods, and an income element, which represented the financ-

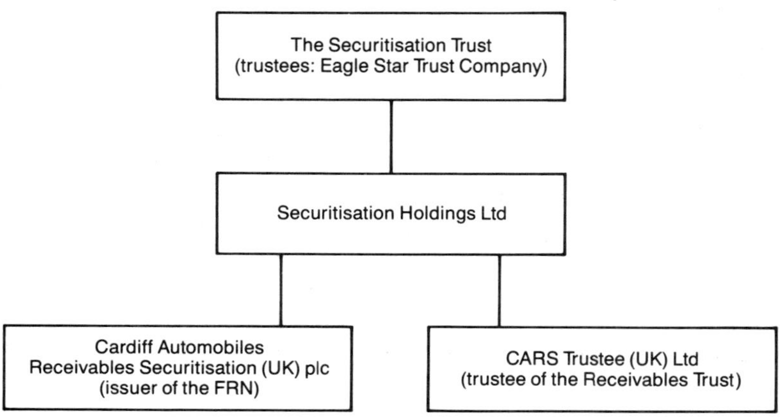

Figure 7.2.

ing cost of the advance. The capital elements were used by CARS (UK) to pay off the principal of the FRNs or to purchase further receivables from Chartered Trust. The income elements were used by CARS (UK) to pay the interest on the FRNs and the costs of credit enhancement, any remainder being required to be passed back to Chartered Trust.

With the defaults and delinquencies inherent in the consumer credit business the precise size and timing of the cash flows from the consumer credit receivables being assigned evidently could not be determined with certainty at the time of assignment. As a result, it proved impossible to use the legal technique of partial assignment to achieve the desired result, since, under English law, partial assignment is only effective if there can be certainty at the time of the assignment as to the precise amounts that will be received by each party in the future. The solution devised employed the legal principles of English trust law, under which it is perfectly possible successfully to operate a trust which distributes monies to its beneficiaries by reference to a formula calculating their relevant entitlements to cash flows as, when and if such flows arise.

CARS Trustee (UK), the Receivables Trustee, became the operator of a trust, the Receivables Trust, which divided any monies received from the hire purchase contracts according to a predetermined set of rules between three parties, CARS (UK), the credit enhancer (UBS) and Chartered Trust, as described below. The principle applied in operating the Receivables Trust was that all monies arising from the securitised hire purchase contracts (including monies from monthly instalments, prepayments, late payments and part payments of instalments, settlement sums from early terminations and net sale proceeds from repossessed motor vehicles) flowed on a daily basis through to the Receivables Trust. All monies were then deposited in an interest-bearing account with UBS—the Guaranteed Investment Contract (GIC)—until the next interest payment date for the FRNs. On each interest payment date sufficient funds were first paid by the Receivables Trust exactly to settle CARS (UK)'s liabilities, including its liabilities under the interest rate swap arrangements (see section 7.7 below). Funds were then paid to the credit enhancer (UBS) to keep the Deficiency and Reimbursement Accounts at their appropriate levels (see section 7.4 below). Finally, any remaining monies were paid over to Chartered Trust.

UBS also provided a start-up loan to CARS (UK) to enable CARS (UK) to pay its initial issuance costs. This loan could be drawn on during the first quarter to meet expenses and was expected to be repaid within the first six months thereafter from the income flowing through CARS (UK).

These somewhat complex payment flows are illustrated graphically in figure 7.3.

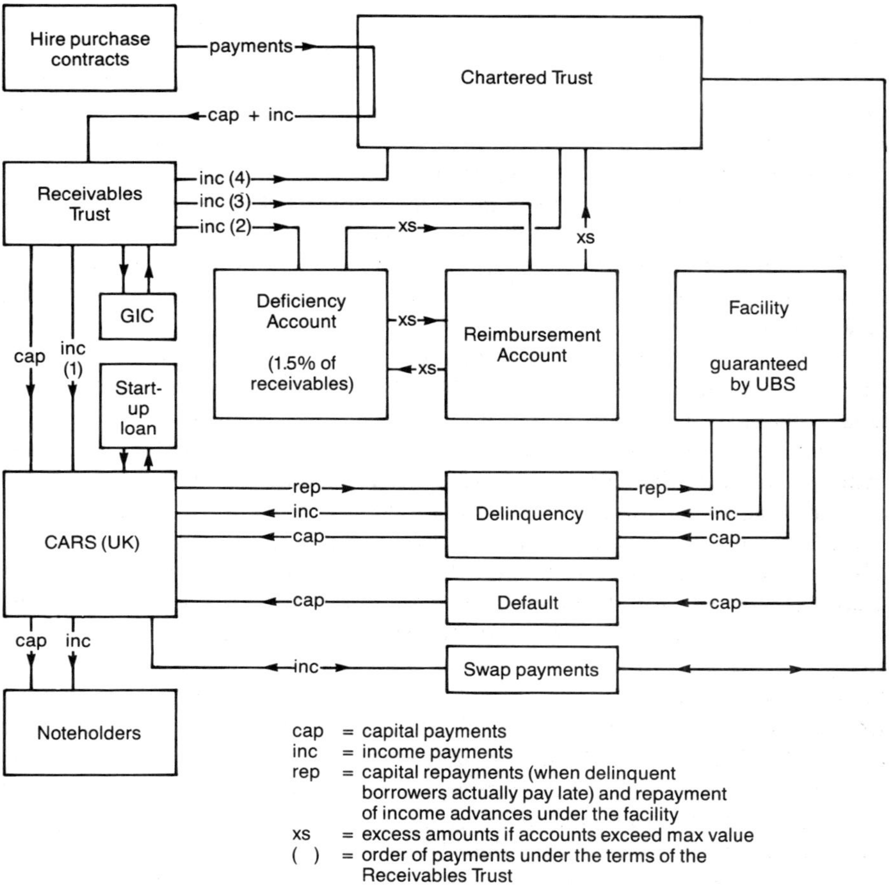

Figure 7.3.

7.4 CREDIT ENHANCEMENT

In order for the transaction to obtain an AAA rating, it was necessary to provide credit enhancement so that noteholders would not suffer if the default rate on the underlying automobile hire purchase loans were for whatever reason to rise above the predicted levels. A line of liquidity was also needed so that any cash flow deficits arising from the inevitable delinquencies (late payments) which regularly occur in consumer credit business could be covered. While it was theoretically possible to use structures involving pool insurance or subordinated notes, the most economic structure was determined to be partial credit support by an AAA rated bank. The institution selected for this role was Union Bank of Switzerland. This mechanism had the advantage that the two separate requirements of providing credit enhancement and of providing liquidity could be combined.

In the US partial credit support is normally provided in the form of a letter of credit. In the UK insolvency law would prevent the directors of CARS (UK) drawing on a letter of credit if the company was close to insolvency and if the directors believed that the company would not be able to repay its debts. These are the very circumstances in which credit enhancement is vitally important. For this reason it was necessary for UBS to make available to CARS (UK) a facility under which, in the event of non-repayment by CARS (UK), there was recourse only to the underlying receivables and not to CARS (UK) itself.

The size of this facility was determined by the rating agencies in the light of the historical performance statistics of the Chartered Trust automobile receivables portfolio. It was set at 15 per cent of the capital value of the portfolio outstanding at any time (subject to a minimum of 1.5 per cent of the initial principal value of the FRNs). This level of credit support was consistent with the rating agencies' approach to automobile loan securitisations in the US.

UBS was not, however, standing in the transaction as first-loss guarantor. There were two layers of protection before the facility provided by UBS, as credit enhancer, would be utilised. The first level of protection against defaults was provided by the margin flowing through the transaction during any given three-month interest period. The second level of protection was provided by a deposit known as the Deficiency Account. At the outset Chartered Trust paid over to UBS £3.28m, a sum equal to 1 per cent of the principal value of the FRNs. This deposit was supplemented in the initial months of the transaction by a further 0.5 per cent of the principal value of the FRNs out of funds generated by the securitised portfolio through the Receivables Trust mechanism. This Deficiency Account, which was at all times maintained at 1.5 per cent of the value of the FRNs outstanding (but with a minimum equal to the amount of the initial deposit of Chartered Trust, in accordance with the Bank of England rules for such contributions to securitised transactions by loan originators), was the direct equivalent of the so-called 'Spread Account' in transactions in the USA and together with monies retained in the transaction during each quarterly period, acted as the first-loss guarantee for the transaction. However, for both tax and Bank of England regulatory purposes and contrary to practice in the USA, it was necessary for this Deficiency Account balance to be owned by UBS and not by CARS (UK). At the end of the transaction UBS was obliged to pay over to Chartered Trust any balance remaining in the Deficiency Account to the extent that it was not required to pay off any outstanding net advances under the facility described below.

The UBS facility was set up to cover the capital element of defaults and to provide liquidity to cover delinquencies. It could also be drawn upon to fund any deficiencies if the income of CARS (UK) was insufficient to meet its expenses in any interest period. Any advances under the facility to meet defaults were reimbursed by payments into the Reimbursement Account by the receivables trustee to the extent that income was, or subsequently became, available, or, in the case of delinquencies, by direct repayments by CARS (UK) when the late payments were received. The net exposure of UBS to CARS (UK), however, could never be greater than 15 per cent of the outstanding principal amount of the receivables.

In the extraordinary event that losses in the transaction were to exceed the levels that could be absorbed by the credit enhancement, those losses would be borne by the holders of the FRNs. There was no recourse whatsoever to Chartered Trust. This enabled Chartered Trust to remove the securitised assets fully from its balance sheet.

CARS (UK) was an investment company (as opposed to a trading company) for the purposes of UK Corporation Tax. As a consequence CARS (UK) was unable to use income to offset capital losses without adverse tax consequences. In normal circumstances in the consumer credit business a certain level of default happens as a matter of course. In a trading company, such as Chartered Trust, part of the margin on performing loans is used to fund losses arising from defaults, but this cannot happen in an investment company without incurring tax charges. The mechanism adopted to resolve this difficulty was to have UBS make capital advances under the facility to cover defaults and delinquencies and for CARS (UK) to make equal deposits out of its income into the Reimbursement Account. Advances from the facility and their eventual repayment from the Reimbursement Account at the close of the transaction were tax neutral.

The rules governing the allocation of funds by the Receivables Trust ensured that no funds flowed back to Chartered Trust from the transaction while there were any real net advances outstanding from UBS to CARS (UK).

7.5 SUBSTITUTION OPTIONS

Securitisations of automobile receivables in the USA have typically been done on a pass-through basis; that is to say that the life of the securitisation transaction is only as long as the underlying hire purchase contracts. Although most of Chartered Trust's automobile hire purchase contracts have an original term of three years, their average is somewhat shorter and even less than equivalent automobile hire purchase loans in the US.

Partly for this reason it was decided that a pass-through instrument was not ideal for financing in the Eurobond market and it was thought than an instrument with a longer life would be more appropriate. Such an instrument would also help to spread the initial costs of the transaction. Substitution options had been used in European mortgage transactions but never in the securitisation of automobile hire purchase receivables in the US. Despite the difficulties of engineering satisfactory substitutions in order to maintain the credit quality of the transaction throughout its life, it was decided that there should be substitution options in the CARS (UK) transaction. By this means, as the underlying hire purchase contracts repaid their principal, in the early years of the transaction CARS (UK) would have the option on each interest payment date on the FRNs to utilise the repaid principal to purchase further receivables from Chartered Trust. To the extent that the option was not exercised, FRNs would have to be redeemed. Chartered Trust had the option of offering further hire purchase loans to CARS (UK), which under the arrangements contemplated could be accepted by CARS (UK).

In a changing environment for hire purchase business three years was considered by the rating agencies to be a satisfactory period during which they could be reasonably sure that Chartered Trust would be able not only to maintain the profile of the business it wished to add to the securitised pool, but also during which it would be able to add sufficient business of identical quality to the original pool so that the substitution options would be fully exercised. It was therefore determined that there should be 12 quarterly substitution options. Taking account of the expected average life of new business added in the final substitution option, it was conveniently demonstrable that the transaction would have a maximum maturity of five years and an average life of around four years.

The rating agencies and UBS insisted that each substitution option could only be utilised if the performance of the existing receivables in the pool had not fallen below certain criteria. All new receivables added to the pool had to meet the pool quality criteria described below and each new tranche was to have business sector characteristics broadly similar, but not identical, to the initial pool. Rules were also set so that the credit quality of the receivables being added to each sector of the portfolio would not deteriorate.

It should be noted that the concept of substitution was to add tranches of new receivables to the pool with similar characteristics to those of the receivables in the initial pool. It was intended that the characteristics of the pool as a whole should remain constant over its life. This would have been almost impossible because even the characteristics of a static pool will progressively change over time as some of the loans mature and defaults occur.

7.6 POOL CRITERIA

Specific criteria were established by the rating agencies for the business that was acceptable for securitisation. The criteria chosen, inter alia, provided that the assets should be cars, three-wheeled vehicles, light trucks or vans, and should be financed by equal monthly-paying standard hire purchase contracts, each originated by Chartered Trust. The contracts should have original terms of at least six months, but not more than five years, and each should expire before the final maturity date of the FRNs. The outstanding principal balance should exceed £500 and be less than £30,000. The first monthly payment at least should have been made, no more than one monthly payment should be overdue and the contract should be amortising normally. In addition, each contract should not come within any category in Chartered Trust's records which might cast any doubt on the creditworthiness of the hirer, such as where fraud was suspected or where there were any legal proceedings. It was also necessary to ensure that the origins of the contracts had a broad geographical spread throughout England, Scotland and Wales. Scottish contracts were limited to 5 per cent of the pool because of the different legal environment in Scotland. However, at the time of its inclusion in the pool a contract could be at any stage in its life, provided it met the criteria above. The net result of these restrictive requirements, which were determined so as to provide a relatively homogeneous portfolio of perfectly performing hire purchase loans for securitisation, was to limit the absolute size of the portfolio of automobile financing business that Chartered Trust was able to put into the transaction.

Securitised contracts related to both new and used vehicles, and to both individual and corporate hirers. For the initial tranche approximately 26 per cent of the outstanding principal balance related to consumer business for new vehicles, 48 per cent to consumer business for used vehicles, 16 per cent to business customers for new vehicles and the remainder to business customers for used vehicles. For each substitution option the mix of business between these four categories was required to be approximately the same as the mix of the initial pool.

Before Chartered Trust takes any new consumer business onto its books the prospective customers are credit scored, using a statistical technique based on the analysis of individual hirer characteristics which have historically proved to be predictive of credit performance. To ensure the continuing quality of the consumer loans the rating agencies required a certain minimum average credit score for all the consumer loans included in each tranche, as well as an undertaking that the credit scoring system would always be applied and would not be permitted to deteriorate over time. Business customers were not credit scored but historically had better credit performance than consumer business. There were also conditions relating to the degree of substitution of business loans in the event of a deterioration in the relatively favourable default experience of the business loans.

Prior to the securitisation interest rates had been generally rising but had recently peaked. Thus contracts included in the pool had a fairly wide spread of yields, although contracts with yields of less than 1 per cent below the swap rate for the relevant swap between CARS (UK) and Chartered Trust were excluded. An important condition, both for the initial pool and for each substitution option, was that the average gross yield (prior to any costs of Chartered Trust) of each tranche of securitised contracts should be at least 4 per cent over the swap rate in order to give an adequate margin flowing through CARS (UK). In fact, as a result of a fairly rapid decline in interest rates in the two months prior to the launch of the transaction, the initial pool had a margin of over 6 per cent above the swap rate.

Chartered Trust was obliged to give a substantial number of warranties relating to the contracts being securitised. The only remedy for breach of any of the warranties given was for Chartered Trust to repurchase the relevant contract for cash.

Approximately 100,000 fixed-rate automobile hire purchase contracts were placed into the securitised pool. While the longest term was for five years, the majority were for three years. However, in hire purchase business early voluntary terminations are commonplace and the average life of the securitised contracts was anticipated to be somewhat shorter than their nominal life.

7.7 INTEREST RATE SWAPS

Because the flow of income from the hire purchase contracts was at a fixed rate of interest and CARS (UK) would have floating-rate interest obligations under the FRNs, it was necessary to introduce interest rate swap arrangements into the transaction to eliminate the interest rate mismatch.

A complex interest rate swap structure was therefore required to eliminate the interest rate risk for principal balances which were of diminishing size on each quarterly interest payment date and which could not be calculated with total certainty in advance as a result of the uncertain prepayment pattern on the hire purchase contracts. Chartered Trust was the perfect counterparty for such a complex swap structure, an arrangement which was permitted under the Bank of England guidelines.

Each tranche of hire purchase loans sold by Chartered Trust had one swap associated with it. The transaction anticipated 13 swaps altogether, including the swap relating to the initial pool of receivables and the swaps relating to the 12 substitution options. All the payments on each swap were designed to fall on interest payment dates for the FRN, so it was only necessary for one net payment to be paid on each such date between CARS (UK) and Chartered Trust. At the time of sale of each tranche of receivables, Chartered Trust calculated the estimated amortisation schedule of that tranche, taking into account expectations of defaults and prepayments. At the time of purchase of each new tranche of receivables, Chartered WestLB, the swap arranger, calculated the fixed rate of interest to be applied to this estimated profile of the relevant amortising swap. The fixed interest rate which had been so ascertained by reference to estimated principal balances was then applied on each payment date for each swap to the actual outstanding principal balance of the relevant tranche to calculate the payments due between the counterparties.

To provide CARS (UK) with insulation from interest rate risk, the balances used for the swap calculations, both for the interest rate estimation at the outset and subsequently for the payments due in practice, were actually the average balances outstanding on the relevant dates at the beginning and at the end of each relevant interest period. The assumption made in such a calculation was that the principal balance of the receivables was amortising regularly throughout the interest period. Because all repayments of interest and principal under the hire purchase contracts received during an interest period on the FRNs were being temporarily invested in the GIC at a rate of interest 50 basis points less than that being paid on the FRNs in the relevant period, the interest rate swap provided an almost perfect hedge to CARS (UK) against interest rate exposure. In order for the transaction to have a AAA rating, UBS guaranteed Chartered Trust's obligations under the swap arrangements.

Prior to securitisation, Chartered Trust had been funding the portfolio in the money markets with short-term deposits and associated interest rate swaps. As a result of arranging the swap between CARS (UK) and Chartered Trust, whereby Chartered Trust became obliged to pay the floating rate interest on the notes and received the fixed-rate income flows from the hire purchase contracts, Chartered Trust was essentially in the same position as it was prior to securitisation. Chartered Trust merely had to cancel the money market funding with which it had previously funded the portfolio but retain the associated swaps.

Since the original interest rate swaps into which Chartered Trust had entered as part of its arrangements for funding the portfolio pre-securitisation had a plethora of payment dates linked to Chartered Trust's money market funding arrangements, it was necessary for Chartered Trust to adjust some of its existing interest rate swaps relating to the portfolio being securitised so that the payment dates on the swaps would coincide with the quarterly interest payment dates on the FRNs.

7.8 CREDIT MANAGEMENT

It was important to Chartered Trust that its manner of conducting its business should be as little affected as possible by securitisation. Chartered Trust, having originated the hire purchase business, continues to service the contracts after securitisation. Although CARS (UK) retains an absolute right to appoint an alternative servicer at any time, it would not be economic for it to exercise that right in the normal course of events. In the UK the servicing charge is liable to VAT.

Servicing hire purchase loans requires far more administration than servicing mortgage loans for a wide variety of reasons, inter alia, because the individual contract size is far smaller and delinquency, default and early terminations are more frequent. By comparison with household mortgage lenders, a hire purchase company is far more regularly engaged in pursuing hirers for late payments, legal actions, repossessions and disposals of repossessed goods. Chartered Trust already had comprehensive procedure manuals, and the rating agencies and UBS agreed that its procedures were thoroughly satisfactory and could be used as a benchmark standard for the servicing and administration of the securitised contracts.

The rating agencies wished to feel satisfied that no distinction would be drawn by the administrator between the manner in which both securitised contracts and non-securitised contracts would be handled. The enquiry systems on Chartered Trust's computer used by branch managers and general staff outside the areas concerned with securitisation were specifically programmed so as not to enable such staff to determine which contracts had been securitised. Chartered Trust had no obligation to notify customers whose loans had been securitised. Hence, in practice neither customers nor branch and general staff would be able to distinguish between securitised and non-securitised contracts. Only staff in specific areas in certain head office departments (such as the legal and accounting departments) were able to distinguish securitised contracts from non-securitised contracts.

One reason for the adoption of the Receivables Trust mechanism as the means of returning profits to Chartered Trust was that Chartered Trust thereby retained an equitable interest in the receivables, although the whole of the receivables were being assigned to CARS (UK). If Chartered Trust were to receive its portion of the receivables it was evidently essential that its servicing role be continued. The only additional servicing that was required was to provide management and accounting functions for CARS (UK) and the Receivables Trust. This entailed ensuring that the monies collected were appropriately allocated and distributed according to the rules of the Receivables Trust, ensuring the various facilities and accounts with UBS and Chartered Trust's clearing bank were properly operated and administered, supervising the operation of the substitution options and the interest rate swap arrangements, seeing that the FRN investors received the due interest and capital repayments, and providing management accounts and a report on a quarterly basis to the various relevant parties. The rating agencies were satisfied that a substitute servicer could be found and that it was not necessary to nominate a substitute in advance.

A practical difficulty which arose during the securitisation exercise related to the manner in which Chartered Trust received monies from hirers. Arrangements had to be put in hand to ensure that payments received from hirers whose contracts had been securitised were separated from non-securitised payments as soon as possible and, when so identified, were passed over to the Receivables Trust. Since no notification of securitisation was being given to affected hirers, payments from both securitised and non-securitised hirers continued to be made to the same collections accounts of Chartered Trust. It was thus necessary to prevent Chartered Trust being able to make payments from such commingled monies until this separation had been effected. The separation of the funds was determined from the debtor's ledger on Chartered Trust's computer system.

The delay involved while funds remained commingled was normally one day for direct debit payments and two days for cash and standing order payments, although theoretically this might occasionally increase by a day or two in the event of some computer failure or a late information transmission from the clearing bank. Working from Chartered Trust's debtor's ledger was the only practical way of rapidly ascertaining the ownership of payments, but it had the disadvantage that it was possible for monies which were, in fact, uncleared funds (such as bounced cheques) to be paid over to the receivables trustee. A mechanism had to be devised for Chartered Trust to recoup such payments as soon as it was known that the funds were not valid when initially transferred. Such occurrences were relatively infrequent and the most practical way of redressing any occasional resultant small overpayment was achieved by correspondingly reducing a subsequent payment between the parties.

7.9 TAXATION

The principal objective in any securitisation scheme is to remove income-earning assets from the balance sheet of the asset originator, while permitting as much of the earnings as possible from the securitised assets to continue to accrue to the originator. As can be seen in the case of Chartered Trust complicated arrangements were required. It is important to any scheme that the structure adopted results in as little additional taxation as possible being incurred beyond that which would have been suffered by the originator were the assets to have remained on his balance sheet. Hence, careful consideration of the tax consequences of the scheme is needed in order to arrive at an efficient structure.

In the UK there are five forms of taxation which have to be considered in structuring a securitisation transaction. These are: Corporation Tax on trading profits, Corporation Tax on capital gains, Stamp Duty, Value Added Tax and Withholding Tax.

The Receivables Trust, described above, was by the nature of its form, activities and purposes, a bare trust and transparent from a taxation point of view, merely directing the flows of funds to its various taxable beneficiaries. CARS (UK) had investment company status for UK Corporation Tax purposes. CARS (UK) did not own the vehicles which were the subject of the hire purchase contracts and was therefore acquiring only the rights to receive regular cash payments from Chartered Trust via the Receivables Trust. At the time of the assignment of the receivables from Chartered Trust, CARS (UK) was purchasing at a discount the right to receive a series of discrete payments in the future. As and when those future payments were received, they became taxable on a cash basis relating to the realised discount profit. Under the terms of the Receivables Trust it was unlikely that CARS (UK) would have significant accounting or taxable profits during its lifetime.

Chartered Trust's income from the transaction was taxable as the normal trading income of the company net of the costs incurred in deriving that income. Hence, in accordance with the objectives of securitisation, such income, although flowing through the hands of the Receivables Trust, was only taxed when it was received by Chartered Trust via the Receivables Trust. UBS was taxed on the fees it received for the provision of credit enhancement and other services it provided and these were treated as normal trading income from its banking activities.

CARS (UK) was a UK-resident company for tax purposes because its transactions and activities took place there. There were no off-shore companies involved in the transaction. As a result, withholding taxes did not enter into the CARS (UK) transaction.

7.10 LEGAL POINTS

Chartered Trust did not notify its customers of securitisation. In the CARS (UK) transaction the securitisation involved more than 100,000 contracts. It was considered impractical to notify 100,000 or more customers that their hire purchase contracts were being securitised. In mortgage securitisations in the UK mortgagors must be notified that their loans are being or may be securitised. There is, however, no requirement for notification for non-mortgage assets. The practical effect of notification is that the assignment of the receivables is then effected on a legal basis rather than on an equitable basis. The assignment of the receivables between Chartered Trust and CARS (UK) was therefore only an equitable assignment.

In the transaction the assignment of the receivables took place with Chartered Trust making written offers to assign without any formal written acceptance, each offer being deemed to have been accepted once payment had been made. It was established that the tripartite assignment arrangements were legally effective, since while the cash consideration was to flow from CARS (UK) to Chartered Trust, the receivables were subsequently to flow in the reverse direction via the Receivables Trust.

The principles of using equitable assignment had already been well tried and tested in mortgage securitisations. There were, however, a number of important legal consequences. Firstly, customers without notice will continue to make payments to the hire purchase company and the hire purchase company will legally continue to be their creditor. Having sold the receivables to the securitisation company, the hire purchase company will then be acting as agent for the securitisation company. Only when notice of assignment has been given will the securitisation company have any direct rights to enforce a contract. Secondly, equitable rights of set-off between the hirer and the hire purchase company could arise when a customer could refuse to make a payment under his securitised contract, claiming that the hire purchase company owed him money, either under another non-securitised contract or under some deposit arrangement (if the hire purchase company were also an authorised bank). It is therefore necessary to exclude from any pool being securitised all contracts where the hirer may also be a depositor and all contracts where any rights of set-off are being claimed. Thirdly, if a customer wants any modification to his contract the securitisation company and the hire purchase company theoretically have to agree jointly to the modification. Finally, if it subsequently becomes necessary for the securitisation company to take legal action against any hirer the hire purchase company will need to be joined in the action. Chartered Trust was permitted by CARS (UK) to modify contracts in accordance with its usual policies but undertook not to modify any contract outside its usual policies. An undertaking was also given by Chartered Trust to be joined in any action against a hirer whose contract had been securitised.

Some 5 per cent of the contracts securitised were originated in Scotland, and were therefore subject to Scottish law. Scottish law does not recognise equitable assignments at all, but conveniently Scottish trust law enabled the transaction for Scottish receivables to follow the transaction for the English receivables very closely. The only substantive difference was that it was necessary for an intimation to be given at the time of assignment for the assignments to be effective, and slight adjustments had to be made to the original English trust arrangements.

It was necessary, however, to consider how a legal assignment could be effected if it were required to enforce a specific contract. This was resolved by arranging for a standing power of attorney to be issued by Chartered Trust so that a legal assignment of any particular contract could be entered into at short notice.

Consideration also had to be given to whether a receiver or liquidator of Chartered Trust would recognise the equitable assignment arrangements, and whether it might be necessary for CARS (UK) to call for legal assignments of all the contracts in the event of the insolvency of Chartered Trust. The advice received was that a receiver or liquidator would have great difficulty in challenging the equitable assignment arrangements, but there might be some timing delay for payments after an insolvency while the arrangements were investigated.

A number of issues arose as a result of the application of the Consumer Credit Act. The first of these related to the position of the dealers in selling the motor vehicles and the quality of the motor vehicles being sold. If a dealer made a misrepresentation about the motor vehicle at the time of sale, the owner of the assets could be liable under section 54 of the Act. Similar liability issues could arise under the Sale of Goods (Implied Terms) Act, if the goods themselves were defective. Historically the hire purchase industry suffers minimal problems relating to customer claims under either Act, but theoretically a huge third party claim could arise. The Bank of England guidelines required that the liability under such claims be passed across to the securitisation company and not left with the originator. The rating agencies would not countenance CARS (UK) accepting open-ended liabilities. The problem was resolved by insuring the event risk.

The Consumer Credit Act also gives rights to the hirer to settle contracts early and obtain ownership of the vehicle by paying all the outstandings under the contract less any rebate of charges to which the hirer may be entitled or, alternatively, to terminate the contract, paying the amount (if any) by which a minimum of half the total amount due under the contract exceeds the amounts already due and paid, returning the vehicle in good condition. The case of early settlements did not present any problems because such payments were passed through CARS (UK) and were always sufficient to pay off all the liabilities of CARS (UK). In the case of early termination, the statutory amount payable is sufficiently large as to make it extremely unlikely that CARS (UK) could incur a capital loss. Were it to do so, such deficit would be funded through drawings on the facility provided by UBS.

If a hirer defaults on a contract, under English law the hire purchase company initially has the right to repossess the vehicle. Chartered Trust undertook to sell repossessed vehicles relating to securitised contracts for the benefit of CARS (UK). However, if the hirer has paid one-third of the amount payable under the contract, the vehicle becomes a 'protected good' and the hire purchase company has to obtain a court order before repossession can take place. Under Scottish law a hire purchase company always has to obtain a court order before a repossession. Chartered Trust undertook to join CARS (UK) in any such court action. However, a hirer can always apply to a court for a time order, which in effect is a rescheduling of his obligations. This rescheduling risk was absorbed by CARS (UK).

CARS (UK) has a strict policy whereby loans are considered in default when four scheduled payments are in arrears. As a result any rescheduled loans rapidly become defaulted loans in CARS (UK)'s books, with consequent drawings on the UBS facility. If these rescheduled delinquent loans do continue to pay, the payments progressively reduce the advances made by UBS to CARS (UK).

7.11 SECURITY

The security for the FRNs consisted of an assignment of CARS (UK)'s rights in the Receivables Trust, including CARS (UK)'s interests in the receivables; an assignment of CARS (UK)'s rights against Chartered Trust under the receivables sale contract, the credit management (servicing) agreement and the interest rate swap; an assignment of CARS (UK)'s rights against UBS under the credit enhancement agreement and the interest rate swap guarantee; together with a floating charge over CARS (UK)'s bank balances and any other assets and investments.

The underlying assets, the vehicles, which gave rise to the receivables were never transferred from the ownership of Chartered Trust. The principal difficulty in transferring the vehicles to the securitisation company arises because the hire purchase contract between the hire purchase company and its customer gives the hirer rights to enjoyment of the asset free of any encumbrances, as required by the Consumer Credit Act. Moreover, at the end of the contract the hire purchase company must be able to pass clean title to the vehicle to the hirer. Had the vehicles been transferred to the securitisation company, the hire purchase company would need to have the right to reacquire the vehicle from the securitisation company at the end of the contract to enable it to pass clean title to the hirer: such a right might be considered an encumbrance over the asset. Secondly, the fact that CARS (UK) did not acquire the vehicles was important to its corporation tax and VAT treatment. Furthermore, because the vehicles were physically located in the UK stamp duty might have been payable if legal title had passed since registration documents existed, albeit that they are not documents of title. Finally, there were practical difficulties in passing title to vehicles which are in the physical possession of third parties. In any case, since the vehicles were mobile and damageable assets are always likely to be in the possession of hirers, an equitable assignment of the vehicles by Chartered Trust to CARS (UK) seemed of fairly dubious commercial merit. Chartered Trust undertook obligations to sell any repossessed vehicles which were the subject of contracts owned by CARS (UK) and to pass the sales proceeds to CARS (UK).

Some, but not all, of the hire purchase contracts were subject to payment protection arrangements, such that if the hirer became ill, unemployed or died, the monthly payments would continue to be met. The benefit of the insurance relating to securitised contracts carrying payment protection arrangements was assigned to CARS (UK).

7.12 COMPUTER REQUIREMENTS

The problems of modifying the computer systems of any company wishing to undertake a securitisation should not be underestimated. Such modification to the software is a very time-consuming task, requiring extensive management participation. In the case of Chartered Trust, work on planning and assessing the required changes to the system started almost one year before the transaction took place. Fortunately, Chartered Trust's system was very well designed in the first place, but it was still a major task.

There are four key elements to the systems requirements for securitisation. The first is ensuring the system is able to generate the statistical information required by the rating agencies and ultimately by the investors. This falls into two categories: historical information on the originator's existing business portfolio and statistical information on the portfolio which will be extracted from the business for securitisation. The second task is for the system to be able to select from the originator's portfolio loans which are suitable for securitisation and transfer the selected loans to the securitisation vehicle. The third task is for the system to be able to keep track of, and account for, the securitisation company, integrating and interfacing those accounts with the accounts of the originator as the circumstances of the securitisation demand. Finally, the computer must be able to provide the management reports to enable the interested parties to monitor the transaction adequately.

In the CARS (UK) transaction, the statistical information about Chartered Trust and its business provided in the offering circular consisted of loan write-off experience by sector; an account payment status report showing the degrees of delinquency; an analysis of deposits paid by hirers at the outset of their contracts; a geographical analysis of business written; together with some historical analysis of Chartered Trust's business record by sector. Further statistical information was required by the rating agencies on a fairly wide range of items, most of which was readily available on Chartered Trust's systems. As regards the securitised portfolio, the system had to be capable of extracting reports for the prospectus on the type of contract by business sector, the distribution by annual yield, the distribution by remaining term and the distribution by outstanding principal balance.

The suite of programmes for extracting loans for securitisation from the originator's portfolio needed careful construction. The system had to be capable of identifying loans which met a number of criteria. The data stored on the loan masterfile in Chartered Trust's system was in fact well formatted and extensive. Since each tranche had to be of a specific size the system needed to be designed to add to or reduce the qualifying loans so as to achieve the requisite tranche size. The rating agencies insisted that the selection process for determining which loans should be securitised should be automated and systematic. Once each tranche had been selected correctly the loans had to be flagged.

Next, the problems relating to accounting for the securitised portfolio had to be tackled. Conceptually, the basic accounting for a securitisation special-purpose company is similar to the accounting for operations carried out through a separately incorporated subsidiary company. Thereafter however, special programmes had to be written to cope with the interfaces between the originator, Chartered Trust, CARS (UK) and UBS, as well as programmes to deal with the mechanics of the Receivables Trust and the various loan and deposit accounts.

In the case of CARS (UK) all this amounted to a considerable amount of modification work being required to Chartered Trust's computer system, although the system had been designed at the outset to handle multiple company accounting. A whole host of small technical problems had to be individually resolved relating, inter alia, to the handling of commingled funds, dealer commissions, different accounting policies (such as provisioning on delinquent loans), different default criteria and even different evaluations of loan values, to mention but a few, each of which took considerable time to resolve.

Finally, the management accounting report set had to be designed for the rating agencies, the credit enhancer, the trustee for the FRNs and the directors of the securitisation company. In the case of CARS (UK), this report consisted of twenty short schedules. In practice, this is relatively easy to achieve since the relevant data should be available if the system has been well designed to cope with the accounting of the special purpose company.

Chartered Trust completed all the above work in about eight months, including systems testing, without any major disruptions to its business, and the systems have worked extremely well since the launch of the transaction.

7.13 CONCLUSION

The CARS (UK) securitisation of automobile receivables has effectively proved that securitisation of assets in the UK need no longer be confined to household mortgages.

It took many months of pioneering work but the FRN issue was very well received by the market. The note carried a coupon of 25 basis points over LIBOR and front-end fees totalled $27\frac{1}{2}$ basis points. The issue was more tightly priced than mortgage-backed securities, and consistently traded well in the secondary market subsequent to launch, although the greater part of the paper was placed immediately into the hands of long-term investors seeking quality paper. The transaction showed that there is a ready appetite for such quality asset-backed securities among investors in Europe. It is therefore likely that securitisation of non-mortgage assets in the European environment will gather pace in the coming years.

Although the pioneering work of preparing for a company's first securitisation is very time-consuming and expensive, once a company has successfully securitised one portfolio of its assets, further portfolios can be securitised more easily and at far lower cost, enhancing the benefits that can be obtained. There seems little doubt that securitisation is a financial technique which will be of growing importance for both financial institutions and companies.

Note: Copies of the CARS (UK) offering circular can be obtained from Chartered WestLB Ltd, 33–36 Gracechurch Street, London EC3V 0AX.

Europe and Beyond

8: Securitisation of UK Real Estate

Nigel King, Salomon Brothers

8.1 SECURITISATION OF UK COMMERCIAL PROPERTY DEBT

Securitisation of commercial mortgage-backed securities has long been a feature of the domestic capital market, with UK financial institutions providing long-term financing in the form of first mortgage debentures which are listed and traded in London. This market has traditionally provided recourse funding at maturities over 15 years where domestic institutions seek to match their long-term liabilities with long-term assets. Domestic issuance has consisted of both unsecured bonds for stronger credit companies and mortgage-backed debentures. More recently, however, borrowers have been able to access a broader pool of capital through issuing secured bonds in the Euromarkets. The Euromarkets provide access to a large pool of capital which can provide financing on a recourse or non-recourse basis at highly competitive rates. With the continued growth of bank lending to the UK property market and the currently limited supply of new equity capital available, the Euromarkets are increasingly being viewed as an important refinancing source in addition to the traditional banking and domestic securities markets. This chapter outlines the development of securitised financing in the context of the rapid growth in UK property lending during the 1980s and the factors which will influence this market in the 1990s.

8.1.1 The background to UK commercial property lending in the 1980s

Between 1980 and 1985 UK property lending was predominantly a domestic affair, where UK institutions and banks provided the bulk of the equity and debt capital for existing investments and developments. The valuation and market fundamentals, together with the lending criteria on UK property, was largely determined by local financial institutions. Development financing in this period was predominantly through the forward funding of developments by UK institutions. In 1980, loans outstanding to UK property companies stood at approximately £2bn, with approximately 21 per cent of this sum being funded by non-UK banking institutions. Here was a local market being driven predominantly by local money.

After 1985, however, the UK market experienced significant and fundamental change. International appetite for debt and equity in the UK market rose rapidly as the soaring rental rates resulting from ever-declining vacancy rates prompted new supply. In the City of London in particular, the relaxation of planning constraints in the late 1980s unleashed a wave of development activity which tripled annual supply from 4.3 million square feet in 1988 to over 14 million square feet in 1990. This period also saw the arrival of new international souces of equity capital for completed investment properties and also risk capital for development. The relaxation of foreign exchange controls in Sweden, together with the arrival of Japanese construction companies, developers and financial institutions brought new buyers for development opportunities and existing investment properties. International investors effectively replaced the domestic institutions as the marginal buyer of UK property in 1988 and 1989.

However, the major market influence during the same period was the sea-change occurring in the source of development funding as the traditional UK institutional forward funders (or forward purchasers) of new developments were replaced by non recourse financing provided by banks and securitised property financings. Loans outstanding to UK property companies escalated from £7.7bn in 1986 to £34.1bn in 1990. By this time the international banks

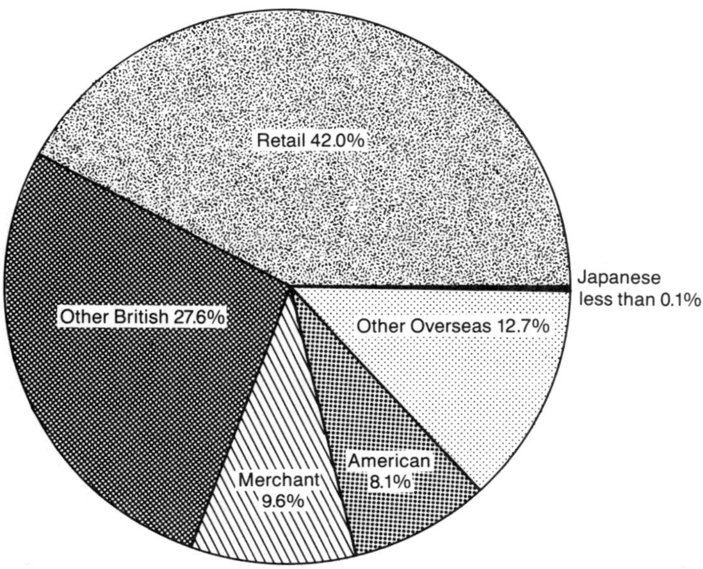

Figure 8.1. Total loans to property companies by type of bank–1980.
Source: Bank of England

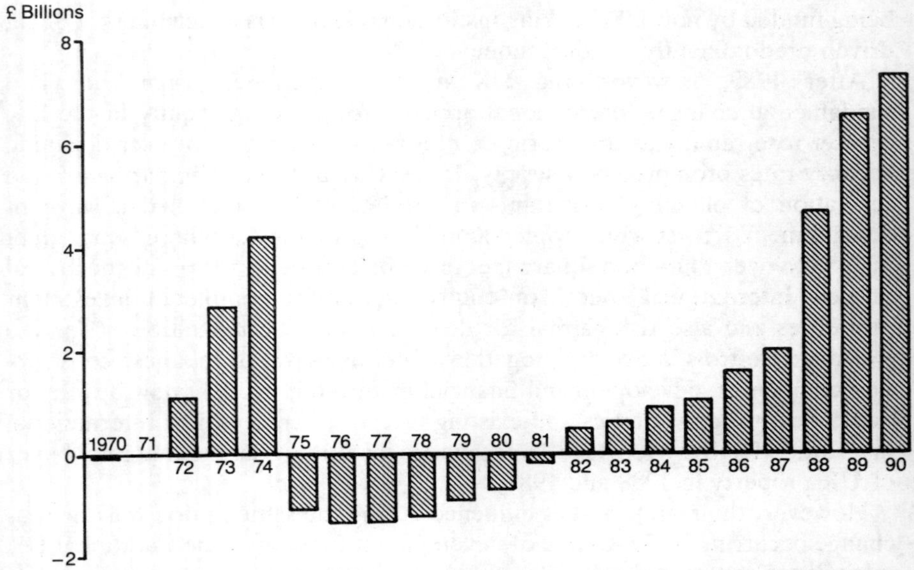

Figure 8.2. Annual change in real loan amounts outstanding to UK property companies 1970–1990 (1970 £ in billions). Source: Bank of England.

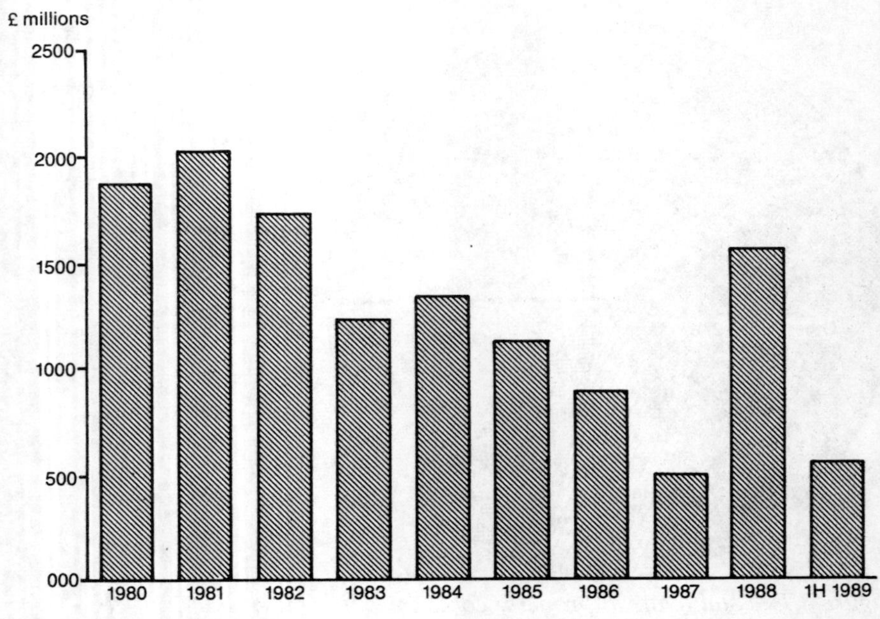

Figure 8.3. Insurance company, pension fund and property unit trust net direct investment in property, 1980–89. Source: CSO Financial Statistics.

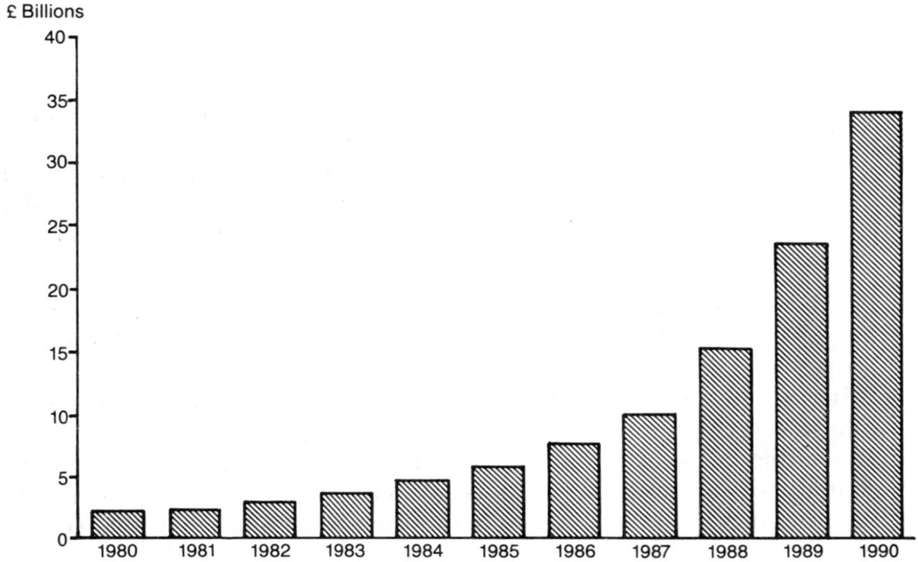

Figure 8.4. Loan amounts outstanding to UK property companies 1980–90. *Source:* Bank of England.

had nearly 35 per cent of the market. During 1991 this figure has exceeded £40bn as existing committed facilities are drawn down to complete further development projects. Here then was a market being driven by local product and global money as the marginal buyers of property and the marginal lenders were increasingly non-UK financial institutions.

1990 also saw the fundamentals for the UK property market starting to deteriorate, with vacancy rates for the central London office market doubling from 5 per cent in 1988 to over 10 per cent in 1990 and short-term interest rates doubling from 7.5 per cent in mid-1988 to 15 per cent in late 1989. With most of the bank lending on a floating-rate basis, many developers prudently hedged part or all of the interest rate exposure on their loan facilities. However, many developers were still caught by the classic two-pronged assault on profit margins—the increased interest burden during construction and the increased carrying cost of holding debt-financed projects longer than planned.

8.1.2 1990—a new reality

1990 will be looked back upon as the year in which many of the major problems facing the UK markets were exposed, in particular:

- Property values, market liquidity and rents all fell in central London with the rapidly increasing City of London vacancy rates.
- Several over-leveraged property companies failed or experienced major financial difficulties and some larger London development projects such as County Hall were beset with major commercial setbacks.
- Some of the major property buyers and lenders in the international capital markets experienced their own domestic problems, such as the secondary banking crisis in Stockholm and the balance sheet bolstering required by the Japanese banking sector to meet the BIS capital guidelines.

Overlaying these issues affecting the availability of global capital to refinance the £40bn of bank debt on property are the slowdown in UK economic activity and the liquidity squeeze generated by the Gulf crisis.

If the total annual net equity investment in UK property by domestic and foreign investors continues at its current rate of approximately £2–4.5bn, the refinancing demands placed on the banks will be very considerable as they continue to refinance the rising unsold inventory of property developers. Securitisation of property debt is set to provide a significantly enlarged role over the next few years as borrowers and their bankers seek to reduce the overall size of bank lending to the UK property sector by accessing the securities markets.

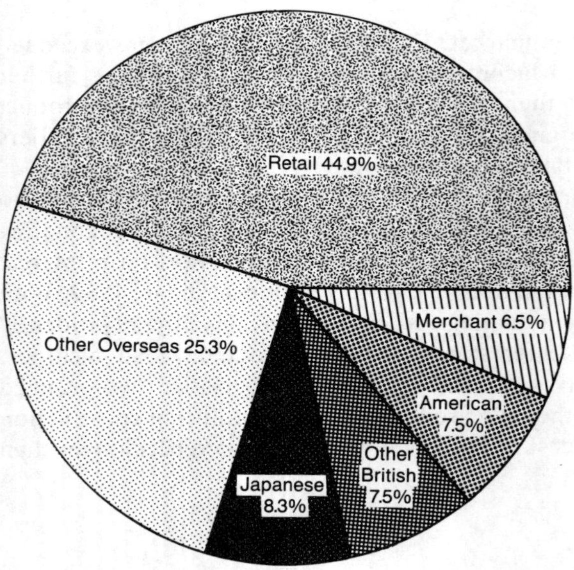

Figure 8.5. Total loans to property companies by type of bank—1989.
Source: Bank of England.

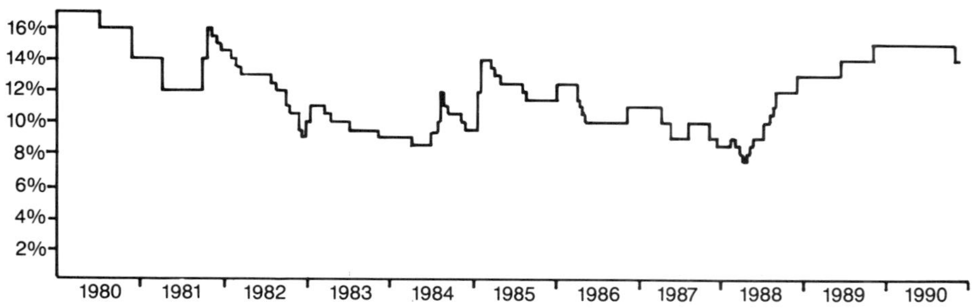

Figure 8.6. UK base rates, 1980–90. Source: Salomon Brothers Inc.

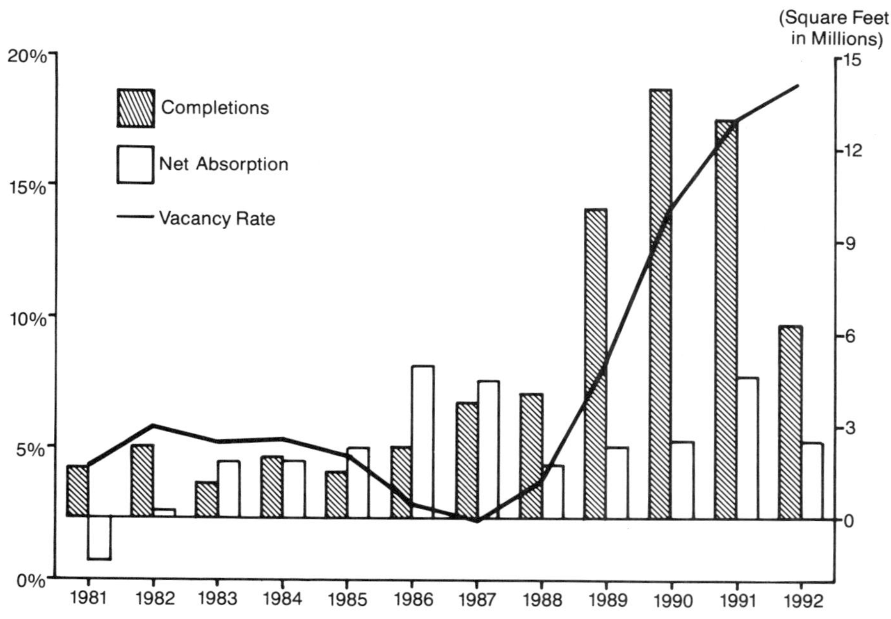

Figure 8.7. Central London office vacancy rate and net absorption vs construction completions 1981–92. Sources: APR, JLW and Salomon Brothers Inc.

8.2 BENEFITS OF SECURITISATION

Securitisation provides many benefits for issuers and investors by fractionalising debt obligations and distributing them in a securitised format to a global investor base.

Securitisation of property debt provides the following major benefits in a global market currently experiencing a major capital shortage:

- *Broad investor base* Borrowers can access a broad investor base which reaches beyond the traditional banking sector, whose appetite for property lending during the next few years may be at best static or could decline.
- *Liquidity* Investors are attracted to securitised debt by the liquidity available in the secondary market. Liquidity will assume an increased importance to investors in a current market characterised by increased volatility in credit spreads and cost of capital together with an increased desire by borrowers to lengthen the maturity of their liabilities.

The securitised markets for property debt can be broadly divided into two major categories:

1. The long-term mortgage market—'Domestic bonds';
2. The international medium-term mortgage market—'Euromarket bonds'.

Domestic bonds are characterised by two key features: (1) a maturity usually exceeding 10 years, and (2) a predominantly UK-based investor audience. Euromarket bonds are sold to an international investor base who buy property-backed securities with maturities between four and twelve years. The major characteristics of each market are outlined in Table 1 and reviewed in subsequent sections.

Table 1 Key features of the securitised debt markets for UK property

	Domestic Bonds	*Eurobonds*
Term	Over 15 years	4–12 years
Typical maximum loan to value	60–65%	60–80%
Typical debt service coverage ratios	Over 1.1 times	Over 1.03 times
Fixed/floating interest rate financing	Fixed only	Either
Type of security	Full coupon bonds	Discount or full coupon bonds
Investors	Domestic UK institutions	International financial institutions
Single or pooled properties	Both	Both
Non- or limited recourse financing	Not available	Available

8.3 THE LONG-TERM DOMESTIC MORTGAGE MARKET

Companies have for many years raised funds through the domestic capital markets, where the UK institutional requirement to match long-term liabilities with long-term assets can be satisfied particularly well with secured bonds or debentures. The UK institutional investors comprise pension funds, life insurance and general insurance companies who have extensive experience in the UK commercial property sector through their direct property holdings. Unlike many European property markets, the long-term fully repairing and insuring (or 'triple net') leases which are widely used in the UK are ideally suited for long-term financing due to the stability of rental cash flow. These characteristics have underpinned a sophisticated market for long-term (over ten years) securities which are sold to domestic financial institutions. These listed securities have been issued as first mortgage debentures for smaller companies, or senior unsecured corporate debt for larger companies such as British Land and MEPC. In the mortgage debenture market, smaller companies such as the Burford Group, together with the largest quoted property company, Land Securities, have raised long-term fixed-rate financing by charging pools of properties.

Tables 2 and 3 summarise the recent domestic issues of debt by UK property companies issued since 1986.

Table 2 Unsecured long-date sterling issues by property companies since 1986

		Coupon %	*Maturity*	*Issue size £m*
4/86	MEPC	10.25	2003	100
	Land Securities	9.50	2007	100
4/87	MEPC	9.875	2004	75
	Land Securities	9.50	2007	100
5/87	Slough Estates	10.00	2007	50
10/88	MEPC	10.50	2032	152
10/88	MEPC	11.625	2032	80
1/89	Great Portland Estates	9.50	2016	100
2/89	Hammerson	10.75	2013	100
8/89	Laing Properties	11.50	2010	75

It is immediately apparent that during 1990 the number of companies accessing this market has fallen off sharply. Historically, the long-term mortgage market has been a source of funds for both the larger and smaller property companies alike. This market is currently effectively closed to smaller companies and only available to larger companies on a selective basis.

The issuance calendars in Tables 2 and 3 illustrate how the combined

Table 3 First mortgage debenture issues issued in the UK since January 1986

		Coupon %	Maturity	Issue size £m
4/86	Great Portland Estates	9.50	2016	25
	Estates Property	10.00	2011	12
	London & Prov. Shop Centres	10.00	2026	50
	Peel Holdings	9.875	2011	35
	Asda Property	10.3125	2011	21
5/86	Estates and General	11.25	2018	10
	London Shop	10.00	2026	20
6/86	Brixton Estates	9.50	2026	30
8/86	Audax Properties	11.00	2021	8
9/86	Scottish Metropolitan	10.25	2016	60
4/87	Estates and General	11.25	2018	7
	City Site Estates	10.50	2017	10
	Town Centre	10.50	2021	15
5/87	Peel Holdings	9.875	2011	100
	Peachey Properties	9.50	2015	30
	Great Portland Estates	9.50	2016	40
6/87	Dares Estates	10.25	2012	15
	London & Prov. Shop Centres	10.00	2026	50
3/88	Audax Properties	11.00	2021	7
4/88	Peel Holdings	9.875	2011	30
5/88	Capital & Counties	9.875	2027	50
	London & Provincial	10.00	2026	35
10/88	Land Securities	10.00	2030	200
11/88	Estates & Agency	11.25	2020	7
1/89	Great Portland Estates	9.50	2016	85
	London & Provincial	10.00	2026	35
2/98	Scottish Metropolitan	10.25	2016	30
	Merivale Moore	10.50	2020	10
	Burford Group	10.625	2014	20
	City Site Estates	10.50	2017	15
	Tops Estates	10.25	2011	27
	Allied London	10.75	2025	35
	Dares Estates	10.25	2012	20
4/89	Peel Holdings	9.875	2011	100
9/89	Capital and Counties	9.875	2027	50
	Town Centre	10.50	2021	35
12/89	Brixton Estates	10.625	2012	80
1/90	Estates & Agency	11.25	2020	9
3/91	Capital & Counties	11.25	2021	80
6/91	British Land	12.50	2016	100
6/91	MEPC	12.00	2016	150

issuance of unsecured and first mortgage debentures collapsed from over £800m in 1989 to under £50m in 1990.

The rapid decline in new issuance in 1990 was investor-driven as UK institutions became increasingly concerned about the deteriorating property market prospects, coupled with the escalating demand from borrowers to refinance short-term bank loans with long-term funding. While the market remains accessible, long-term funding is likely to be available only on a selective basis to larger companies and could be relatively expensive.

Given the current low level of net new equity investment into the UK property market, a key factor in 1991 will be the depth of demand from this domestic investor base.

8.4 SECURITISED COMMERCIAL PROPERTY FINANCING IN THE EUROMARKET

The first securitised property financing executed on a completed investment property was issued in June 1986 for Billingsgate City Securities plc as a single asset property company. Initially owned by Berisford plc, the headquarters building of Midland Montagu was refinanced with three security types which consisted of secured discount bonds with a maturity of 20 years together with preferred stock and equity. The discount bonds and preferred stock were sold to UK institutions while the original owners of the property retained the residual majority equity position. This transaction received a mixed reception as the first single-asset property company and the securities were finally redeemed in August 1989.

In early 1988 the Euromarket funding source was accessed for the first time for development financing as Salomon Brothers pioneered the first securitised funding for a major London office development. A £125m deep discount bond issued by a joint-venture partnership between Greycoat plc and Sir Robert McAlpine & Sons Ltd funded the construction of an office development of 360,000 square feet at Victoria in London's West End. The financing incorporated several novel features, including (1) the pre-funding of coupons during construction; (2) a below market 8.25 per cent coupon capable of being serviced by the projected rental income; and (3) a seven-year maturity to provide both construction and permanent financing. The securities were sold to a broad group of international investors and the development has proved to be very successful for the development partnership.

These Euromarket securities enabled domestic borrowers to access a global pool of property investors, including banks, financial institutions, fund managers and corporations, through private placements and publicly listed eurobonds.

Although there is no set structure for these securities, each was designed to satisfy the prime objectives of the issuer. Property companies have realised the benefits from accessing capital pools outside of the banking sector using customised financings. In this way these companies have also diversified their exposure to the actions of any one group of lenders and obtained attractive borrowing terms.

Specific transactions have been structured to satisfy a range of the following requirements: high loan-to-value, non-recourse funding, coupon payments funded exclusively from rental income, and fixed or floating interest rates. A range of different solutions have been used to meet each investor's specific objectives. Several examples of successful and innovative financings follow which illustrate how each individual borrower's requirements were satisfied using Euromarket financings.

In all of these transactions, several features tend to distinguish the offering terms of Euromarket issues from domestic bond issues, including:

- Euromarket investors' willingness to accept higher loan-to-value exposure than domestic bond investors, where loan to value typically does not exceed 65–70 per cent.
- Unless interest payments or bond coupons are guaranteed by third parties, eurobonds typically require high credit quality tenants to ensure reliability of debt service.
- Whereas domestic bonds are invariably full coupon securities, where debt service is fully covered by rental income, many eurobonds have some features designed to address shortfalls between income and total debt service. Such features include deep discount bonds, where investors receive a below-market paid coupon rate together with an interest accrual feature or over-collateralisation to fund interest shortfalls.

From the major public transactions listed in Table 4 we have reviewed the significant features of some of the larger transactions.

8.4.1 June 1986—Billingsgate City Securities plc

In June 1986 the first securitised property financing to be carried out on a single investment property was issued for Billingsgate Securities plc, a single asset property company. Montagu House is the City headquarters of Samuel Montagu, which has since been incorporated into Midland Bank as Midland Montagu. A joint venture development between S&W Berisford and London and Edinburgh Trust (LET), the property was completed in September 1985. By 1986 Berisford had purchased the LET interest in the development, and wished to reduce their exposure to the property while maintaining an equity interest.

Table 4 Major UK securitised property eurobond financings

Issue	*Size (£m)*	*Date*	*Property*	*Loan to value*	*Lead manager*
Billingsgate	35.5	Jun 1986	Montagu House	44%	Goldman Sachs
Greycoat plc	50	Apr 1987	Unsecured	–	Salomon Brothers
Greycoat Victoria	125	Jan 1988	123 Buckingham Palace Road	81%	Salomon Brothers
LEP House[1]	130	Jul 1988	LEP House	87%	Salomon Brothers
Bechtel House	35.5	Aug 1988	245 Hammersmith Road	95%	Salomon Brothers
Kings Cross House	55	Apr 1989	Kings Cross House	112%	Kleinwort Benson
Greycoat plc	150	Mar 1990	One Finsbury Circus	88%	Salomon Brothers
BHH	90	Sep 1990	Portfolio Financing	108%	Banque Paribas

Notes

[1] An initial amount of £75m was issued, with provision for further issues of up to £55m.

Montagu House is a modern office building with 185,000 square feet of net lettable space which is fully let to Samuel Montagu on a 35-year lease with standard upwards-only rent reviews. The term of the lease began in March 1985, with an initial rent of £5m per year in June 1986. The building, which was valued at £79m, had an implied capitalisation rate of 6.2 per cent. In March 1988 the property was revalued to £110m.

The financing was structured to reduce the Berisford interest in the development at the same time as maintaining full equity control in the longer term and matching payments to rental income. The issuance of debt was carried out through the creation of a single asset property company, Billingsgate City Securities plc, floated on the Luxembourg Stock Exchange in June 1986. The London Stock Exchange did not at this time permit the listing of single asset property companies, the company being listed there only in June 1988 following a relaxation of this requirement.

Three types of Security were created, consisting of (1) secured discount bonds, (2) cumulative preferred ordinary shares, and (3) ordinary shares, with the latter retained by Berisford. The financing was a successful example of a layered securitisation with different levels of risk receiving different rates of return. Most of the securities were sold to UK institutions. The preferred stockholders were entitled to receive a fixed percentage of the net rental income and capital appreciation with Berisford as the common equity holders retaining any Capital Gains Tax liability.

The discount bonds raised £35.5m at a 67.6 per cent discount to their nominal face value of £52.5m and had a term of 20 years. Security was provided in the form of a first fixed and floating charge against the property and a letter of credit equivalent to three semi-annual interest payments. The coupon was a nominal 6⅝ per cent, with an issue yield of 10.6 per cent.

The 25.8 million preference shares were issued at £1 each with an initial yield of 5.9 per cent and were entitled to 30.44 per cent of net rental income after debt service due on the first mortgage bonds. The preferred shareholders had the right to instruct the directors to sell the property or wind up the company annually after December 2001, although this triggers a call option enabling the ordinary shareholders to repurchase the preferred shares.

The transaction enabled Berisford as ordinary shareholders to derive full gearing by raising some 75 per cent or £61.3m of the value of the property in return for approximately 30 per cent of the equity value. The first mortgage bonds and preferred stock were successfully distributed but received a mixed overall reception and were redeemed in August 1989, when Midland Montagu tendered for the outstanding securities to acquire absolute ownership of the property.

8.4.2 January 1988—Victoria II

In January 1988 Salomon Brothers placed the first and largest securitised property development financing to be carried out in the UK. The £125m secured note issue was secured against the sole property asset of a new special-purpose company, Greycoat Victoria plc. This joint-venture development between Greycoat Group plc and Sir Robert McAlpine & Sons Ltd undertook the development of 123 Buckingham Palace Road. With construction completion and cost overrun guarantees provided by the parent companies, the financing resulted in a debt structure that minimised the cash equity commitment by the developers. At the time of the offering, the property had already been partially leased to the Secretary of State for the Environment for 23 years, with the first rent review due in 1993.

The property comprises a twin-building office complex with a small amount of retail space and forms the second stage of a development built above the platforms of Victoria Station. The development was completed in March 1991 and contains a total of approximately 380,000 square feet of net lettable space, with the ownership interest in the form of a 250-year headlease from British Rail.

The principal amount due at maturity of £125m was equal to 80.6 per cent of the estimated £155m value of the development when fully let and income-producing. The high loan-to-value for the development financing was justified by the high quality of the scheme, which has since proved to be very successful. For investors who required a full coupon rate of interest on their investment, the discount mortgage notes with a coupon of 8.25 per cent were combined with income notes from Salomon Brothers to create a full-coupon security which could be purchased on either a fixed- or floating-rate basis when combined with an interest rate swap from Salomon Brothers. This structure ensured a high degree of marketability for the offering.

The bond proceeds were invested in fixed rate deposits at high short-term interest rates and enabled approximately 90 per cent of the projected development costs (including capitalised interest) to be debt-financed.

8.4.3 July 1988 – LEP House

In July 1988 Salomon Brothers completed a deep discount bond issue to refinance LEP House for LEP (St Paul's Vista) Ltd. The property is a new 200,000 square feet net lettable office building located near St Paul's Cathedral in the financial district of the City of London, and had been completed to the shell and core stage in March 1988. The property is fully let to Swiss Bank Corporation on a 25-year lease.

LEP Group plc, as the developer, was seeking to refinance an existing bank construction loan and decided to raise funds through the issuance of debt secured against the assets of the subsidiary company, St Paul's Vista Ltd. The ownership interest of LEP group plc was in the form of a headlease granted by the City Corporation for 150 years. The high quality of the occupational tenant enabled a high loan-to-value of up to 87 per cent to be raised. At the time the bonds were issued, LEP Group were in negotiations with Swiss Bank Corporation regarding the settlement of the first rent review. There was therefore some uncertainty as to the final outcome of this review and consequently the amount of financing which could be raised. The offering was therefore structured as a two-tranche offering, with the final amount raised being determined by a further valuation of the property to be carried out after the first rent review.

The two tranches of notes were comprised of initial notes and rent review notes to be issued at a later date on settlement of the rent review negotiations. The principal face value of the total offering was an amount up to £130m issued in an initial tranche of £75m. The rent review notes could be issued within a 12-month period from the initial issue date, and investors committed to purchase £75m of the initial notes and up to £32 million of the rent review notes. The amount of rent review notes were subject to a maximum of a loan-to-value not exceeding 87 per cent of the post-review valuation.

With a maturity of seven years and a coupon of 7.30 per cent, the notes were issued at a price of 80.6 per cent of face value to raise gross proceeds of £60.45m. The financing was also designed to be off-balance-sheet to LEP Group plc through the use of an innovative capitalisation structure.

As with the 123 Buckingham Palace Road issue, investors could purchase these notes either as fixed-rate discount bonds or as full-coupon fixed- or floating-rate securities to enhance the marketability of the offering.

8.4.4 August 1988—Bechtel House II

In August 1988 Salomon Brothers brought to market a deep discount bond issue for London and Edinburgh Trust plc (LET). The issue was secured against the assets of a subsidiary company, 245 Hammersmith Road Investment Ltd, a special-purpose company (the SPV) which owned Bechtel House II. The freehold property consisted of a fully-let 165,000 square feet office building which was completed in 1982 and is situated in the centre of Hammersmith, four miles from Central London. The occupational lease to Bechtel Ltd expires in March 1997, with the final rent review occurring in 1992. The short-term nature of the Bechtel lease presented a financing challenge due to the uncertainty regarding refinancing. With a seven-year maturity, a refinancing or sale of the property would be required just two years before the expiry of the Bechtel lease, which could produce uncertainty as to investment value.

The issue consisted of £35.5m secured deep discount notes with a maturity of seven years and a 6.25 per cent coupon which could be fully funded from current rental income from the property. With a principal amount due at maturity equal to 95 per cent of the £37.3m appraised value of the property, debt investors were able to accept such a high loan-to-value due to the put option available to the SPV.

A contingent put option was granted by LET to the SPV which required LET to purchase the property for the appraisal value of £37.3m if the SPV had not effected a sale or refinancing of the property within six months prior to the maturity of the notes. The put option is therefore exercisable only within the last six months of the term of the bond, with the repayment of principal being made from these proceeds unless alternative arrangements have been made. Investors could therefore look to the parent company LET for further security for repayment of principal.

8.4.5 April 1989—Kings Cross House

A well-known securitised transaction was the funding of the Kings Cross House development in April 1989. Fully leased to National Westminster Bank, the property was sold to a single asset company (the SPV), Kings Cross House plc, for £45m. Speyhawk plc, the original owner, retained a call option to repurchase either the property or the company at a given price at any time. As Speyhawk plc had no direct interest in the single-asset company, the property was 'owned' but completely off-balance-sheet. Speyhawk plc retained all the benefits of property ownership in terms of asset growth and management control (through a management agreement) but without the need to retain the debt on-balance-sheet.

The financing consisted of a full-coupon ten-year £55m non-recourse bond issue, secured against the property valued at £49m. The offering was placed mainly with Japanese institutions. The £55m face value of the bonds exceeded the £49m valuation of the property, which reflected the uncertainty surrounding a pending rent review. The SPV also had additional collateral because part of the financing proceeds were retained within the SPV. Speyhawk plc received £45m from the purchase price, of which approximately £5m was loaned back to the SPV as a subordinated loan and combined with the remaining £10m from the bond issue to purchase an annuity. This annuity funded the shortfall between the initial rental income and the coupon rate of interest at 12.1 per cent.

8.4.6 March 1990—One Finsbury Circus

In March 1990 Salomon Brothers executed a landmark bond financing on behalf of Greycoat plc. Secured by a first mortgage against One Finsbury Circus, a prime city property recently let to British Petroleum, the £150m issue was the largest securitised property financing ever executed in the UK. It also delivered a financing which matched existing rental income to coupon payments. The 12-year term of the bond provided financing beyond the first two rent reviews in 1994 and 1999.

Designed by Sir Edwin Lutyens, the property is located in the financial district of London and was the subject of an extensive redevelopment. Entirely reconstructed from within, the external facade and major internal features were retained to provide 192,000 net square feet of prime modern office space. The lease to British Petroleum is for an initial period of approximately 34 years on the entire building, except for a small sub-letting to National Westminster Bank plc for use as a branch office.

The financing was a direct issue of the parent company Greycoat plc but was specifically designed with limited recourse and with stepped coupons which could be serviced directly from rental income. The deep discount bond satisfied these requirements with a principal amount due at maturity of £150m against the appraised value of £170m. During the first six years of the financing the coupon was set at 6.25 per cent, rising to a market rate of 12.50 per cent for the second six-year period. In years 7 through 12 of the financing, the projected rental income following the first rent review will be sufficient to service the full market rate of interest. Greycoat plc guaranteed to make up any shortfalls between the rental income and the coupon rate during this final six-year period where the coupon steps up from 6.25 per cent to 12.5 per cent.

For investors who required a full coupon rate of interest, the deep discount bonds were combined with the income notes to provide full coupon-paying certificates. The income notes were issued by Salomon Brothers to provide, in conjunction with the 6.25 per cent coupon paid by the discount bonds, the 12.50 per cent market rate of interest to the investor. In this way, investors could buy the securities either as a fixed-rate discount bond in sterling or as a full-coupon paying security in sterling or any other major currency.

Greycoat also benefited from an interest rate swap arranged with Salomon Brothers in mid-1989. Correctly anticipating a significant rise in interest rates, Greycoat hedged this exposure through a customised interest rate swap to fix the interest rate on the financing some eight months in advance of the issue date. This swap was unwound at the closing of the transaction to provide an extraordinary profit for Greycoat of £15.8m, which reduced their overall funding cost to gilts flat (about 12.40 per cent).

8.4.7 September 1990—BHH AAA-rated issue

A more recent example of a financing, which brought a structure previously unseen to the UK markets, was the BHH issue in September 1990 of £90m guaranteed floating-rate notes due in 1995. This was the first AAA-rated asset-backed debt to be issued in the UK and secured by mortgages over a pool of industrial buildings. The issue, paying a rate of three-month LIBOR plus 0.375 percentage points, was rated AAA/Aaa. Security was provided both by a fixed mortgage over a portfolio of 33 properties valued at £83.6m and the guarantees of both principal and interest from Financial Security Assurance (FSA). Westinghouse Credit Corporation provided 20 per cent first-loss reinsurance cover to FSA on the principal amount.

Following issuance, the net proceeds of £82.2m were deposited in an interest-bearing account of BHH Investment Properties. £62.7m, or 75 per cent of the value of the property portfolio, was then paid to BHH Investment Properties Ltd to refinance existing loans. The remainder of the proceeds were used to fund the shortfall between the total rental income from the property portfolio of £7.4m per annum and the full coupon floating rate interest due on the notes.

8.5 CONCLUSIONS

Reviewing these euromarket transactions highlights several factors which distinguish them from domestic bonds, namely:

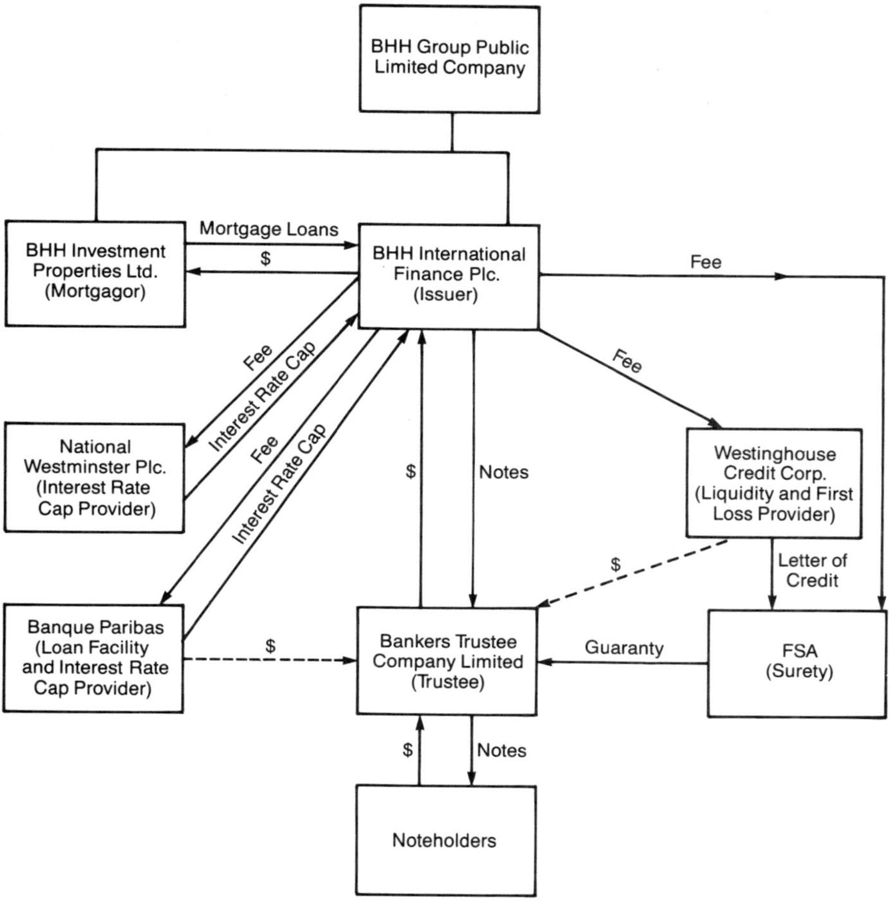

Figure 8.8. BHH Group Public Limited Company.

- The Euromarket bonds can provide somewhat more flexibility than domestic bonds in achieving specific borrower requirements, such as limited recourse, off-balance-sheet, cash flow matching, etc.
- The domestic bond investors usually prefer full-coupon securities so that overall leverage can be constrained by the current rental income available for debt service. With eurobonds, the borrowers can issue discount securities to overcome initial cash flow shortfalls from lower yielding properties in order to maximise financing proceeds.
- While Euromarket investors will accept more principal risk exposure in terms of higher loan-to-value financings than domestic bond investors, they will seek correspondingly higher returns.

In a current market environment, where many investment and development companies are seeking to refinance their short-term bank liabilities, the eurobond market offers a viable route to recapitalise with longer maturity debt. The 1990s will be a decade of significant growth in securitised financing for UK property as the currently high levels of bank debt are recapitalised with new equity and domestic and eurobond securities.

9: Pioneering Securitisation in the French Market

Blaine Roberts, Bear Stearns & Co. Inc.

The first issuance of asset securities requires a real pioneering effort. Among the many issues that have to be addressed are the following:

1. management information issues;
2. legislative issues;
3. regulatory issues;
4. taxation issues;
5. accounting issues;
6. credit enhancement;
7. rating issues;
8. structuring issues;
9. underwriting;
10. marketing;
11. pricing and trading.

In a pioneering effort, where asset securitisation has never been done before, a massive effort is required to tackle each of these. France was not an exception.

9.1 ADDRESSING SECURITISATION ISSUES IN FRANCE

France, as with most other nations that have not yet witnessed asset securitisation, lacked a legal and regulatory framework prior to legal changes enacted 23 December 1988. The principal impediments generally found in most countries are three-fold:

1. there are limitations and restrictions on the assignment of loans or in legal participations in the cashflows from such assets;
2. there do not exist bankruptcy remote and otherwise safe special purpose vehicles to perform the functions of a trustee;
3. there are usually a variety of tax problems.

In the case of France, the Code Civil permitted the assignment of debt under two articles (1271 and 1690). However, these require either participation of the debtor or an expensive notification process that made securitisation impractical. The 'Loi Dailly', enacted 2 January 1981, introduced the *bordereau* for credit institutions to assign debts for commercial activities but was quite limited, and debts could only be sold to other credit institutions.

9.2 THE 'TITRISATION' LAW

The purpose of the 'titrisation' law of 23 December 1988 was to overcome these problems as well as to address items (2) and (3) above. The basic components of the titrisation law are the creation of three new types of entities and the establishment of controls and oversight by two existing ones. The law created *fonds communs de créances* (FCCs), *societés de gestion* (SGs), and *dépositaires*, and it established control and oversight responsibilities with the Commission des Opérations de Bourse (COB) and the Banque de France.

The FCC is a vehicle that has no legal personality. Thus, it cannot be taxed and functions like a grantor or unit trust in the US or the UK. Debts are transferred to an FCC by means of a document, a *bordereau*, that identifies the particular debts or, more practically, identifies the computer tape or system that contains the requisite information. The law also states that notification by a simple letter to debtors is sufficient; however, it is not necessary for the validity of the transfer nor does it have to be proven that debtors were notified.

The other positive aspects of the FCC are that there may be different types of shares, and there is no restriction on principal and interest on the shares or how principal and interest from the debts is allocated to the share units. Thus, the law allows for considerable flexibility in structuring or financial manufacturing.

The French framework had several limiting aspects. Presumably with the aim of protecting investors, the law placed several restrictions on the FCCs that have limited the development of the market in France to some extent.

First, the FCCs may only acquire debts from a financial institution. The rationale for this is not entirely clear, but it can be circumvented by a financial institution acquiring the debts as an intermediary step. This portion of the law is a nuisance that introduces another player to the securitisation process for those debts held by non-financial institutions.

Second, the debts acquired by the FCC must be of the same nature, but may be from more than one financial institution. For example, the debts must all be personal loans or automobile loans but not a mixture.

Third, the debts must be acquired all at the same time, and there is a one time issuance of units or shares in the FCC. Hence, the FCCs are 'closed'. The purpose of this is to limit the activities and scope of the FCC.

Fourth, the debts must have an original maturity of more than two years. This eliminates the securitisation of revolving lines of credit, such as credit cards, under the French framework.

Fifth, the FCC has limited investment powers. About the only things an FCC can do is invest cash flows in French treasury securities, or equivalent, between the time of receipt and a payment date to unit holders and to sell the debts upon final liquidation of the fund. It cannot borrow or pledge the debts for any purpose.

The second component of the law is the *societé de gestion*, which must be a French company whose explicit purpose is to manage FCCs. The SG is required to have at least FFr1.5m in equity capital and any seller of loans to an FCC managed by the SG can only own less than one-third of the SG.

The first responsibility of the SG with respect to a proposed FCC is the arrangement of continued servicing of the debts. Normally this would be continued by the seller, who would be paid a primary servicing fee as agreed by the SG.

After the establishment of an FCC, the SG determines the investment of cash flows, prepares various reports, carries out any liquidation of the debts, and represents the FCC in any legal matters. The SG instructs the *dépositaire* on the payments to various shareholders. In these regards, the SG acts as a pseudo-trustee and master servicer and must be able to reconcile and verify cash flows from the debts. This generally requires substantial technology and financial acumen that must be demonstrated prior to establishing an FCC.

The third component of the law is the *dépositaire*. This must be a registered French financial institution that is the depository for the debts assigned to the FCC and any cash or intermediary investments.

The Commission des Opérations de Bourse must approve the establishment and the liquidation of an FCC. The COB is required to notify and consult with the Banque de France in this process. In particular, it is the responsibility of the COB to ensure that all the requirements as to the structure of the FCC are met.

The units of the FCC are classified under the law as *valeurs mobilières* which makes them negotiable instruments. The units have a proportional share with all other units of the same class. The minimum denomination is FFr10,000 and not more than 5 per cent can be sold to mutual funds (SICAVs) related to the seller of the debts. The intent of the law is that the units be sold to institutions and not to individuals. The law requires some form of credit enhancement for the units that can be obtained by (1) a letter of credit or similar financial guarantee, (2) over-collateralisation, or (3) by issuing subordinated units, *parts spécifics*, that bear all the initial risks of cash shortfalls.

9.3 TAXATION ISSUES

Transfer of the debts to the FCC is not subject to value added taxes nor is any remuneration to the SG or the *dépositaire*. The FCC, having no legal status, cannot be taxed. Institutions transferring debts to an FCC will be subject to usual capital gains taxation if there is a capital gain.

Income and capital gains for individuals investing in an FCC falls in the same category as that for equity shares and bonds. Income and capital gains are taxed at the normal progressive tax rates unless the investor elects to subject such income to a flat rate of taxation, which is currently 15 per cent plus a 1 per cent social security contribution.

Taxation of income and capital gains for French business entities investing in an FCC is subject to normal rules and rates. Income from an FCC for a non-profit institution in France is subject to company taxation at a rate of 10 per cent.

For non-French investors, there is a 15 per cent withholding tax for interest income or for capital gains. However, the withholding tax can generally be avoided. Investors have to demonstrate that they are non-French in the same way they do to avoid withholding for French treasury securities. In the case of a liquidation at the end of the FCC, non-French investors may be subject to some withholding taxes. However, there are various tax treaties that may eliminate these as well.

9.4 ACCOUNTING ISSUES

The regulatory accounting treatment for financial institutions in France is considered to be more lenient than in many other countries. If a financial institution retains a subordinated share in an FCC, then the expected loss must be expensed immediately. However, for risk-based capital calculations, only the amount of the subordinate issue is counted as an asset. In contrast, in the UK and the US, if a financial institution retains a subordinated share, the expected loss does not have to be expensed right away; instead the entire amount of the assets are included in the risk-based capital calculation even though the senior shares are sold. The senior shares are risk-weighted according to the underlying loans, the subordinate shares at 100 per cent.

9.5 MANAGEMENT INFORMATION SYSTEM ISSUES

The technology of information management is the core of asset securitisation. Generally speaking, this requires substantial systems development. Systems have to be built or modified to be able to select and analyse the potential assets in the balance sheet. Further systems are needed to manage the securitisation transaction.

For rating, marketing, pricing and trading securitised assets an historical database is necessary. Information on the following items has to be assembled:

1. payment history: delinquency, defaults, recoveries and prepayments;
2. loan characteristics: purpose, age, maturity, fixed or floating coupons, amortisation schedule, prepayment provisions, collateral and geographical location;
3. borrower characteristics: financial data, social and demographic information;
4. loan commitment and drawdown procedures: credit scoring, approval procedures and record-keeping practices.

9.6 DEALS PRICED

As of 1 July 1990 there have been four FCCs priced as shown in Table 9.1. All issues have units rated triple A by Moody's. The first, CAC Titrisation, was not a real securitisation of assets, but was four asset-backed bonds with a guarantee of the Caisse des Dépôts, whose credit alone is sufficient for a triple A rating. It is a floating rate issue and was placed privately.

The first real securitisation in France was adapted from the US senior/subordinate structure but was noteworthy for several reasons. The units of CL FCC 90–1 were a new product in a new market that did not exist. The units were fixed coupon, monthly pay, variable cashflow securities. All in all the execution of CL FCC 90–1 was one of the most successful of a new issuance.

The structure was collateralised by fixed-rate, unsecured consumer loans issued in France—loans that are rarely securitised in the US. The senior

Table 9.1

Designation	*Amount (FFrm)*	*Tranches*	*Date*	*Underwriters*
CAC Titrisation	485	4	15 Dec 1989	Caisse des Dépôts
CL FCC 90–1	1000	2	3 April 1990	Bear Stearns and Crédit Lyonnais
CB 1	1000	2	7 June 1990	Société Générale and Merrill Lynch
Valora 13,000	200–1000	1	1 July 1990	Caisse des Dépôts

shares comprised 87.5 per cent of the issue and the subordinate shares consisted of the remaining 12.5 per cent. The senior shares were rated Aaa by Moody's while the subordinate shares were rated Baa3 (investment grade). The rating on the subordinate shares represented among the highest ratings accorded to an unsecured subordinate share, which was accomplished through a unique structuring ploy.

The senior shares were sold 50 per cent in France and 50 per cent in Europe outside of France. The senior shares were priced at 70 basis points over the equivalent average life French treasury (BTAN) and were sold out in two days. This was substantially better pricing than would have been achievable through a comparable issue in the US market.

Since issue, the senior shares have traded 1.5 times over, indicating that not only was the initial pricing a success, but the instrument has become a trading vehicle. The shares have held the issue spread over the course of their first six months, with active markets being made in London and Paris.

The third issue was also a securitisation of fixed-rate, monthly pay personal loans and used a senior-subordinated structure. The publicly sold senior units of CB 1 are floating rate units that pay quarterly. An interest rate swap with Société Générale was used to convert monthly pay fixed collateral to quarterly floating. The subordinated units were rated B2 by Moody's.

The fourth issue was the securitisation of one note from Crédit Local, the amount of which would be determined by the sale of the units to range between FFr200m and FFr1bn. These units were sold to the general public. They have a fixed rate accrual and a three-year bullet maturity. This use of an FCC permitted the loan seller to issue, in effect, a zero coupon bond and for a maturity of less than five years, circumventing the requirement that corporate debt be five years or longer.

In sum, the securitised asset market in France has begun, but it has not surged. Prospects for further securitisation remain promising.

9.7 PROSPECTS FOR THE FUTURE

How the market develops in France in the near term will depend on both supply and demand factors. On the supply side, sellers often assess the value of asset securitisation in a single dimension—the relative cost of funding. This is particularly true in markets where securitisation is a new tool. Solely on this basis securitisation can be very attractive. However, over and above funding costs there are several other facets of value for issuers that include:

1. the strengthening of the capital position and the improved return on equity through improved capital ratios;
2. the elimination or reduction of interest rate risk through match funding;

3. the potential optimization of tax and profit positions;
4. the added borrowing efficiency afforded by opening additional markets for funding;
5. the liquidity and flexibility provided to the balance sheet;
6. several other benefits related to the use of state-of-the-art financial technology and the frontiers of financial engineering.

While these facets are difficult to measure accurately, they add significantly to the value of securitisation.

On the demand side, all the forces at work in international financial markets suggest a broadening and deepening demand for securitised assets. For a portfolio manager, the first requisite for investing and managing a portfolio in a dynamic world is information. Information and data feeds on a real time basis continue to become more widely available as the cost of information technology continues to decline. The second requisite for the portfolio manager is liquidity, that is, broad markets with narrow bid–ask spreads. This is clearly the case in the US; there are also active markets made in the UK, and the CL FCC 90–1 traded actively.

Provided these requisites are met, then the fundamentals of portfolio management suggest a much greater degree of portfolio diversification than currently exists around the world. As economic markets become more and more intertwined, from such forces as the EEC goals for 1992 and the recent developments in Eastern Europe, the efficiency of more financial diversification will increase further. Consequently, the candle of asset securitisation that has been lighted in France should glow ever brighter in the future.

10: Securitisation in Italy

Anthony Cutcliffe, Citicorp Investment Bank

Italy has the fifth largest economy in the OECD, with a gross domestic product of nearly $1,000bn. The strength of the Italian economy is shown by continuing real growth: 3.2 per cent in 1989 and in the region of 2.5 per cent in 1990. However, Italy faces a huge public sector deficit amounting to 98 per cent of GDP which successive governments have been unable to cut. The deficit is financed by government borrowing which swamps all other forms of borrowing in Italy. Indeed, the Italian capital markets are still relatively underdeveloped as a result of the government's funding needs.

10.1 THE BANKING SYSTEM

The Italian banking system is characterised by a large number of institutions owned indirectly by the Italian state.

Italian banks are divided into commercial banks which are majority owned by the Istituto per la Ricostruzione Industriale (IRI, the state holding company), the public law credit banks (such as Banco Nazionale del Lavoro, Istituto San Paolo di Torino) which are majority owned by the Treasury, and the savings banks (such as Cassa di Risparmio di Torino). In all about two-thirds of the banking system is held in the public sector. All these institutions lend short-term money (up to 18 months) and have Banca d'Italia restrictions on longer-term lending. Institutions which offer long-term funds include special credit institutions (such as IMI) and the *credito fondiario*—the separate mortgage sections of the short-term banks.

The other institutions which play an important role in the consumer credit markets are the finance companies. Most finance companies are either bank subsidiaries (both domestic and foreign banks) or subsidiaries of corporates, such as the automotive captive finance companies. Finance companies in Italy are not subject to Banca d'Italia supervision and are restricted only in their ability to book long-term assets, by the willingness of the market to lend to them, and the costs associated with obtaining funds. Nevertheless, because of the banks' limits on medium-term assets, many finance companies only borrow with a maximum maturity of 18 months.

One of the most significant events to affect the Italian banking system was the passage of the so-called Amato law in July 1990. The law enables the public sector banks to transform themselves from trusts, foundations and associations into joint stock corporations. The law opens the way for stock market quotations, though there is a limit of 49 per cent of the amount of equity which can be floated. Bank mergers will be more easily accomplished. Indeed, one of the first results of the Amato law is the announcement that Cassa di Risparmio di Roma will acquire a majority stake in Banco di Roma to create the largest bank in Italy.

Most of the Italian banks are regionalised and relatively inefficient. Italian labour laws make it difficult to reduce costs by shedding surplus labour. This means that banks will continue to be relatively inefficient and will not be able to build their weak capital base from retained earnings. For this reason any equity offerings by banks are unattractive to most Italians. The only Italians willing to purchase bank equity for such low returns are the big industrial corporations. The Banca d'Italia has made it clear that it does not want a major bank to be controlled by a corporate.

Given the above constraints many Italian banks will have the following choices in order to meet BIS requirements:

- raise quasi-equity such as subordinated debt;
- reduce asset growth;
- securitise assets.

The first of these will probably not provide a complete solution to the bank's needs, as subordinated debt, perpetual preferred stock and its many variants usually count as Tier 2 capital. Many banks will be constrained by Tier 1 capital.

Many banks will reduce their asset growth, but securitisation will enable them to continue to generate new customer relationships and increase earnings while still achieving the required Cooke ratios.

10.2 CONSUMER CHARACTERISTICS

The growth in the Italian economy has led to a much higher standard of living in Italy. The results of the growth in real disposable income will transform the consumer sector and in particular Italian attitudes to consumer spending, saving and finance.

At nearly 30 per cent of disposable income, Italy currently has one of the highest savings ratio in the OECD. Many individuals still have a traditional attitude to borrowing, in particular towards using credit to purchase consumer goods. However, greater confidence in the ability to repay debt and a greater need for consumer goods will stimulate a preference for financing rather than cash purchase of durables and will thus reduce the savings ratio as has happened in particular in the US and the UK. This translates into a propensity to spend future income. As a result of the increase in credit the consumer will become more sophisticated and increasingly sensitive to interest rates.

Both of these trends pose dangers and opportunities to financial institutions in Italy. Combined with financial liberalisation and increasing foreign competition from new entrants the effect on Italian institutions will be severe. Margins will decrease: few institutions will be able to get away with paying low deposit rates on savings and lending to good credits at penal rates. Institutions will have to cut costs to compete with their more efficient foreign equivalents. The Italian banks have one competitive disadvantage, however: Italian labour laws make it very difficult to reduce staff numbers.

In summary, consumer assets and consumer debt will grow very quickly over the next few years, but increased competition will force down margins on those assets. Undercapitalised banks will find it difficult to grow assets at the necessary rate to meet consumer demand without resorting to off-balance-sheet financing methods.

10.3 THE AUTOMOBILE LOANS MARKET

The Italian car market is the second biggest in the European Community, with in excess of 2 million new cars purchased annually. Autoloan originations in Italy are now approaching L5,000bn ($4.5bn) p.a. The autoloan market in Italy is divided between three types of institution: the banks, the captive finance companies (i.e. subsidiaries of the major car manufacturers such as Fiat-Sava) and the independent finance companies (such as Compass, owned by Mediobanca and Citifin, owned by Citibank).

The banks have about a 50 per cent market share. They market directly to their client base and do not use dealer networks as they are prevented from paying dealer commission by Italian banking laws.

Captive finance companies such as Fiat-sava and Fin Renault have just over a quarter of the market. They obtain business directly through their dealer networks. Their key competitive strengths are the manufacturer's power over their dealers and low-interest-rate (or interest-free) dealer promotions.

The independent finance companies also solicit business through the dealer network and rely on speed of service and high dealer commissions to obtain business.

Typically autoloans are monthly-pay fixed-instalment contracts with a maturity of up to five years. Required downpayments vary with vehicle type, age and depend also on the lender. Some lenders require charges over the cars, others believe that the benefits of a charge are limited and the costs of registration do not provide sufficient benefit.

10.4 THE MORTGAGE MARKET

The Italian mortgage market is less developed than in most other Western European countries, although the level of home ownership is about average for Europe. In 1987 60 per cent of Italians owned their own homes, compared to 64 per cent in the UK and 41 per cent in West Germany.

Most Italians stay in the same property for life rather than trading-up every few years as in the UK. Perhaps this accounts for the high proportion of second homes in Italy (7 per cent). Many people will buy a weekend cottage when they can afford one.

Even now 70–75 per cent of home purchases are financed by savings. Those people who do obtain mortgages will typically provide a 50 per cent downpayment and obtain a mortgage with a 15-year contractual term.

The biggest source of mortgage finance in Italy is the mortgage banks (Istituto di Credito Fondiario), although foreign institutions are becoming increasingly important.

Traditionally mortgages in Italy were fixed-rate semi-annual-pay mortgages with a contractual term of 15 years. As Italian interest rates have declined and are much more stable than ten years ago, variable-rate mortgages have become more popular. Variable-rate mortgages are generally monthly-pay, with interest rates based on either the Italian prime rate or the Interbancario (Italian domestic interbank rate) with a contractual term of 15 to 20 years. One distinguishing feature of the Italian market is the high number of ecu-denominated mortgages. Borrowers prefer the lower interest rate payable on ecu mortgages while believing exchange rate risk to be small because of Italy's EMS membership. About a third of originations in 1989 were ecu-denominated. This trend may be followed in the UK now that Britain has joined the EMS.

10.5 SECURITISING MORTGAGES IN ITALY

Italy is one of the more difficult markets in which to securitise mortgages because of the formidable tax, legal and regulatory problems. Other obstacles to securitisation in Italy include the lack of information on consumer assets, the time taken to repossess properties and assumability of mortgages.

10.5.1 Legal and tax problems

Italy, along with much of Europe, has a legal system based on the Napoleonic Code. This means that, unlike in the UK, if something is not specifically permitted by the Civil Code it is probably illegal. There is currently no legal framework for securitisation to take place, and as yet there is little discussion of a possible 'titrisation' law as in France. In trying to sell or assign assets the following difficulties are encountered. First, it is difficult to sell financial assets (such as mortgages) without notifying the obligor. If notification is not given, then the transfer is not treated as a true sale as the mortgagor can refuse to pay monies to anyone other than the seller, hence creating risk on the seller. Once such notification has been given, the purchaser takes a two-year insolvency risk on the seller. If the seller goes into bankruptcy in that period, the seller's creditors may have the right to take possession of the assets. Second, legal transfer of charges attracts a stamp duty of 0.5 per cent for all assets except mortgages. For mortgages, transfer of the charge attracts a 2 per cent stamp duty. Further, fixed charges over assets need to be notarised, and subsequent transfer of the same assets requires the charges to be notarised again. Each mortgage or charge which is transferred needs to be separately notarised: 'block' notarisation is not possible. As a result there will be a separate notary file for each mortgage or charge transferred.

Interest payments from Italian residents to non-residents are subject to withholding tax, as are payments to residents on bond issues, other than for certain supranationals such as the European Coal and Steel Community.

10.5.2 Regulatory problems

It is impossible to create thinly capitalised special-purpose vehicles in Italy to issue bonds. In general, any company issuing debentures must have equity at least equal to the amount of debt issued.

The Banca d'Italia tightly controls the Lira eurobond market using a queuing system and there is no domestic corporate bond market. (The government bond market is, however, the third largest in the world.) Issuers in the market tend to be supranationals, governments, AAA-rated companies or other well known corporates. It is not clear whether the Banca d'Italia would give the go-ahead to a long-dated, amortising, uncertain-life-structured bond issue. There is still a perception that the relatively small eurolira bond market needs careful nurturing.

The Banca d'Italia has issued no rules on securitisation. It is still unclear whether transactions which meet French or even UK regulatory standards would be granted Italian regulatory off-balance-sheet treatment.

10.5.3 Information problems

Most Italian banks still retain manual files and have not yet begun to change to computer files. As a result most banks are still unable to say clearly what the losses and delinquencies are on their consumer asset portfolios. They cannot track how much money has been received from a specific portfolio on a monthly basis, or give several years' historical data to enable comparisons between lenders and to enable 'worst case' scenarios to be established.

10.5.4 Repossession problems

Although net losses on Italian mortgages have historically been very low, a potential problem faced when structuring a transaction is the time taken to repossess a property in Italy. Many lenders in Italy do not start the legal process required to repossess a property until at least three payments are delinquent (in the case of semi-annual instalments, when the loan is 18 months delinquent). Under Italian law, if a finance company wants to repossess a property, it has to apply to the courts for an auction to take place. The judicial process is also quite slow, so it can take four years to repossess a property. This creates many headaches for the structurer to ensure timely payment of interest and principal to the investor.

10.5.5 Assumability problems

Most mortgages are assumable in Italy. If a house is sold, the mortgage is sold with it. This means that if the house is sold, then the lender's initial credit checks on the original owner are useless. The lender must then rely on an individual over whom he has no control for repayment and on the value of the house itself.

10.6 THE CHARIOTS SECURITISATION

The first securitisation carried out in Italy was Chariots (No. 1) Ltd. The transaction was a L220bn securitisation of Italian autoloan receivables for Citicorp Finanziaria SpA. Citifin, a Citibank subsidiary, had been active in lending to finance car purchases (and other assets) since 1974, and is one of the largest of the free finance companies in Italy.

10.6.1 Aims of the transaction

The transaction had three main aims:

- to achieve off-balance sheet treatment for Citibank NA;
- to provide matchfunding of assets and liabilities;
- to diversify Citifin's funding sources.

Off-Balance-Sheet Treatment
Citibank NA has a policy of securitising its consumer assets worldwide. In 1990 transactions have been completed in the US, the UK, Germany, Spain and Hong Kong as well as Italy. The Chariots transaction was part of this global policy.

Matchfunding of Assets and Liabilities
As discussed above, the structure of the Italian banking system is such that it is difficult and expensive to borrow money for a period above 18 months. Although most of Citifin's autoloans have a contractual life of four years, the average life is considerably shorter. Citifin typically finances its assets by borrowing 18 months' money, approximately equal to the average life of the assets. This minimises Citifin's interest rate risk but does not remove it entirely. One of the aims of the transaction was to remove interest rate and repayment risk on the assets from Citifin by matching the payment characteristics of the autoloans to the funding.

Diversification of funding sources
The transaction enabled Citifin to raise funds from investors in more than 10 countries, diversifying funding away from the Italian banking market.

10.6.2 Structure

Citifin obtained a limited-recourse fixed-rate loan from Banca Commerciale Italiana, London Branch (BCI). Repayment of the loan to BCI was contingent upon the performance of a specific pool of autoloan receivables. In turn a special purpose vehicle based in the Cayman Islands, Chariots (No. 1) Ltd ('Chariots') made a fixed-rate limited-recourse loan to BCI. At the same time Citicorp arranged a letter of credit provided by Bayerische Vereinsbank AG to Chariots. Repayment of the loan from Chariots to BCI was dependent upon BCI being repaid by Citifin, and in the event of non-payment, Chariots had the benefit of the Bayerische Vereinsbank letter of credit.

Finally Citicorp arranged a syndicate of banks to make a loan to Chariots.

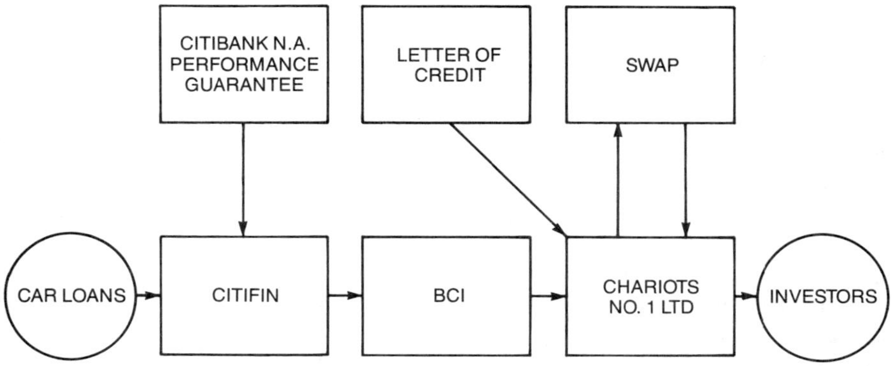

Figure 10.1. The Chariots structure.

This loan was made on a floating-rate basis. Chariots entered into an interest rate swap with Bayerische Vereinsbank to convert the fixed-rate interest payments received from BCI into floating-rate interest payments with which to pay the investors (see figure 10.1).

The transaction was legally structured as limited-recourse loans from BCI to Citifin and from Chariots to BCI. However, investors were not taking Citifin risk because of a Citibank NA guarantee of Citifin's obligations.

10.6.3 Accounting Treatment

The transaction achieved sale treatment for Citibank NA as the risks and benefits of the portfolio were transferred from Citifin to BCI, from BCI to Chariots and ultimately to the investor group. Citifin received the proceeds of sale and retained the servicing and will obtain 'excess servicing' on an ongoing basis from the difference between cashflows from the autoloans and the obligations to BCI.

10.6.4 Credit Protection

The credit protection was determined on the basis of the quality of the underlying asset portfolio, with its low delinquency and historic net loss experience. The protection against losses comes from a combination of the excess spread on the portfolio which is built up in a spread (or 'reserve') account and a letter of credit provided by Bayerische Vereinsbank for 12 per cent of the portfolio's initial amount. The letter of credit declines quarterly subject to the performance of the portfolio.

10.6.5 Payment Characteristics

Chariots issued two tranches of debt. Tranche A had a contractual life of just under one year and was repaid quarterly. Tranche B had a contractual life of four years and received no principal payments in the first year, but was then repayable quarterly. Interest was payable quarterly on both tranches at a margin over LIBOR. The tranching enabled Chariots to obtain a lower overall cost of funds, which was passed on to Citifin.

Both tranches of debt had the unusual feature of fixed amortisation schedules, despite the fact that Citifin passes principal repayments and prepayments on to BCI as they are received. This was done by reinvesting prepaid principal and prepayment penalties. Particularly on future transactions, this structure could reduce the yield premium investors require in asset-backed financings by removing the uncertainty associated with the exact timing of investor prepayments on many other autoloan securitisations.

10.6.6 Rating

Unusually for a structure that is legally a loan, a rating was obtained from Moody's Investor Services on the transaction of Aa2. The rating enabled Citicorp to attract a more diverse group of institutions into the transaction, many of whom were not familiar with the Italian autoloan market.

The rating on the transaction was based on the quality of the receivables, the 12 per cent of credit from Bayerische Vereinsbank and the ratings of BCI and Citibank NA.

10.7 WHERE NEXT?

In 1990 Citicorp, in addition to Chariots, arranged several other transactions in Italy for trade receivables and for mortgages. Swiss Bank Corporation also arranged one transaction.

1991 may see many more transactions for autoloans, for mortgages (both lira- and ecu-denominated), for trade receivables and other assets. However, many Italian banks will be concentrating their resources on transforming themselves into joint stock corporations as a result of the Amato law.

The growing competition within the Italian marketplace will, for many lenders, make securitisation an increasingly important part of their financial strategy. Many leasing and factoring companies which are owned by Italian banks but which are not regulated by the Banca d'Italia may also come under pressure to reduce assets from their balance sheets. 1991 may also see the first securitisation of their assets.

Many financial institutions will start to diversify their portfolio risk by selling assets originated in their home country and by purchasing assets from other EC countries. This trend has already started in the insurance industry in Europe, with many European insurance companies (including Italian insurers) providing reinsurance on UK mortgage pool policies.

11: Securitisation in Australia and New Zealand

Jeff Connor, Bankers Trust Australia Limited

The development of asset-backed markets in the Antipodes has been much less spectacular than in the USA. To date the markets have been dominated by issues supporting Australian state government programs to provide finance for residential housing mortgages to low-income borrowers. Thus, this chapter will concentrate on housing mortgage securitisation in Australia.

11.1 FINANCE PROVIDERS

Banks The major providers of housing finance in Australia are the banks. The majority of these operate under the (Commonwealth) Banking Act 1959 and are supervised by the Reserve Bank of Australia (RBA). It is also usual to include the banks owned by the state governments in this category, although for constitutional reasons they are not legally governed by Commonwealth legislation. They do, however, report to the RBA and voluntarily comply with its regulatory guidelines.

Traditionally the major banks' operations were split between trading banks and their savings bank subsidiaries, with each arm subject to different regulations. The savings bank was the vehicle through which most housing lending was conducted. Although there is now no regulatory distinction between the two types of bank, the separate vehicles are still mantained by the major banks.

As at October 1990 total bank assets exceeded A$320bn. This included $65bn in housing finance to individuals, $62bn in fixed loans, $7.5bn in leases and $4bn in credit card receivables.

Building Societies Building societies are co-operatively-owned organisations which principally raise deposits from the general public to channel funds into housing loans. They operate under state, not Commonwealth, legislation and the degree of regulation and control varies from state to state.

As at October 1990, total assets of building societies amounted to $21.6bn, of which \$9.4bn was housing finance to individuals and \$2.4bn was other loans to individuals.

Credit unions Credit unions are another form of co-operative organisation regulated under state laws. They traditionally developed on the basis of a common bond among members either through employment or community interest. Of their total assets of \$8.5bn, only \$1.5bn comprised housing loans, \$5.3bn of the total was other loans to individuals.

Finance Companies Finance companies borrow mostly through debentures and note issues to lend funds for a variety of purposes. Most major finance companies are owned by licensed banks. Of their \$40bn assets only \$600m was lent for housing. Of the balance \$6.3bn comprised other loans to individuals, \$10bn lease receivables and \$18.6bn other loans, including wholesale financing and factoring.

Life offices The involvement of life offices in direct mortgage lending is insignificant, with \$0.9bn in housing and \$1.3bn in other mortgage loans as at October 1990.

The commonwealth and each of the state governments have established schemes to provide mortgage finance to low-to-middle income earners.

11.2 MORTGAGES

11.2.1 Types of mortgages

Adjustable-rate mortgages By far the most common type of home mortgage in Australia is the adjustable-rate mortgage (ARM). The ARM is the main product offered by savings banks and building societies, and is used for over 90 per cent of their housing lending. The features of a typical ARM are:

- The loan has an original term of around 25 years.
- Principal is repaid over the life of the mortgage (i.e. the mortgage is amortising).
- Payments are due monthly in arrears.
- The interest rate and/or the payment may be reset on short notice at the discretion of the mortgagee.
- The loan is prepayable at the option of the mortgagor, at little or no cost.
- The loan can be made for a very high proportion of the valuation of the property (over 90 per cent is not uncommon), depending upon type of property, location, mortgagor and mortgage insurance.
- The loan is non-portable.

The interest rate payable on an ARM has historically been set with regard to the mortgagee's cost of retail funds, as well as competitive and political pressures. Until April 1983 the interest rate payable on housing mortgages was subject to a commonwealth government-imposed ceiling. The ceiling has been removed for new loans, but stays in place, at 13.5 per cent per annum, for then existing loans.

When the interest on an ARM is changed, mortgagors are commonly given the option to alter the monthly payment accordingly, or to alter the loan term to maintain the same monthly payment.

Interest-only mortgages Interest-only mortgages generally pay interest only for three to five years, at either a fixed or floating rate, and repay principal in a single repayment on maturity. Interest-only loans are commonly used to finance small-to-medium sized industrial, commerical, retail and residential investment properties, as well as larger owner-occupied residential properties.

Interest-only mortages are prepayable, although generally there are imposed prepayment charges, which may be substantial for fixed-rate loans. An increasingly common prepayment charge is based on the net present value of loss of income caused by changes in interest rates.

Graduated payment mortgages Under a graduated payment mortgage (also generally known as a low-start mortgage) the payments made by the mortgagor in the early life of the loan are not sufficient to pay interest at the rate accruing on the loan, resulting in an initial period of negative amortisation. The payments increase annually by a fixed percentage over the life of the mortgage or for a given number of years. The payment increases eventually reverse the initial negative amortisation and enable the repayment of principal in full. In other aspects, the mortgages are conventional (e.g. secured against the property, prepayable, long-term).

Graduated payment mortgages are offered in limited amounts by various banks and building societies. At present, graduated payment mortgages are offered by the New South Wales and Queensland governments to low-to-moderate income earners, as part of the respective states' Department of Housings' Home Loans Programme.

Indexed mortgages Payments on indexed mortgages are linked to an index—usually the consumer price index (CPI). Typically the mortgagor pays interest at a base rate, or real rate of interest, adjusted for any change in the CPI. Indexed mortgages generally have a long term to maturity, are subject to prepayment, and an amortising nature.

The state government of Victoria offers indexed mortgages to low-to-middle income earners as part of its Home Opportunity Loans Scheme. The interest charge is equal to a base rate of interest plus the current inflation rate. During the first five years of the loan no change is made to the rate. Repayments are tailored to the income level of the mortgagor and are initially set at approximately 27 per cent of eligible income. The state governments of South Australia and Western Australia have offered similar schemes.

11.2.2 Mortgage characteristics

No reliable data on the prepayment behaviour of Australian mortgages is publicly available. The normal industry view is that the average life of ARMs is five to seven years.

Mortgages are generally illiquid instruments. Prohibitive stamp duty was levied on the transfer of mortgages until various state governments eliminated the duty in the mid 1980s. However, no significant secondary market has developed following these changes. The lack of standardisation of loan terms and lack of uniformity of documentation remain two of the main impediments to a deep secondary market in unsecuritised mortgages.

The credit quality of residential mortgage loans is generally good. The chance of recovery in the event of default is high, the mortgage is secured against property and land, and there is usually protection available because of the loan to valuation ratio and/or mortgage insurance.

11.3 CAMPBELL COMMITTEE AND MARTIN REVIEW GROUP

The 1981 Committee of Inquiry into the Australian Financial System ('Campbell Committee') and the Martin Review Group (1984) identified a number of impediments to the establishments of an Australian Secondary Mortgage Market (SMM). These included the following:

1. *Political interference in housing interest rates* Australian investors were reluctant to purchase adjustable-rate mortgages or mortgage-backed securities in an environment where the government's political goal was to maintain low housing interest rates. Investors were concerned in particular that the government would intervene to hold down rates on their mortgage pools during a period of rising interest rates.
2. *Transaction taxes* State stamp duty on conveyances of property and marketable securities imposed a double tax on the industry. First, duty was levied on the transfer of mortgages into a pool in preparation for their securitisation. Second, duty was also payable on the assignment of mortgage-backed securities in the secondary market.

3. *Building society restrictions* State restrictions confined building societies to initiating or purchasing mortgages over real estate within the state of their formation, which limited their capacity to participate in a national SMM.
4. *Non-trustee investments* Mortgage-backed securities did not have trustee investment status. Potential investors, such as government superannuation funds, pension funds and other groups whose investments were governed by state trustee legislation were, therefore, prohibited from investing in mortgage-backed securities even though they could acquire mortgages in the underlying pool collateralising such securities.

The Campbell Committee and the Martin Review Group both recommended that a SMM be established in Australia. Based upon this, New South Wales, Victoria and Queensland have removed many of the restrictions that were identified. Queensland had also attempted to regulate the industry by making these concessions available only to mortgage-backed securities that comply with additional criteria linked to prudential and registration requirements. Although the Campbell Committee and Martin Review Group recommended against the establishment of a GNMA, FNMA or FHLMC-style government agency, New South Wales and Victoria have each provided official impetus to the SMM by sponsoring the formation of two of the major issuers—FANMAC Ltd (originally called First Australian National Mortgage Acceptance Corporation Ltd) and the National Mortgage Market Corporation Ltd (NMMC). Also, significant support for the industry has been provided by the Housing Loans Insurance Corporation, which offers mortgage and pool insurance backed by the guarantee of the Commonwealth government (although refer to section 11.7 for proposals to privatise HLIC).

11.4 ISSUERS AND SECURITIES IN THE AUSTRALIAN MORTGAGE-BACKED MARKET

The Australian mortgage-backed market now approaches something in the order of $6.2bn. The three principal issuers (and their approximate market shares) are FANMAC (50 per cent), the NMMC (14 per cent) and MGICA Securities Limited (MSL) (15 per cent). There are also a number of other small issuers, including State Bank of NSW, Security Pacific Securities Australia Limited, Secured Asset Funding Entity Limited (SAFE), Town & Country Building Society, ANZ McCaughan and Capel Court.

11.4.1 FANMAC

FANMAC was incorporated in September 1985. 26 per cent of its issued share capital is owned by the New South Wales government; the balance is held by a variety of Australian and overseas financial institutions.

FANMAC has issued over \$3.2bn of securities (which includes an offering of A\$50m in the Eurobond market) and is by far the dominant issuer.

Early domestic issues FANMAC commenced its domestic programe in December 1986 with an issue of A\$50m of FANMAC Premier Trust (Australia) No. 1 Bonds. The proceeds from the subscription of the bonds were used to purchase graduated payment mortgages originated by participating co-operative housing societies under the New South Wales Home Loans Programme.

Domestic bond issues nos. 1–10 represent undivided beneficial interests in separate trust funds supported by separate distinct pools of assets. The bonds pay 'interest' (i.e. distribute trust income) semi-annually at a fixed rate on principal outstanding from time to time.

Reductions of the mortgage pool balance arising from prepayments and net amortisation may be passed through to the bondholders. There is, however, a call protection period of approximately 12 months from original issue date during which no principal can be passed through. As an alternative to passing through principal repayments, FANMAC has the option of either purchasing replacement mortgages or repurchasing bonds in the market.

The fixed rate payable on the bonds is reset every four or five years depending on the issue. Bondholders have a put option exercisable on these reset dates.

FANMAC Bonds are rated AAA by Australian Ratings and AA+ by Standard & Poor's by virtue of the credit support provided by the State of New South Wales. This is provided through the HPAA or HPAF Trusts and consists of obligations (supported directly by the State of New South Wales) to:

- purchase bonds from those bondholders exercising their put option;
- purchase all mortgages remaining in the trust on the business day immediately preceding the maturity date of the bonds or, if requested, when the pool size falls below a specified level;
- purchase defaulting mortgages if requested;
- cover any income shortfall on each 30 June;
- subscribe for bonds which are issued on any interest payment date to cover any cash flow shortfall and which the bond underwriters fail to subscribe for whatever reason.

Subsequent domestic issues Bond issues after no. 10 have been unsecured debt obligation of the FANMAC trustee with a limitation on the trustee's liability to the assets of the relevant FANMAC trust and the interest of the unitholders in the trust is subordinated to the right of the bondholders to full payment from the trust.

Bond issues nos. 17 and 18 removed the put option and are promoted as an average life security. Bond issues nos. 19 and 20, the latest to date, are three-tranche serially prepaying collateralised mortgage obligations.

Euromarket issue In January 1987 a FANMAC subsidiary—FANMAC Overseas No. 1 Limited—made a A$50m Eurobond offering. In contrast to the early domestic issues, the bonds represented debt obligation of FANMAC Overseas. FANMAC Overseas applied the proceeds of the issue towards acquiring a premier unit in the FANMAC Premier Trust (Overseas) No. 1 (The FANMAC Overseas Trust), which premier unit was charged in favour of Bankers Trustee Co. Ltd for the bondholders. The bond was thus grafted onto a similar structure used for the early domestic FANMAC issues. As with the domestic issue, support was provided by the State Bank NSW in its capacity as trustee for the HPAA/FANMAC Trust (Overseas) No. 1 (the HPAA Overseas Trust) and by the New South Wales government. The issue was supported by an over-collateralised mortgage pool—there being A$50m of mortgages held in the FANMAC Overseas Trust and A$30m in the HPAA Overseas Trust.

11.4.2 National Mortgage Market Corporation Ltd (NMMC)

The NMMC was formed in December 1984. Its share capital is divided into A and B-class shares. The B-class shares represent 26 per cent of its authorised capital and are held by the Victorian government and South Australian and Western Australian government entities. The A-class shares represent the balance of the authorised capital and are held by 49 shareholders (as at 30 June 1989) who are leading participants in the mortgage and finance markets.

Aussie Macs The NMMC has issued over $4.6bn of debt-based instruments known as 'Aussie Macs', of which $657m were outstanding as at 30 June 1990. There are two classes of Aussie Macs. The first comprises short-term promissory notes with a maturity not exceeding 185 days and a face value of not less than $50,000. The second class is composed of longer-term Aussie Macs with a term of three-to-five-years depending on the period required by the investor.

The purpose of the Aussie Mac programme is to enable a mortgage originator to reliquify by discounting Aussie Macs issued to it by the NMMC. The mortgage originator is under an obligation to place the NMMC in sufficient funds to redeem the Aussie Mac certificates on their maturity. This obligation is secured by the pledge of qualifying mortgages by the mortgage originator to the NMMC.

The Aussie Mac constitutes a debt obligation of the issuer (i.e. the NMMC). However, the NMMC's obligations in respect of given Aussie Macs are not directly secured by the relevant underlying mortgage pool. Instead Aussie Mac holders are simply unsecured creditors of the NMMC. To the extent that an amount owing by a defaulting originator is recovered from enforcement of the NMMC's security, the proceeds must be shared between all of the NMMC's creditors, including the holders of Aussie Macs relating to other mortgage pools and its general trading creditors.

National Mortgage Bonds (NMBs) The NMMC has launched a number of series of National Mortgage Bonds. These are rated AA+ by Australian Ratings and qualify as authorised trustee investments in NSW and Victoria. To date NMBs with a face value exceeding $255m have been issued by the NMMC, with the last issue occurring in May 1989.

Unlike the Aussie Mac, the NMB represents an undivided beneficial interest in a trust. Each series is created pursuant to a separate trust and different series are not fungible. Interest and principal payments on the mortgages are made to the originator which is required to pay them to the trustee. In the case of any mortgage delinquency, originators are required to pay to the trustee monthly payments due but not received for the first four months.

Mortgagors have the right to prepay their mortgages early although these prepayments are not passed on to bondholders but reinvested in a Guaranteed Investment Contract (GIC) provided by the State Bank of Victoria, under which interest is paid at the rate that was payable on the mortgages. To the extent this is out of market, the cost is borne by the mortgagor in the form of a prepayment penalty.

Other credit and cash flow support includes:

- primary mortgage insurance on certain loans;
- pool insurance provided by HLIC;
- bank standby and overdraft facilities provided by State Bank of Victoria.

The NMB is marketed as equivalent to a debt instrument, and holders are promised regular payments of 'interest' and a 'repayment' of principal on maturity. The underlying mortgages comprise three-to-five-year fixed-rate, fixed-term interest-only mortgages provided by approved mortgage originators.

Low-Start loan programmes NMMC manages the low-start loan programmes for the state governments of Victoria (Home Opportunity Loans), Western Australia (Keystart Loans) and South Australia (Home Start

Loans). Under the Victorian scheme, short-term securities worth $139m and Indexed Victorian Housing Bonds worth $329m have been issued.

In 1990 National Housing Securities Ltd—a special-purpose vehicle managed by NMMC—was established to act as central fundraiser for these state government programmes.

11.4.3 MGICA Securities Ltd (MSL)

MSL, now called Australian Mortgage Securities Ltd, has issued nearly $900m of MGICA Mortgage Securities (MMSs). Each MMS represents a beneficial interests in a designated pool of mortgages held on trust for MMS-holders. The underlying pool is composed of fixed-rate mortgages returning periodical payments in excess of the 'interest' due to be passed to the MSS-holders.

As with NMBs, MSLs are 'bullet' securities and mortgagors prepaying must pay an amount sufficient to cover lost income from reinvesting the principal under a GIC with Chase AMP Bank. Alternatively the trustee may use the principal proceeds to repurchase MMS in the market.

The credit rating of MMSs is provided by, inter alia, primary mortgage insurance, mortgage pool insurance by MGICA Ltd, and a limited standby credit facility provided by Chase AMP Bank and Australian Mutual Provident Society to enable the trustee to meet payments of 'interest' and to redeem each series of MMSs on a timely basis. Reflecting these enhancements, MMSs have been assigned a AA credit rating by Australian Ratings.

MSL has recently advised changes to the MMS structure effective from Series 15 onwards, including:

- provision for fungible tranches;
- reduction in credit and cash flow support levels;
- increases in maximum mortgage sizes;
- removal of the Chase AMP Bank GIC (proceeds of repayments will now be reinvested in authorised investments).

MSL has also announced its intention to issue passthrough securities guaranteed by Financial Security Assurance Inc. to fund mortgages originated by Credit Unions.

11.4.4 Secured Asset Funding Entity Ltd (SAFE)

In November 1990 Bankers Trust Australia Ltd (BTAL) launched the first $100m issue for SAFE, a special-purpose company incorporated to facilitate a variety of securitisation initiatives. The SAFE bonds are fixed-rate 'bullet' debt obligations with payments of principal and interest guaranteed jointly by State Government Insurance Commission (of South Australia) and Financial Security Assurance Inc.

The proceeds of the first bond issue were on-lent to another special-purpose company (SPC) to allow it to purchase a portfolio of residential and commercial mortgages from Town & Country WA Building Society.

The structure is designed to enable SAFE to issue further bonds with identical cash flow and primary credit characteristics to raise funds to on-lend to other special-purpose companies to allow the securitisation of a variety of asset types from a number of different originators.

Subsequent bond issues have been \$200m in April 1991, the proceeds of which were on-lent to an SPC to purchase a portfolio of residential and commercial mortgages from St George Building Society, and \$180m in June 1991. These proceeds were on-lent to an SPC to purchase a portfolio of credit card receivables from David Jones Ltd.

SAFE Bonds are rated AAA by Standard & Poor's, Moody's and Australian Ratings, and are authorised trustee investments in all states.

11.4.5 Other Issues

Security Pacific Mortgage Trust Bonds

Security Pacific Securities Australia Ltd (SPSAL) offers 'bullet' medium-term MBS (called MTBs) that securitise interest-only fixed-rate mortgages. The SPSAL structure is similar to that used by NMMC.

The credit and cash flow enhancements include:

- primary mortgage insurance;
- Housing Loans Insurance Corporation pool insurance;
- a liquidity facility and mortgage purchase obligation from Security Pacific Australia Ltd (which are guaranteed by Security Pacific National Bank, Los Angeles).

Mortgage prepayments may be used to purchase MTBs in the market or deposited with SPAL under a GIC. The GIC ensures that interest on the deposits will be paid at the interest rate which had been payable on the prepaid mortgage.

The \$300m MTBs are rated A+ by Australian Ratings.

State Bank Mortgage Bonds

The State Bank of New South Wales (SBNSW) launched its Mortgage Bond Trust in 1986 and it was relaunched late in 1988. At that time \$160m of medium-term MBS and \$40m of short-term MBS were offered.

The information memorandum provided by SBNSW describes the MBS as beneficial interests in the trust fund. The MBS are either fixed-income, bullet securities having terms of up to five years, or short-term discount securities.

Town & Country Housing Bonds
Town & Country Housing Bonds (the 'bonds') are issued by Town & Country Housing Bonds Ltd (the 'issuer'), which is owned by Chase AMP Bank group, Town & Country WA Building Society and National Mutual Life Nominees Ltd. The bonds are issued pursuant to a trust deed are bullet debt instruments secured by a floating charge over all of the issuer's underlying property and assets which will include mortgages and other authorised investments.

The mortgages are over residential properties with no restrictions on the maturity date or nature of the mortgages, e.g. the mortgage may pay interest-only during their term or amortise principal over the life of the loan. As the mortgages do not necessarily mature on or before the bonds. Chase AMP Bank has provided a mortgage take-out facility on maturity of the bonds. Chase AMP Bank Ltd has also provided a term standby credit facility to ensure timely payment of interest. The facility is limited to 10 per cent of the face value of bonds. In addition, Town & Country WA Building Society ensures that the issuer has sufficient non-defaulting mortgages to meet certain ratio requirements covering principal and interest obligations on the bonds.

The bonds are rated A+ by Australian Ratings. There are two issues totalling $150m.

11.5 INVESTORS AND SECONDARY MARKETS

There are approximately ten investment banks and other fixed-income securities specialists involved in the distribution and/or market making of asset-backed securities. Primary distribution is generally through dealer panels of three to four participants by way of 'bought deals'.

While industry figures are not available, it is widely believed that market turnover of the corporate and mortgage-backed bonds is between $400m and $600m per day (compared with commonwealth bond turnover in excess of $1bn per day and semi-government securities trading of around $5bn per day).

Of the 60 or so institutional investors involved in the market the insurance funds (life, general and superannuation—i.e. pension) are generally believed to hold over half the paper on issue. Other investors include the banks, building societies and friendly societies.

11.6 OTHER AREAS OF SECURITISATION

11.6.1 The Australian asset-backed securities market

The asset-backed securities market in Australia is still in its infancy. There has been considerable local interest in the potential offered by asset-backed securitisation, particularly by investment and merchant banks in relation to the financial receivables of their corporate clients and by the trading banks in relation to their credit card consumer debt portfolios. The interest of the banks in this area has particularly strengthened with the advent of capital adequacy as these classes of receivables are weighted at 100 per cent, and so the banks will gain the most from removing these rather than housing mortgage assets from their balance sheet. The only asset-backed security which is widely traded is the SAFE issue which funded a portfolio of credit card receivables originated by David Jones Ltd, a major retail department store. There have been a number of private issues.

BULLETS

In June 1988 Bankers Trust Australia Limited (BT) launched BULLETS (Bonds Undertakings and Loans of Local Entities Trust). As the name implies, the product involves the packaging of illiquid local government and public authority loans into marketable fixed-interest investments.

BULLETS are undivided equitable interests in a trust structured to resemble fixed-interest-rate bonds, i.e. investors are promised a fixed 'coupon rate' payable semi-annually in arrears and a repayment of principal on a specified date.

To meet the cash flow needs of the trust and to overcome expected mismatches of interest and principal between the underlying pool of loans and the BULLETS, BT has agreed to provide an overdraft credit facility for the trust and an underwriting facility for the issue of short-term units.

A pool insurance policy is provided by SGIC (of South Australia) and the BULLETS are rated AA+ by Australian Ratings. In excess of $400m BULLETS have been issued. Currently around $260m of these remain on issue in the hands of a number of institutional investors.

LION Trust

The LION Trust was established by J. B. Were & Son to permit borrowers, who would not otherwise be able to do so, to tap the promissory note market. Since the stock market crash, though, its operations have been wound down. Nevertheless, it suggests a likely debt-based structure for asset-backed securities in Australia.

Under the scheme, a borrower would issue a promissory note in favour of

Lion Securities Ltd (LSL), supported by a letter of credit from an Australian trading bank. LSL would then reliquify its position by issuing its own matching promissory notes known as a Liquid Interest-bearing Obligation Notes (LIONs). The borrower's promissory note and the letter of credit would then be deposited with the trustee to be held for each LION-holder as security for LSL's obligations thereunder.

Pooled Unlisted Mortgage Assets (PUMA) Fund
Established by Schroders Australia Mortgage Securities Ltd, a wholly-owned subsidiary of Schroders Australia Ltd, the PUMA fund will issue fixed-rate medium term notes (MTNs) and utilise the proceeds to acquire interest-only, fixed-rate residential and commercial mortgages.

Investors will be entitled to semi-annual interest payments out of income of the trust and repayment of principal from redemption proceeds of the trust's assets and will have an unsecured interest in the trust's assets.

The Housing Loans Insurance Corporation (HLIC) is to provide a pool policy which covers both defaults and losses of prepayment penalties. Prepayment of underlying mortgages is allowed, with penalties based on loss of income.

A guaranteed investment contract (GIC) will be provided by an AAA-rated financial institution to cover reinvestment risk. A similarly rated financial institution will provide a liquidity redemption facility of up to 60 per cent of the principal balance of the original mortgage pool to enable the trustee to make full and timely payment of principal on the MTNs.

Moody's has assigned a prospective Aaa rating to PUMA MTNs.

The Leasing Trust of Australia (LTA)
LTA was established by Macquarie Bank Ltd in January 1990 as an off-balance-sheet funding vehicle for lease receivables. The assets of LTA will be originated by various financial institutions acting as agent for LTA, with the first agent being Esanda Finance Corporation Ltd, a subsidiary of the Australian and New Zealand Banking Group Ltd.

Funding of LTA will be through the issue of a variety of short- and long-term securities constituting debt obligations of LTA. In addition, as each agent originates business and subsequently settles with LTA it must simultaneously subscribe for income class units equal to 10 per cent of the assets settled with LTA.

The equity provided by each agent must equal or exceed at all times 10 per cent of the assets of LTA. If at any stage the ratio falls below 10 per cent, LTA must cease writing further business until the ratio is restored by way of further equity subscription or repayment of leases.

The funding structure of LTA is to be actively managed by Macquarie Bank Ltd so as to minimise costs and maximise profit margins. State Bank of

New South Wales has provided a three-year standby liquidity facility equal to 10 per cent of the lease assets of LTA.

Australian Ratings has assigned a rating of AA/A.1+ to LTA.

11.6.2 New Zealand

Since 1984 the New Zealand government's deregulation of its financial markets has provided a regulatory environment more conducive to asset-backed securitisation. Specific initiatives include the removal of interest rate and exchange controls and the removal of stamp duty, as well as the removal of the requirement for certain institutions to hold a certain portion of their assets as government securities.

Despite these changes there has been no development of a domestic asset-backed securities market. Perhaps what is needed is a commitment from the government to the development of such a market similar to that evidenced by the New South Wales government's commitment to FANMAC. The obvious vehicle in New Zealand would be the Housing Corporation (the government's housing policy agency), which is the largest mortgage lender in the country, with assets in excess of $3.5bn.

GMBS No. 1

In the one securitisation which has occurred in New Zealand, Bankers Trust New Zealand Ltd raised US$100m for United Building Society by securitising a portfolio of its residential mortgages. The society avoided the problem of the lack of a domestic market by issuing the securities into the euromarkets as a US dollar bullet bond.

An international AAA rating was achieved through an unconditional guarantee of principal and interest from Financial Security Assurance Inc.

The bonds were actually issued as debt obligation of a Cayman Islands company which on-lent the proceeds to a New Zealand special-purpose company. A similar structure was used by Bankers Trust Australia Ltd to raise US$100m for Town & Country WA Building Society through GMBS No. 3.

11.7 OBSERVATIONS ON THE AUSTRALIAN MORTGAGE-BACKED SECURITIES MARKET

Participation by banks

With such large volumes of mortgages potentially available for securitisation the domestic secondary market has been characterised as having considerable scope for growth. In Australia, the banks have not participated by securitising their mortgages in any significant volume which has hampered the market's development.

Risk weighting for capital adequacy purposes

Risk weighting for capital adequacy purposes is unlikely to change in the short term because under the Reserve Bank of Australia (RBA) capital adequacy guidelines, residential mortgages have a 50 per cent risk weighting. The banks need only hold half as much capital against these as for other private-sector loans. There is, therefore, little incentive for the banks to remove such mortgages from their balance sheets by securitising them. Their priority instead in the short term is to securitise their 100 per cent risk-weighted assets (such as credit card receivables).

Even given a desire to securitise assets to reduce capital requirements, it remains unclear what will satisfy the RBA that the desired result has been achieved. Despite some general observations from the RBA, there exists no clear guide as to practical requirements. From the general comments delivered to date it appears that the required degree of 'distancing' from the bank will be in direct conflict with the banks' strong desire to maintain its relationship with its clients.

From the point of view of investors in mortgage-backed securities, the RBA has indicated that only securities based on pools of bank (rather than, say, building society) residential mortgages and satisfying certain other criteria would be treated as having a 50 per cent risk weighting; while all other mortgage securities would receive a 100 per cent weighting.

Changes in non-bank financial intermediaries

Following deregulation there has been a significant reduction in the number of independent building societies. Some have become banks, others have been taken over by banks and there has been a spectacular collapse of one society.

For those that remain there is considerable talk of tightening regulation and creating uniformity between the states. Included in some proposals are a capital-adequacy-style risk-weighting which would mirror the approach taken by the RBA. In the absence of such regulation, some building societies nonetheless attempt to show that they comply with the RBA guidelines as evidence of prudent management.

In the wake of the collapse mentioned above and the general deterioration in credit condition, the NBFI's ability to access their traditional retail and their wholesale banking funding has been impaired and any opportunity they may have had to access the emerging unsecured medium-term note market has disappeared for the immediate future.

Changes in credit markets: government and semi-government securities
The Commonwealth government and its agencies have consistently run budgetary surpluses over the last few years and have substantially reduced their borrowing programmes. As a result there has been a reduction in the number of Commonwealth bonds on issue.

In the 1980s the semi-government securities (i.e. principally those issued by state government central borrowing authorities) played a bigger role in Australian capital markets. This development was assisted by increased volumes on issue and concerted efforts by the authorities to improve the marketability of their bonds, including debt consolidation programmes and the adoption of dealer panels to market and trade stock.

In the late 1980s the rate of new borrowings by the semi-government authorities began to decline.

Changes in credit markets: corporate bond market
Promoters of asset-backed securities are hopeful that these securities will fill the vacuum resulting from the growing shortage of Commonwealth and semi-government securities. They compete with medium-term unsecured debt obligations of the banks and (to a lesser degree) a few major corporates. The banks ability to access this market in their own names must be one factor affecting their views on the viability of securitising their assets.

Changes in credit markets: investor sophistication
The ability of the Australian fixed-interest security investor to assess and price the potentially complex credit and cash flow characteristics of asset-backed securities can be critical to the success of the market.

In relation to cash flow risks, FANMAC and its promoters have expended considerable time and effort in the education process. Its initial offerings had call protection and put options to limit the prepayment risks. Series 17 did away with the put option and traded as an average life security. Series 18 was a three-tranche serial-pay CMO. Despite these efforts it is questionable whether the market prices the inherent prepayment options fairly.

The market remains a fairly unsophisticated assessor of credit risk. Rating agencies play an important role here although it appears to be advantageous to have an easily understood credit (for example the ultimate NSW government risk for FANMAC and the unconditional guarantees from SGIC and FSA on SAFE bonds).

Growth and changes in investable funds
The combined effect of a number of years of changes to the Australian government's retirement and industrial relations policies will result in a massive growth in funds under management by superannuation funds. Securitisation provides a means for these funds to be channelled into areas of lending

traditionally dominated by the banks and other financial intermediaries by way of direct mortgage lending.

Interest rate mismatches
As discussed earlier, the vast majority of residential mortgages in Australia have variable interest rates. The way in which the mortgage interest rate may vary without reference to any common benchmark, and the way in which either the payment or the term may change in response to an interest rate change, together with the long-term, amortising and prepayable nature of ARM, make the efficient securitisation of these mortgages a challenge.

To date the major private issuers have attempted to sidestep this problem by principally securitising fixed-rate fixed-term commercial mortgages; however, the size of their operations has been constrained by a shortage of suitable stock.

Real growth could occur under a couple of scenarios. First, if borrowers and lenders accepted either fixed-rate or market-linked floating-rate mortgages the resulting loan would be easier to securitise.

An alternative approach is that adopted in the GMBS and SAFE structures. Investors are presented with fixed-term, fixed-rate securities but the assets supporting the issue include traditional ARMs. The potential mismatch between the revenues generated by the asset pools and the corresponding interest obligations on the bonds is overcome through the use of a variety of swaps and cash flow management techniques.

Risk management products
The development and maturing of financial markets has enabled better liability management techniques to be used in structuring securitisation transactions.

Privatisation of the HLIC
The proposal by the Commonwealth government to privatise the HLIC has generated a considerable amount of controversy in the industry, which to some extent has become polarised over the issue. On the one hand, FANMAC, the NMMC and the Mortgage Bankers' Association have opposed the move, arguing that the HLIC provides pool insurance to 70 per cent of mortgage-backed issues that carry insurance. They argue its commonwealth government guarantee has done much to underwrite investor confidence in mortgage-backed securities and so has been crucial to the development of the market. On the other hand, its major competitor, MGICA Ltd, believes the privatisation of the HLIC would have no discernible effect on the market as investors look principally to the quality of the originator and its loans rather than to the pool insurance.

Non-uniform legislation
New South Wales, Victoria and Queensland have sought to underwrite the development of the Secondary Mortgage Market (SMM) by sponsoring two of the major issuers and by offering stamp duty concessions and trustee investment status for qualifying mortgage-backed securities. Their respective approaches, however, have tended to be uncoordinated and designed principally with a narrower vision in mind of fostering an SMM only within their own jurisdictions. As a result, an issuer faces a patchwork of legislation with quite disparate requirements with respect to both stamp duty and trustee status. For example, a recognised institution under the Victorian Act must apply afresh for the relevant approvals under the Queensland legislation if its securities are to qualify for any of the benefits conferred thereunder. Consequently, despite the progress to date, the SMM tends to be partitioned along state boundaries. A national SMM can only come into existence once the legislation of each state has been brought into line and the disparities worked out. This should then broaden the potential market for a particular state's securities, which in turn should strengthen the SMM.

Political decisions
With the major issuers to the market being FANMAC and NMMC it is clear that state-government-sponsored programs play a dominant role. The future direction of the markets will be influenced by the various state governments decision as to:

- the provision of government-assisted housing lending; and
- the funding of these programs (central borrowing authorities versus securitisation initiatives).

The funding decisions for these programs are often driven by the balance between state governments' total funding requirements (i.e. for all their activities) and the constraints imposed on their ability to borrow money in their own name by the Loan Council agreements (under which the aggregate level of borrowings by the public sector is regulated).

The increasing need for various state governments to raise funds and the possibility that securitisation provides for doing so outside of Loan Council constraints bodes well for this area of securitisation.

Past history indicates, however, that it would be optimistic to expect the various state governments to adopt a consistent approach and a number of different developments could therefore be expected.

Conclusion
Whilst it appears unlikely that we will see a significant push by the major Australian banks to securitise large amounts of their assets in the immediate future, the prospects for asset backed securitisation in Australia appear quite

good. Institutional investors with fast growing amounts of funds under management are becoming increasingly aware of the opportunities provided by securitisation. The main areas of activity should relate to state government initiatives and assets originated by non-bank financial intermediaries and other areas outside the banking sector.

Credit Enhancement

12: Credit Enhancement: Introduction and Overview

Stephen L. Wenman, Special Risk Services

12.1 THE ROLE OF CREDIT ENHANCEMENT

Credit enhancement offers the issuer of a security a better opportunity to access the liquidity of the capital markets which in normal circumstances might be closed to him. If the underlying structure of a security is new and not easily understood, credit enhancement can make the issue more marketable. Credit enhancement dramatically reduces the amount of research and analysis an investor has to perform to make an investment decision. The investor can base his decision on the guarantor or insurer's rating rather than having to dig through the structure. An investor offered two issues of equal complexity, one enhanced to a rating of Triple A and the other without credit enhancement, will have a strong incentive to choose the credit-enhanced issue. Capital markets are highly competitive and investors have a vast quantity of choices. Thus, the more easily understood a particular issue, the better recognised its name and the better its rating, the more likely it is to be selected.

When an issuer decides to access the capital markets for funding, he looks to launch an issue which will produce the lowest yield possible. Many basis points can be lost if investors cannot easily understand an issue, do not recognise the name of the issuer or have no information about its financial condition. In addition, a low rating can reduce the liquidity of an issue which can then cause an increase in the yield. Credit enhancement can be used in the structuring of an asset backed issue to establish a finer yield to the issuer by eliminating or reducing the impact of these factors.

In the situation where a potential issuer prefers not to release his financial information to the public or is unknown to the market, credit enhancement of an issue can eliminate potential illiquidity in trading (which can adversely effect future issues) or higher yields which would otherwise be caused by lack of information or name recognition of the borrower. A potential investor need only look at the name and financial condition of the guarantor to make his investment decision. An example of this is an issue for the Rockefeller Foundation which took place several years ago, where the foundation, as a private institution, was not willing to disclose its financial statements to the market. In spite of the high credit standard of the foundation, without detailed financial information the market could not make a proper assessment of the issue nor could the rating agencies grant a rating despite the issuer's well recognised name. Thus to raise funds in the capital markets, the foundation gave Aetna Life access to its financials and Aetna subsequently provided a triple A guarantee to the issue. In this case, credit enhancement enabled a triple A security to be issued without releasing the financial information of the foundation to the market. The issue subsequently traded partly on the name of the foundation and partly on the financial security provided by the credit enhancement.

Credit enhancement can give an issuer anonymity in the capital markets by enabling the company to raise funds through a special purpose company (SPC). The SPC receives the assets from the company in exchange for cash raised in the capital markets. The SPC can raise funds in the market at competitive rates because it has credit enhancement. The SPC is not supported by its parent (or the company who set it up) so the originator can remain anonymous and the funds are raised on the strength of the credit enhancement. This method is successful for firms who wish to preserve their financial privacy as in the case mentioned above, for firms who are unknown in the market and firms who wish to remain anonymous because of difficulties in their local markets or with parts of their balance sheet. Special-purpose companies are also useful in achieving off-balance-sheet funding: this will be discussed later in this chapter.

The anonymity endowed an issuer who has purchased credit enhancement is particularly attractive to institutions who have had an actual or de facto reduction in their rating. The institution may or may not have had an actual downgrading but the capital markets treat it as if it had. Such a rating decline could be due to shocks in the issuer's home markets such as a rapid decline in property or equity market values or even political difficulties. In many cases, the institution will undoubtedly recuperate in time but will suffer short-term liquidity difficulties due to the fact that it will not be able to fund at pricing levels to which it is accustomed. Credit enhancement can be used in this situation to bridge this credit difficulty. The institution could thus release an issue at a price very near its original cost of funding.

'Guilt by association' can even be an issue. An institution that has the misfortune of being merely associated with a market which has had a downturn could have difficulty when attempting to raise money in the capital markets. Even if the institution is unaffected by the difficulties, the issue cost and subsequent liquidity of its paper can be adversely affected by mere association. The enhancers of an issue will make a detailed analysis to determine the nature of the situation and the condition of the issuing institution. Then the credit enhancement put in place will remove any doubt that could be held by the market about the condition or vulnerability of the issuer.

In the case of an institution which has been affected suddenly by adverse changes in its market which have put its balance sheet at risk, the institution may still have a substantial portfolio of assets which remain of high quality. This company could securitise those assets using credit enhancement and raise funds in the market at an acceptable cost while preserving financial anonymity; that is, without revealing to the market the extent to which the rest of the balance sheet is at risk. The cost of credit enhancement would be based upon the quality of assets to be used as collateral, not those on the institution's balance sheet which may be at risk.

Credit enhancement has played an important role in developing securitisation as a method of balance-sheet management. Securitisation enables a company to continue to earn from assets without having to carry regulatory capital. With many financial institutions under pressure from the approaching deadline set out in the Basle Accord for capital adequacy, the securitisation of a variety of assets is being widely considered. However, securitisation would not be a useful solution to the capital adequacy problem if off-balance-sheet status could not be achieved. Credit enhancement provides the financial 'comfort' so that a structure can be developed where the investor has no recourse to the originator, which is a requirement for off-balance-sheet status, yet has protection against inherent risks from the third-party provider of the credit enhancement.

To summarise, credit enhancement is appropriate when the markets do not have sufficient information about the issuer or the assets underlying the issue (or the time to obtain the information), or where there is lack of recourse to an institution with a sufficient rating and the assets backing the issue cannot stand on their own. Credit enhancement can reduce the costs of issuing a security and improve subsequent liquidity eliminating the need for the market to have extensive financial information about the issuer. Credit enhancement can provide a credit rating, a 'marketable' name to support the issue or a more marketable structure so it can achieve a finer yield in the markets than it would otherwise on its own.

Credit enhancement can also be used to arbitrage differences in regulation. Banks have a capital requirement ranging from 0 to 8 per cent depending upon the class of asset on the balance sheets. Insurance companies have a different regulatory system which is based upon premium income rather than balance sheet size or exposure to risks. Thus, insurance companies have a cost advantage in certain businesses. For instance, it is more efficient for an insurance company to take the actual credit risks on mortgages, but for banks to purchase mortgage-backed securities. This is because if a bank provided a financial guarantee, it would be 100 per cent risk-weighted, but buying an asset-backed security only has a risk weighting of 50 per cent (that is, a capital requirement of 4 per cent). (This could possibly rise to 100 per cent risk-weighting in 1993.)

Credit enhancement is a way to disintermediate credit risk and funding. In a sophisticated financial market it is no longer necessary that an institution providing liquidity be required to accept the underlying credit risk; in fact the regulations of financial institutions make it inefficient to do so. The risks can be transferred to those institutions with the capacity and interest to carry them efficiently. Then institutions, such as banks, who are most efficient at providing liquidity and funding should be able to do so without keeping the risks which they do not carry efficiently. The cost of funding in the capital markets would then fall because each institution involved in a transaction would be providing the service it does most efficiently in creating a whole transaction. This type of structure would be better priced than having a single institution perform the whole transaction, being efficient in some aspects and inefficient in others.

12.2 METHODS OF CREDIT ENHANCEMENT

There are several methods of credit enhancement available to an originator once he has decided to pursue the concept of securitisation. Each of these different methods has its particular attributes which makes it more or less appropriate or attractive for a particular type of transaction or for a particular role in a transaction. Many transactions have been issued where there is more than one type of enhancement in the structure. Usually asset-backed structures are complex, having many different, interdependent features. Thus, several types of credit enhancement can be incorporated into a single transaction to make it as cost-efficient as possible. For example, to insure or guarantee a particular portfolio might be very expensive if 100 per cent of the value of the underlying portfolio were paid in cash to the originator. However, that cost could drop significantly if there were some level of over-collateralisation in the portfolio. That is, if the issuer received less than the value of the assets in cash and left the remaining value of the assets in the vehicle in the form of 'risk equity'. The risk equity could also be supplemented with a small amount of cash.

The different kinds of enhancement are grouped in five categories. They are:

- over-collateralisation;
- senior/subordinated structures;
- bank guarantee or letter of credit;
- guarantee issued by a US monoline insurance company;
- indemnity issued by a rated insurance company.

Over-collateralisation and senior/subordinated structures are forms of 'self-enhancement' or 'self-guarantee'; that is, there is extra cash flow from the assets themselves which forms the security for the bondholders. In contrast, bank guarantees, US monoline guarantees and insurance indemnities are all external guarantees; they differ from one another in the areas of coverage, timing of payments and pricing.

Three of these methods are currently most widely used in the markets: insurance, guarantees from US monolines and senior/subordinated structures.

12.2.1 Over-collateralisation

Over-collateralisation is the simplest of the different methods. The originator includes a greater value of assets as collateral in the issue than cash received. This method is rarely used owing to its high cost and its especially inefficient use of capital. However, there are certain classes of assets and structures where it may play an important role when used in addition to other methods.

12.2.2 Senior/subordinated structures

The senior/subordinated structure splits the issue into two tranches: A notes and B notes. The A notes, the senior notes, have the first right to the cash flows and principal from the collateral; the B notes have second right and are paid only once the A noteholders are satisfied. As a result of this structure the A notes can be triple-A-rated if the rating agencies perceive that enough of the risk is borne by the B notes.

What can be attractive about this structure was that the credit enhancement costs are spread over time; the credit enhancement costs are simply the higher coupon on the B notes. For those companies who had a very high cost of capital which they used as the discount rate to determine the present value of the B bond costs, as compared to the up-front cost of insurance, this form of credit enhancement was economically attractive. However, as with the bank guarantee, the originator's profits are at risk since the B noteholders are fully protected by surplus cash in the vehicle company and this has to be used before they can suffer any losses.

12.2.3 Bank guarantee or letter of credit

The bank guarantee may guarantee principal or interest on the loan or, more likely, guarantee against excessive losses on the collateral. In this way it is more like the insurance product than a monoline guarantee, but it is generally written in quite a different way. The bank product bases its coverage on the amount of cash that is produced by the pool. The insurance product normally indemnifies on the basis of losses which arise out of any individual asset, once some particular aggregate loss position has been reached. Therefore, there may be situations where the insurance product would pay a claim because a particular asset has suffered a loss where the bank product would not, because there would be sufficient cash coming out of the vehicle to offset the effect of losses before they reached the bondholders.

The pricing of the bank letter of credit works out much closer to that of insurance because banks can issue a partial guarantee on the collateral. Thus they can charge against the value of this partial exposure rather than the full value of the issue. This capability exists in part because bank regulators take no account of the probability of loss when assessing capital usage. Therefore a guarantee on the first 15 per cent of losses on the portfolio attracts the same capital weighting as the last 15 per cent. This regulatory issue enables banks to issue partial guarantees at reasonably attractive rates.

There are, however, disadvantages in using bank guarantees. The first is the shortage of triple-A-rated banks available in the market. The second is that the profit back to the originator is at risk and is subordinated to the bank's position. Finally, there could be a comparatively high deposit against the first loss position.

12.2.4 Guarantee issued by a US monoline insurance company

The traditional monoline product guarantees 100 per cent of the structure, unlike the insurance product or the bank letter of credit. Although one of the monolines has expanded its product range to include partial guarantees.

The monolines do not underwrite any non-financial guarantee business, unlike the large multiline insurance companies. They therefore must be very protective about their capital base since they cannot diversify out of their portfolio of financial risks. The assets a monoline guarantees must be investment grade before the application of the monoline guarantee. Although the structure does not actually have to be publically rated before the transaction occurs, the rating agencies will have to assess the structure to determine the investment grade of the transaction, providing a 'shadow' rating for the transaction. Thus, the monoline product is best used for credit enhancement in the form of upgrading structures and 'wrapping' transactions than for transferring risk.

In most monoline-enhanced structures some other mechanism has to be used to take the substantial part of the risk before the US monoline can wrap the issue with its guarantee. This process will be expanded later in this chapter. That additional layer of cover is not required by a multiline insurance structure. The monolines can be effectively used to wrap a structure to a rating of AAA where subordinated debt, overcollateralisation or pool insurance has brought the structure up to investment grade.

With a monoline guarantee, the issuer receives a triple A rating based on the AAA rating of the monoline, rather than on the structure of the transaction. The monoline will do all the analysis and research that would otherwise have to be performed by the rating agencies if another structure had been used without a monoline guarantee to 'wrap' the transaction.

The greater price often quoted by the US monolines is due to the strict regulatory environment in which they exist. The particular regulations that govern their activities and capital structure are very specific with regard to the rating of the assets guaranteed and the capital reserved by the monoline. In this way monolines are somewhat between banks and insurance companies with regard to their capital requirement. Although a monoline does not have to reserve as much as a bank for a certain exposure, the capital requirement is based upon the total exposure, not the premium paid. This practice ensures their security as triple-A-rated institutions in lieu of the size and diversity of the multilines, but often leads them to quote annual pricings on the paper they guarantee which are substantially higher than those the multiline insurance markets would offer.

12.2.5 Indemnity issued by a rated insurance company

A policy of indemnity is not a guarantee. Such a policy issued by an insurer will protect the value of the collateral which underlies structured financing or a bond issue but it will not, in general, guarantee the bondholders that they will get paid their principal and interest payments, although it could provide that cover if required.

The performance of the assets that support the bond is the single biggest consideration as to whether the bondholders are paid what they are owed, but there are other risks. For example, there are documentation risks, liquidity risks and there may be problems with withholding tax. Insurance indemnities do little about these and the financial structure of the issue must accommodate them elsewhere. The principal advantage of insurance is that, in applying itself to only one specific risk, namely the credit risk, it will typically be less expensive than a full guarantee on principal and interest offered by the US monolines although it may not necessarily be less expensive than either a letter of credit or a subordinated issue.

There are other advantages with the insurance product. There is more triple-A capacity in the insurance market than in any other enhancement market. Thus, if the enhancement structure is insurance-based then it will be easier to maintain the rating of the structure in the case of an insurer being down-rated. Usually several insurers will be involved in a single structure. If one is down-rated, it can be shifted around within the structure and another insurer, one with the required rating, can be moved to the other's place. In the case of a letter of credit, if the bank is down-rated, the rating of any securities it has guaranteed will also be down-rated.

The fact that there are usually several insurers used in an insurance-based indemnity structure has another advantage. Many investors have investment limits set for any one issuing or guaranteeing institution. Thus, with a structure with many participants, those limits are less likely to cause liquidity difficulties. On the other hand, with a structure that is enhanced by a single institution, either a monoline or a bank, an investor may prefer not to buy more paper which is enhanced by that institution merely because the investor has reached the limits for that particular institution. This can then cause a discount in the trading price of an issue or decrease its liquidity and could require that subsequent issues are released at higher interest rates to compensate for the loss of liquidity. The size of the capital and reserves, often in the billions of pounds sterling, of the large diversified multilines also supports the acceptability to the investor.

However, as insurance policies are not a guarantee on principal and interest the rating agencies will have to look deeper into the structure. They will have to be content that the amount of insurance that the issuer is buying to protect the asset is sufficient given the performance of that type of collateral. The following three chapters discuss in greater detail the three most widely used methods of credit enhancement. Chapter 13 compares and contrasts the products offered by the banking industry, senior/subordinated debt structures and letter of credit. Chapter 14 expands upon the nature of the guarantees offered by the US monoline insurance companies. Finally, chapter 15 explores the characteristics and applications of the insurance-based credit enhancement.

13: Bank Enhancements and Subordinated Debt

Mark Lewis, Union Bank of Switzerland

Asset-backed security investors potentially face five distinct financial risks: credit, liquidity, interest rate, maturity and reinvestment risks. However, an array of financial institutions are willing to absorb these. As a result, rating agencies are able to give higher credit ratings than would otherwise be the case, which will widen the potential investor base and lead to an overall lower cost of funding for an issuer.

The involvement of the multiline and monoline insurance companies in absorbing risk is discussed in other chapters. This chapter will discuss the involvement of two alternative sources of financial risk intermediation—banks and subordinated debt investors.

13.1 BANK ENHANCEMENTS

This section aims to provide an insight into the products that banks can provide to mitigate the five inherent risks mentioned above for asset-backed security investors.

13.1.1 Credit protection

Letters of credit, committed lines of credit and partial guarantees are different legal forms of what is essentially the same bank product. As legal systems throughout the world vary, so the title of the product may also vary, but its basic nature remains the same. That nature is essentially to protect investors from credit risks arising from the underlying asset portfolio. For example, Bayerische Vereinsbank provided a letter of credit for Chariots, the first Italian loan securitisation, while Union Bank of Switzerland provided a partial guarantee (a 'Garantia a Primera Demanda') and a committed loan facility for the first Spanish and UK auto-loan securitisations respectively. In each case, however, despite differing security, tax and cash flow structures, the investor is given a better degree of credit protection from losses on the underlying assets by the addition of 'credit enhancement'.

Facility structure
Banks have dominated credit enhancement for assets such as credit cards, auto-loan receivables, leases and trade receivables. However, structures have been developed in the US, where banks have credit-enhanced mortgages, although to date insurance companies have dominated this sector of the market in the UK. As an example of a credit enhancement structure, section 13.4 describes Union Bank of Switzerland's partial guarantee for Citibank's first Spanish securitisation. This transaction was unusual in that it was not rated. However, the investors placed great reliance on UBS's rating and its enhancement. Although the details may vary from other securitisations in Europe, the general principles portrayed in this example are similar to other bank credit-enhanced transactions.

The four key variables in a credit enhancement structure are:

- size of the credit protection facility;
- size of the reserve account;
- yield of the assets;
- quality of the credit enhancer.

Size of the credit protection facility
In rated transactions the size of the credit protection facility is determined by the rating agencies to give the required rating level. Thus, for example, in the CARS (UK) transaction the first UK securitisation of autoloan receivables, which was rated AAA/Aaa by Standard & Poor's and Moodys, the initial level of credit enhancement was 15 per cent of the total transaction size. In the Chariots transaction the first Italian securitisation of autoloan receivables the initial rating was set at Aa by Moodys and the level of credit enhancement was 12 per cent. However, the size of the credit protection facility is essentially set with reference to past and future expected losses on the asset pool and the transaction structure as a whole.

Size of the reserve account
The purpose of the reserve account is to give the credit enhancer first-loss protection against losses and remove a risk which may be borne by investors. The reserve account will be held in the form of cash or liquid instruments and will be used to offset credit losses on the underlying assets. As the reserve account must be fully depleted before the credit enhancement is utilised, this represents a layer of credit enhancement for the credit enhancer!

The amount in the Reserve Account may be capped as was the case in the CARS (UK) transaction. (The effect is that the credit enhancer does not have

100 per cent clawback of 'excess' transaction cash flows; i.e. the credit enhancement cannot fully use past profits from the assets to subsidise future credit losses on the asset pool. In the CARS (UK) transaction, this was important to improve the capital efficiency of the transaction for Chartered Trust.) The reserve account in the Chariots transaction, however, was unlimited in size. In addition, amounts in the reserve accounts may be increased by the originator placing an initial deposit into it. Until recently most UK residential mortgage-backed securities had reserve or escrow accounts in which on the initial transaction closing dates were placed between 0.2 and 0.1 per cent of the initial issue size as a first-loss cash deposit. This amount would be placed on deposit by the originator upfront and there would be no additional amount available from the mortgage cash flows. However, recent UK residential mortgage transactions have moved towards the structure of a lower upfront deposit plus ongoing deposits from the mortgage cash flows. The benefit for investors of a reserve account structure is that as any amounts in the reserve account revert to the originator at the end of the transaction, the originator has an ongoing interest to ensure the wellbeing of the transaction (i.e. this incentivises the originator to keep credit losses at a low level).

Yield of the assets

In transactions where the ongoing assets' cash flows are used to offset credit losses, the higher the yield of the assets relative to the investors' yield, the more the credit enhancer and the investor will be protected. In the CARS (UK) transaction the 'after-swap' yield gap between the assets and the notes was set at a minimum of 4 per cent. Clearly there are strong relationships between the size of the credit protection, the size of the reserve accounts and the yield of the assets, and these can only be negotiated between issuer and credit enhancer on a case-by-case basis.

Quality of the credit enhancer

If the securitised assets fail to perform adequately, this is likely to be in times of severe economic stress. The investor is therefore dependent for the quality of the transaction on the quality of the credit enhancer. For this reason, credit enhancers are financially sound with high credit ratings. Indeed, if a credit-enhanced transaction is required to have AAA rating, it is extremely likely that the credit enhancer will be AAA-rated itself. Investors also prefer and place a premium on those institutions whose AAA rating is more certain. This point is important especially in light of the significant number of AAA banks downgraded in recent years. Indeed, depending on the structures, many investors rely solely on the strength of the credit enhancer when assessing whether or not, and at what price, to buy an asset-backed security.

How banks analyse these facilities

It is important that arrangers and issuers provide banks with as complete an information package as possible. The more information is available, the more accurately a bank will be able to assess the credit risk which in turn may reduce an element of the risk premium (i.e. greater certainty leads to lower costs). The basic elements of analysis for a bank are described below. (A more detailed checklist of the various criteria needed to evaluate an asset-backed securitisation appears in section 13.5 at the end of this chapter.)

1. *Assets* Since an asset-backed securitisation transaction looks to the underlying assets to service the debt and repay the principal, the quality and performance of those assets are vital. A typical review of the assets would therefore look to their historical track record to see if they have been paying off with an acceptable level of arrears and defaults, and whether the cash flow can be used and is sufficient to cover the debt service. Additionally, it is crucial to determine whether the assets display an adequate diversification in terms of the demographic and geographical distribution of the underlying obligors. The quality of the assets may be improved by external factors, e.g. reserve accounts, various insurances etc.
2. *Originator/servicer* Securitisation represents a disintermediation between the original lender and borrower. However, a linkage between the lender and the borrower is maintained and the common thread is the lender's role as the originator and servicer. It is essential that the procedures and personnel of the originator and servicer reflect sound and prudent judgement, since they are the front line in deciding who receives the loan and how efficiently and promptly money is collected. In the case of deficiencies or arrears, it is generally the servicer's policies which determine whether forbearance is warranted or whether the collateral will have to be foreclosed upon and sold.
3. *Administration* A securitisation is a complex transaction involving multiple parties. The paperwork underlying the structure is massive, and it requires sophisticated control to keep track of the various cash flows, to ensure that the different parties are paid in a timely fashion, and that the credit enhancer and liquidity provider pay up on their commitments as they are due.
4. *Structural elements* By now, securitisation may well seem 'old hat' in the US. Yet this is a relatively new financing technique in Europe, and there are a host of recurring legal and structural issues which require the unwavering attention of the army of lawyers and accountants called forth in every transaction. In addition, as these transactions may involve multinational and transnational parties and/or assets, the legal and accounting structure of several countries may have to be considered.

5. *Transaction analysis* This is an analysis of the transaction structure ensuring that cash flow from the assets eventually finds its way to the investors and how the credit support is structured.

13.1.2 Liquidity protection

Liquidity facilities are committed lines of credit for the purpose of bridging temporary shortfalls of cash to the investors. These shortfalls arise because the underlying assets do not generate sufficient cash flows in a given period to meet the investors' interest obligations because of arrears of payments from the underlying borrowers. The liquidity facility provider is generally repaid either by increased cash flows from the assets (i.e. the underlying borrower catches up payments, collateral is sold etc.) or, in the worst case, from payments by the credit enhancer.

The liquidity facility can be provided by the credit enhancer and wrapped up into a single facility as was the case in Chartered Trust's securitisation in the CARS (UK) transaction or by separate institutions, as is the case with UK mortgage-backed securities, where banks tend to provide the liquidity facility and insurance companies provide credit enhancement in the form of pool insurance. In Citibank's first Spanish securitisation, Citibank Espana was the liquidity facility provider and Union Bank of Switzerland was the credit enhancer. Clearly the ultimate risk for the provider of the liquidity facility is the quality of the ultimate take-out (i.e. the credit enhancer, which is generally AAA-rated) and the cost of this facility for an issuer is commensurate with its risk (i.e. lower risk, lower cost). In UK mortgage-backed securities the size of the liquidity facility at AAA level for a 'prime pool' is approximately 3 per cent (the size is a function of the maximum expected level of arrears and the length of time that arrears are outstanding). The size of liquidity facilities would be different for other assets and countries. For example, consumer loan arrears in the UK tend to be recovered or finally written-off within six to twelve months of the first non-payment, while mortgage arrears in Italy may take more than two years to be recovered or finally written-off.

13.1.3 Basis risk protection

Temporary shortfalls of interest to the investors may arise because the basis for setting the rate of interest on the underlying assets is different from that of the underlying securities. For example, in Chartered Trust's UK autoloan securitisation, the assets bore fixed-rate interest while the investors received interest based on floating-rate LIBOR. The mismatch was solved by incorporating an interest rate swap into the structure (described in chapter 7). The swap was guaranteed by Union Bank of Switzerland to ensure the transaction's AAA/Aaa rating.

Conversely, UK mortgage-backed FRN securities bear interest on a floating basis set with reference to LIBOR, while the underlying mortgages also generally bear interest on a floating basis but at a level set by the originator. That latter rate is set not solely by reference to LIBOR, but will involve concerns such as market share for the originator and the originator's competitors' mortgage rates. In the event of LIBOR being near to or greater than the rate on the mortgages, it is possible that the expenses of the issuer (which includes interest to the investor) will be greater than its income for a short period.

This temporary shortfall of interest can be bridged by drawings under a basis risk facility which is provided for the purpose of meeting such interest shortfalls. The issuer will be able to run a shortfall for as long as bridging funds are available. At a certain point in time, if the bridging facility is fully utilised, the issuer will not be permitted to run any more shortfalls and will be required to raise the charging rate on the assets to a level whereby shortfalls do not occur and the bridging facility is repaid. In UK mortgage-backed securities, the appropriate mortgage rate is calculated by reference to the 'threshold rate' calculation, which if a basis risk facility is used will include the requirement to repay the basis risk facility.

13.1.4 Maturity risk protection

Securities have been issued where the underlying assets may mature after the stated maturity of the notes. However, to ensure the investor is repaid on a timely basis a financial institution may agree to purchase the outstanding assets at the standard maturity of the issue. The maturity guarantee or 'put' has been successfully used in four UK residential mortgage-backed security issues (for HMC Mortgage Notes 101 PLC and HMC Mortgage Notes 102 PLC), with AIG Financial Products Corporation, a wholly-owned subsidiary of American International Group, a AAA-rated insurance company serving as put provider in both cases.

13.1.5 Reinvestment risk protection

Most securitisations pay investors on a regular basis—for example, every three, six or twelve months. However, the assets may generate cash flows on a more regular basis. The issuer and therefore the investor bears a reinvestment risk (i.e. that funds will be invested at a sufficient rate and with creditworthy counterparties). Therefore cash funds need to be reinvested until the interest payment date. In a rated transaction the funds need to be held with an appropriately rated institution or held in appropriately rated short-dated securities. It is possible to fix the rate at which funds are reinvested through a guaranteed investment contract (GIC). The benefits for an issuer are twofold:

- Greater certainty of cashflow.
- The rating agencies assume low reinvestment rates (e.g. 5 per cent below note rate LIBOR for an AAA-rated three-month coupon floating rate note transaction) in their worst-case scenarios which negatively impact on the sizing of the credit enhancement levels. A guaranteed investment rate provided by an appropriately rated counterparty will effectively reduce the required credit enhancement level.

Union Bank of Switzerland provided a GIC in the CARS (UK) transaction. Investors receive interest at LIBOR plus 25 basis points per annum, with LIBOR reset every three months; principal redemptions will be received by the investers only (if at all) at the end of each three-month period. However, the special-purpose vehicle receives principal and interest income on a daily basis which must be reinvested until the end of each three-month period. Union Bank of Switzerland agreed to receive the deposit of the daily cash flows at a fixed rate below the note LIBOR rate, where LIBOR is set as the beginning of the three-month period.

13.2 SUBORDINATED DEBT

An alternative to bank or insurance company provided liquidity and credit enhancements is the issue of subordinated debt maturing with or after the senior-ranking debt. Thus, for example, a special-purpose vehicle may purchase £100m of assets of which £90m is funded by the senior-ranking investors and £10m by the subordinated debt investors. In the UK mortgage-backed securities market, National Home Loans and Household Mortgage Corporation have both utilised subordinated debt to enhance the credit and liquidity profile of their securitisations. In these transactions, the subordinated debt served both a credit and liquidity protection function.

In France, bank-originated securitisation issues have tended to use subordinated debt, which has proved to be a very efficient means of providing credit enhancement. This is because bank originators have been allowed to provide the entire subordinated debt layer themselves and the capital weighting applied to the subordinated debt has been deemed by the French regulatory authorities to be identical to the capital weighting applied to the original loans. This would not be the case for a UK-regulated institution.

	Before securitisation	*After securitisation*
Loans on balance sheet	£100	£10
Capital required	£8	£0.80

Where the originator holds the subordinated debt, he effectively retains all the risk and reward of the underlying asset pool but the process of securitisation reduces the capital requirement for those assets by a substantial degree and thereby enhances the return on capital employed. Although the UK and US regulatory authorities do not allow such treatment, this treatment for banks is expected to be maintained for the present in France.

In structuring terms, subordinated debt works in a manner that the subordinated debt holder will not receive payments of principal and interest due until the senior noteholders have been paid principal and interest (i.e. subordinated debt can act as both credit and liquidity support for the senior investors). The subordinated debt may or may not be rated. For example, the subordinated debt of Cetelem's securitisation of unsecured personal loans (the issuer's name was CB 1) was rated B2 by Moody's although to date the subordinated debt has not been rated in National Home Loans' and Household Mortgage Corporation's securitisations.

13.3 COMPARING BANK ENHANCEMENTS WITH SUBORDINATED DEBT

We have now examined a number of techniques for financial risk intermediation. To some extent these are 'horses for courses' although the different methods do compete in certain areas. For example, FSA, a US monoline insurance company, have guaranteed a UK commercial property securitisation. Yet, in today's environment it is difficult to see a bank wishing to credit-enhance a UK commercial property securitisation. But banks dominate credit enhancement of assets such as credit cards, autoloans and other short-dated receivables, although globally subordinated debt has been increasingly used as a credit enhancement technique for both longer- and shorter-dated assets.

For the first-time issuer, bank enhancement has significant advantages. Investors may be unfamiliar with the deal structure or the originator's name but would take comfort that the transaction will stand significant levels of credit stress if a well known bank stands behind the deal. After all, banks do not enter transactions expecting to lose money! In this respect, the better the quality of the bank, the better the transaction will be received. Indeed, for AAA-rated transactions, the bank is likely to be AAA-rated. A first-time issuer may take many months to bring the transaction to market. A bank credit enhancer will be able to give the issuer a degree of comfort that enhancement will be available on the day of the launch (i.e. bank credit enhancement is a product of a negotiated agreement). However, subordinated debt investors may not be willing to purchase subordinated debt on the day of launch (obviously this is not correct where the originator is also the purchaser of the subordinated debt).

A bank with experience of securitisation techniques will in fact be able to assist the issuer to bring a transaction to market through its understanding of the basic enhancement products and the underlying assets. Banks tend to have strong analytical capabilities; therefore, with transactions involving complex cash flows such as credit card securitisations, banks will be in a strong position to analyse the assets and provide a cost-competitive facility to an issuer. Finally, most securitisations involve banks in one form or another indeed, while we have analysed five areas of potential bank intermediation, subordinated debt is not appropriate for the intermediation of all five risks. In a complex transaction, it is often more efficient to minimise the numbers of parties involved. It follows that if a single bank can provide all the necessary enhancements for a particular transaction this may prove to be the most cost-effective method of structuring the transaction.

However, for repeat issuers with substantial issue volume, continual dependence on banks may bring disadvantages (e.g. banks may impose product credit limits or have volume constraints for an individual client). Subordinated debt also enables an issuer to diversify its investor base by sourcing higher risk/return profile investors. Bank enhancement also suffers from the fact that the ongoing rating of the securities will be dependent on the rating of the supporting bank—a problem encountered in many US securitisations with bank downgradings. Subordinated debt deals do incur downgrading risks but this will only occur through a reassessment of the asset and structural risks. Yet bank downgrading risk can be mitigated first by the possibility of replacing or upgrading the enhancer in the event of a downgrade. This is by no means certain to occur and is therefore a potential risk for the investor. For this reason, investors prefer to see a bank credit enhancer whose rating and credit quality are perceived as certain. Second, the US asset-backed market has recently developed the cash-collateralised credit enhancement structure. This structure is identical to the traditional credit enhancement structure except that a cash loan is provided upfront and held in escrow instead of a loan commitment. In this way, the transaction can avoid bank downgrade risk although the downside is the reinvestment loss on the cash deposit for the issuer. Whether or not this structure is more efficient depends on the balance between the reinvestment loss on the one hand and reduced issuing costs on the other hand. Therefore, in terms of cost, whether bank enhancement or subordinated debt is cheaper depends on a range of factors, namely: complexity of the transaction, familiarity of the assets and the transaction structure in the marketplace, maturity of the assets, credit structure supporting the credit enhancer or subordinated debt provider.

A disadvantage of reliance on subordinated debt as a means of credit enhancement is the subordinated debt may not always be available at an acceptable price at the time of launch of the issue. For many potential issuers this may not be a problem if they have the ability to hold or 'warehouse' assets pending securitisation. However, for these issuers, reliant on securitisation as the primary means of funding, the problem can potentially be significant. As investors worldwide become increasingly constrained by credit quality, pricing and liquidity factors over the next few years, this is bound to have an effect on market demand for subordinated debt. As the supply of asset-backed financings increases in Europe and beyond over the next few years (as the author of this chapter believes it inevitably will do) the search for new and cost-effective supplies of bank enhancements and subordinated debt finance will become more difficult.

The conclusion for any potential issuer is that bank enhancements and subordinated debt can form a valuable part in the securitisation armoury. The cost-effectiveness and suitability of each method can, however, be assessed only on a case-by-case basis and compared with the other enhancement methods detailed elsewhere in this book.

13.4 APPENDIX 1: THE FIRST SPANISH AUTOLOAN SECURITISATION

The parties in the transaction of the first Spanish autoloan securitisation were as follows:

1. Citifin Espana, (99.99 per cent owned by Citibank Espana, which is in turn 99.8 per cent owned by Citibank Overseas Investment Corporation) which acted as:

   - originator and grantor of the sub-participations in the contracts;
   - provider of the peseta interest rate hedge (a hedge is required because the assets are fixed rate and the banks will receive floating rate based on MIBOR (the Madrid Interbank Offered Rate);
   - liquidity facility provider, designed to provide short-term bridging finance to cover shortfalls of scheduled payments to the banks in the event of arrears under contracts; the facility is repaid either from cash flows from the contracts, from the reserve account or from the UBS guarantee;
   - servicer of the contracts, whose duties include processing payments maintaining records and documentation, pursuing and monitoring bad debt and delinquent obligations, and holding the transaction accounts.

2. Citibank NA, acting as
   - guarantor of Citifin Espana's obligations.

3. Citicorp Investment Bank, acting as
   - structurer, arranger and sole distributor of the sub-participations to a group of banks.

4. Union Bank of Switzerland, acting as
   - credit enhancement provider in the form of a partial guarantee facility (a 'Garantia a Primera Demanda'). The purpose of the facility is to provide limited recourse credit to ensure that banks receive scheduled interest and principal as due despite arrears and defaults under the contracts.

The transaction size was 7 billion pesetas and had the benefit of a 0.7 billion pesetas (10 per cent) partial guarantee facility. The transaction did not require to be rated because it was a private placement of loan sub-participations to a group of banks. The securitised contracts constituted a pool of fixed-rate peseta, level-instalment, monthly-payment motor vehicle retail instalment contracts with a maximum four-year contract life relating to the purchase of new automobiles originated by Citifin Espana throughout its Spanish dealer network.

At the end of each quarter, Citifin Espana assesses 'Available Funds', i.e. amounts which have been received from the contracts and any reinvestment proceeds thereon. Available funds will then be distributed in the following order of policy:

1. servicing fee due to Citifin Espana payable quarterly in arrears based on the actual balance of the portfolio outstanding on the prior quarter date;
2. principal repayments on Citifin Espana liquidity facility advances;
3. interest on Citifin Espana liquidity facility advances charged quarterly in arrears;
4. interest due to the banks payable quarterly in arrears based on the actual balance of the portfolio outstanding on the prior quarter date;
5. principal due to the banks;
6. UBS's guarantee fee payable quarterly in arrears based on the undrawn balance of the facility at the prior quarter date;
7. principal repayments on the guarantee;
8. a utilisation fee based payable to UBS on the amount of drawing on the guarantee payable in quarterly arrears.

If there are sufficient available funds after payment of the above, any excess will be allocated to an account held with Citibank (the reserve account). The purpose of the reserve account is as a 'first-loss credit cover' for the liquidity and guarantee facilities. The reserve account has no cap on the amount of funds which can be held in the account.

If there are insufficient available funds on the quarterly payment date to pay any of the items set out in 1–8 of the order of priorities above, three additional sources of funds are available in the following priority:

First, Citifin Espana's liquidity facility: to the extent that there are cash flow shortfalls which are attributable to contracts not more than three months in arrears, then Citifin Espana will make funds available in an amount equal to the shortfall. The limit of the amount available under the liquidity facility will be equal to the then available amount of the UBS guarantee outstanding. As can be seen from the order of priorities, Citifin Espana will recover any advances made under this facility in priority to all other payments except the servicing fee to the extent that the corresponding arrears are deemed to be recoverable. Interest on liquidity facility advances will be payable quarterly in arrears and will be paid from the deal cashflows.

Second, if the liquidity facility becomes fully drawn, funds will be drawn from the reserve account to the extent available.

Third, UBS' guarantee facility, which will be drawn upon to the extent that shortfalls of cash as set out in 1–8 of the order of priorities detailed above, are not satisfied by liquidity facility advances or by draws from the reserve account.

The Guarantee Amount will amortise quarterly based on the lesser of:

- 10 per cent of the principal portfolio balance outstanding on the prior quarter date but in any event not less than the lower of 700,000 pesetas and the principal portfolio balance outstanding on the prior quarter date and;
- the guarantee amount on the prior quarter plus any reimbursements for previous draws minus any amounts drawn under the guarantee. The 'available guarantee amount', i.e. the extent to which the banks can draw on the guarantee facility equals the guarantee amount minus liquidity facility draws.

A utilisation fee based on the level of drawings on the guarantee will be charged and payable quarterly in arrears and will be paid solely from the deal cash flow.

UBS looks solely to excess cash flows from the contracts, including recoveries, for reimbursement of guarantee drawings. UBS's guarantee facility is protect by amounts in the reserve account and by the benefits of Citifin Espana servicing and the related Citibank NA guarantees.

The guarantee facility will terminate upon the earlier of full repayment to the sub-participating banks or 57 months.

13.5 APPENDIX 2: DETAILED INFORMATION REQUIREMENTS

Although details may vary from asset to asset, the main information criteria described below should be provided to bank enhancers when structuring an asset-backed financing.

Asset information

Current asset information will include:

- *Yield of assets* Required in order to determine the excess cashflow available over and above the issuers' funding costs. Typically a credit enhancer will look for a minimum level of spread between the yield of the assets and the financing costs which is related to future maximum expected credit losses on the pool of assets.
- *Original term distribution* Provides an indication of the seasoning of the pool of assets. Generally, the more seasoned the pool the better the quality.
- *Remaining term distribution* Together with prepayment expectations used to determine the expected average life of the funding.
- *Loan-to-value ratios* In mortgage-backed transactions this is the key figure which provides an indication of the credit quality of the assets.
- *Collateral/asset type distribution* The quality of the asset is important especially in the event of forced sale.
- *Delinquency profile* Current payment performance of the pool together with historical information will form the basis to determine likely future performance. In cash flow analysis used to determine the level of liquidity shortfall.
- *Current principal balances* Level of exposure to any one individual.
- *Original principal balance*
- *Insurance* (if any) Credit protection available for the credit enhancement provider.
- *Debtor type/profile* E.g. new and used automobiles may have differing risk profiles borne out by historical delinquency and write-off data.
- *Geographical concentrations/distributions* Used to assess the risk imposed by assets on an aggregate basis due to demographic, socio-political and economic influences in a particular geographical region.

Historical pool information

Historical information is useful because of its guide to future asset performance. Information will include:

- write-offs (net and gross), i.e. after sale of collateral, if any;
- recovery profiles;
- delinquencies;
- total portfolio balance (asset type, geographic breakdown, debtor type);
- total portfolio size;
- major changes in group strategy which may have had an impact on any of the above.

Originator/servicer information

Organisational issues

- *History and prospective growth* Description of business strategy (i.e. willingness to achieve growth to incur lower credit losses).
- *Management* Key officers, organisational chart and operating procedures.
- *Branch/subsidiary organisation* Description of geographic location and processing responsibilities (i.e. underwriting, servicing, collecting).
- *Department organisation* Functional breakdown (loan underwriting, collections, servicing etc.).
- *Credit and control procedures*
- *Goals and objectives* Market share emphasis of strategy and account solicitation methods versus competitors. Competitive strengths and weaknesses.

Origination and distribution

A Overview of lending and servicing:

- account solicitation methods and production history by source, loan type, region; marketing history by volume, loan type, region;
- application review/process;
- credit/management review;
- approval process;
- documentation of credit (e.g. verification of employment, credit bureau checks, collateral appraisal);
- payment calculations (e.g. simple interest);
- billing cycles;

- delinquency status and controls;
- account treatment (i.e. income recognition, delinquency and charge off policies);
- computer systems.

B Lending criteria and modifications:

- loan to value;
- credit underwriting (i.e. payment-to-income ratios, job history, income etc.);
- loan terms and conditions;
- pricing practices;
- arrears and enforcement procedures (including extensions and rewrites);
- credit servicing/approval/authority;
- insurance protection;
- exposure limits.

C Servicing:

- General servicing issues:
  - expansion/modifications proposed for separate securitisation servicing;
  - adequate resources (experienced staff, computer hardware/software commitment).
  - Will securitisation assets be given the same attention as non-securitisation assets?
  - Will new or updated procedures be created to reflect securitisation servicing and accounting?
  - Will all staff be adequately informed of changes due to activities?

- Administration:
  - monitoring frequency;
  - audit controls;
  - credit and management reviews;
  - computer systems/document storage;
  - collection procedures—current;
  - collection procedures—default and arrears.

- Loan tracking:
  - transaction flowchart;
  - loan account number tracking.

- Other information required:
  - copy of annual report and accounts;
  - list of insurance providers;

- list of contingency insurance providers;
- list of insurance policies and what they cover.

Structural elements

Tax considerations
Tax considerations to assess the negative impact, if any, of:

- VAT, sales tax;
- stamp duties;
- corporation and income taxes;
- capital gains tax.

Legal considerations

- security package (e.g. assignment, sub-participation, fixed or floating charge rights from security package, ability to perfect security package);
- consumer protection laws (e.g. Consumer Credit Act in the UK).

Regulatory considerations
E.g. impact of regulatory authorities such as the Bank of England.

Accounting considerations
Accounting impact for both the issuer and the enhancer.

14: The Role of the Monoline Financial Guarantor

Theodore V. Buerger
Financial Security Assurance

One spur to development of the asset-backed market has been the availability of first-loss credit enhancement and 100 per cent guarantees from insurance companies dedicated to providing these products. These specialist insurers are known as 'monoline' financial guaranty insurance companies, because their only business is financial guarantees, and they take on no other risks, as do the property/casualty and life insurers (which are 'multiline').

14.1 A BRIEF HISTORY

Although surety bonds to guarantee performance of specific financial obligations date at least to the last century, the modern financial guaranty industry began in the United States in the early 1970s, when the Municipal Bond Insurance Association (MBIA), an association of several major US insurance companies, and the American Municipal Bond Assurance Corp. (AMBAC) issued the first municipal bond insurance policies.

Except for final underwriting decisions, most MBIA operations were originally conducted on its behalf by Municipal Issuers Service Company (MISC), a partnership that acted as the exclusive general manager and general agent for MBIA. The principals of MISC were responsible for persuading the insurance company members of MBIA to enter the municipal bond insurance business and for developing and expanding the concept of municipal bond insurance. Later in the 1970s, another partnership, S&B Insurance Services Company (S&B), became the first company to structure corporate debt and bank obligations to qualify for financial guarantees from insurance companies. Aetna Life and Casualty was the first major provider of such guarantees.

Certain of the principals of MISC and S&B, along with other experts in law, structured finance and fixed-income markets, helped to form Financial Security Assurance (FSA) in 1985.[1] FSA was the first monoline financial guarantor to emphasise secured corporate and asset-backed obligations. It remains the dominant monoline guarantor of non-municipal securities. Capitalised originally by a group of major corporate and institutional investors, FSA was sold in 1989 to U S WEST Capital Corporation, the financial services arm of U S WEST, Inc., one of the regional telephone companies created by the break-up of the Bell System. In 1990, the Tokio Marine and Fire Insurance Co. Ltd became a minority shareholder in FSA.

FSA was followed into the field in 1987 by Capital Markets Assurance Corporation (CapMac), a subsidiary of Citicorp. Financial Guaranty Insurance Company (FGIC), primarily a US municipal bond insurer, also insures corporate structured securities. Although there are substantial barriers to entry for additional competitors, including the necessity of raising adequate capital and the highly specialised expertise required, a small number of other monolines, including existing municipal bond insurers, may soon offer guarantees for securitisations in the international market, because demand for the product will undoubtedly rise as securitisation spreads to more countries.

14.2 FINANCIAL GUARANTY INSURANCE

Financial guaranty insurance companies charge a premium to guarantee that the payment obligations of another party in a financial transaction will be fulfilled. The financial guarantor may be thought of as 'renting' its high credit rating to the issue it insures. In this way, the insurance serves to improve an issue's marketability, thereby reducing the cost of funds.

The most important thing to understand about a responsible monoline guarantor is that it is not in the business of taking on primary credit risks. The issues it insures have already been structured to investment-grade levels through such means as over-collateralisation, third-party first-loss facilities, spread accounts, recourse to the seller, or senior/subordinated structuring. (In the last case, ordinarily, only the senior portion of a 'senior/sub' will be insured; the subordinated piece typically will not be.)

Two kinds of monoline financial guaranty insurance (FGI)[2] are available for asset-backed issues. The first, a partial guaranty, insures against defaults in the underlying collateral ('asset-risk') up to a specified percentage of the pool, usually in the range of 7 to 15 per cent . Alternatively, the insurance may be applied as an unconditional and irrevocable 100 per cent guaranty, covering not just a portion of asset risk but *all* asset risks and *all* securitisation risks, including the risks of bankruptcy consolidation, legal or regulatory changes, lawsuits, fraud and performance failures by servicers, trustees, swap counterparties, guaranteed investment contract (GIC) providers, portfolio managers or other essential parties to a given asset-backed transaction.

From the investor's viewpoint, a partial guaranty is comparable to other first-loss protections, like those provided by first-loss letters of credit and senior/subordinated structures. But there is generally added strength if the guarantor is a monoline insurer committed to this line of business. The insurer will normally protect itself through a mechanism like a spread account, so that its own risk is not worse than investment grade. The rating agencies will evaluate the transaction structure and the amount of insurance provided, and then assign a rating to the partially insured issue. If it deems the amount of coverage sufficient, the issue will be assigned the insurer's triple-A rating.

In the case of a 100 per cent guaranty, there is total coverage. As for all Aaa/AAA monoline financial guarantors, rating agencies review each transaction to assure that the insurer's underwriting standards are maintained. These standards should require not only that the issue be structured to an investment grade level before being insured but that it contain additional protections to minimise the guarantor's ultimate losses in the unlikely event of default. FSA is the major provider of these 100 per cent 'wraps'.

The appropriateness of a partial or 100 per cent guaranty will depend on a number of factors, including premium and the trading value of the insurer's name. In general, the more unfamiliar the assets are to the market and the newer or more complex the structure, the more investors will prefer the comfort of 100 per cent coverage. Conversely, when investors can quickly and cost-effectively make themselves comfortable with the size of a partial guaranty and the body of documents, legal opinions, representations, warranties and other assurances attesting to the transaction's soundness, they may

	Coverage	
	without 100% guaranty	with 100% guaranty
Asset risk		
Senior/subordinated issues	7–15%	100%
Issues partially enhanced by seller or third party	7–15%	100%
Securitisation risk		
Senior/subordinated issues	Depends on structure, documentation, legal opinions, etc.	100%
Issues partially enhanced by seller or third party		100%

be satisfied with partial coverage. Table 14.1 summarises the differences in coverage provided by partial and 100 per cent guarantees.

Premiums for FGI are paid by the issuer on a non-refundable basis and frequently in a single instalment at the time of the issuance of the policy, regardless of the term of the insured obligation. Premiums are deemed to be earned for accounting and regulatory purposes ratably over the term of the insured obligation.

14.3 BENEFITS OF 100 PER CENT FINANCIAL GUARANTY INSURANCE

Because the 100 per cent guaranty is the most prevalent form of FGI in the international market, it bears additional discussion.

14.3.1 Issuer benefits

In addition to a favourable funding rate, 100 per cent FGI offers a number of benefits to issuers, including the following.

A broadened market

Securities with 100 per cent insurance may appeal to investor classes that would not otherwise show an interest. For example, certain investors might be reluctant to purchase an issue backed by foreign assets because of unfamiliarity with the legal, credit, or other issues relating to those assets or their securitisation structure. Such investors might purchase the same issue if it is fully guaranteed by a monoline insurance company they recognise. Indeed, in any transaction whose complexity could deter investors, a 100 per cent guaranty confers a marketing advantage by simplifying the investor's decision-making process.

The substitution of the guarantor's name for that of the issuer (or asset seller) allows the issuer to raise funds without increasing its 'name-in-the-market' exposure and to retain capacity within its traditional funding sources. Guaranteed securities that replace rather than augment existing funding programs decrease market saturation in the issuer's name and may thereby improve secondary market pricing of such programs.

Also, monoline insurers sometimes provide marketing support for the issues they guarantee. They will consult with the underwriters at an early stage of the transaction about the most advantageous market, type of debt instrument, call protection and other factors that can result in the most efficient borrowing. They also maintain ongoing advertising and educational efforts to improve the marketability of the issues they insure.

Guarantor expertise
A monoline insurer that specialises in structured financings must have an abundance of knowledge about all the economic, accounting, structuring, rating agency and legal elements of an asset securitisation, not just of the asset quality. Because it is given opportunities to see many more transactions than it actually insures, it is likely to have a broad perspective on the market and the mechanisms that make for successful securitisations. The guarantor can assist at every stage in structuring a transaction that, however complex, will function smoothly until its maturity.

Timeliness
The use of 100 per cent FGI usually reduces the time required for the credit-rating agencies to rate an obligation. This benefit may be particularly important to an issuer seeking to take advantage of a temporary market situation, an issuer previously unrated by the rating agencies or an issuer involved in a complex transaction. Some guarantors will manage the entire rating agency process and arrange for delivery of all required rating letters at closing.

Favourable disclosure, tax or accounting treatment
Some insured transactions also benefit from reduced disclosure requirements or advantageous tax or accounting treatment. Even though such factors in a transaction are not risk-related, they add value that may be reflected in the insurer's premium.

Willingness to guarantee long-term obligations
Banks have generally declined to write standby letters of credit or guarantees that extend beyond seven years. Monoline insurers will do so in appropriate transactions. (This holds for partial monoline insurance as well.)

Less risk of downgrade
Although the risk of downgrade is borne by the investor, issuers generally wish to avoid association with debt instruments that become problems for investors. The reduced risk of downgrade for issues with 100 per cent guarantees is explained in more detail in the following section, 'General Benefits of FGI'.

14.3.2 Investor benefits

Due diligence
100 per cent guarantors are in a position to provide due diligence more cost-effectively than investors. The guarantor consolidates tasks that would otherwise have to be carried out individually, and hence with duplication of effort, by multiple investors. This review encompasses not only the detailed

process of reviewing asset quality (described in section 14.4) but also the review of all securitisation risks discussed in chapter 2.

The guarantor's standards may be more conservative than the minimum rating agency requirements. For example, FSA often imposes self-correcting mechanisms that will correct transactions should they deteriorate, even though such mechanisms may not be required to meet the rating agencies' minimum requirements. Partially guaranteed issues rarely have any more protection for investors than the absolute minimum required by the rating agencies.

Monitoring and surveillance
Asset-backed issues are notorious for the amount of ongoing monitoring and surveillance required to assure not only that assets are performing but that all the 'moving parts' of a transaction are functioning as intended. If the insurance policy covers 100 per cent of principal and interest, the monoline insurer *guarantees* the performance of all structural elements and other third parties. It therefore shares the investor's interest in seeing that all facets of a transaction work properly until maturity, and it maintains a staff dedicated to keeping up with the stream of compliance and performance reports attached to these issues. It may also stipulate the proper form for the reports.

If something does go wrong, the guarantor has the standing to do something about it, and can frequently invoke remedies that it required to be built into the transaction at the outset. This could mean replacement of servicers or downgraded first-loss providers, capture of excess cash flows or, in some cases, mandatory infusions of collateral.

Liquidity
Investors in the secondary market can buy insured securities without having to duplicate the due diligence of the original investor. In addition, the guarantor's ongoing market development efforts can broaden investor awareness of its guaranteed issues.

14.4 GENERAL BENEFITS OF FGI

Whether the scope of FGI coverage is full or partial, the presence of a monoline guarantor provides attractive benefits to investors.

14.4.1 Ratings durability of the monoline guarantor

Recent downgrades in the banking sector have brought home the importance of ratings durability in asset-backed securities. The investor must be concerned not only with the current rating of a guarantor but also with the likelihood that the rating will be maintained. A number of powerful forces work to keep the monoline insurer's triple-A claims-paying rating in place.[3]

First, monoline guarantors are regulated by various jurisdictions in which they write business. Specifically, all the existing Aaa/AAA monoline financial guaranty insurance companies are subject to the insurance law of the State of New York. Article 69 of that law limits the business of each financial guaranty insurer to financial guarantees and related lines (such as surety, residual value and credit insurance); requires that each such insurer maintain a minimum of capital and surplus; establishes contingency, loss and unearned premium reserve requirements for each such insurer; and limits the size of individual transactions (single risks) and the volume of transactions (aggregate risks) that may be underwritten by each such insurer. The law also restricts how the insurance company may invest its capital reserves, and it prevents asset stripping by limiting the payment of dividends.

The regulatory regime governing monoline guarantors is comparable to that of banks. Both employ risk-weighted methods to measure capital adequacy. The main difference is that the risk-weightings applied to monolines make finer distinctions in terms of the quality of the credits being reserved against. For example, the FGI rules discriminate between investment grade and non-investment grade credits and between secured and unsecured obligations, requiring more capital for the lower quality and unsecured. This causes monoline guarantors to focus virtually exclusively on high quality risks.

Second, rating agencies revisit the monoline insurer's rating each time it insures a new asset-backed transaction. For example, Standard & Poor's Corporation has a specific capital adequacy model that it applies to monoline guarantors. Under this model, S&P assigns a 'shadow rating', reflecting the rating it would assign if the transaction were not insured, to every guaranteed issue. It calculates a 'capital charge' equal to the amount of losses the insurer would be conservatively expected to suffer in a depression environment. Moody's Investors Service also examines insured issues on a case by case basis and continuously monitors capital adequacy.

In addition, the rating agencies regularly review the insurer's overall book of business to assure diversification by geography, transaction types, maturities, industry segments and collateral asset categories. The company's ability to pay all claims is tested against a simulated four-year worldwide depression. Ability to pay is calculated on the basis of statutory capital, surplus and contingency reserves, without drawing on the unearned premium reserve, which is created by the accumulation of premiums paid at the outset of transactions.

In pursuit of the highest quality for its guaranty, the guarantor will conduct its own additional tests for capital adequacy and diversification and will reinsure its exposures.

Third, the monoline nature of the business is itself protection. All financial institutions take credit risk in some form, but the monoline financial guaranty insurer faces no potential losses from other risk-assumptive lines of business, as do banks and companies that issue property/casualty and life insurance policies.

Fourth, instalment premiums paid to the insurer create a predictable earnings floor from year to year, insulating the guarantor from the normal corporate pressure to generate earnings anew each year.

Fifth, event risk is virtually absent, because both New York insurance law and common sense preclude any type of leveraged restructuring of a monoline financial guarantor. Regulation limits indebtedness and payment of dividends, thereby preventing excessive leverage and asset stripping. Regulation aside, any restructuring that would impair the monoline's triple-A rating would be self-defeating, because that rating is its most powerful means of attracting future business.

14.4.2 Asset analysis and diligence by the monoline guarantor

The guarantor conducts detailed file reviews and meets on-site with management, collection officers and servicing staff. In addition, in analysing historical asset performance, the guarantor may have access to loss development information that investors can rarely obtain from offering circulars. It has the time, resources and, perhaps most important, motivation to seek out hidden correlations in the data that might otherwise be missed. For example, it may be in a position to discover that lenient underwriting standards were disguised by a strong local economy.

In addition, the guarantor will use computer simulations, similar to those of rating agencies, to determine the level of losses the transaction will survive given a variety of catastrophic economic scenarios. On the basis of these, it determines the levels of overcollateralisation and other protections necessary to protect both investors and the guarantor, even in a 'worst-case' economic depression.

14.5 DISADVANTAGES OF MONOLINE INSURANCE

Issuers comparing monoline insurance with alternative products, such as multiline insurance or bank guarantees, will need to consider the relevance of certain comparative disadvantages of FGI:

- To qualify for FGI, an asset-backed issue will normally have to be of investment-grade quality without the guaranty. In some cases, the cost of accomplishing this through spread accounts, over-collateralisation or other means will be justified by the reduced interest rate on the insured securities. If not, FGI is not indicated.
- Even beyond the investment-grade qualification, the issuer must be able to demonstrate exceptional transaction quality. The monoline industry's loss rate of 0.009 per cent of outstanding par value insured from 1985 to 1989 attests to the level of quality the industry demands.
- Monoline insurers cannot engage in 'tie-in' business, as when a multiline insurer provides property insurance to the issuer.
- Because the monoline must dedicate capital to each transaction on the basis of specific risk-weighting rules of regulators and capital requirements of rating agencies, it sometimes charges a higher premium than a multiline for the same level of coverage and, for transactions involving significant risk, would be required to charge premiums far greater than those of bank letters of credit. The issuer must weigh the cost differential against the marketing value of a 100 per cent guaranty from an Aaa/AAA monoline guarantor.

14.6 THE GUARANTOR AS ARCHITECT

At each stage in the development of the asset-backed market, pioneering transactions have depended upon financial guaranty insurance. The monoline financial guarantor is often a creative force behind innovative transactions, spending the time to understand collateral that has not been securitised before, working with issuers and their advisers to design the structural elements that will protect investors and make the issue marketable, and identifying and overcoming legal and regulatory obstacles.

Often the willingness of a monoline insurer to provide a guaranty makes a new type of transaction possible. FSA, for example, was involved in the first home mortgage securitisation in the UK, the first international securitisations of Australian and New Zealand home mortgages, the first structured Euromarket financing to repay bank debt, the first repackaging of perpetual floating rate notes (FRNs) into fixed maturity FRNs, the first rated securitisation of a pool of UK commercial mortgages and the first Aaa/AAA variable rate notes (VRNs).

A guarantor's international reputation enables it to bring unfamiliar issuer names to foreign markets. This allows issuers to take advantage of better interest rate conditions that arise abroad and to free up borrowing capacity in their home markets.

Figure 14.1 illustrates a transaction in which a 100 per cent guaranty has enabled a UK mortgage originator to obtain ongoing financing in the US commercial paper (CP) market.

On the funding side of this transaction, the guarantor was instrumental in establishing a special-purpose lending entity, whose purpose is to obtain funds to lend by issuing commercial paper in the US. A consortium of international banks provides backup liquidity. This part of the structure looks like a conventional US commercial paper facility.

By adding its guaranty, the guarantor assured that the commercial paper would be rated A-1+/P-1. As a result, the securities have the highest possible ratings and are trading in the most liquid market in the world, the US commercial paper market. The cost of funds is thus very low.

The guaranty is not only in favour of the CP holders but in favour of the banks as well. If the banks advance money, they will benefit from the guaranty just as the CP holders would.

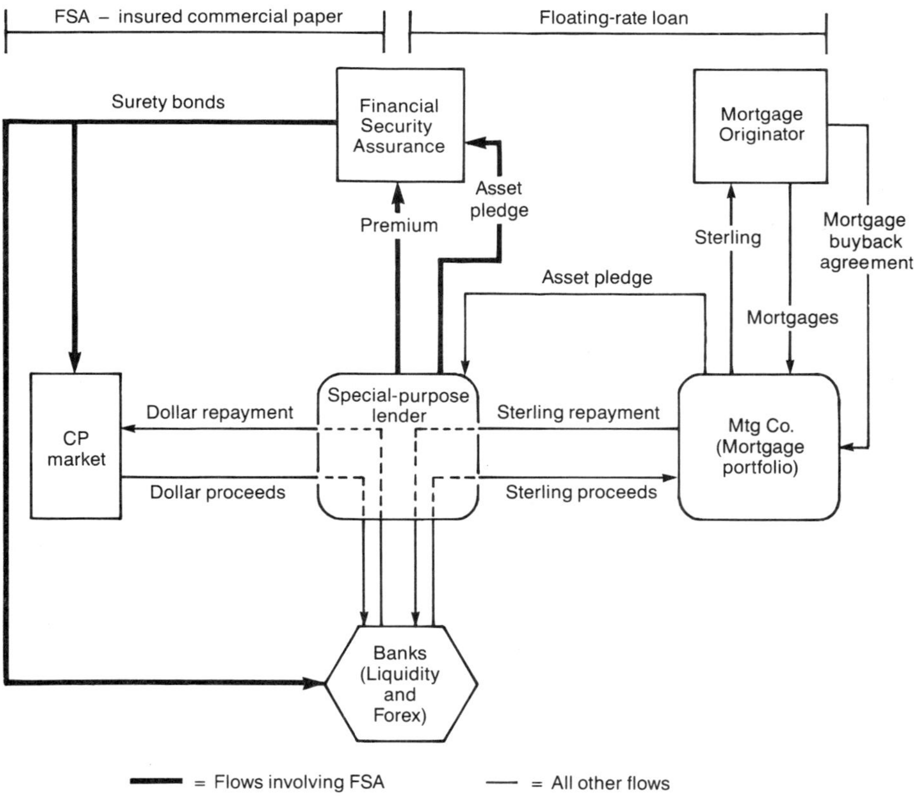

Figure 14.1 Principal flows in an illustrative transaction.

On the other side of the transaction, there is another special-purpose company, this one a funding vehicle set up by the mortgage originator. It borrows from the lending entity, but it borrows in dollars rather than sterling. To accomplish the conversion, the liquidity banks take a second role by providing a foreign exchange facility. They sell dollars for sterling in the spot market and buy dollars for sterling in the forward market. Now there is sterling available to purchase sterling-denominated mortgages, and dollars to pay interest on the commercial paper.

The originator receives the cash, which it uses to originate more mortgages. The mortgages are transferred to the funding vehicle,which pledges them as collateral to the lending entity, which pledges them in turn to the guarantor. Dollar assets now balance dollar liabilities on the commercial paper side of the transaction, and sterling mortgages collateralise sterling loans on the loan side of the transaction. Currency risk has been eliminated at a cost that simply reflects the difference between dollar rates and sterling rates plus a small dealer commission amounting to 3/10 or 4/10 of a basis point.

Despite the complexity of this transaction, it has been very worthwhile for the originator, which generally relies on UK floating-rate bank lending or domestic securitisation. But because of its complexity, it probably could not have been done without a 100 per cent guaranty from a monoline insurance company capable of structuring it.

As more and varied types of assets are securitised, as the asset-backed market becomes more global in scope, and as new structuring methods continue to emerge, the monoline guarantor has growing importance because of its ability to create simplicity by providing an unconditional, irrevocable, 100 per cent guaranty. An asset-backed issue bearing such a guarantee is a secured debt instrument that is of investment grade quality in its own right, and it is coupled with a 100 per cent guaranty from a regulated entity that values its Aaa/AAA credit rating above all else. Such issues provide the greatest certainty, short of some government/sovereign securities, that principal and interest will be received in full and on time.

1 The author was a senior vice president and general partner of S&B and was a founder of FSA.

2 Throughout this chapter, the terms 'financial guaranty insurance' and 'FGI' refer exclusively to products of monoline insurance companies as defined in Article 69 of the New York State Insurance Law.

3 It should be noted that many multiline insurers are also extremely well capitalised relative to the risks they have taken on. Provided that they are subject to a strong regulatory system and consider their ratings to be an essential part of future business opportunities, they may also exhibit the exceptional ratings durability of Aaa/AAA monoline financial guaranty insurers.

15: Insurance-based Credit Enhancement

Stephen L. Wenman, Special Risk Services

15.1 CHARACTERISTICS OF INSURANCE-BASED CREDIT ENHANCEMENT

There are four essential characterstics of insurance-based credit enhancement:

- the coverage that is offered in comparison with other products;
- the pricing of that coverage;
- the way in which the coverage is underwritten;
- the structure of the industry that offers this form of enhancement.

In discussing these characteristics, insurance will, where relevant, be contrasted with alternative routes: senior/subordinated structures, financial guarantees and bank letters of credit.

15.1.1 Coverage

An insurance policy is quite different from a letter of credit or a financial guarantee in so much as the cover that it provides is conditional. That is, the policy will set out certain conditions which it will expect to see observed in the origination of the securitised assets. Should it later transpire that one of these assets causes a loss, and it was not originated in line with the policy conditions, then the policy will void cover on that particular asset and the originator who has ceded it to the securitising vehicle will have to repurchase it. (For many of these policies rating agencies require that should the originator become bankrupt and therefore be unable to repurchase an asset which was written outside policy conditions then, within limits, the insurers will indemnify the investors for any losses that may result.)

Insurance cover will not pick up liquidity shortfalls in the cash flow which result from a default on the collateral in the pool. For example, if a mortgagor defaults on his borrowing then there is an immediate cessation of cash to the vehicle company which has issued the bond. The insurance policy will not immediately pay out to make good this cash shortfall. Instead, the originator of the assets must wait to see whether the borrower will recommence payments and so make good his arrears. If not, the originator (or his administrator) will pursue that borrower for the recovery of the collateral and it will be sold. The insurer at this stage hopes that the proceeds of the sale will cover the debt to the vehicle. If it does not then the insurer will pay the difference between the value of the asset sale and the total indebtedness at that time. This indebtedness will also include the value of any short-term borrowing that has had to be entered into to maintain the liquidity of the bond issue. The net effect, as far as the credit risk is concerned, is no different than had a guarantee or a letter of credit been purchased. The mechanism is perhaps a little more complicated, but the complication is in practice small compared with the complexities of the remainder of a typical securitisation. Insurance has, in fact, proved simpler to employ than senior/subordinated structures, which involve a large amount of cash flow analysis at the time that the security is structured.

We have so far discussed how insurance covers the credit risk associated with mortgage-backed securities. Insurance does not cover a number of other risks that may be inherent in a structure, such as documentation or tax risks. Nor will it normally cover more than a first-loss proportion of the overall size of the pool. This layer of cover is determined by the rating agencies. It is possible to buy 100 per cent cover, if required, but it is normally avoided because of increased cost (although this is modest given insurance underwriters' marginal pricing practice) and the use of capacity. In contrast, financial guarantees will normally pick up documentation risk—but rarely tax risk—and will usually (there are exceptions, such as the partial guarantees issued by CapMac) cover 100 per cent of the issue size.

15.1.2 Pricing

The fact that insurance cover for asset-backed securities is partial in nature is compensated for, first, by price and, second, by the capacity and depth of the insurance industry. As far as prices are concerned, insurance-based credit enhancement is less expensive than the alternatives. If, for example, we look at a mortgage-backed security in the UK, where mortages are written to the rating agencies' criteria, then we would expect an insurance policy which would typically be constructed with a first-loss deductible of, say, 0.5 per cent to 1 per cent of the total pool size, to be priced at approximately 40 basis points for AAA cover. This is *not* a per annum cost but is paid flat, once only, for the life of the deal. On a per annum basis over the average life of a mortgage-backed security, the cost amortises to some 6–7 basis points per year. Financial guarantees are typically more expensive than this, although they have generally not been used in the residential mortgage-backed security market in the UK. What is known of their pricing methodology would suggest that the likely cost of such guarantees would lie between 40–60 basis points per annum, and this would be possible only after the risk associated with the first 4–6 per cent of the value of the mortgage pool had been transferred by some other mechanism, such as conventional insurance or over-collateralisation. Only when this had happened would the financial guarantor wrap the whole issue with his guarantee.

It is difficult to compare the cost of an insurance policy with a letter of credit because we have not seen many letters of credit being provided in the same sort of market where the insurers have been active. However, the pricing we have seen on pools of personal loans and leases suggests that the pricing for letters of credit is more competitive than in the case of financial guarantees but still not quite as competitive as insurance policies. This situation results from the fact that banks can issue letters of credit which provide partial cover only; i.e. they cover only the layer of risk which the rating agencies have determined they wish to see covered rather than the total issue size. Since the total exposure is less they can charge accordingly. Most financial guarantors wish to guarantee an entire issue and not provide merely a partial guarantee.

It may be argued that there is in reality little difference between providing say, the first 15 per cent of an issue on a first-loss basis and guaranteeing the entire sum. However, with both letters of credit and financial guarantees every effort is taken to ensure that the real risk is already taken out before the letter of credit or guarantee is provided. This is done by such measures as subordinating all excess cash flow in the vehicle to any losses and providing a cash escrow sum to reinforce the cash flow.

As a result, the cost of banks' letters of credit and financial guarantees are, in the main, charges for the volume of capacity which is used, and not to cover expected losses. Financial guarantors could, in fact, provide guarantee capacity slightly cheaper than the banks on a pound-for-pound basis. This results from differences in the way the two industries are regulated: the capital allocation which a financial guarantor has to make is normally less than of the banks.

The difference in regulation is also the main reason why insurance can be priced cheaper than either bank letters of credit or financial guarantees. Insurance companies are regulated by a quite different method from banks and financial guarantee companies. Typically their capital allocation will depend on the amount of premium that is charged rather than the overall exposure. This results in substantially lower capital costs. As we have seen, the cost of an insurance policy for a mortgage pool might by typically 7–8 basis points a year over the life of that issue—substantially below that of the competitors. On pools of personal loans and leases the pricing difference is not quite so dramatic; in a recent comparison, insurers were charging 65 basis points against a letter of credit cost of 75 basis points per annum, on a similar pool. The real difference may be larger than this since the banks will normally want to subordinate all excess cash flow to losses, whereas insurers may be willing to cap the amount of cash that is taken, thereby ensuring at least a minimum level of profitability for the originator. For example, in mortgage-backed structures that use surplus cash flow, such usage has been kept at between 1.25 and 2 per cent of the issue size.

15.1.3 Underwriting

What do insurers look for when they are deciding to underwrite a pool? The two most important factors they will focus on are the value of the assets that secure the borrowing and the ability of the borrower to meet his monthly or quarterly interest payments. The emphasis on whether they regard assets or income as more important will vary depending on the nature of those assets. For example, for automobile pools, where the assets are expected to depreciate fairly rapidly, most of the focus will be on the borrower's ability to repay and the skill of the originator to lend without incurring defaults. Conversely, when lending on mortgages a great deal of emphasis will be put on securing the right value of the properties to ensure that there is substantial collateral over and above the lender's position.

To investigate this process in more depth let us see the various factors that an insurance underwriter would investigate when underwriting a mortgage pool. They include:

- the loan-to-value ratio;
- the relationship between the borrower's income and the cost of the mortgage;
- the historical loss rate of the pool;
- the levels of arrears of payments on a pool;
- the amount of substitution of new mortgages into the pool as that pool amortises;
- the amount of further advances that are likely to be made to borrowers in the pool;
- the product criteria (e.g. whether the mortgages are fixed or floating or have a deferred element);
- the geographical spread of the portfolio (to ensure that there is no undue concentration within the pool);
- the length of time between when the mortgage is originated and when it enters the pool (the seasoning of a pool).

15.1.4 The structure of the industry

The industry that provides insurance policies for securitisation is comparatively widespread in Europe, although the spread is much wider on the reinsurance side than on the primary side. To date some half-dozen or so companies have been involved in taking a primary underwriting position. This small number is a reflection on the limited number of companies that have the required rating. (This needs to be either double-A or—preferably—triple-A standard.) It is also because of the still modest size of the structured finance market in Europe and the reluctance on the part of some companies to underwrite policies for the very long term that mortgage-backed securities (the largest single asset market) can involve. Such companies are aware that even though the mortgages in a particular security may have a theoretical life of, say, 25 or even 35 years, the average life of one of these securities is much shorter, and will typically be anything between five and ten years. Insurers often draw as much comfort from the incentives structured into some of these bonds for an originator to call an issue, as the investors do. Even so, insurers know that they can be on risk for a long term if the call fails to be exercised. Some companies simply do not want to undertake that long term exposure.

It is to be hoped that in the future more companies will come in as primary insurers. The underwriting results of this type of business have been profitable. As the underlying quality of the business comes to be recognised it is likely that other companies will be drawn in. Unfortunately the number of triple-A companies has been reduced recently but the technology has been developed by Special Risk Services (SRS) to upgrade double-A companies to triple A. This greatly expands the number of participants who can potentially underwrite this business. However, if an issue is going to be rated triple-A by the rating agencies then we are still dependent on using a triple-A company to upgrade the double-A company. This need not necessarily increase the overall cost of the deal because of the differences in pricing the pool to double-A and triple-A standards but it does mean finding triple-A companies who will be willing to take credit risk on other insurance companies. This is a wider field than those who are purely willing to take risks on the underlying assets, but it is not unlimited and there is a continual quest for additional capacity.

The number of reinsurers who participate is a great deal larger than the number of primary underwriters. Indeed, it is said that it is the participation of the reinsurers that provides the depth in this market. Reinsurers in most European countries have at one time or another participated in asset-backed securities. The depth of the reinsurance market partly resides in the fact that at this level it is not necessary to use rated companies and partly because insurance companies can participate in quite small amounts per issue and can therefore spread their risks very effectively. Many of the reinsurers will be underwriting, for example, only 2.5 to 5 per cent of the original risk.

The depth of reinsurance allows the primary writers to write far more risk than they would otherwise be able to do. The investors see only the primary underwriter, who is legally and technically at risk for the full sum insured, but the underwriter would not be able or willing to write the sort of exposures that are required of securities structures unless he knew that he could syndicate a substantial amount of it.

Reinsurance capacity is not only available on a deal-by-deal basis. Insurers may enter into long-term commitments to provide forward capacity (a treaty), and this gives insurers a product which originators of assets will find particularly useful. Committed capacity gives security to the originator that, barring a collapse of the capital markets, he will be able to securitise over the coming year at a moment of his choosing. Forward commitments to buy capacity will also result in reduction in management expenses. Instead of having to negotiate separate capacity for each securitisation, there can be one major negotiation at the beginning of the year. This will arrange the parameters of the capacity and the sort of assets that the originator wishes to securitise. Having secured agreement at the beginning of the year the originator can then continue to originate assets knowing that credit enhancement capacity will be available when he needs it. Most originators who operate this system actually purchase the credit enhancement as they originate the assets, rather than waiting until they securitise, finding such enhancement can also provide support to the banking lines which are funding the assets before they are securitised, and, if necessary, enabling the originator's capital resources to be stretched.

The question is often asked: 'What is the danger of "event risk" in an insurance-based structure?' In other words, how resistant are these structure to the possibility of downgrading of the insurance company. The answer is twofold. First, because the insurance companies that underwrite this class of business are generally large composites, with assets running into billions of pounds, they have enormous financial strength from which they can defend themselves against temporary setbacks. Second, the financial insurance part of the business is usually a very small percentage of their overall underwriting, so it is unlikely that any particular problems with credit enhancement will result in a downgrading.

However, downgradings do happen, though they are relatively rare. At the time of writing there have been two such incidents in the UK market. One was the placing of Eagle Star on credit watch as a result of a takeover bid. This would have also resulted in the securities which they were enhancing also being put on credit watch. Instead, another insurance company was found to stand behind Eagle Star in order to support the rating, and this was done at no cost to the originator. It is one of the attractions of using the insurance market that the industry is a co-operative one and likes to support its good name. Therefore in times of difficulty the market will be keen to help. Similarly, in the other incident, the downgrading of Royal, Sun Alliance was brought in to backstop the issues that Royal had guaranteed.

To summarise, insurance-based credit enhancement provides deep, widely spread capacity at an economic price. It also has the ability to enter into long-term commitments with originators of assets, providing a security of enhancement into the future and low administration costs.

15.2 DEVELOPMENT OF THE INSURANCE-BASED CREDIT ENHANCEMENT MARKET

15.2.1 The USA

The insurance-based credit enhancement market started in the USA approximately 15 years ago. It did so for much the same reasons that it thrives today, namely to increase the ease of understanding of an issue and reduce the complexity and risk inherent in the investment decision.

In the late 1970s and early 1980s municipalities in the US started to raise money through the capital markets. These local government instruments were invested in by retail investors who were attracted by their tax-exempt status. The decision to invest was already difficult, with nearly 14,000 different issues available, thus making a thorough credit analysis nearly impossible for the investor. As these bonds were held by investors for whom safety was critical, the creditworthiness of the issues was paramount. In response to this the Municipal Bond Insurance Association (MBIA) and subsequently financial guaranty companies were incorporated to offer a guaranty for the investor.

As the municipal bond market grew, other non-government institutions, such as corporations, became interested in accessing the capital markets to increase their liquidity. Previously only well known names could easily achieve fine yields in the capital markets; unknown names, in spite of their financial strength, would trade much more poorly. Hence it was logical that the same credit enhancement used for municipal bonds could be applied to corporate issue with the same effect: the issuers could achieve a yield on the basis of their creditworthiness rather than on name recognition.

CIGNA, Fireman's Fund and Aetna were the US multiline insurers leading the development of credit enhancement for the non-tax-exempt commercial paper markets. These insurers offered enhancement to a wide range of corporates that otherwise would not have been able to achieve reasonable yields had they issued debt straight into the market. The credit enhancement was attractive to corporations who were unrated, unknown in the markets or undercapitalised. Credit enhancement could take unrated debt or low-rated debt and raise it to AAA where it would have much greater liquidity.

In the late 1980s, regulators in New York State introduced legislation ensuring that the financial guarantee business could not jeopardise the reserves of the multilines and put their other, traditional business at risk. The legislation required that insurers participating in the financial guarantee business allocate that business to a separate entity that did only financial guarantee business. Because of this legislation, FSA and CAPMAC emerged and became, with FGIC, the leaders in the development of the financial guarantee business. It is interesting to note that even though the insurance legislation was not a national requirement but only a New York State requirement, all the major insurers who had business operations in New York were nevertheless forced to comply.

Mortgage securitisation started in the US through government agencies such as the Government National Mortgage Association and the Federal National Mortgage Association raising funds on the capital markets. These issues carried a direct US government guarantee, as in the case of GNMA or 'Ginnie Mae' as it is better known, and an implicit government guarantee in the case of FNMA or 'Fannie Mae'. Fannie Maes actually trade at approximately 10 basis points worse than Ginnie Maes because FNMA is not a government organisation; thus, although the market expects an implicit guaranty, it is not an actual guaranty as there is with GNMA. These organisations were set up well before securitisation became popular with the purpose of providing mortgages to veterans and other less well-off people. They accessed the capital markets in the same way as the municipalities and the corporations but with the backing of the US government, trading with very high liquidity in the same way as US treasury bonds.

The success of the mortgage-backed issues subsequently encouraged the development of other asset-backed issues. 'Sallie Maes' were issued by the Student Loan Marketing Association, the agency which issues the US-government-guaranteed student loans. These loans were sold through local banks and were guaranteed from inception, like Ginnie Mae and Fannie Mae mortgages, then allocated directly to the pool to be securitised. Again, no additional credit enhancement was necessary.

Banks became interested in accessing these markets to fund their mortgage lending. Their mortgage portfolios are not insured by the US government so additional credit enhancement is necessary. This came in the form of a letter of credit or a guarantee issued from a US monoline. The level of guarantee was usually 13 per cent of first losses, which was twice the level of defaults that occurred in the Depression of the 1930s. Today, where the load-to-value is higher, more complex structures are used.

15.2.2 Europe

The development of the asset-backed securities market and the necessary credit enhancement began in Europe several years after the market had already taken off in the US. In the early 1980s there was neither the desire nor the need to raise funds through the mechanism of securitisation. However, from the mid-1980s (particularly the late 1980s) this changed. First in the UK, subsequently in France, Sweden, Italy, Spain and Germany, asset-backed markets began to develop. The reasons behind this development were different from the drive that led to the growth of the US market. There the primary motivation was the imbalance between the location of funds and the need for funds to finance mortgages, due to the regulation of banking in the US. In Europe this was not the problem. However, by 1986 the deregulation opportunity within the UK led to the creation of the first of what came to be called the centralised lenders. These were rivals to the traditional sources of housing finance in the UK, typically the building societies and the banks, and were designed specifically to borrow money on the wholesale markets and lend it retail. At that time there were considerable cost advantages to wholesale funding. By the end of the 1980s these funding needs had been added to by a general requirement in the banking community to improve capital ratios. Securitisation was one very good way of doing this.

A credit enhancement market had to develop at the same time if these securitisation issues were going to be successfully launched. For example, in the UK, where the European market began, the early issues in this market were all pool-insured. They had to be: there were no government guarantees available, unlike in the US, and it was quite clear from the attitude of the UK government at the time (and probably in the future) that no guarantees would be likely to be forthcoming. Indeed, the attitude of the regulatory authorities was suspicious towards this new type of funding and there was no particular wish on their part to encourage it overtly.

The early issues were marked by the concentration of credit enhancement capacity in one insurance institution. It was able effectively to monopolise the market at the beginning because it was then the only multiline insurer that had a triple-A rating. Other UK insurers subsequently achieved ratings and new techniques were developed, particularly by Special Risk Services, the broker which developed much of the credit enhancement capacity in this area, which enabled triple-A structures to be created while using double-A-rated risk-carriers. However, by the beginning of the 1990s this growth was beginning to slow as several of the companies which had been rated triple A began to suffer downgradings. In spite of this, the amount of capacity available to the mortgage-backed market continues to increase from year to year.

Insurers were well placed to take advantage of the start of the mortgage-backed market. UK insurers have been involved for many years in insuring mortgages and therefore to underwrite pool policies was only an extension of their existing practice. Almost uniquely in Europe, UK insurers had been insuring the top-slice risk of mortgages for lenders. In other words, if a building society would normally lend to 75 per cent load-to-value (LTV), then they were able to exceed this figure provided that they could purchase insurance against the risk of default. This meant that lenders could sometimes originate mortgages up to 95 or even 100 per cent of LTV.

As a result of this involvement by British insurers over the years, they had a broad experience of lending practices in the mortgage industry and the sort of underwriting conditions that led to either a profit or a loss. For those who understood mortgage-backed securities it was very attractive to extend this underwriting knowledge to the enhancement of the lending below 75 per cent LTV. Although the premium rates were apparently much finer, the risks were also substantially reduced. In fact, because the whole bond issue did not have to be insured, but only that layer which was determined by the rating agency, the insurers managed to get a similar premium, as a percentage of their risk, as they did on the top layer but retained the benefits of having substantially more equity ahead of their position than with top-slice insurance. Since many of the insurers were already writing the top layer for their securitising lenders, participating in the pool policy was a way of generating extra income for the same risk. To date the profitability of the pool account is a great deal better than the top-slice MIG account, which runs into substantial losses every five years or so.

Credit enhancement through insurance was not the only technique used. Some originators were sufficiently frustrated by the pricing policies of some insurers that they started to explore other methods. Principal among these was the development of senior/subordinated structures. These were not seen until 1987 in the UK, but once present they grew rapidly and at one point in 1989 they were taking about 40 per cent of the market. However, the subordinated route did have some disadvantages for issues. To begin with, issuers had to subordinate their entire cash flows to any losses. This meant that potentially they would have no profitability from the securitised assets if mortgage defaults are high. More seriously, the capacity in this market proved to be ephemeral and investors in the subordinated tranches appeared to be easily scared once conditions became a little tougher in the underlying mortgage market. By 1990 the percentage of issuers who were pursuing the senior/subordinated route had substantially reduced.

Elsewhere in Europe the senior/subordinated structure continues to exercise a hold over some originators. For example, in France, the second largest securitisation market in Europe, subordinated debt has been the favourite method of credit-enhancing issues. This is because French regulatory authorities have written the rules in a way that makes it an attractive option to pursue. Typically a French originator can issue a subordinated tranche and then repurchase it with a capital write-off equal only to the expected historical loss on the assets plus a normal 100 per cent weighting on his holding of the subordinated tranche. This means that a French originator who chooses to securitise in this manner can achieve substantial improvement in his capital ratios while at the same time holding what is likely to prove the entire risk associated with those assets that he has now securitised. This procedure is not allowed in some other European countries since it effectively weakens the balance sheets of banks, even if such weakening is not apparent from the published numbers. As can be seen, under such a mechanism, once the originator has securitised some assets he has liberated capital which can then be used to support new lending. However, at the same time he is likely to be retaining the credit risk from the original assets. In other words, the originator is now increasing his overall exposure to his own capital, not improving it as was the apparent object of the exercise.

If securitisation were in time to become a sufficiently widespread mechanism for funding of banking institutions, this treatment of subordinated bonds would result in competitive advantages to those banks who were allowed it. We would expect therefore to see, in a couple of years or so, a European-wide agreement outlining how lenders must treat their subordinated layers of securities issues should they wish to repurchase them.

That the widespread support for the senior/subordinated route is the result of local regulation rather than economic logic is seen in the credit enhancement routes that have been taken by other European nations. The securitisation market in Italy is only just starting, but so far there have been two issues—'Chariots' and 'Auriga'—which have employed respectively personal autoloans and corporate autoleases as the form of collateral. Both have used bank letters of credit as the credit enhancement mechanism. These operate in a very similar way to insurance in that they transfer the risk away from the originator to the supplier of the letter of credit.

A further development in the Italian market is likely to be the securitisation of mortgages. Here most originators expect to use the route of insurance as credit enhancement since the duration of an issue will be sufficiently long that it is unlikely to be an attractive deal for a bank.

In northern Europe Germany and Sweden have so far seen securitised issues. The 'Osprey' transaction in Sweden employed triple-A insurance capacity and it is widely expected that the mortgage originators in Scandinavia will continue to use this route. In the 'KKB' transaction in Germany, a bank letter of credit was used to enhance an autoloan portfolio.

In conclusion, we can see that as the European market has developed three main methods of credit enhancement have all been used: namely, insurance, senior/subordinated structures and bank letters of credit. Which one is used depends on local regulation, which varies the attractions of these products to different originators. In addition, the types of assets may have characteristics that make one form of credit enhancement more attractive than another. If one looks forward then one can probably see a rosier future for insurance and bank letters of credit than for senior/subordinated structures. This is because investors are increasingly wary of what is high yield paper and demanding higher spreads in order to be persuaded to buy it. In some cases the global pressure on corporate cash flow means that there are fewer investors who are prepared to except subordinated paper. However, insurance and bank letters of credit may also come under pressure. Pricing may move out slightly since both communities are currently suffering from downgrading. This means that not only is available capacity squeezed but those players who are left in the market may well feel that they have an ability to raise prices that would be curtailed in a more competitive market.

A great deal of effort will be devoted in the future to develop structures which enable lesser-rated credit enhancers to be employed in triple-A structures while at the same time growing the present level of capacity to ensure that there is proper competition within the market. But despite the problem with ratings it is expected that both banks and insurance companies will continue to be players in this market. Banks may suffer as their ability to price competitively is eroded by increased capital requirements whereas insurers do not yet have these problems. In the long term it is expected that the financial strength of the insurance community and its ability to spread risk, internally through its traditional technique of building portfolios of small lines on a multiplicity of risks, and externally via reinsurance, will lead to its pre-eminence in the market.

The Rating Agencies' Approach to Securitisation

16: Standard & Poor's View

Lionel J. Marsland-Shaw, Standard & Poor's Corporation

Any review of rating agency criteria for asset-backed debt needs to be put into perspective in terms of the framework within which an agency operates and the manner in which it approaches the subject matter. It is to be hoped therefore that the following will provide some enlightenment as to the philosophy used by Standard & Poor's Corporation (S&P) in its assessment and evaluation of asset-backed, or securitised, issues. There will also be particular emphasis on specific areas of securitisation as well as a review of assets already used to collateralise debt issues and an attempt to gauge what may occur in terms of assets and market developments in the future.

16.1 ANALYSING AN ASSET-BACKED TRANSACTION

The essence of an evaluation of an asset-backed transaction is to ensure that the quality of the assets and the structure itself can withstand the worst-case stress situations that S&P criteria envisage, with the intent that investors will receive payment on time and to the extent required. The severity of this stress analysis must, of course, be viewed against two factors. First, whether or not the issue is expected to achieve investment grade, i.e. the minimum level at which principal is not considered to be at risk. Second, the particular rating applied to an issue insofar as the level of investors' risk is concerned.

One aspect of an asset-backed structure that may be deemed a disadvantage is that the framework of the issue is fixed at the outset. Thus, it becomes difficult to alter that structure subsequently, which removes a certain amount of flexibility for the issuer. Consequently, although the desired rating can be 'targeted' when drawing up a structure, the level and extent of protection built into it has to be adequate from the beginning because the vehicle has little ability to adapt to changing market or economic conditions. It should also be remembered that in these types of transactions S&P is rating the issue not the issuer. An AAA rating on one issue does not necessarily mean that all issues by that same entity will receive an AAA, nor does the rating address the unsecured creditworthiness of the issuer.

16.1.1 S&P methodology

The keystone of S&P's methodology is often referred to as the 'weak link' theory, and that concept, together with ratings' consistency are two important features of an S&P rating. Given the accepted wisdom that a chain is as strong as its weakest link, that principle can be applied to the structure of an asset-backed issue when considering the strengths or weaknesses of any specific transaction.

Moreover, S&P may not rate all parties who perform a function within an issue. Consequently it will make the assumption that such parties may become insolvent during the life of an issue. The problem that then arises is that the rated bonds are expected to perform irrespective of the insolvency of any unrated party to the structure. It is in order to resolve this concern that the issuer is established in a special-purpose vehicle and that so much importance is attached to its ability to be as far removed as possible from insolvency. Consistency of ratings (i.e. the basis on which all ratings are established) is paramount because of the need to give investors the ability to make comparisons worldwide and be certain that any given rating has the same implications wherever it is applied.

16.1.2 The three-pronged approach

As an inherent part of S&P's methodology, the evaluation of any structure relies upon an analysis, incorporating what is called a 'three-pronged approach', that focuses on the following main areas:

- quality of collateral;
- financial mechanisms;
- legal considerations.

A major concern in evaluating the quality and sufficiency of collateral is the asset itself. The ability of the asset to pay the investors is the linchpin of the issue and it is important to understand the potential credit risks inherent in that asset, as well as how the asset can be used to assure value to the investors. A variety of over-collateralisation scenarios are employed, depending on the assets concerned and whether their value derives from being market-to-market or cash flow based.

Although currently UK transactions have been cash flow based, this does not preclude the possibility of a market value transaction if parties can be found to make a price in the relevant assets. If the collateral itself is insufficient to meet the requirements of the transaction, irrespective of the valuation technique applied, there must be some means of covering any such shortfall.

While the origins of securitisation have their roots in the US, a great many issues have now been completed outside that original market, and asset-backed debt is a funding tool used in a number of countries. A point that should be emphasised is that although S&P rates such issues in a number of different legal jurisdictions, and while detailed criteria may differ to take account of local markets and practices, the underlying principles remain constant in the way in which such transactions are evaluated.

It is helpful to all parties involved in the rating process if the principals concerned have a comprehensive appreciation of S&P methodology. Development of the rating process is repetitive, requiring interaction between the parties, and it should be remembered that each iteration may add to the passage of time between the conception of a deal and its completion. That said, successive transactions founded on a similar base become a much more straightforward process for all involved.

Understanding how the collateral is to be structured to ensure that the investor receives interest and principal in full, under all conditions, is critical. The nature of the asset and how it operates within its own market will receive close consideration, with a view to ensuring that its performance is adequately assessed for the purposes of an issue. Equally important is the consideration of funds flow and where a liquidity shortfall could occur.

Liquidity needs can arise owing to a number of events. For example, shortfalls may be due to a timing mismatch of payments on the collateral relative to payments in the issued securities, resulting from a mismatch in the interest rate on the funding versus the interest rate on the securities. Similar shortfalls may also occur as a result of market-related risks, such as an inability to remarket short-term debt, or to reinvest cash produced by the assets at a rate needed to pay investors.

The legal jurisdiction of both the issuer and the assets should be addressed in all cases at an early stage. This is an area that may require extensive work depending on both the issuer's and S&P's familiarity with the jurisdiction. Legal opinions are usually sought on a variety of matters, depending on the issue structure, the assets and particular national laws.

16.1.3 Documentation

Following an assessment of the credit aspects, attention will then turn to the documentation. S&P examines all draft documents relevant to the rating of the transaction and comments on aspects which affect the full and timely payment of the issue under all foreseeable circumstances. Although, as a general rule, final documentation is not available until signing, it is wise to have S&P's tacit approval of the documents prior to launch, and, at a minimum on all areas which might be considered material in a prospectus. If the documents are subject to substantial changes at any time, S&P would expect to see copies of the revised drafts before the final documentation is completed. S&P and its legal advisers should have approved drafts of all necessary legal opinions prior to signing of the documents.

When S&P has applied a public rating to an asset-backed issue, that rating is subject to surveillance for the term of the issue. The structure will provide that the issuer submits regular reports on the performance of the issue to both the trustee and the rating agencies, as well as to other interested parties; the reports will cover such things as arrears performance of the assets, liquidity and credit enhancement usage. The fact that an issue has an AAA rating at sale does not necessarily mean that such a rating remains in place if there is a marked deterioration in asset performance during the life of the transaction.

The rating is subject to change if the performance varies from expectations, if any party to the transaction fails to perform as expected, or if rating changes occur on supporting entities.

As a part of S&P's ongoing due diligence process, a review of the administrator of the collateral will be carried out, at least annually, to assess its ability to continue servicing a rated issue. Any significant changes affecting a servicer or administrator will also be monitored (for example, a change of ownership or installation of new computer systems), and, depending on the impact of such changes, a visit may be prompted as a consequence.

16.1.4 Third-party ratings

Devising an asset-backed structure will often require, sometimes by necessity, the use of parties unconnected with the issuer to provide some form of financial support for the transaction. Such support can take a variety of shapes: borrowing facilities, guarantees, letters of credit, insurance policies and swaps, to name but a few. Given the nature of S&P's analytical approach, such parties will need to carry an S&P rating. It is the nature of the use of these ratings in asset-backed issues which earns them the nomenclature of 'supporting ratings'.

The term refers to parties which play a monetary role within a structure, regardless of whether that role is long- or short-term in nature. The level of supporting rating necessary for any particular transaction will depend not only on the nature of its use but also on the rating targeted for the issue.

S&P will almost inevitably not rate all the participants in an issue, and thus from the rating viewpoint, unrated entities cannot be certain to perform their roles. Knowing the strength of the supporting entity, by dint of a rating already applied, helps in assessing the various aspects of the structure where the party is involved. From S&P's standpoint, where this not the case, and an unrated entity were an essential link in the chain of the structure, its ability to perform its financial responsibilities to the requisite level of stress would be unknown.

However, that does not preclude an entity with a lower rating, or even without a rating at all, from taking a monetary role in the issue; what it does mean is that such parties may need to have a form of credit support available to reassure S&P that the overall strength of the structure is not impaired.

One of the most common functions performed by a supporting rating is that of being a provider of a liquidity or a revolving credit facility. This position is usually taken by a bank, where it sustains the availability of funds for the issue for items such as short-term arrears. Similarly, a guaranteed investment contract (GIC) provider is a supporting rating—the purpose of a GIC is to assure the issuer of a guaranteed rate of income on cash which is surplus to current requirements, thereby boosting income levels sufficiently to match the rate necessitated by the level of the coupon on the issued securities.

The third use is in debt issues with a maturity shorter than that of the assets. In this situation there would normally be a provision that one or more entities rated as high as the issue will buy out remaining assets at or before the issue's maturity.

16.2 STRUCTURES

Notwithstanding the apparent similarity of many public issues, identical structures as between different issuers are not common. Consequently it is necessary that a rating agency is able to adapt to specific or customised modifications to the basic principles of securitisation, and to evaluate them.

Such changes to what may have become established practice or ways of thinking arise for a number of reasons. The fundamental nature of an originator's product may make it more flexible in designing cash flow arrangements or, conversely, certain characteristics may necessitate further complexities to enable the structure to perform to a required standard. Similarly, while obtaining off-balance-sheet treatment for an asset is an often-quoted reason for securitisation, this need does not hold for every issuer. Depending on the particular circumstances of the issuer/originator it is equally valid to issue asset-backed securities simply to obtain an improved rate of return on capital or equity.

In addition to these and a variety of other issuer considerations, it is necessary to take into account the local market, both in terms of asset performance and the prevailing legal jurisdiction. This latter point is especially relevant when the transfer of title or control of the asset is considered. One of the major concerns when assessing the strength of a structure is whether the trustee, in whatever form that role is included, has both the ability to foreclose and realise the value of the underlying assets, and, if necessary, vary the charging rate on the related debts to ensure the continued cash flow for the investors. S&P has evaluated asset-backed issues in a number of different jurisdictions, and is always willing to recognise the need for change to adapt to local circumstances, which, combined with its depth of experience, gives it an insight into the problems that can be encountered when moving across borders.

One advantage of asset-backed financing is the ability to create matched funding. However, that can require certain other precautions to be taken when it is considered how asset-backed commercial paper needs to be structured in order to ensure that investors are protected from the misalignment of the maturity of a long-term asset compared to that of the issued paper. Viewed from the rating perspective, it becomes necessary to make sure that mechanisms exist within the documentation to provide immediate liquidity and credit cover, as well as an ultimate source of repayment where this situation exists.

Similar concerns will also arise when the relative interest rates of the asset and the issued security are of a different tenor. That is to say, where one is variable and the other fixed. Therefore, to enable fixed-rate assets to support the cash flow of floating- or variable-rate bonds (or vice versa), a form of interest rate swap will be required. This will need to be provided by a supporting rating of the appropriate level if the swap is an integral part of the structure.

16.3 ASSETS

The range of potential assets which can be securitised is vast. A look at the types employed to date in the US market gives an indication of the variety available, from mortgages on residential and mobile homes, to autos, credit cards and boat loans. Asset-backed finance outside its natal boundaries has a long way to go to catch up with its American peer as far as different assets is concerned.

However, in view of the relatively short time the non-US market has existed, it has demonstrated a remarkable resilience and strength, given that asset-backed finance was relatively unknown outside the USA only three or four years ago. A review of non-US issues shows what assets have been used so far. Residential mortgages in the UK (including both a commerical paper issue and a floating-rate note issue based on a portfolio that was totally in arrears), Canada, Sweden and Australia, commercial property in both the

UK and Australia, autoloans (both UK and French originated), synthetic bonds, repackaged corporate bonds and whole loans ... Quite a respectable beginning in such a short period of time.

S&P has always expressed a willingness to assess different assets, and endeavours to apply its expertise and experience as appropriate when asked to consider a 'new' variety. This has established the need to adopt a methodical approach to evaluating the quality, risks and performance of assets in general. Fundamental to this philosophy is a requirement to obtain and evaluate as much data as possible to broaden the understanding of the nature of the particular asset. Some, such as mortgages, are much more homogeneous in nature and more readily lend themselves to analysis on a generic basis. Others are usually far more lender-specific; that is to say, the underwriting approach, for example, can differ significantly between lenders, which in turn impacts the quality of the assets and their performance. Furthermore, some unique assets do not lend themselves easily to rating evaluation methodology and require much more research to establish a base from which a methodical analysis can be achieved.

Establishing and collating the raw data is a major initial step in coming to terms with an asset that is unfamiliar to securitisation. One of the biggest problems faced by S&P in this sort of research is the amount of information available. This applies both in terms of the length of time that records have been kept, as well as the detail of what information has been recorded. Bear in mind, of course, that most originators may not have envisaged securitisation at the outset and therefore may well not have had a need to capture data in any depth or detail. In a situation where available data is less than desired, S&P is usually able to make some worse-case deductive assumptions in order to arrive at appropriate criteria.

Key elements in reviewing and researching any asset which is a candidate for financing are the markets in which it exists and the jurisdiction by which it is governed. One fundamental aspect to remember here is that, notwithstanding any similarity between cultures of different countries, it is almost inevitable that laws have been drawn differently or underwriting concerns addressed in another way, such that these changes can render using the same evaluation approach difficult to apply. For instance, countries whose legal system operates from a common law base tend to adopt a vastly different judicial system from those where the law is codified. Similarly, the social culture of a country and the factors which influence borrowers' behaviour may be at opposite ends of the spectrum. France and the UK provide an obvious example of disparate legal systems, the former with its Napoleonic code and the latter with centuries of common law precedents. Contrast also the historic approach by US mortgagors, with their great reliance on fixed-rate loans, to those in the UK, who until relatively recently were accustomed only to variable-rate mortgages, despite the cyclical and volatile nature of UK interest rates. The breadth of Standard & Poor's experience in these areas gives it a distinct advantage in its analysis.

16.3.1 Mortgages—residential and commercial

To date, residential mortgages have been the staple diet of UK-based securitisation vehicles, although recent developments have provided the first indications of a parallel move towards using commercial properties.

Market conditions in the UK over the period from early 1988 through to late 1990 led to what can only be described as an explosion of residential mortgage products, designed to provide a cushion for mortgagors against then prevailing high interest rates, but also destined to aggravate competition amongst lenders. The withdrawal of joint MIRAS availability led to a surge in borrowing at about the same time that lenders were devising products to maximise individuals' earnings potential by using increased income multiples, greater loan-to-value property ratios and refraining from asking too many questions about levels of income. These factors, combined with the hybrid products for deferring interest due, in part or in whole, for varying periods of time, changed the face of the market almost beyond recognition.

It is interesting to note, however, that this phenomenon of product development has been largely confined to the UK. Deferred interest mortgages have been available in France for example, but are not particularly common and apparently frowned upon in some quarters. Furthermore, other countries becoming involved in securitisation do not appear to have ventured into the more esoteric areas of mortgage finance.

The impact of such developments can be seen clearly when reviewing the structures and credit enhancement levels of UK issues launched during that period. Mechanisms had to be created to fund the deferred interest elements on loans, cash flow structures became more complex, other legal issues had to be addressed and the overall amounts of credit enhancement increased.

The latter arose partly as a result of the rating agencies' view that many of these new mortgage types had a significantly different risk profile to a standard annuity or endowment mortgage.

It was partially in expectation of the by-products of such increased risk that S&P introduced a liquidity test into structures that contain provisions to substitute new mortgages. The intent and effect of the test is to monitor the levels of arrears for loans classified as more than two months past due as a proportion of all expected interest due over a defined, preceding period; the trigger level so set can vary with each issue. A result in excess of the criterion level puts up a warning flag that arrears levels may be rising faster than originally anticipated and allows time for remedial action if appropriate.

In Australia, the securitisation of mortgages has involved mainly non-standard, rather than standard, residential mortgages—as well as pools of small commercial mortgage loans. Two state governments, New South Wales and Victoria, have established programmes for securitising government-subsidised residential mortgage loans. Apart from these, there are several programmes backed by mixed pools of small commercial and some standard residential mortgage loans. Most of these issues have included 100 per cent pool insurance and partial liquidity facilities to cover mortgage arrears and any mismatches between bond and mortgage maturities. From a rating perspective, S&P expects criteria development to continue, in conjunction with its subsidiary, Australian Ratings, for both existing and future structures.

Commercial mortgage pools have been used in asset-backed issues in the US for some time, and since commercial investment property has now made an appearance in the UK market, pools of commercial mortgages may not be far behind.

It is not, however, simply a matter of transferring residential mortgage criteria to portfolios of commercial mortgages, as there are a substantial number of different factors to be taken into account, not the least of which are legal.

Consideration will also be given to the types of property concerned, for example whether they are retail shops, light industrial units or factories, the prevailing market for such properties, provisions of leases if appropriate, and the implications of tenancies if they also exist. All these factors will have a bearing on the ultimate view taken as to the proportion of financing that the properties can support from a rating perspective.

16.3.2 Autoloan receivables

Securities backed by autoloans have long been common in the US but only first made an appearance in the European market in January 1990 with the securitisation of French autoloans. This was followed by an Italian transaction and then by a UK issue in July 1990, although both the UK and French issues came after a fairly lengthy period of gestation.

The analysis of risk for UK loans is complicated by the necessity of evaluating, amongst other things, the impact of the Consumer Credit Act 1974 (CCA), due to the fact that the majority of autoloans will be for a value of less than £15,001 and therefore come under the auspices of the CCA.

At the time of the French issue, launched via an offshore vehicle, no equivalent legislation existed, although now the 'Niertz Law' provides increased protection to consumers and may serve to complicate any such future issues.

The CCA implications cover a relatively wide area from the need for the lender to have the appropriate government licence, and the rights of borrowers to terminate or withdraw from credit agreements, to liability for the quality of goods supplied and how a borrower can apply for relief in the event of encountering difficulties in making payments. Viewed from a rating agency standpoint it may be possible to cover some of these risks by structural modifications or simply by increased credit enhancement levels, but it should be emphasised that without satisfactory legal comfort to support these points no amount of increased credit cover will suffice to achieve a rating.

There are therefore signs of developing markets in Europe for autoloan securitisation, but for the moment the UK and France appear to be the most promising. However, for the French market the difficulties of operating within the framework of the French 'titrisation' law may tempt other issuers to go offshore. An offshore structure does, however, prevent the securities being sold in the French domestic market and gaining a listing on the Paris bourse, because that in turn requires conformity to the securitisation law.

Evaluating consumer assets like autoloans has to be done much more by reference to individual pools of loans as performance is more lender-specific. This arises because different lenders may target diverse markets, e.g. new vehicles via dealer stocking facilities or individuals seeking second-hand cars. An evaluation of a book of autoloans depends on a number of factors, the principal ones being underwriting criteria and standards, geographical concentration, proportion of new versus second-hand vehicles and seasoning of the loans.

Considerable emphasis will be placed upon individual lenders' underwriting processes and controls, and the review will include a detailed analysis of any credit scoring system used. Further, S&P will look at how the scoring system was established and how it is updated and maintained.

Geographical concentration can cause risks if it exposes the portfolio to increased economic risk by being heavily biased to one area, and thus a regional economy.

Evidence to date indicates that autoloan performance varies significantly as between the financing of a new and second-hand vehicle, irrespective of the sophistication of any credit scoring system and 'good' underwriting. It therefore becomes important to analyse as much data as possible in relation to the historic performance of loans originated by a lender to gain an understanding of the loan book, and have some indication of its likely future development.

16.3.3 Credit card receivables

At the time of writing there has been only one public issue backed by credit card receivables originated in a country outside the US that has seen issues of asset-backed debt, and this occurred in Australia. The reasons for this lack of activity are not immediately apparent as far as the UK is concerned, although it is worth remembering that the majority of the stock of UK credit card receivables is concentrated in the hands of a few large financial institutions who may have no need to shed these assets for a variety of reasons. As far as the rest of Europe is concerned, only France really has the legal infrastructure to securitise readily, but under legislation credit cards are implicitly prevented from being used, as they do not meet the minimum maturity rule of two years. For the remainder of the 'securitised' world, only time will tell if such assets are sufficiently attractive. Potential in other markets is difficult to gauge, for while there is an apparent supply of receivables, a need or incentive to securitise has yet to appear.

As far as UK card receivables are concerned, these would be caught under the CCA, so that similar considerations would need to be addressed as in the case of autoloans. The most obvious features to be incorporated in any credit card structure would be to take account of the revolving nature of the asset and the monthly stream of repayments, as well as the redrawing element. However, it is also likely that the nature of credit card receivables will raise matters not previously encountered in the UK, but that does not mean the concerns cannot be resolved. Consumer legislation similar to the CCA, where it exists in other markets, will also need to be taken into account.

16.4 FUTURE DEVELOPMENTS

One of the most obvious questions about asset-backed finance is where its future lies. From a standing start in 1987 the UK mortgage-backed market rose to over £8bn in value in 1990, with a range of other assets starting to appear. France has made a steady if somewhat slower start but is gaining momentum. Italy came into the fold with its autoloan transaction, and may prove to be another strong source of securitisation. Australia is already developing well, albeit in slightly different fashion from its European cousins, and Scandinavia, via Sweden, has had its first essays into the securitisation market.

If appearances hold true, the gospel of asset-backed finance, both in terms of its concept and its applicability to a range of assets, is set to spread to other countries slowly but surely. It is difficult to predict the next country to enter the market, as is the most likely asset to be used. What does seem to be aparent, however, is the increasing trend towards using securitisation as a funding method, whatever the underlying motive, and unless regulators, be they financial or accounting, block such transactions completely, asset-backed debt seems to have a sound future.

17: Moody's View

Donald Selzer, Moody's Investors Service Limited

Over the past two decades a more efficient technology for lending, known as 'securitised lending', or simply, securitisation, has evolved. This technique has had a profound effect on the business of financial intermediation. In the USA, securitisation has revolutionised the country's financial services industry. In Europe, financial institutions have begun to study and to adapt securitisation to their purposes.

The opportunities resulting from the technology, particularly its potential as a more efficient form of financing, are placing strong pressures on financial intermediaries to use securitised lending as a competitive tool. The possibilities are particularly attractive for lenders desiring to capture major shares in a European-wide consumer loan origination market without having a proportional amount of capital, and for intermediaries wishing to underwrite, distribute and trade securitised assets.

17.1 BENEFITS OF SECURITISATION

Numerous factors are motivating financial intermediaries to use the financial tool of securitisation. For issuers, the securitisation of financial assets improves returns on capital by converting a spread banking business into off-balance-sheet, less-capital-intensive sources of income. Depending upon the type of structure utilised, securitisation may also offer the originator lower borrowing costs, reduced leverage, immediately available capital for expansion or reinvestment, diversification of funding sources and improved asset/liability management. For investors, asset-backed debt and equity securities offer high ratings and high yields at a time when traditional corporate bonds are declining in credit quality. For consumers, the increased competition that securitisation fosters is forcing loan originators and underwriters to share the cost savings generated by the use of this technique with them.

17.2 WHY SECURITISATION EXISTS

Securitisation first was developed in the US banking market, where flows of capital were heavily regulated. The costs associated with creating special structures and educating various participants and investors regarding these transactions were willingingly absorbed by issuers faced with deficiencies of capital increased by regulations such as restrictions on inter-state banks. Securitisation was a viable alternative source of funding because capital flows inefficiences created an opportunity for the originator to securitise notwithstanding the costs.

Over time, securitisation has gradually become accepted as yet another source of funding for lenders and as a balance-sheet and profit-generating mechanism. It allows an entity to isolate various risks, retaining some and off-loading others to parties willing to accept them, while at the same time retaining many of the economic benefits associated with the securitised assets. The entity can also use securitisation to allocate capital against each portfolio as it wishes.

Take, for example, a financial institution, which has existed for many years and is involved in many different lending markets worldwide. An investor in the debt of that entity takes on various risks, including the following:

- *interest rate risk*—the risk that its cost of funds will increase without a corresponding increase in its return on assets;
- *maturity/funding risk (asset/liability mismatches)* the risk that assets or liabilities will mature and no alternative investment or source of funds, respectively, can be found, while the corresponding assets or liabilities to be funded or refinanced remain outstanding;
- *credit risk*—the risks associated with debtors unable to filfill their obligations as agreed;
- *the risk of excessive costs*—the risk that the costs of generating revenue exceed the margins on the revenue that is being produced (e.g. personnel expenses are too high, the cost of modernising systems or buildings is too great);
- *managerial risk*—the risks created by strategic and day-to-day decisions detrimental to the organisation, that increase the probability that the institution will become insolvent.

Each of these risks is magnified by competition and by the economic environment.

The capital of the financial institution described above provides the investor with protection against these and many other risks. When a securitisation of assets occurs, the institution sells a relatively homogeneous portion of its portfolio of assets to a special-purpose issuer that typically has minimal capital (usually a special purpose corporation or trust). The same investor that invested in the institution's debt is now asked to invest in the securitised debt (or equity) instrument offered by the minimally capitalised issuer, at a yield that is often less than the yield paid by the financial institution for its own funds. Why do investors purchase such an instrument?

They invest in the security of the newly created issuer because the risks mentioned previously are absorbed by a third party rather than by capital funds. These risks are not eliminated by securitisation, rather, they are passed on to other entities.

For instance, *interest rate risk* that might exist in the financial institution is eliminated for the special-purpose issuer by matching (or tying) the interest to be earned by the investor to the interest to be earned on the securitised asset (or vice versa). That, for example, may be accomplished by requiring that the minimum mortgage rate charged to a mortgagor (whose mortgage is part of the securitised pool of assets) be set high enough so that the resulting payments will be at least sufficient to cover the funding costs and expenses of the special purpose issuer. Thus, the interest rate mismatch risk is absorbed in part by the borrowers whose debts were securitised.

If a perfect match is not feasible, an alternative must be found to lessen the remaining risk. One method might have the issuer purchase a guaranteed investment contract (GIC) that provides for any cash held by the issuer to earn interest at a rate tied to the interest rate paid to the issuer's creditors. A second method might have the originator of the assets provide the special purpose issuer with sufficient funding to set up a reserve fund, which in part is used to cushion these mismatches. In the first example, the GIC provider assumes the risk; in the second, the issuer is provided with quasi-equity that serves this function.

Maturity and funding risks might be managed by matching the maturity of the assets to the maturity of the special purpose issuer's obligation. To the extent the assets redeem early, the issuer is required to redeem its security early. Mismatches created by liabilities that mature prior to the maturity of the asset may also be covered by asset put options purchased from or by letters of credit issued by a creditworthy third party. Mismatches created by assets that might redeem prior to the repayment date on the securitised debt might be covered by a GIC. In the first example, the investor absorbs the risk of early repayment of the asset; in the second, the put or letter of credit provider absorbs the mismatch risk; in the last, the GIC provider is paid to assume the reinvestment risk resulting from early redemptions.

Credit risk is usually passed along to third parties, such as insurance companies, banks or sophisticated investors, or it remains with the originator of the assets. Insurance companies may issue pool policies or indemnity policies. Banks may issue letters of credit or subordinated loan facilities. The originator or investors may purchase a subordinated securitised debt (or equity) issue offered privately that is junior in point of security to the senior security of the special purpose issuer sold publicly. Each of these entities has agreed to assume the risk that the borrowers will default on their obligations, thus protecting the senior investor from the consequences of such a default.

The risk of excessive costs is usually absorbed by the administrator of the assets. Substantially all risk of excessive costs remains with the administrator in return for a level of remuneration usually determined by reference to the outstanding balance of the securitised pool of assets, notwithstanding the actual cost to the administrator of administering the assets and affairs of the issuer. If the administrator's collection costs increase, it cannot pass that expense on to the special purpose issuer. If the computerised systems used are more expensive to operate than had been expected or if they do not generate the efficiencies of scale anticipated, the costs of the systems cannot be allocated to the issuer. As stipulated in the documentation creating the special purpose issuer and the securitised obligation, only those costs and expenses directly related to each loan in the asset pool or certain operations of the special purpose issuer are allocated to it.

Managerial risk might be mitigated by limiting the discretion of the administrator of the assets (normally the originator and seller of the assets) in managing the asset pool and by obligating a third party at the outset to provide for asset and issuer administrative functions if the original administrator becomes insolvent. Methods of handling arrears and collections are normally agreed at the outset. Fixed procedures are created that control the receipt and payments of funds. The time periods within which all actions to be taken are stated in great detail before securitisation. Finally, a trustee may be appointed to oversee the functions being performed for the special purpose issuer by the administrator of the pooled assets. As a consequence of these controls, the discretion of the administrator is limited, and in fact is restricted to what amounts to a clerical role. The administrator can no longer use these assets to further its own financial and competitive goals with the flexibility it had when it owned the assets. Managerial risk remains with the financial institution originating the assets and with the trustee. If the originating institution fails, by ensuring that an administrator of last resort is obligated to take over the managerial functions, the risk of an interruption of asset administration is mitigated.

Each of the risks discussed above is usually allocated to a third party instead of being allowed to remain with the special purpose issuer. In return for assuming its allocated risk, each risk-taking entity normally requires compensation, which depends in part on the perceived magnitude and uncertainty of the risk, as well as on the cost of capital funds to be allocated to servicing the risk (i.e. the level of profit required by the entity on capital allocated to the risk). Securitisation takes place because the compensation—required by the third parties absorbing the various risks—in aggregate is less than the financial institution's cost of retaining these risks.

17.3 THE IMPACT OF ASSET SECURITISATION ON CORPORATE FINANCIAL HEALTH

Although securitisation is often used to take advantage of a relatively low-cost funding opportunity, the financial institution selling the assets may be, to a degree, modifying its own risk profile. The specific structures used by some institutions to securitise assets are, at times, not significantly reducing their overall credit risk. In fact some structures may be increasing it by the retention of significant off-balance-sheet residual risks relating to the assets securitised and by a shift in the institution's asset mix to assets of lower credit quality. There is a risk that the seller is transferring one of the stronger parts of its balance sheet to the special purpose issuer, thus diluting its own financial strength.

In its analysis of the impact of securitisation on a corporation's credit quality Moody's focuses on two key issues:

- How does a specific securitised transaction affect the financial institution's credit quality.
- How does the general trend of securitisation affect the credit quality of the financial sector as a whole?

In answering the first question, Moody's focus is not on whether a sale of assets is arbitrarily put on or kept off the balance sheet, but is on assessing the fundamental residual credit risks left with the originator from the asset sale and the amount of the firms' equity base that should be allocated to support the transaction. To this end, Moody's Structured Finance Group analyses the securitised transaction in detail, including structural protections furnished by the reallocation of risks to third parties, legal issues, collateral quality and support agreements, in order to rate specific structured transactions and to evaluate the residual risks left with the originator. (That analysis is discussed more fully below.) The industry specialist is then responsible for examining the credit quality of the financial institution and factoring the residual risks of securitised asset sales into the determination of its rating.

The second issue Moody's focuses on—that is, how the general trend toward securitisation affects the credit quality of the financial sector of which the financial institution is a part—is much more global in scope. Addressed within the rating process, Moody's forms its opinion of the impact of securitisation on the financial sector as a whole based on its own analysis and on the insights gained from meetings with major issuers, intermediaries and public policy-makers. The outlook thus formed is factored into specific rating conclusions.

17.4 RATING A SECURITISED TRANSACTION

For a securitised transaction to qualify for Moody's highest ratings, the transfer of risks from the special purpose issuer to third parties must be complete. Residual risks remaining with the issuer must not result in a default by the issuer on its obligations to the investors who own the rated security.

In making rating decisions for securitised transactions, Moody's reviews all vulnerable aspects of the structure that may result in an interruption or cessation of promised cash flows to the investor and analyses each in terms of the probability of its occurrence. The amount of possible loss associated with these defaults is also considered as is those features of the structure that mitigate the vulnerable points. This is what is known as the 'composite risk approach'.

The three general areas to which Moody's applies its approach in reviewing a structured transaction are the following:

- *regulatory and legal risks*—weaknesses resulting from the legal environment of relevant countries, primarily insolvency issues relating to third parties;
- *collateral credit risks*—the possibility and potential amount of losses on those assets which are relied on to furnish cash flows to the issuer of the structured transaction, and the effect that any losses might have on the issuer's ability to make interest and principal payments to investors;
- *cash flow deficiencies*—structural vulnerabilities resulting from mismatches in the timing and amounts of cash inflows and outflows of the issuer, especially in stressful economic environments.

These general areas of review are, in practice, intertwined, but have been used to simplify the description of the rating process.

17.4.1 Regulatory and legal issues

A number of legal and regulatory considerations must be reviewed in rating a transaction utilising the securitisation of assets. Normally, these include issues of insolvency and conveyance, which are applicable to any type of structure. They include:

- the impact that the insolvency of the originator, the administrator, or

other third party will have on the ability of the issuer to meet its obligations to investors;
- the impact that an issuer's insolvency will have on investors (if the issuer is not insolvency-remote);
- the impact that various forms of assignment of assets from the originator to the issuer (and trustee) will have on payments to investors;
- the impact that consumer protection laws under which the assets were originated will have on the ability of the lender to collect sums owed;
- the impact that regulators and accountants and their treatment of the transaction will have on the viability of the structure. The tax and stamp duty implications for the issuer are also reviewed.

Insolvency of third parties

The insolvency of third parties may have a significant impact on the ability of the issuer to meet its obligations to investors, unless the transaction is structured properly. If the administrator of the securitised assets is no longer able to manage the day-to-day servicing of the assets, arrears and losses could increase considerably because late payments are not followed closely and, in fact, may be missed entirely simply because no one informs the borrowers' banks that a payment is due. The insolvency of the originator of the assets could, in certain circumstances, result in its liquidator reclaiming certain assets sold or monies paid by the insolvent party to the issuer. There may also be a delay or a loss of funds passing through the accounts of the administrator. In a few cases, the administrator's insolvency may cause an acceleration in the debt obligation of the issuer. In its analysis, Moody's assesses the likelihood of such circumstances occurring, and the amount of losses that could result.

Issuer's insolvency

The insolvency of an issuer might result if: (1) cash flows to the issuer from the collateral or from any other source are not sufficient to meet the obligations of the issuer, or (2) the liabilities of the issuer (including contingent and prospective liabilities) exceed its assets.

The first instance is considered in our analysis of collateral and cash flow; the second may result from the way in which the issuer's accountants and lawyers structure the various liquidity and funding facilities. If loan facilities are worded improperly, or are paid down at speeds that do not match the amortisation of the capitalised initial expenses, liabilities may not have corresponding assets, and the issuer may become insolvent because liabilities exceed assets, even though it has ample cash flow to meet its obligations. In such a circumstance, the directors of the issuer would be faced with a decision either to continue trading, with the possibility of exposure to personal liability because of wrongful trading, or to declare the company insolvent and expose the investors to the possibility that the sale of the assets held by the issuer will not generate enough funds to pay all creditors. Therefore, funding facilities must not create a liability of the issuer that is not perfectly matched by an offsetting asset.

Forms of assignment

The analysis of the impact that various forms of assignment have on the transaction varies considerably, depending on the type of collateral securitised. With each type of asset, Moody's analyses the extent to which the borrower and others retain rights with respect to the originator. These rights, if significant, may seriously impede the ability of the issuer or the trustee to enforce the obligation of the borrower and the cash flows between the borrower and the investor. In addition, Moody's reviews the form of assignment to determine whether it is possible that the assets securitised by the issuer will be included in the insolvency proceedings if the originator becomes insolvent. If the sale of the assets is not considered to be a 'true sale', the issuer (and the trustee) may lose unrestricted access to these assets, and, as a result, lose any possibility for repayment.

Consumer protection laws

Consumer protection laws may have a significant impact on the ability of both the issuer and the administrator to enforce an obligation against the borrower. If a consumer protection law is systematically violated, even inadvertently, the borrower documentation for the entire collateral pool may be unenforceable.

Among the most significant of typical laws are the licensing of providers of credit, the requirements for disclosure to the borrower of the borrowers' obligations under the credit agreement and the consequences to them for failure to make required payments, and the need for their consent to tranfser the benefit of their obligation to another party, such as the issuer. If the licensing requirement has not been met, in some countries the debt may be unenforceable. Inadequate disclosure to the borrower, even if inadvertent, may also result in the contract being unenforceable. If the borrower's consent is needed to transfer his or her loan to the issuer, failure to do so properly may render the issuer and trustee unable to transfer servicing to the designated substitute asset administrator upon the originator's insolvency. Other consumer protection provisions might include borrowers' rights of cancellation of the loan agreement in certain circumstances without paying the entire principal balance of the loan, or the right to seek recourse of the lender if the asset purchased using the loan proceeds is defective.

Regulators and tax authorities
The objectives and the goals of regulatory authorities sometimes clash with the desire of financial institutions wishing to securitise their assets. Laws and regulations often stimulate changes in the structures of proposed transactions that may create additional credit risks, unless adequate protections are in place.

Taxation of the issuer must be considered carefully. Taxes incurred by the issuer which are not offset by cash profits could result in the issuer being unable to meet other obligations. If taxes are imposed not only on profits but also on interest paid to creditors, the special purpose issuer may be unable to meet payments to investors.

Stamp duties may also cause liquidity problems. Withholding or interest deduction rules may cause difficulties in meeting cash payments. Many other aspects of the regulatory environment in which the issuer exists that might affect its credit quality must be considered as well.

17.4.2 Collateral analysis

If principal and interest payments to investors are dependent on both the timing and amounts of cash flowing from the collateral, the predictability and variability of the cash flow generated by the assets must be assessed. To qualify for Moody's highest ratings, the credit quality of the assets that collateralise the issuer's obligations and the amount and quality of any credit enhancement protection against arrears and losses on such collateral must be sufficient to withstand an extremely harsh economic environment.

For instance, when reviewing consumer auto or credit card receivable backed transactions, Moody's examines the record of both the originator and the administrator by looking at their history of arrears, defaults and recoveries. It then determines whether the records provided are a reliable indicator of future performance. The predictive value of the historical data is directly related to the consistency of the originator/administrator's underwriting standards and collection procedures and to the economic environment at the time the portfolio performance was measured. The final step in the process is to judge how the assets would perform in the worst possible economic environments, with the severity of the test depending on the rating level. If the receivables are generated in conjunction with the manufacture of a product, Moody's analysts must consider what the impact would be on the quality of the receivables pool in the event the manufacturer becomes insolvent.

The special purpose issuer of an asset-backed security relies on the financial institution to originate the assets it purchases and, generally, has neither the employees nor the facilities to administer the asset pool and to collect arrears. A designated party, often the financial institution that sold the assets to the issuer, is responsible for the ongoing administration of the portfolio. The responsibilities of the administrator may go beyond normal duties, such as setting interest rates, operating the direct debiting scheme, and managing collections. Such additional responsibilities may include advancing funds to the issuer to provide for liquidity if borrowers are in arrears, obtaining all necessary insurance policies, remitting cash flows to the trustee and the issuer, reinvesting temporarily idle cash in short-term investments, and administering the day-to-day affairs of the issuer.

In rating such a transaction, the administrator's quality is important in determining how the securitised pool of assets will perform during adverse economic conditions. It is relevant from two perspectives: (1) the administrator's operational quality; that is, how well equipped is the administrator to carry out its day-to-day responsibilities; and (2) the administrator's credit quality, that is, its capability to fulfill the financial responsibilities, if any, it takes on as administrator.

When the asset administrator's sole line of business is the origination and administration of assets similar to those being securitised, Moody's recognises the potential link between a high level of arrears and losses for the asset pool and the insolvency of the administrator. A poorly performing pool increases the cost of administration and therefore decreases the likelihood that a replacement willing to bear this expense can be found. Unless a third party is obliged to be administrator of last resort, no one may be willing to act in this capacity upon the insolvency of the original administrator. Even when the asset administrator's financial strength is not solely dependent on the origination and administration of the assets securitised, an administrator of last resort may be needed if the original administrator is rated at a level that does not support the rating on the security.

At this stage, the guarantee, insurance policy, letter of credit, or structure is reviewed. What collateral risk does it cover? Is the credit enhancement it provides complete enough to adequately protect the investor at the rating level the transaction is structured to achieve?

In a fully supported transaction, in which all principal and interest payments to be paid by the issuer are guaranteed in full, an insurance company, bank or other party completely absorbs the risk of the collateral and the structure and makes payment to the investor if the issuer does not. The only relevant collateral issue is whether the rating of the guarantor is sufficient to support the rating of the structured security. Much of the analysis in this kind of structure centres on whether there are any exceptions to the guarantee, whether the guarantee is enforceable, and whether the guarantee will pay within the necessary time period required to ensure continuous cash flows to investors.

17.4.3 Cash flow analysis

For certain types of collateral, the third phase of our analysis involves the modelling of the structured transaction. Securitisation structures are often complex. Therefore, the ramifications of various environments and nuances in the loan documentation may not be readily evident, unless modelling is undertaken.

There is no one 'worst case' environment, because what is stressful to one structure may be a strength in another. The interactions of many different variables have to be reviewed at all points in the potential life of the transaction in order to understand the impact of economic variables on the structure.

Once Moody's is satisfied that a model reflects the structure outlined in the legal agreements, various loss, arrears, redemption and interest rate scenarios are used to stress for shortfalls. In each transaction the analysis seeks to answer the same question—will mismatches in the timing or amounts of cash flowing between the collateral and the investor result in a delay or default in payment to the investor?

Shortfalls resulting from structural defects or weaknesses could occur under many different circumstances. One of the more substantive risks for asset-backed securities often occurs because the collateralised notes pay interest and principal on a quarterly basis, while borrowers representing the underlying assets pay interest on a monthly basis and may be allowed to prepay the principal at any time. Therefore, the amount of interest earned on receivables during the quarter may be less than the amount of interest payable on the notes.

Senior/subordinated structures

Senior/subordinated structures (also known as A/B or senior/junior structures) use certain cash flows and principal distributions otherwise due to the holders of an obligation of the issuer which is subordinated to the rated security, to provide credit enhancement for the collateral backing the securities. Currently, three variations of the senior/subordinated structure are being used in the various securitisation markets: one employs an initial deposit and reserve fund for liquidity and maintenance of credit support; another maintains credit support by shifting interests in the collateral pool between the junior and the senior investors as redemptions and losses occur; and the third (most commonly used in Europe) maintains credit support by using all interest and principal cash flows from the collateral to pay the interest and principal due on the senior obligations before paying interest on the junior obligations.

Some senior/junior structures do not place any restrictions on the amount of credit losses the subordinated security will bear, while others limit the credit enhancement to the original principal balance of the subordinated security—a significant distinction that must be recognised when modelling the structure. The structure that does not place any restriction on the credit enhancement available from the subordinated tranche has all cash flows that would otherwise be paid to the junior security available for this coverage. The structure that does restrict the credit enhancement usually limits credit protection to the par amount of the junior security, and/or limits the maximum loss that will be covered from particular types of risk (e.g. special hazard, fraud).

17.5 CONCLUSION

Many different types of assets are being considered for securitisation throughout Europe. The structures are quite varied, but generally use assets with predictable and regular cash flows to fund a regular payment to investors.

The extent of the benefits of securitisation is often determined by the strategies of the asset originator, the regulatory scheme in which the originator of the securitised assets operates, and the ease with which the various risks normally associated with the ownership of the assets can be transferred to third parties. The risks that must be transferred from the special purpose issuer in order to protect its creditworthiness not only include credit risks of the collateral but also the numerous other risks that operating companies generally have. The cost of this transferral of risks determines the viability of securitisation for a financial institution contemplating its use. The issuers of asset-backed securities tend to be special purpose issuers set up solely to hold assets and to fund their purchase by the issuance of debt or equity in the form of notes or preferred shares. The tax and regulatory schemes of the various countries typically restrain the options available, as does the need to isolate the risk of the investor from that of the originator and seller of the assets to the special purpose issuer.

As a financing technique, securitisation has many benefits, but it may also alter the financial institution's own credit risk profile. Moody's therefore conducts a careful review to determine what the impact of securitisation might be on the institution's credit quality, and how its competitive environment might be altered.

The transfer of risks to third parties is used in lieu of capital to provide protection to investors in highly rated structured securities. For an asset-backed security to qualify for Moody's highest ratings, this transfer of risk must achieve a composite risk level equal to the risk levels of highly rated debt issuers worldwide.

Technical Issues

18: Legal Issues

18.1 THE UNITED KINGDOM

Simon Robinson, Slaughter and May, London,
Eilís Ferran, St. Catharine's College, Cambridge

The term 'securitisation' is often used in the UK to describe transactions in which a special-purpose vehicle acquires a pool of assets out of the proceeds of an issue of securities, the securities being secured on the assets so acquired. The securities are listed in Luxembourg or, occasionally, in London. To date the assets that have been the subject of securitisation in the UK have usually been mortgages of residential property in England and Wales, although Scottish mortgages were included in at least one issue and non-mortgage assets have also been securitised. The securitisation market is highly specialised and the sophistication of its participants is reflected in the wide variety of structures that have been adopted. Notwithstanding the diversity of structures, it is possible to identify some patterns, particularly in relation to mortgage securitisation, which is the most developed sector of the UK market. Accordingly, this chapter focuses first on mortgage securitisation before looking at the securitisation of other assets. The law is stated as at 27 September 1991.

18.1.1 The corporate structure of mortgage securitisation issues and authorisations required

Although it would be possible for an originator of mortgages to issue mortgage-backed securities, a typical structure involves the use of a special-purpose vehicle company which is established specifically to make the issue. The use of a special-purpose vehicle company facilitates the exclusion of the securitisation transaction from the originator's balance sheet (or that of its group) and can insulate the originator from risk in respect of that transaction. It can also help to secure a high (usually triple A) rating for the securities. There are a number of legal requirements that must be satisfied in relation to the structure and organisation of the special-purpose vehicle company which, in practice, will usually be a UK registered company.

First, it must be a public limited company, which was either incorporated as such or as a private company and re-registered. This is made necessary by Section 81 of the Companies Act 1985 (the '1985 Act') which makes it an offence for a private company to offer its securities to the public. Section 81 of the 1985 Act is subject to an exception for debentures which, under the terms of issue, must be repaid within five years of the date of issue and which are issued to professional investors (Section 195 of the Financial Services Act 1986, as amended by Section 202 of the Companies Act 1989). However, this exception does not apply to a typical issue of mortgage-backed securities where, as discussed below, the maturity date of the securities is more than 25 years from the date of issue (but see section 18.1.11 below). Although Section 81 of the 1985 Act is to be repealed when Part V of the Financial Services Act 1986 comes into force (expected in late 1991), it is expected that certain restrictions will continue to be imposed on the ability of private companies to issue their securities to the public. The exact nature of these restrictions is presently unclear as Part V is expected to be amended so as to implement a number of European Community directives before coming into effect.

Secondly, it must satisfy the compulsory minimum share capital requirements imposed on public companies, incorporated as such, by Sections 101, 117 and 118 of the 1985 Act and on private companies, re-registering as public companies, by Section 45 of the 1985 Act. These are that it has an allotted share capital of at least £50,000, of which at least one-quarter must be paid up on initial allotment or, as the case may be, at the time of the decision to re-register.

Thirdly, if it is registered as a public company on its original incorporation, before it commences business the vehicle company must obtain a certificate from the registrar of companies entitling it to do business and to exercise any borrowing powers. This certificate is not required if the vehicle company is incorporated as a private company and then re-registered as a public company, although in that case there are other formalities to be satisfied.

A key question that has to be determined at the outset of any mortgage securitisation is whether the originator of the mortgages wishes to remove the portfolio of mortgages which is to be sold to the issuer from its consolidated balance sheet. If it does, it has to ensure that the vehicle is not a subsidiary undertaking required to be consolidated with the originator under the requirements of the 1985 Act, as amended by the Companies Act 1989. Although the 1985 Act does provide exceptional circumstances in which a subsidiary undertaking does not have to be consolidated, it is unlikely that any of these exceptions would apply to a mortgage securitisation.

The requirement imposed on a reporting enterprise to prepare consolidated accounts for itself and its subsidiary undertakings is relatively new. It stems from the European Community Seventh Company Law Directive on consolidated accounts of 13 June 1983 (83/349/EEC) which was implemented into English law by the Companies Act 1989 by means of amendment to the

1985 Act. The relevant provisions came into force on 1 April 1990 and apply to financial years commencing on or after 23 December 1989. The new rules are tighter than those they replaced in a number of respects and many existing structures which were deliberately designed to be off-balance sheet may now require consolidation as a result of the change in the law. However, it is clear that certain structures which have been developed for the purpose of mortgage securitisation issues still fall outside the consolidation net set by the new statutory requirements. A commonly used structure in off-balance sheet mortgage securitisation issues is for all the shares in the issuing vehicle to be held by a holding company and for the shares in the holding company to be held by an independent trustee on a discretionary charitable trust. In some issues the holding company is dispensed with and the trustee holds the shares in the issuing vehicle on a discretionary charitable trust. One advantage of involving a holding company in the structure is that it can facilitate a series of securitisation issues, each made by a separate wholly-owned subsidiary of the holding company, without the need to establish a separate charitable trust in each case.

Common to both of these variations is the feature that neither the originator, nor any other member of its group, has an interest in any of the ordinary or preference shares of the issuing vehicle or, as the case may be, the holding company. This feature results in all but one of the tests set by the 1985 Act for determining whether an entity is a subsidiary undertaking being inapplicable. The remaining statutory test is not dependent on a shareholding in the relevant entity by the originator or another member of its group but, instead, is based on a right to exercise a dominant influence over the entity. This test is limited in its practical effect by the fact that the right has to be formally granted, either by provisions in the relevant entity's memorandum or articles or in a control contract, and it is almost impossible to conceive of circumstances where it would be satisfied unless that was deliberately intended by the parties involved. A provision in the vehicle's articles whereby the originator is given the right to nominate a director or directors of the company does not, of itself, constitute the grant of a right to exercise a dominant influence, as that phrase is defined by the 1985 Act. Consequently, there is still some scope for an originator (provided it has no interest in the share capital of the vehicle or its holding company) to exert a degree of management control without that giving rise to a parent/subsidiary undertaking relationship under the 1985 Act.

However, it should be noted that the new statutory rules will not be the last word on consolidation requirements. In an exposure draft of a proposed statement of standard accounting practice issued by the Accounting Standards Committee in May 1990 (ED 49, entitled *Reflecting the Substance of Transactions in Assets and Liabilities*) it is stated that there are circumstances in which mortgage securitisation vehicles which are not caught by the new statutory requirements may still have to be consolidated as if they were subsidiary undertakings in order to give a true and fair view of the financial position of the reporting enterprise and its group. Broadly speaking, a securitisation will remain on-balance sheet under ED 49 (notwithstanding that the vehicle is not a subsidiary undertaking and the mortgages have been effectively sold to it) if the vehicle is directly or indirectly controlled by and is a source of benefits or risks for the reporting enterprise (or any of its subsidiary undertakings) which are in substance no different from those that would arise if the vehicle was a subsidiary undertaking. ED 49 specifies a number of criteria which will determine whether or not a securitisation vehicle is in this position. These criteria are considered further in chapter 20.

The inclusion of an entity which is not a subsidiary undertaking in consolidated accounts requires the use of the true and fair view override under Section 227(6) of the 1985 Act (as amended by the Companies Act 1989). Section 227(6) provides that if, in special circumstances, compliance with the provisions of the 1985 Act as to the matters to be included in consolidated accounts or in notes to those accounts is inconsistent with the requirement to give a true and fair view, the directors must depart from that provision to the extent necessary to give a true and fair view. There remains some dispute whether this override, even as amended by the Companies Act 1989, allows a full consolidation of the relevant entity or whether it permits only the inclusion of the assets and liabilities of that entity in the accounts in a manner falling short of a full consolidation. The argument in favour of the latter approach is that the override does not relate to the definition of a 'group' for accounting purposes and, therefore, it does not permit the consolidation of entities falling outside that definition. In any event, the form in which the proposals contained in ED 49 will be adopted as an accounting standard remains to be seen.

Related to the consolidation requirements imposed, or to be imposed, by the 1985 Act and accounting standards are the capital adequacy requirements to which building societies and banks are subject. The capital adequacy of UK institutions authorised under the Banking Act 1987 is regulated by the Bank of England. Its supervisory policy on the treatment of loan transfers and securitisations involving banks is set out in a Notice issued by its Banking Supervision Division in February 1989 (BSD/1989/1). There are a number of strict conditions that have to be satisfied before a bank can exclude mortgages which have been sold to an issuer of mortgage-backed securities from its risk-asset ratio. These conditions include the following:

- the vehicle must have no formal recourse to the seller for losses;
- the transfer must not contravene the terms and conditions of the loans and all necessary consents must have been obtained;
- the seller must have no residual beneficial interest in the principal amount of the loan which has been transferred;

- the seller must have no obligation to repurchase any of the mortgages (although it can have an option to do so); and
- where payments are to be routed through the seller, it must be under no obligation to remit funds to the vehicle unless or until they are received from the borrower.

Where the seller continues to administer the mortgage portfolio on behalf of the vehicle, arrangements must be in place which ensure that its role is seen by the market to be nothing more than that of an agent; for instance, the seller/servicing agent must not fund the vehicle, intentionally bear any losses arising from the effect of interest rate changes on the scheme, or bear any of the recurring expenses of the scheme (although it can enter into interest rate swap agreements at market prices with the vehicle and it can make a one-off contribution to the vehicle's credit-worthiness and lend to it on a long term subordinated basis).

For building societies, capital adequacy is regulated by the Building Societies Commission. The conditions which it has set are presently contained in its Prudential Note 1988/2 entitled *Capital Requirements for Off-Balance Sheet Mortgage Lenders*, which was issued in May 1988. The Commission has undertaken a revision of this Prudential Note and in August 1991 published a consultation draft of a revised Note. The conditions that have to be satisfied before a building society can exclude mortgages which it has sold for the purposes of securitisation from its risk-asset ratio are broadly similar to those imposed on banks. The underlying purpose of these conditions is to ensure that the vehicle company is fully distanced from the building society and that it carries the credit and other risks involved without recourse to the society.

In some respects the capital adequacy requirements relating to securitisation can be viewed as somewhat academic for building societies since, as yet, none of them has issued mortgage-backed securities (although a number have investigated the possibility of securitising their mortgage assets). However, the fact that the regulatory framework has already been put in place is an indication of the interest which building societies have shown in the funding opportunities offered by securitisation and demonstrates that there is an expectation that they will become active participants in the market in future.

The vehicle company set up for the purpose of the securitisation also requires a board of directors. Under Section 282 of the 1985 Act, a public company must have at least two directors but there is no requirement that they hold shares in the company. The conditions imposed by the Bank of England and the Building Societies Commission for the exclusion of securitised mortgages from capital adequacy calculations include restrictions on the composition of the boards of off-balance sheet vehicle companies. No more than one officer of the bank or, as the case may be, the building society may be a director of the vehicle. The company must also have a qualified company secretary. The acceptable qualifications for a secretary of a public company are specified in Section 286 of the 1985 Act and include being a solicitor, a barrister, a member of any one of a number of professional accountancy bodies or of the Institute of Chartered Secretaries and Administrators.

The vehicle company must obtain a number of authorisations which are specifically related to the kind of business in which it is intended to engage. One of the most important of these is the obtaining of 'qualifying lender' status for the purposes of the Mortgage Interest Relief at Source (MIRAS) Scheme. Mention should also be made of the need for the vehicle company to be registered under the Data Protection Act 1984 and for it to obtain a licence under the Consumer Credit Act 1974. Registration under the Data Protection Act 1984 is required for the vehicle lawfully to hold to the originator's computer records relating to the relevant mortgagors (for example in the event of the originator becoming insolvent or otherwise unable to administer the mortgages on the vehicle's behalf). Failure to register when required to do so by the Data Protection Act 1984 is a criminal offence. A Consumer Credit Act 1974 licence is required not because the vehicle will make consumer loans of £15,000 or less (but see section 18.1.8 below) but because it may engage in other businesses such as debt adjusting or debt counselling, in respect of which a licence is required.

At one stage in the development of the market in the UK there was a concern that securitisations could be collective investment schemes within the definition of that term in the Financial Services Act 1986 with the result that the requirements as to authorisation of such schemes imposed by that Act and the regulatory regime established thereunder would apply. The time and costs involved in ensuring regulatory compliance would, it was generally assumed, have effectively precluded the development of the UK mortgage securitisation market. Partly as a result of representations from participants in the market, that Act was amended in 1988 with a view to making clear that securitisations are not covered by the collective investment scheme regulatory regime (Section 76(6)(f)(i) of the Financial Services Act 1986 inserted by Financial Services Act 1986 (Restriction of Scope of Act and Meaning of Collective Investment Scheme) Order 1988 (SI 1988, No. 803)). The exemption applies where the rights or interests of the participants in the scheme are represented by debt securities issued by a single body corporate and, although there are some technical disputes on the wording of the relevant provision, the general view is that the structure of the typical mortgage securitisation described in this chapter satisfies these requirements.

18.1.2 Acquisition of mortgages and related security by the issuing vehicle

The mortgages and related securities have to be sold to the issuing vehicle by the originator. The pool may comprise only mortgages in respect of which the originator is the original mortgage lender or it may include, or comprise, mortgages which it has acquired from other companies within its group or from third-party mortgage lenders. The terms of the mortgages have to be reviewed closely to ensure that they can be transferred without the need to seek the borrowers' specific consent and are otherwise suitable for securitisation. Particular difficulties may arise in circumstances where it is proposed to include mortgages originated by a number of different lenders in a securitisation pool.

The issuing vehicle can acquire the legal title to the relevant mortgages from the originator or can acquire them in equity only. Practice has differed on this point but it is now usual for the mortgages to be transferred in equity only. Provision is included for the vehicle's title to be perfected in certain circumstances relating, broadly speaking, to the solvency of the originator. Although an equitable transfer of the mortgages is inherently less secure than taking full legal title, the market and, in particular, the rating agencies are now prepared to accept that, given the peculiar structure of a mortgage securitisation and the relationship between the originator and the vehicle, the practical risk taken by the vehicle in accepting equitable transfers is usually slight. A major advantage of equitable transfers in relation to mortgages on registered land is that they are considerably cheaper and adminstratively simpler than full legal transfers. Legal transfers of mortgages on registered land must be completed by registration at the Land Registry; although in the past practice has varied, substantial fees are now payable in respect of these transfers. This cost consideration does not apply to mortgages on unregistered land as their legal transfer does not require registration but there can be complications where a mortgagor requests a further advance from his originator if the legal title to the mortgage has been transferred to the vehicle. It is therefore now also more common for mortgages on unregistered land to be transferred to the vehicle in equity only (i.e. by an agreement to transfer), but with provision for the title to be perfected in certain circumstances.

In normal circumstances it is prudent for a transferee (whether legal or equitable) of a mortgage to give notice to the mortgagor that his mortgage has been transferred. The main risk if such notice is not given is that the borrower can continue to pay the transferor, his original mortgagee, and he cannot be obliged to pay again in the event that the transferor fails to remit the payments to the transferee. However, this eventuality is unlikely to occur in the absence of fraud or mistake on the part of the transferor. It is generally accepted that the risk of an originator of securitised mortgages failing to remit payments to the vehicle is usually minimal and, as a result, it is not the practice for notices to be given to the mortgagors that their mortgages have been transferred, thus avoiding the costs, administrative inconvenience and possible perceived disruption of the originator–borrower relationships that giving notice might involve.

The omission to give notice enables the mortgagors to continue to exercise any rights of set-off they may have against the originator. The risk that the vehicle's income may be less than anticipated as a result of the exercise of set-off rights by mortgagors is more significant for deposit-taking institutions such as banks and building societies (since there can be a number of different financial relationships between the parties from which rights of set-off may arise) than for specialist mortgage financing companies (since there will usually be only one financial relationship between the parties in this case, namely, the mortgages).

Although provision is included for the issuing vehicle's title to the mortgages to be perfected and for notice to be given to the relevant borrowers where, for example, the security provided as backing for the issue is in jeopardy, the actual process of vesting of the legal titles to the mortgages in the vehicle could take some time. This is particularly the case in relation to registered land where, as mentioned above, the transfers require registration at the Land Registry before being fully effective. Until the registrations are effected, the issuing vehicle has no personal right to exercise the powers of the legal owner of mortgages on registered land. However, if the security is in jeopardy or there is some serious threat to the solvency of the originator, the vehicle will want to have the power to act immediately as if it were legal owner (and the trustee for the issue will usually require this). Accordingly, the originator is required at the outset to provide an irrevocable power of attorney (under Section 4 of the Powers of Attorney Act 1971) in favour of the issuing vehicle authorising it to exercise the powers of the legal owner in circumstances where it is entitled to call for a transfer of the legal titles to the mortgages. The originator is also required to provide an irrevocable power of attorney to such effect in favour of the trustee for the issue.

The mortgages used in mortgage securitisation are often endowment mortgages where the repayment of the capital advanced to the borrower is to be met out of the proceeds of an endowment policy. The originator will have an interest by way of security in the endowment policies and this interest must be transferred to the issuing vehicle. Again the transfer can be legal or equitable but it is now usual for the transfer to be made in equity only, with no notice being given to the relevant insurance companies. Provided the equitable transfers are made in writing, it is possible under both Section 136 of the Law of Property Act, 1925 and the Policies of Assurance Act, 1867 for them subsequently to be converted into legal transfers by the giving of notice in writing to the relevant insurance companies. The originator's interest in other insurance policies relating to the relevant mortgages, i.e. buildings insurance and mortgage indemnity insurance in respect of any mortgage loan where the value of the advance exceeds, say, 75 per cent of the valuation of the property must also be transferred to the issuing vehicle. The vehicle may also become a co-insured under other miscellaneous contingency insurances (e.g. cover for a building policy being void through non-disclosure by the borrower).

Pension-related mortgages, which provide for the capital advanced to be repaid out of the proceeds of a pension policy, are sometimes securitised. Under Inland Revenue rules no security interest can be obtained in a pension policy and therefore pension policies cannot form part of the originator's security for a loan. A borrower on a pension policy mortgage will be required to obtain separate whole-life insurance to cover the risk of his death during the currency of the loan. That insurance policy will be assigned by way of security to the originator and hence, to the issuing vehicle.

18.1.3 Investigation of title

In normal circumstances, a person proposing to acquire a mortgage would be advised to approach the transaction as if it were a transfer of the land itself and, therefore, its advisers would undertake a full investigation of the vendor's title to the mortgages, including appropriate searches at the Central Land Charges Registry and HM Land Registry. This procedure is not followed in a mortgage securitisation (where typically 2,000–3,000 mortgages are transferred) and investors are informed in the prospectus that neither the issuing vehicle nor the trustee for the issue has conducted an independent investigation of title. Instead, the originator is required to give warranties as to its title to the mortgages (but not as to the creditworthiness of the mortgagors). It is also required to undertake to accept a re-transfer of any mortgage in respect of which, in the opinion of the issuing vehicle or trustee, there occurs a material breach of warranty or some other prejudice to the vehicle's interests which would have been disclosed by inspection (e.g. structural defects). A put option onto the originator is often the only remedy for breach of warranty as the issuing vehicle's right to claim damages from the originator is usually excluded. However, if the originator is a bank or a building society particular care would have to be taken in the drafting of these warranties so as to ensure that they do not place such a degree of risk on the originator as to result in the vehicle having to be included in the originator's capital adequacy calculations.

18.1.4 Funding for the issuing vehicle—the proceeds of the issue

The issuing vehicle funds the acquisition of the mortgages and related insurance policies, etc., out of the proceeds of the issue of securities. To date the majority of issues of mortgage-backed securities have been listed in Luxembourg but some have been listed in London. Listing in either Luxembourg or London enables the securities to qualify for the 'quoted Eurobond exemption' from the obligation to deduct basic-rate income tax on interest payments. The London Stock Exchange has now taken steps to encourage listing in London by formulating a specific listing policy for asset-backed securities. This policy was published in April 1990 and took effect by means of amendment to The Stock Exchange's listing rules. The listing rules now require, *inter alia,* that the issuer of the securities should normally be a single-purpose undertaking and that there should be a trustee or other appropriate independent party representing the interest of the holders of the debt securities. The information to be included in the prospectus relating to the issue includes details of the following:

- the assets used to back the debt securities;
- the risks involved and the means whereby they are sought to be addressed;
- the issuer's rights to the assets backing the issue;
- description of the structure of the transaction and explanation of the flow of funds;
- details of the originator and other parties to the transaction.

The documents used to market the mortgage-backed securities, which are primarily an invitation telex, an offering circular and an allotment telex, are based on forms which are generally familiar to the eurobond market. If the securities are listed in London, the offering circular must comprise listing particulars which means that, *inter alia*, the general duty of disclosure imposed by Section 146 in Part IV of the Financial Services Act 1986 must be satisfied. Where the securities are listed in Luxembourg, the offering circular must (pending implementation of Part V of the Financial Services Act 1986) comply with the requirements for a full prospectus specified in Part III of, and Schedule 3 to, the 1985 Act. Although there is an exemption from the obligation under the 1985 Act to produce a prospectus where securities are offered to professional investors, this can only be used by issuers which are oversea companies or by UK companies in respect of securities which must be repaid within five years of the date of issue. This exemption has not been available in most of the mortgage securitisations to date in the UK, where typically the issuer has been a UK registered company and the contractual maturity of the securities has usually been at least 27 years. Under the Companies Act

1985 (Mutual Recognition of Prospectuses) Regulations 1991 an offering circular prepared in one Member State is, in certain circumstances, deemed to be a prospectus satisfying the requirements of the 1985 Act but those regulations do not apply to an offer of eurosecurities unless they are the subject of a generalised campaign of advertising or canvassing. A typical offer of mortgage-backed securities could not be so described.

As mentioned above, Part III of the 1985 Act is due to be replaced by Part V of the Financial Services Act 1986 at some point in 1991, and it is expected that Part IV of the Financial Services Act 1986 will also be amended at that time. At the time of writing the effect of these changes is somewhat uncertain. One expected change is that wider exemptions from the need to produce a prospectus will be made available for issues of securities which are marketed only to professional investors.

One item that is usually included in the offering circular is a statement relating to the average life of the securities. This statement is expected by the market but in view of the fact that it relates to a matter which is subject to factors outside the control of the issuing vehicle, such as the rate of early repayment of mortgage loans, it has to be clearly stated that the calculations are provided by way of illustration only and that they are therefore to be viewed with caution.

Care has to be taken to ensure that other marketing documents (such as drafts of the offering circular circulated to the management group) do not infringe any other marketing restrictions imposed by the Financial Services Act 1986. Where such documents are investment advertisements they will, prima facie, be subject to the requirement imposed by Section 57 of that Act to be issued only by or with the approval of an authorised person. By virtue of an exemption order made under Section 58(3) of the Financial Services Act 1986 (Financial Services Act 1986 (Investment Advertisements) (Exemptions) Order 1988, reg. 9) there are exemptions from Section 57 for investment advertisements issued to persons who may be broadly described as being considered to be sufficiently expert to understand the risks involved. Where it is intended to take advantage of these exemptions, it is essential to ensure that the circulation is strictly limited to persons who fit within the specified categories: these categories include authorised persons and exempted persons under the Financial Services Act 1986, governments, local authorities and public authorities, companies exceeding a specified size and certain of their directors, officers and employees.

As conditions of the obligation of the managers to subscribe the securities, the issuing vehicle, and probably also the originator, will be required to provide warranties in the subscription agreement covering a range of matters, including that the vehicle is a 'qualifying lender' for MIRAS purposes and has (or at the very best has applied for) a Consumer Credit Act 1974 licence and a Data Protection Act 1984 registration. The managers' obligations under the agreement will also be subject to a number of conditions precedent, which will usually include the obtaining of an acceptable rating for the securities.

UK mortgage-backed securities have usually been floating-rate notes, although the market has seen examples of fixed-rate securities. Interest is usually payable quarterly on floating-rate mortgage-backed securities. If definitive individual notes are issued they will be in bearer form, although a registered option may be included in order to cater for US investors. However, notes usually now remain in global form for the life of a securitisation issue in order to facilitate repayment of principal on early redemption of the underlying mortgages. Under current UK tax law, interest on bearer notes can be paid gross but, in the absence of relief under an appropriate double tax treaty, interest on registered notes must be paid net of basic-rate UK income tax (presently standing at 25 per cent). Although a provision for grossing up in the event of the imposition of withholding taxes is usually considered to be essential for euromarket securities, the strictly limited flow of funds into the issuing vehicle means that it is not included in the terms of mortgage-backed securities, including bearer notes.

Mortgage-backed securities commonly have a stated final maturity which is at least 27 years from the date of issue, although there have been a few issues of five-year notes and of commercial paper. The period of 27 years is significant in that it is likely to be two years after the final maturity date of the mortgages, which in the UK are commonly for a term of 25 years. The two-year extension allows the issuing vehicle a reasonable period to implement any necessary enforcement procedures for mortgages which are in default on final maturity. Where, as is discussed below, provision is included for the substitution of mortgages into the mortgage pool in the first few years of the issue, the final redemption date is usually correspondingly extended: for example, if there is a five-year substitution period, a 32-year maturity period would be usual.

Although the standard term for a mortgage loan in the UK is 25 years, in practice the average life of a mortgage has historically been around seven or eight years. The provisions for redemption of the notes usually reflect this and they are structured so as to maintain a balance between the interest payments being made by mortgagors and the interest payments the vehicle is required to make in respect of its mortgage-backed securities. As discussed below, provision can be included allowing, for a specified period, new mortgages to be substituted into the pool in replacement for those that have been redeemed. Such a provision enables the actual life of the issue to be prolonged which, *inter alia,* facilitates the recovery of the initial expenses of the issue over a longer period than would otherwise be possible.

The notes usually contain provisions for both optional and mandatory redemption by the issuing vehicle. Typically, mandatory redemption provisions are structured to reflect principal funds that will become available from mortgage redemptions so that the issuing vehicle will be required to make redemptions where the amount of capital receipts, net of amounts used to purchase and cancel notes and (where permitted) to purchase new mortgage loans and/or to make further advances, in a given period exceeds a specified figure. There is no clear practice relating to whether partial redemption of notes are made pro rata or by drawings. Where there is a two-tier structure comprising Class A and Class B mortgage-backed securities (this structure is described further below in the context of credit risk) there can be complex provisions establishing an order of redemption between the two classes. The (more risky) Class B notes will generally always be redeemed pro rata. There have also been examples of 'slow pay/fast pay' issues involving the division of the securities into a number of classes and the establishment of a strict order of redemption between the various classes.

The notes are invariably constituted by a trust deed. A two-tier structure can be accommodated in a single trust deed and the trustee can act for the holders of both Class A and Class B notes. The trustee could be placed in a difficult position in the event of a conflict between the interests of the Class A noteholders and the Class B noteholders and in anticipation of this, the trust deed should provide for the trustee to have regard only to the interests of the Class A noteholders in such circumstances.

One of the main functions of the trustee is to hold the security on which the notes are secured. In practice the terms on which the security is provided are set out in a separate document, usually referred to as a 'deed of sub-charge and assignment'. This terminology reflects the nature of the underlying transaction.

The first element in the security package is a charge on the issuing vehicle's interest in the mortgage pool. Where the mortgages have been transferred to the issuing vehicle in equity only, the trustee's interest is also necessarily equitable. In English law, the trustee's interest is technically an equitable sub-mortgage. Like the issuing vehicle, the trustee will want to ensure that it can obtain a legal sub-mortgage in the event of the security being in jeopardy and therefore provision for its, as well as the vehicle's, title to be perfected in certain circumstances is included. As mentioned above, irrevocable powers of attorney are given by the vehicle and the originator in favour of the trustee allowing it to exercise the powers of the legal owner of the mortgages in the event of the security being in jeopardy. This is intended to ensure that the noteholders' interests will not be prejudiced by any delay in the vesting of the legal title to the sub-mortgage in the trustee. The issuing vehicle's interest in the related life insurance and other insurance policies are also charged in favour of the trustee and the benefit of its contractual and other rights are assigned to the trustee by way of security. Finally, the typical security package also includes a first floating charge over the whole of the vehicle's undertaking and assets. This is intended to be a 'catch all' so that all of the issuing vehicle's assets are secured in favour of the noteholders by way of either a fixed or floating security. It is also a safeguard against the appointment of an administrator of the issuing vehicle's affairs since, under the Insolvency Act 1986, no administrator can be appointed where there is in place an administrative receiver of the company appointed by or on behalf of the holder of a floating charge on the whole (or substantially the whole) of a company's property.

The security in favour of the trustee has to be registered at the Companies Registry within 21 days of creation under Part XII of the 1985 Act. The detailed requirements relating to this registration obligation are to be amended by Part IV of the Companies Act 1989 (which is expected to be implemented in 1991) but the substance of the obligation i.e., registration within 21 days of creation, and the main consequence of failing to comply with it (i.e. invalidity against specified categories of persons) will be unchanged.

18.1.5 Funding for the issuing vehicle—other sources

Because of the requirements imposed on the funding of public companies by the 1985 Act the issuing vehicle must raise at least £12,500 in share capital. Other start-up funds are also frequently injected into it, commonly by the originator by means of a subordinated loan, to enable it to meet the costs and expenses of the issue and, very often, to provide it with a further capital cushion; this can be a rating agency requirement. Care has to be taken in structuring this subordinated loan to ensure, as far as possible, that it will not be held to be invalid in the event of either the vehicle's or the originator's insolvency on the grounds that it contravenes the principle of *pari passu* distribution of assets which generally applies in the event of insolvency. The need for such care to be taken came into prominence as a result of the 1975 decision of the House of Lords in *British Eagle International Airlines* v. *Compagnie Nationale Air France*. Structures have been devised which are intended to deal with this difficulty but the matter is still not free from doubt.

To the extent that the issuing vehicle's capital funds (share capital, any retained earnings and subordinated loan capital) are represented by assets other than intangibles (such as issue expenses), they are often known as the vehicle's 'tangible capital'. The tangible capital constitutes a cushion against loss and, to the extent it is invested in liquid funds, a ready source of liquidity.

During the life of the issue there will be an inflow of funds to the vehicle, representing interest payments from borrowers, MIRAS payments from the Inland Revenue and capital payments in respect of redeemed mortgages. From the outset, stringent restrictions are imposed on the vehicle with regard to the application of these funds. Whilst it will be allowed to retain some of the funds for expected expenditures, the issuing vehicle will usually be expected to deposit the bulk of the interest and MIRAS payments in specified bank accounts except to the extent that it is allowed to invest a proportion in specified liquid short-term securities. It may be permitted, at least for a time, to use a specified part of capital to make further advances and/or to purchase substitute loans or to purchase and redeem notes but the balance will also have to be deposited or invested.

The funds which an issuing vehicle may have from these various sources are not considered to be sufficient to enable it to obtain the triple A rating which the market usually demands. It is therefore necessary to build into the structure of a mortgage securitisation a series of 'enhancements' which are designed to protect the issuing vehicle against the various risks perceived to be involved.

The risks faced by an issuer of mortgage-backed securities can be divided into three categories, namely:

- credit risk;
- liquidity risk; and
- revenue risks.

Broadly, credit risk is the risk of loss resulting from defaults by mortgagors; liquidity risk is the risk that there will be a delay between the payment of interest (or sometimes principal) on securities by the issuing vehicle and the receipt of interest (or sometimes principal) from mortgagors by the issuing vehicle; and revenue risks comprise interest basis risk (i.e. an adverse interest differential between the interest rate receivable on mortgages and the rate payable on the securities) and re-investment risk (i.e. an adverse differential between the rate of return on the vehicle's liquid funds and the rate of interest payable on the securities). Different strategies have been devised to address these various risks.

Credit risk

An established means of dealing with credit risk is the adoption of a two-tier structure. This involves the issuing vehicle in making a second issue of securities (commonly referred to as Class B notes) at the same time as the issue of the main securities (commonly referred to as Class A notes). The Class B notes are structured so as to rank in point of security behind the Class A notes. Deficiencies resulting from defaulted mortgage loans (i.e. credit risk) are to be borne by the Class B notes and to the extent that such deficiencies are not made good by subsequent receipts by the vehicle, the principal of the Class B notes may, at final maturity or earlier redemption, be written down and the issuing vehicle's obligations reduced accordingly. Class B notes are usually listed but no rating is usually sought from any rating agencies. The Class B notes will often be held by the originator itself.

Another recognised method of protecting against credit risk is through insurance. The issuing vehicle can take out a pool policy whereby the insurer undertakes to indemnify the vehicle against credit risks. For this to be acceptable to the market and the rating agencies, the insurer itself has to have an appropriate rating for its claims' paying ability. The cover is usually limited to a specified proportion of the mortgage pool and the vehicle will usually only be able to claim on it in respect of any shortfall over and above the proceeds on enforcement, the surrender value of any relevant endowment policy and the proceeds of any relevant mortgage indemnity policy. If there is a provision in the pool insurance for an excess or deduction, the issuing vehicle must be able to establish that this can be met out of its tangible capital.

Recently there have been a few issues of securities backed by mortgages that were in default when the securities were initially issued. In order to minimise the credit risk and to achieve a triple A rating for the securities, these issues have been guaranteed by financial guarantee insurance policies issued by insurance companies which themselves have a triple A rating in respect of their claims-paying ability.

Liquidity risk

Liquidity risks will be met out of the issuing vehicle's liquid funds and, where the two-tier structure described above is used, through deferral of the interest payable in respect of the Class B notes. In addition, a specific liquidity fund may be established or the issuing vehicle may have the right to draw on a liquidity facility provided by an appropriately rated lender. The liquidity facility is, in effect, a form of overdraft and the lender will usually expect to be given security which ranks in priority to the Class A notes and, where used, the Class B notes. The market has also seen other variations such as an immediate right under a pool policy which is intended to provide protection against liquidity risk.

It may be noted in passing that an issuing vehicle's exposure to liquidity risk in respect of payments of principal on A Notes is usually minimal.

Revenue risks

In the simplest type of mortgage securitisation, where the mortgage pool is comprised solely of variable rate mortgages, any shortfall between the rate of interest payable by the borrowers and the interest payments and other expenses which have to be met by the issuing vehicle could, in theory, be met by an increase in the mortgage interest rate. Provision may be included in the securitisation documents requiring the interest rate on the mortgages to be increased in certain circumstances and allowing for the trustee for the issue to do this if necessary. However, it may be commercially unacceptable for one mortgage lender to move very far out of line from the rest of the market on its interest rate policy as it could result in borrowers prepaying their mortgages and refinancing elsewhere. Moreover, the terms of variable-rate mortgages may themselves impose restrictions on the lender's unilateral power to alter the interest rate. The Statement of Practice on the Transfer of Mortgages issued by the Department of Environment and HM Treasury (the 'Statement of Practice') is also relevant in this context as this requires the same policy on interest rate setting to be adopted in respect of securitised mortgages as is applied in relation to the originator's other mortgages. The Statement of Practice is considered further below. Other arrangements are therefore usually also put in place to cover this risk. These can include an agreement by the originator to provide temporary loan funding to cover any shortfall, although this would result in the mortgages having to be included in capital adequacy calculations (where applicable). Alternatively it may be possible to address the risk through a parallel loan or swap mechanism provided the counterparty is sufficiently highly rated or, if it is not, provided its obligations are guaranteed by a third party of sufficient standing. Additional arrangements, such as the creation and setting aside of special interest capitalisation funds and swap and cap provisions, are required in more complex cases where deferred interest rate mortgages and fixed-rate or stabilised-rate mortgages are included in the mortgage pool. Such arrangements need, in all cases, to be structured very carefully, bearing in mind their possible impact on the rating of the securities and such matters as accounting and applicable capital adequacy implications.

Re-investment risk

The risk of the issuing vehicle receiving a lower rate of return on its investments and deposits than its prevailing interest rate can be met, at least in part, by the vehicle entering into an agreement with an appropriately rated bank whereby the bank guarantees to provide a specified rate of return in respect of any monies deposited with it. This does not obviate the risk entirely as the guaranteed rate of return will not be as high as the mortgage rate. The remaining risk has to be met from other sources such as the vehicle's tangible capital and, where used, Class B notes. The requirements relating to the redemption of securities by the issuing vehicle out of sums representing, broadly, the proceeds of redeemed mortgages, also tend to limit the extent to which a re-investment risk can arise.

18.1.6 Rating

To date, most issues of Class A mortgage-backed securities in the UK have been assigned an AAA rating by Standard & Poor's Corporation; some have also been rated Aaa by Moody's Investors Services. Before giving a triple A rating, the rating agencies have to be satisfied that there is virtually no risk of the issuing vehicle becoming unable to meet its obligations to the holders of the rated notes. In determining this, they make projections based on 'worst-case scenarios', which typically are based on assumptions as to such matters as rate of default and decline in house prices which are much higher than the actual levels which have historically been experienced in the UK housing market. The fact that the quality of the mortgage pool is assessed on these worst-case scenarios has a strong impact on the structure of mortgage securitisation as it results in the need for the inclusion of the various 'enhancements' described above.

If the issuing vehicle is permitted to purchase substitute mortgages, this power will be subject to restrictions relating to the characteristics of the substitutes. The purpose of this is to ensure that the substitutes will be of sufficient quality so as not to jeopardise the ratings of the notes. The rating agencies will also monitor the rating of any counterparties to swap transactions to which the issuing vehicle is a party and of providers of insurance and guarantees. If they are downgraded, this could result in a consequential downgrading of the mortgage-backed securities; for example, MFC's issues were put on creditwatch when Eagle Star's long-term rating was downgraded.

18.1.7 Administration

Issuers of mortgage-backed securities do not personally administer the mortgage pool and arrangements for this have to be included in the securitisation documents. It is usual for the originator to undertake administrative functions on behalf of the issuing vehicle and it will be appointed as the vehicle's agent for this purpose. Where the mortgage pool contains mortgages which were originally advanced by third-party mortgage lenders, not in the same corporate group as the issuing vehicle, the original lenders also have to undertake some administrative responsibilities.

The Statement of Practice is relevant to the arrangements for the continued administration of the mortgage pool. This Statement of Practice prevents the transfer of mortgages on residential property to a body outside the original mortgage lender's corporate group without the consent of the borrower obtained in accordance with the Statement of Practice. It applies, therefore, to all securitisations which are intended to take mortgages off the consolidated balance sheet of the original lender. In practice an off-balance sheet mortgage securitisation can only satisfy the requirements of the Statement of Practice by having an arrangement whereby the original lender continues to conduct arrears cases as the agent of the vehicle. The arrangement between the original lender and the issuing vehicle must specify that the vehicle's policy on handling arrears will be identical to that of the original lender and that the vehicle's policy in exercising any discretion in setting of mortgage interest rates will be identical to that of the original lender.

The status of the Statement of Practice as a regulatory code is somewhat uncertain. Although there is no precise basis on which it could be legally enforced, the Housing Minister, on presenting the Statement of Practice to mortgage lenders in November 1989, invited them to adopt it; all of the major mortgage lenders, including the specialist lending companies which are the principal participants in the mortgage securitisation market, have stated that they will do so. It may therefore be that a court would now hold that mortgages offered by the mortgage lenders which have made this public declaration are effectively on terms which include adherence to the Statement of Practice unless such terms are expressly and effectively excluded (the Unfair Contract Terms Act 1977 being inapplicable as a mortgage is an interest in land).

There is, in addition, a further Code of Practice on the Transfer of Mortgages which has been formulated by the Building Societies Association and which would probably apply in a similar way in the event of a building society becoming involved in mortgage securitisation. This code covers similar ground to the Statement of Practice and the Building Societies Association has stated that there are not thought to be any conflicts between the two.

One aspect of administration that needs to be resolved at the outset is the arrangements with regard to storage of and access to the title deeds relating to the mortgage pool. The originator may be allowed to retain physical possession of the deeds provided it agrees to hold them to the order of the trustee and undertakes to permit the trustee immediate access to them at all times. Alternatively, the deeds may be deposited with a third-party depositary.

18.1.8 Further advances and substitutes

In the UK it is relatively common for a borrower to request a further advance at some stage after a mortgage loan has been made to him. If the mortgage has been securitised in the intervening period, this can give rise to some difficult commercial and legal questions. The main commercial questions relate to whether the issuing vehicle is to fund the further advance. This will depend upon the issuing vehicle having power to do so under the terms on which the securitisation has been established and upon it having sufficient available capital funds from the proceeds of prepaid mortgages and enforcement steps. The main legal consideration is to ensure that any further advance which is funded by an issuing vehicle has the benefit of the same security as the original advance. There are statutory provisions allowing for a further advance to be tacked on to the security for an original advance but there is some uncertainty whether they can apply in favour of an issuing vehicle, where, as is usual, it has only an equitable title to the mortgage and the legal title remains with the originator. The specific concern is that there is a view that the person making the further advance should do so in the same capacity as the original advance was made, i.e. as owner of the legal and equitable estates. Structures have been adopted to meet this concern which involve either the making of the advance by the originator from funds provided by the issuing vehicle or the transfer of the original loan back to the originator and the acquisition of the enlarged loan by the issuing vehicle. The latter procedure was used in early securitisations but it is now usual for the former procedure to be adopted. This procedure is considered to be effective on the basis that the right to tack remains with the originator notwithstanding the equitable assignment to the vehicle of which the borrower is unaware.

As a further advance could involve an amount of less than £15,000 the requirements of the Consumer Credit Act 1974 are also relevant. In addition to the licensing requirement already discussed, there are a considerable number of detailed requirements imposed by subordinate legislation relating, *inter alia*, to the form and content of regulated consumer credit agreements and the procedures whereby they are concluded. Failure to comply with these detailed requirements renders a loan unenforceable without a court order. The making of a further advance by an originator, rather than the issuing vehicle, can support the arguments that the original and further advance are 'unitary' and, as such, for an amount in excess of £15,000 so that the Consumer Credit Act 1974 and the rules and regulations made thereunder are inapplicable, although the position on this point is not entirely clear.

The structure of some low-start mortgage schemes, where there is an element of deferral of interest, involves the payment of the deferred amounts by the mortgagee to the borrower at the same time as the receipt by the mortgagee of the monthly mortgage payments, these mortgage payments being calculated on the basis of standard rate of interest applicable to the mortgage. This structure was developed to ensure that a borrower could obtain full MIRAS relief and, although changes to the MIRAS rules have now made it unnecessary, there can still be cases where mortgages incorporating this structure are included in the pool of securitised mortgages. Difficult questions arise in such cases as to whether the payments made by the originator should be treated as further advances. Views on this point differ but, if they are classified as further advances, it is then necessary to consider whether they can be effectively tacked onto the original security and whether there are any Consumer Credit Act 1974 difficulties of the kind outlined above.

Where the issuing vehicle is not allowed to make further advances the originator may be entitled to require a mortgage to be transferred back to it in the event that it receives a request from the relevant borrower for a further advance. Alternatively, the original mortgage may remain in the securitised pool and the originator may make the further advance on the basis of a second mortgage.

Provision is included in some mortgage securitisations allowing the issuing vehicle to acquire substitute mortgages out of available capital funds. As mentioned above, there will be restrictions on the types of loans that may be purchased by the issuing vehicle as substitutes. These restrictions will be intended to ensure that the substitutes are of sufficient quality so as not to affect adversely the rating of the securities.

18.1.9 Insolvency

The commercial desirability of a triple A rating from the rating agencies means that a mortgage securitisation has to be structured as to ensure that the risk of the issuing vehicle becoming insolvent is virtually nil. This risk can therefore be almost entirely discounted by investors, although it is something that the prospective directors of the issuing vehicle should consider before accepting their appointment. In particular, their advisers should inform them of their potential personal responsibility for the issuing company's debts under Section 214 of the Insolvency Act 1986 in the event of wrongful trading.

The possible insolvency of the originator of the mortgages is a more significant source of concern. There are provisions under the Insolvency Act 1986 whereby the transactions of a company which has gone into liquidation or administration can be unravelled. The rating agencies have to be satisfied that the sale of the mortgages and the assignment of the related policies to the issuing vehicle and the granting of security over the assets in favour of the trustee will not be put at risk in the event of the originator's liquidation or administration by virtue of an application of these provisions. The solicitors to the issuing vehicle are required to address this point in the opinion which they provide for the purpose of the securitisation. This opinion is also required to address the *British Eagle* difficulty outlined above and to provide an assessment of the likelihood of the subordination provisions proving to be effective in the event of insolvency.

18.1.10 Profit extraction

The final issue arising in a mortgage securitisation relates to the methods used to extract profits from the issuing vehicle. There are a number of alternatives. If the structure is on-balance sheet, profits can be extracted through the payment of dividends to the originator in respect of its shares; but if the structure is off-balance sheet, more complex structures have to be devised. Some profits can be remitted to the originator in the form of fees in respect of the administration services which it provides or in the form of interest on the loans which it makes available to the issuing vehicle. Another alternative is for the issuing vehicle to pay a price for the mortgages which is in excess of par, the par amount being payable at closing and the balance being payable at periodic intervals throughout the life of the issue. A third option is to establish a swap mechanism whereby the originator agrees to meet the issuing vehicle's costs and the vehicle agrees to pay the interest due from the borrowers to the originator. It is not feasible for the originator to seek to transfer only part of its rights to the mortgage pool to the issuing vehicle so that it can claim part of the interest payments since this is treated by the Inland Revenue as resulting in there being two qualifying lenders, which makes the MIRAS scheme practically unworkable. The choice of methods used to extract profits from a securitisation vehicle are invariably influenced strongly by taxation considerations.

18.1.11 Innovations in mortgage securitisations

The techniques involved in mortgage securitisation in the UK are still evolving and it is quite likely that by the time this book is published new products will have been brought to the market. In particular, there may be further developments in relation to short- or medium-term mortgage-backed securities. There is an obvious difficulty in using mortgages which have a maturity of around 25 years as security for, say, five-year notes as there is a serious capital liquidity risk on the issuer. A structure involving the grant of a put option on a portfolio of conventional (in the sense of having a maturity date of more than 27 years) mortgage-backed floating rate notes held by the issuer of five-year notes and exercisable on the maturity date of the five-year notes has been used by HMC to deal with this liquidity problem. The obligations of the put counterparty were guaranteed by a triple A-rated guarantor; Standard & Poor's was satisfied that in the circumstances the five-year notes could be assigned a triple A rating.

This structure provides a good example of the way in which products can be developed to meet the demands of originators and investors.

18.1.12 Securitisation of non-mortgage assets

Although most securitisation activity in the UK has involved mortgage assets, in principle, there is no reason why other assets which have a cash flow cannot also be securitised. One of the first examples of asset securitisation in the UK involving non-mortgage assets was the issue of five-year floating rate notes backed by motor vehicle hire purchase contracts made by Cardiff Automobile Receivables Securitisation (UK) plc ('CARS (UK)') in July 1990. These notes are listed on The London Stock Exchange and have been rated AAA by Standard & Poor's and Aaa by Moody's.

The structure of the CARS (UK) issue illustrates how the techniques and structures developed for mortgage securitisations can be adapted for securitisations of non-mortgage assets. The issuing vehicle is a wholly-owned subsidiary of a holding company, all of the shares in which are held on a discretionary charitable trust. The originator continues to administer, for a fee, the securitised pool of hire purchase contracts under a credit management agreement. It also continues to hold the legal ownership of the motor vehicles and the legal title to the assets which form part of the backing for the securities. These assets comprise the unsecured monetary obligations of the hirers under the hire purchase contracts, the proceeds of certain related credit protection insurance policies and the net proceeds of sale of any motor vehicle following repossession. In the absence of default on the notes, no notice of the securitisation assignment is to be given to the hirers and it thus takes effect in equity only. The sums payable by the hirers under the contracts are fixed monthly amounts; the risk of the issuing vehicle being unable to meet the interest payments on the floating-rate notes is addressed by guaranteed interest rate swap agreements. There is no provision for grossing-up but there is provision for mandatory redemption under certain conditions and also for the purchase of substitute assets during the first three years of the issue so as to prolong the life of the issue and restrict the operation of the mandatory redemption terms. The structure also incorporates a subordinated start-up loan agreement, a guaranteed investment contract and a revolving credit facility.

As in the case in mortgage securitisations, it may become the established practice for issues of securities backed by non-mortgage assets to be represented throughout their life by a single global note; certainly, in the CARS (UK) issue, barring exceptional circumstances, it is intended that no definitive notes will be issued.

More flexibility with regard to the structuring of the security package may be available in a securitisation of non-mortgage assets than in the case in mortgage securitisations, since, as has been discussed, the latter are subject to the constraints of real property legislation and complications such as the need to comply with the MIRAS scheme. For example, in the CARS (UK) issue the assets which form part of the backing for the securities are not assigned to the issuing vehicle itself but to another wholly-owned subsidiary of the holding company. This subsidiary, which acts as the receivables trustee, holds the assets on trust for the issuing vehicle, and certain others including the originator. Broadly, the terms of the trust provide for payments to be made to the issuing vehicle so that it is in a position to meet its obligations to the noteholders and thereafter to the other beneficiaries, including the originator. This structure facilitates the extraction of profits from the securitisation. The issuing vehicle's interest under the trust is charged in favour of the trustee for the noteholders. The trustee for the noteholders also has a fixed equitable security interest in the issuing vehicle's various contractual rights and its bank accounts and a floating charge over all of its other assets. The benefit of this security package accrues not only to the noteholders but also, in specified circumstances, to certain others including the originator, although in the event of enforcement all interests in the security (apart from amounts payable to any receiver and the trustee for the noteholders by way of fees, costs or expenses) are subordinated to the interests of the noteholders.

Where non-mortgage assets which are the subject of securitisation are consumer credit agreements regulated by the Consumer Credit Act 1974, the restrictions imposed by that Act (e.g. in respect of an owner's right to recover possession of an asset from a defaulting hirer without a court order) have to be taken into account in structuring the issue to the satisfaction of the rating agencies and so enabling the securities to obtain the required triple A rating.

18.2 FRANCE

Peter L.R. Deckers, Slaughter and May, Paris

18.2.1 Legal and regulatory framework

The securitisation ball only started rolling in France with the passing on 23 December 1988 of law (the 'Law') n° 88–1201, the third part of which creates a specific category of mutual securitisation fund, the *fonds commun de créances*. The law was supplemented by a web of delegated legislation and regulations including the following:

General

- decree (the 'Decree') n° 89–158 of 9 March 1989;
- regulation (the 'Regulation') n° 89–01 of the *Commission des Opérations de Bourse* (COB) published on 5 August 1989;
- instruction (the 'Instruction') of the COB published in September 1989;

Accounting

- regulation n° 89–07 of 26 July 1989 of the Banking Regulation Committee published on 19 August 1989;
- instructions n° 89–06 and 89–07 respectively dated 22 and 12 September 1989 of the Banking Commission;
- document (the 'Accounting Document') n° 80 of the National Accounting Council published in December 1989;

Tax

- instruction (the 'Tax Instruction') 5 I–3–89 of 17 October 1989 of the Tax Legislation Department of the Tax Administration;

- decree n° 89–801 of 27 October 1989;
- Finance laws (the 'Finance Laws') for 1990 and 1991;

Rating
- decision (the 'Rating Decision') of 23 August 1991 of the Minister of Finance;

Listing
- general decision n° 90–01 of 5 February 1990 of the Securities Exchange Council.

In addition, various replies of the Ministry of Justice to the written questions of various members of parliament indicate the authorities' approach on a number of points.

18.2.2 Characteristics of the securitisation fund

Constitution
The fund is established by the signature of the fund's *règlement* (regulations) by a management company and a custodian. The fund has no legal personality. The management company and the custodian are described in section 18.2.3 below.

The fund's regulations constitute the central contract which defines the rights of the certificate holders both in terms of payments and as against the founders. This instrument determines basic constitutional matters such as the name and duration of the fund, describes the roles of the founders (management, including the provision of information and accounts and master servicing for the management company and the custody and supervisory tasks of the custodian) and contains the detailed provisions regarding the calculation of payments to be made to certificate holders, the characteristics of the certificates, the credit enhancement mechanism and the distribution of any surplus on liquidation.

Object
The exclusive object of the fund is the acquisition, prior to certificates representing interests in the fund being issued, of loans of the same type, whose initial term exceeds two years and which are neither untransferable, nor doubtful nor disputed. These loans may be acquired only from *établissements de crédit* (which covers a considerable number of different types of financial entities, the main category being banks) or *Caisse des Dépôts et Consignations.* Once the certificates in the fund are issued, no further loans may be acquired.

Once acquired, the loans can only be disposed of by way of a single transaction if the amount of assets remaining in the fund is less that 10 per cent of the amount of the fund's certificates when initially issued (see 'Liquidation' below). In the event of the portfolio acquired containing defective loans, even if they fail to comply with the legal requirements in that, for example, their initial term was less than two years, it would not be possible to extract those loans from the fund or add loans complying with the legal criteria: post-issue substitution of loans is not envisaged.

Advances to the fund are expressly prohibited, as is the purchase by it of its own certificates. The prohibition on advances will tend to be honoured in the breach: the Accounting Document, for example, actually requires 'liquidity advances' to be accounted for as debts of the fund.

The fund's investment policy as regards money received by the fund pending its distribution to certificate holders is required to be described in the fund's regulations and is limited to: French Treasury bonds; SICAV shares or units in investment funds (*fonds communs de placement*) other than venture capital or forward market funds; and securities capable of being traded on a regulated market other than *fonds communs de créances* certificates or securities granting access directly or indirectly to the share capital of a company.

COB approval

No fund can issue its certificates unless the COB has previously approved the documents relating to the fund and satisfied itself as to the management and financial capacity of the management company. The COB's approval is granted after consultation with the *Banque de France* and cannot be issued unless an approved rating agency has rated the fund's certificates in the manner required by article 35 of the Law (see 'Rating' below).

The documents which are required to be supplied to the COB and to the *Banque de France* by the management company are listed in the Instruction and depend on whether the fund's certificates are to be the subject of a public offer or a private placement. In its rather quaint 'civil service' approach, the Instruction requires the documents to be sent to the COB and to the *Banque de France* by registered mail with postal acknowledgment of receipt.

The notions of public offer and private placement are dealt with in the Regulation. There is presumed to be a private placement where the certificates are not to be traded on a stock exchange and are to be held by corporate entities registered with the management company and where the number of certificate holders cannot exceed 25 at any time during the life of the fund. Certificates which are privately placed cannot be held by a SICAV. Any other certificates are presumed to be the subject of a public offer.

In the case of a public offer, the documents required by the COB in the Instruction are the following:

- as regards the management company, its constitutional instrument (*status*), the names of its shareholders and the number of shares held by them, a description of its technical and human resources and full details of its officers;

- the name(s) and registered office(s) of the proposed transferor(s) of the loans to the fund and, if more than one, the percentage and nominal value to be transferred by each;
- the rating document required by article 35 of the Law;
- the prospectus (or, where it is decided to deal with each of the different classes of certificates by way of separate prospectus, the prospectuses) for the issue;
- details of the auditor of the fund;
- where appropriate an information memorandum dealing with any certificates which are to be privately placed;
- the name and registered office of any guarantors of loan debtors (see 'Credit enhancement' below);
- copies of drafts of all contracts between the various entities taking part in the transaction (see section 18.2.3 and section 18.2.4 below);
- a detailed description of the guarantees and the circumstances in which they would operate; and the establishment procedure adopted (see 'Effective date' below).

The most important document, the fund's *règlement*, is not referred to in the Instruction but would, in practice, be set out *in extenso* in the prospectus, although this is not stated in the Instruction's requirements regarding the contents of the prospectus.

Effective date

In the case of a public offer, the Instruction provides two alternative procedures for the establishment of the fund to become effective. The first is that after receipt of the COB's approval, the underwriters of the issue pay or irrevocably undertake to pay the subscription monies not later than the last day of the subscription period and the custodian issues a certificate as to such payment or undertaking and sends it to the COB. The management company then acquires, on behalf of the fund, the loans described in the prospectus or such other loans as may be substituted, with notice to the rating agency, to ensure that loans transferred comply with their description in the prospectus and the legal requirements. Notice of such purchase is given by the management company to the COB by registered mail with postal acknowledgment of receipt. The fund is thereupon regarded as established and the certificates may then be publicly placed within the following month.

The second alternative is that after receipt of the COB's approval and the constitution of underwriting groups, notice of which is given to the COB, the certificates may be publicly placed during a subscription period not exceeding one month. At the end of the subscription period the management company acquires the relevant loans, with notice, in case of substitution, to the rating agency. The fund is regarded as established on the loan acquisition date, the acquisition being notified by the management company to the COB by registered mail with postal acknowledgment of receipt.

In both cases (unless, in the first case, the underwriters have actually paid the subscription monies to the fund) the chronology of loan transfer prior to certificate issue requires the loan transfer to be made on credit terms. While in most issues adopting the second alternative there will only be a scintilla of time between the two events it is not difficult to imagine circumstances in which the loan transfer has gone ahead but the issue of the certificates cannot proceed.

Certificates

The Law has deemed certificates of *fonds communs de créances* to be *valeurs mobilières* (securities) thereby conferring upon them all the features of debt or share securities. Their minimum denomination has been set at FFr10,000 and they may be in registered or bearer form although in fact dematerialised and accordingly being evidenced in any event by accounting entries (with the custodian, if registered, and with members of the French clearing system, SICOVAM, if in bearer form).

Rating

The Rating Decision has designated three agencies whose rating would be recognised in respect of *fonds communs de créances*: Euronation France Agence d'évaluation financière (A.D.E.F.), Moody's France S.A. and Standard & Poor's—Agence d'évaluation financière (Se P Adef). Article 35 of the Law requires the agency which is rating the certificates of a fund to issue a document assessing the characteristics of the loans and of the certificates (or each class, if more than one) and assessing the risks inherent in the loans. Since the COB's procedures for the approval of the fund require this document to have been issued and rating agencies may prefer to rate securities once issued, a provisional rating document may be issued to enable the COB to grant its approval, with a definitive rating being given once the certificates are issued.

Listing

Article 11 of the Regulation requires the management company to apply to the *Conseil des Bourses de Valeurs* (French securities exchange council) not later than one month after the end of the subscription period for a listing of fund certificates whose denomination is less than FFr 1 million.

Credit enhancement
Fonds communs de créances are required to provide for the risk of non-payment by the debtors of the loans transferred to be reduced in at least one of the following three ways:

- a guarantee from a credit institution (*établissement de crédit*) which does not exclude the loan transferor, or by an undertaking governed by the insurance code, which institution or undertaking cannot defer the payment of sums due to the fund;
- the issue of specific certificates bearing the initial risk of loan-debtors' default (these certificates may not be subscribed for by undertakings for collective investment in transferable securities or by individuals);
- the transfer of loans to the fund in a higher amount than that of the certificates.

The regulations of the fund must expressly state the loan-debtor default cover and in deciding whether or not to authorise the fund, the COB is required to take this cover into account.

In practice the third alternative will be little used, if at all, since the amount of the discount representing the prospective loan loss cover which the transferor of the loan portfolio to the fund would have to suffer is not eligible for deduction in the transferor's tax accounts. The tax authorities' reasoning is based on the likelihood that in exchange for accepting such a discount, the transferor will be entitled to any liquidation surplus (see 'Liquidation' below) and will therefore have an asset compensating, at least in part, the loss resulting from the discount. The transferor will only be able to provide against its right to liquidation surplus as and when the risk of default by loan-debtors becomes probable.

The relationship between the characteristics of the loans transferred (in particular the prospective loan loss rate) and the credit enhancement provided will always be critical in the rating assessment of each class of fund certificates.

Liquidation
The management company is required by the Law to wind up the fund within six months after the discharge of the last outstanding loan. Where the credit enhancement mechanism consists of a third-party guarantee or of the transfer to the fund of an additional number of loans, the entirety of the fund's certificates are likely to be redeemed well before the last of the loans is discharged. Similarly, where the credit enhancement is provided by a subordinated class of certificates, all the senior certificates are likely to be redeemed well before the discharge of the last loan.

The Decree accordingly allows a sale by the fund of the remaining loans subject to all the remaining loans being sold in a single transaction and the amount of the fund's remaining assets being less than 10 per cent of the amount of the certificates when initially issued. No guidance is given as to whether, for the purpose of this calculation, loans which have one or more instalments in arrears (even to the extent of being written off on a normal accounting basis) nevertheless continue to constitute assets of the fund or as to whether the amount of the issue refers to the nominal value or the issue price of the certificates or the net proceeds of the issue.

The most likely purchaser of the remaining loans will in practice be the transferor of the loans since it will in all probability have continued to service the loans and will require to remain in full control of the final stages of any doubtful loans, particularly where the debtors in question are still its customers.

The Law requires the regulations of the fund to specify the manner of allocation of the liquidation surplus. In the event of any surplus arising on the liquidation of a fund, after settlement of all sums due to all certificate holders, it may be distributed in the manner provided for in the fund's regulations, either by way of a premium to the certificate holders or to a third party, such as a guarantor, or to the transferor of the loans. The Law provides that the transfer agreement may provide for the transferor to be entitled to any liquidation surplus.

No fund may be wound up without the authorisation of the COB after consultation with the *Banque de France*.

18.2.3 Dramatis personae

There are three major roles in French securitisation, namely, the management company, the custodian and one or more transferors, although two of these, as well as others, may be played by the same entity. The founders are the management company (*société de gestion*) and the custodian (*dépositaire*).

Société de gestion

A management company is required to have as its sole object the management of French securitisation funds. The management company of a fund is its legal representative and represents the fund in all its relations with third parties including legal proceedings, whether as plaintiff or defendant. Accordingly, in addition to performing what is known as the master servicing task in the Anglo-American system, it also performs the trustee function in acting on behalf and protecting the interests of certificate holders *vis-à-vis* third parties.

The Regulation requires a *société de gestion* to have adequate resources in terms of organisation, technical and financial support and the reputation and experience of its officers. A share capital of not less than FFr 1.5 million is regarded as adequate financial support. In addition, no transferor of loans to a fund, or any entity associated with any transferor, can hold more than 33 per cent, less 1 share, of the shares of the management company of such fund.

Until the French securitisation market acquires a certain size, management companies may have no commercial incentive to incur the overhead and other costs of all the human and technical resources required to operate securitisation funds. The COB's requirements may accordingly be satisfied on the basis of subcontracting arrangements pursuant to which the management company has access to the requisite know-how, hardware, software, operators and other resources required to ensure proper management of the fund.

Dépositaire

A custodian is required to be an *établissement de crédit* (credit institution) or any other institution approved by the Minister of Economy. Its registered office must be in France. In addition to being a founder of the fund, the custodian has a dual role, custody and supervision. It is the custodian of all the fund's assets, including the contracts representing loans transferred to the fund and any agreement entered into by the *société de gestion* in the name of the fund, any cash or investment accounts of the fund and the books, registers and other records pertaining to the fund, such as a register of certificates where they are in registered form. The *dépositaire* will therefore systematically be responsible for the fund's bank accounts.

In addition, the custodian is required to play a supervisory role in respect of the management company's decisions and reporting obligations. It is accordingly in a possibly conflicting position of receiving instructions from the *société de gestion*, for example, requiring payment to be made to the clearing system on behalf of certificate holders and of having to ensure that the instructions comply with the regulations.

Certain of its functions will be subcontracted—for example, the custody of agreements representing the loans transferred to the fund, which are likely to be scattered in branches of the transferor(s) throughout France and to remain there after the transfer of the loans, although to the custodian's order, to enable primary servicing to continue to be effected by the transferor notwithstanding the transfer.

The transferor

French securitisation is available only to an *établissement de crédit* and to *Caisse des Dépôts et Consignations*. Since the Law requires the consent of the debtor of any loan transferred to the fund to permit primary servicing of that loan to be effected by an entity other than the transferor, the latter will in most cases continue to service the loans transferred by it. The management company therefore has no access to the loan debtors so that, from the debtor's point of view, the securitisation of his loan is without practical consequence. If it were not for the Law's requirement that the debtors must be notified of the securitisation of their loans, they would not even know that their loan had been transferred to a *fonds commun de créances*. The transferor therefore acts as the management company's debt collecting agent but in fact behaves as a principal and continues to take all important decisions in case of failure by the debtor to pay or if the debtor requests a change in the terms of his loan. The keystone principle is that the transferor must continue to treat securitised loans in the same way as its own loans. Account officers in local branches are not necessarily informed of the securitisation since knowledge of the securitisation might lead them to adopt a discriminatory approach which may be adverse to the interests of the certificate holders. As regards defaulting debtors, the fund is therefore entirely dependent on the transferor's internal systems and procedures to ensure, for example, that where a change of terms is agreed with the debtor this is documented by a new loan agreement (with a prepayment of the securitised loan) rather than by way of an amendment which, if accepted for a sufficient number of loans, would have an adverse effect on the amount or frequency of payments and require a downgrading of the fund's rating.

Ancillary roles

Where the credit enhancement mechanism is a third-party guarantee, the guarantor is required by the Decree to be an *établissement de crédit* or governed by the French insurance code. The main purpose of such a guarantee being to obtain a high rating for the certificates, the guarantor will tend to be a highly rated company.

As mentioned earlier (under *'Société de gestion'*), the management company may subcontract a number of its tasks. The higher that number and the less substantial the management company, the more the subcontractors will themselves need to be substantial.

Although not strictly ancillary, each fund is required to have an auditor (*commissaire aux comptes*) whose task includes the auditing of the annual accounts and the verification of the accuracy of a number of reports which the management company is required to publish at regular intervals (see Information requirements' below).

The issue of the certificates may be required to be fully underwritten by one or more underwriters (see 'Effective date' in section 18.2.2 above).

Multiple roles

It would be quite possible for the same entity, an *établissement de crédit*, to be, in respect of the same fund, shareholder in the management company up to 33 per cent less one share, custodian, transferor, subcontractor to the management company and to the custodian, arranger (although this term has been rejected by the COB) and underwriter of the issue of certificates, guarantor of the certificates and purchaser of the subordinated certificates. The loans transferred by it to the fund would nevertheless cease to feature on its balance sheet (although the guarantee would be shown as a contingent liability).

Rigidity
In the same way that no mechanism is provided for the substitution of sound loans for defective ones after they are transferred to the fund, there is no mechanism for the replacement of the custodian, the management company or, without the debtors' consent, the primary servicer. Subcontracting, particularly in the case of the management company, is the only way of ensuring that it has all necessary resources so as to avoid the need for it to be replaced but the position is not absolutely secure.

18.2.4 Contractual structure

In a public offer, the documentation is likely to include the following:

- The regulations of the fund entered into by the management company and the custodian (see 'Constitution' in section 18.2.2 above).
- The transfer agreement entered into between the transferor/primary servicer and the management company/master servicer and which describes the loans to be transferred, contains a number of representations by the transferor, defines the primary servicing obligations, both in terms of information to be provided and payments to be made to the *société de gestion*, and may provide for the transferor's entitlement to any liquidation surplus in the fund.
- The *bordereau* (transfer form) which legally transfers the loans to the fund and is delivered by the transferor to the *société de gestion*, takes effect as between the transferor and the fund and as against third parties on the date inscribed on the *bordereau* upon its delivery. The Decree prescribes the minimum contents of the *bordereau* and provides that where loans are transferred by reference to data stored on a computer, the *bordereau* need only mention their means of identification, their number and their aggregate amount.

  The Law provides that the delivery of the *bordereau* automatically transfers to the fund the benefit of any guarantees or security attaching to the loans transferred. The Law also provides that whenever any legal or regulatory provision requires the particulars of the owner to be stated, the name of the fund may be substituted for that of the certificate holders.

Since the fund has no legal personality the owners of the loans are the certificate holders. Where the debtors' obligations are secured over real or personal property, the transferee of the loans and of the security would in certain cases require to be registered to enable the transferee to exercise the rights of a secured creditor as against the secured property. To avoid the considerable inconvenience of registering all certificate holders (including their transferees from time to time), not to mention the impossibility of doing so in the case of bearer certificates, the Law has allowed the name of the fund to be recorded instead. There nevertheless remains the apparent conflict between the provision of the Law which stipulates that guarantees and security automatically follow on the transfer of loans by a *bordereau* and the provision which envisages that where registration is required, the transfer of security is not so automatic.

- Where the management company subcontracts some or all of its functions, it will enter into one or more agreements with subcontractors. It is important, so as to avoid subcontractors acquiring direct rights against the fund, for the fund not to be regarded as accepting the subcontractors.
- As regards the issue of the certificates, the fund, acting through its management company, would appoint arrangers (this terminology being officially disapproved of) and enter into an underwriting agreement with one or more underwriters.
- The prospectus contents are prescribed by the Instruction and divided into two parts, namely, general information and specific information. There is a good deal of overlap between the two types of information: since the prospectus also contains the regulations of the fund, substantial aspects of which are summarised in the information required by the Instruction, the resulting document is somewhat repetitious.
- Where there is a class of certificates which are to be privately placed such as subordinated certificates, there may also be an information memorandum relating to this class.

There is a chronological difficulty where the transfer of the loans to the fund takes place at the end of the subscription period (see 'Effective date' in section 18.2.2 above) in that the documents which have to be in place at the time of the COB's approval and of the launching of the issue of the certificates (in particular, the prospectus, regulations, transfer agreement, underwriting agreement and rating document) can be based only on a temporary selection of loans, the definitive selection being effected at the end of the subscription period, immediately prior to the transfer of the loans and the issues of the certificates. The transfer agreement nevertheless requires the price and the subject matter of the transfer to be sufficiently ascertainable for the agreement to be enforceable.

18.2.5 Information requirements

Holders of publicly placed certificates are entitled to the following information and reports.

At the end of each accounting period in respect of each fund under its management the *société de gestion* prepares, under the supervision of the *dépositaire*, an inventory of the fund's loans, a statement of the amount of cash and investments representing cash, the balance sheet, the profit and loss account, the annex specifying the accounting principles applied and, where applicable, a list of the guarantees or security obtained. This information is certified by the auditor.

Within three months after the end of each accounting period, the *société de gestion* issues a report including the information described above and a management report specifying:

1. the undertakings for collective investments in transferable securities (UCITS) holding certificates, indicating the percentage held by reference to the assets of the relevant fund, distinguishing the UCITS referred to in Article 26 of the Law (associated with the transferor) from the other UCITS (SICAV and *fonds communs de placement* are required by the Decree to report to the *société de gestion* of any fund, on a six-monthly basis, the number of certificates held in such fund);
2. the aggregate principal amount of loans with a prepayment clause and the percentage of total loans which they represent;
3. the changes in the rate of prepayment;
4. the aggregate principal amount of loans which are the subject of payment defaults and result in rights under any guarantee or other credit enhancement mechanism being exercised, and the percentage of total loans which they represent, where such percentage exceeds 25 per cent of the initial default cover amount;
5. the average life of the fund's loans;
6. the proportion of loans repaid as a percentage of the initially acquired principal balance of loans;
7. a detailed analysis of the results of the fund and of the factors having an effect on such results;
8. stock exchange price movements in respect of listed certificates;
9. a summary of the circumstances in which the various mechanisms covering the risk of defaults by debtors have been invoked and the extent of the remaining coverage if the payment defaults have exceeded the 25 per cent level specified in paragraph 4 above;
10. the amount and the percentage of expenses and management commissions paid during the relevant accounting period.

The auditor verifies the accuracy of the information contained in this report.

Within six weeks after the end of each half-year in the relevant accounting period the *société de gestion* prepares, under the supervision of the *dépositaire*, an inventory of the assets of each fund under its management.

Two months after the end of each first half-year of the accounting period, the *société de gestion* issues, under the supervision of the *dépositaire*, and after verification by the auditor, the fund's loan inventory, the amount of cash and the investments representing cash as well as the information described in paragraphs 1–5 above.

Each month the *société de gestion* issues a statement containing the information described in paragraphs 3–5 above in respect of any fund under its management in which the certificates or any class of certificates have a nominal value of less than FFr 1 million.

These documents and information and the annual report and accounts of the *société de gestion* are transmitted to certificate holders which expressly so request and are generally made available to the public at the premises of the *dépositaire* and of all the institutions appointed to receive applications for subscription. A copy of such documents is also sent to the COB, to the *Banque de France* and, at its request, to the relevant rating agency together with such other documents or information as these entities may require.

18.2.6 Accounting treatment

The main accounting principles which apply to securitisation funds are contained in the Accounting Document and are the following.

The loans transferred to the fund are recorded in its balance sheet in an amount equal to their nominal value. Any difference between their purchase price and that value is credited to an adjustment account also apprearing on the asset side of the balance sheet. Such difference is written off or up through the profit and loss account in the manner specified in the fund's regulations. The preferred method is on the basis of the initial actuarial rate, as revised on each calculation date to reflect actual loan loss experience. Other methods, such as following the proportion of repaid principal, may also be used.

Interest on the loans is recorded in the profit and loss account on an accruals basis. Interest which has accrued or which is due but unpaid is recorded as an asset on the balance sheet in the related assets account.

In the event of the credit enhancement mechanism proving insufficient, a provision for risk is made. On the date provided for in the regulations of the fund for resorting to the credit enhancement mechanism, the relevant loan is recorded, in the amount then due by the debtor, under 'doubtful loans', although not in the balance sheet but by way of information in the annex to the accounts.

Liquidity advances to the fund, upon being notified by the primary servicer, are recorded as debts (see 'Object' in section 18.2.2 above).

Where the enforcement of a third-party guarantee involves subrogation rights the rights against the guarantor are substituted for those against the debtor of the relevant loan.

The amount of doubtful loans is recorded in the profit and loss account as a financial expenditure: since, where the credit enhancement mechanism consists of either the transfer of additional loans or subordinated certificates, their amount will be correspondingly reduced, this will give rise to financial revenue in the profit and loss account.

The fund's certificates are recorded as a liability in the fund's balance sheet in an amount equal to their denomination, different classes being shown separately. Any premium paid on the issue of the certificates and recorded in an adjustment account appearing as a liability on the balance sheet of the fund is written off on the same basis as the adjustment account for the loans.

Interest payable on the certificates is recorded in the profit and loss account on an accruals basis. The portion thereof which has accrued or which is due but unpaid, in the case of ordinary certificates, and the portion thereof remaining unpaid, in the case of specific certificates, is recorded in a related liabilities account.

The various commissions and remuneration which are calculated by reference to the balance of the loans are recorded on an accruals basis. The expenses incurred in the establishment of the fund and the issue and placement of the certificates (although the issue and placement expenses may be included with the issue premium in the adjustment account relative to the certificates) are recorded as an asset on the balance sheet of the fund in an unallocated expenses account. Such expenses are written off through the profit and loss account on the same basis as the adjustment account for the loans.

18.2.7 Taxation

The principles outlined below originate in particular from the Tax Instruction and the Finance Laws. These principles are not exhaustive and are subject to legislative or regulatory modification or change in their application by the tax administration.

Transfer of loans

The transfer agreement, being an agreement under hand, is not required to be stamped. If it was presented voluntarily by the parties, it would only be subject to the minimal fixed stamp duty payable on unspecified agreements as provided for by article 680 of the General Tax Code.

Pursuant to paragraph 8° of article 260C of the General Tax Code, any gain realised on the transfer of the loans is exempt from value added tax and the option provided for in article 260B may not be exercised in respect thereof.

Any difference between the book value and the transfer price of the loans is a gain or a loss, as the case may be, which is an addition or a deduction in the determination of the transferor's taxable profit (or loss) for the financial period in which the transfer is made.

The non-deductibility of any discount on the transfer by way of credit enhancement of an amount of loans greater than that of the certificates issued has already been referred to (see 'Credit enhancement' in section 18.2.2 above).

The fund

The fund is a co-ownership which has no legal personality and accordingly does not fall within the corporation tax provisions.

Certificate holders

Notwithstanding its lack of legal personality, which would normally result in the certificate holders being liable to tax at the time of receipt by the fund of amounts in respect of the loans, certificate holders are only liable to tax upon sums becoming payable to them by the fund.

The tax treatment of certificates is potentially different according to whether they are issued for more than five years ('long certificates') or for five years or less ('short certificates'). Long certificates are treated like bonds and short certificates like negotiable debt certificates with potentially different consequences on the taxation of any redemption premium and of capital gains.

- *Individual certificate holders resident in France for tax purposes*
  Income from the certificates is taxable for any holder who has not elected to subject such income to a flat rate of taxation, at the progressive rates applicable to his income. Income from the certificates falls within the kinds of income from shares and bonds in respect of which certain allowances are available pursuant to article 158–3 of the General Tax Code.

  Income from the certificates received by a holder who has elected to subject such income to a flat rate of taxation is subject, with effect from 1 January 1991 to taxation at a flat rate of 18.1 per cent (including the 1 per cent social security contribution, the 1 per cent exceptional social security withholding (*prélèvement social exceptionnel*) and the 1.1 per cent general social security withholding (*contribution sociale géneralisée*)).

The treatment of any redemption premium depends on the duration of the certificates and also varies according to the proportion which the premium bears to the denomination of the certificates.

If the fund's regulations provide for the liquidation surplus to be distributed among certificate holders, the amount received is taxable for any holder who has not selected taxation at a flat rate, at the progressive income tax rates. Where a holder has selected such taxation, the flat rate is 35 per cent, with effect from 1 January 1991, plus the 3.1 per cent social security contribution and withholdings.

Capital gains realised on the sale of long certificates are taxed at 16 per cent, where the total sales of *valeurs mobilières* (securities) by a tax payer exceed a prescribed annual amount (FFr 307,600 for 1990).

Capital gains realised on the sale of short certificates are taxable in the same manner as if they constituted income.

- *Business entities as certificate holders*

The transfer of certificates held by a business entity is subject to the tax rules applicable to securities in its investment portfolio. The capital gains or losses rules applicable to securities in the investment portfolio in accordance with article 39 *duodecies et seq.* of the General Tax Code will apply to certificates held over two years.

Income on certificates and any share in the fund's liquidation surplus are subject to taxation in accordance with the normal rules and rates.

- *Non-resident certificate holders*

Unless the actual beneficiary produces evidence of a tax residence or registered office outside France, income is subject to withholding tax at the rate of 15 per cent. There seems to be a considerable divergence of views as to the nature of the evidence required to be produced to ensure that payments are in fact exempted.

Capital gains on the transfer of certificates held by a person not resident in France for tax purposes are not subject to taxation in France.

As regards duty, certain consequences follow from the fact that the fund does not have legal personality. No capital duty is payable on the subscription of certificates. Transfers of certificates are not subject to transfer duty unless the transfer is effected by notarial instrument or voluntarily presented for stamping, in either case the duty being only nominal. Where any liquidation surplus is distributed to certificate holders a duty of 1 per cent is payable on the basis that property is being divided among its co-owners. In addition, purchase and sale transactions relating to certificates are exempt from stamp duty applicable to stock exchange dealings (paragraph 6° of article 980 *bis* of the General Tax Code).

Servicing
Pursuant to paragraph 8° of article 260C of the General Tax Code, remuneration arising from the primary servicing of loans is exempt from value added tax and the option provided for in article 260B of such code may not be exercised. The commissions received by the *société de gestion* are exempt from value added tax (paragraph 1° of article 261C of the General Tax Code) but may be liable thereto if the *société de gestion* exercises the option provided in article 260B of the General Tax Code. The *société de gestion* is exempt from value added tax on the whole of its operations unless it exercises the option provided for in article 260B of the General Tax Code.

18.2.8 The state of the art

At the end of July 1991 there were over 20 funds in existence. The following is a sample of what the French market has produced so far.

- 'CAC-Titrisation', a fund formed in December 1989 and guaranteed by *Caisse Autonome de Refinancement* and *Caisse des Dépôts et Consignations* which securitised 27 loans made by the French stock exchange council's predecessor, the *Compagnie des Agents de Change*, to French stockbroking companies. The certificates were not listed.
- 'CL FCC 90–1', formed in May 1990 which was the first fund to be listed (ordinary certificates). It is a senior-subordinated structure implemented by the Crédit Lyonnais—Bear Stearns joint venture and securitises personal loans.
- 'Valora 13000 juillet 1993' formed in July 1990 securitises a single loan by *Caisse des Dépôts et Consignations* to *Crédit Local de France*. The only credit enhancement is that the debtor is a AAA risk. Interest is capitalised so that there is a single payment at the end of the three-year duration. As with the first fund, this is essentially sovereign French risk. The certificates are listed.
- 'ABM–1', formed in January 1991, acquired 12 corporate loans and is insured in part by AGF and UAP.

All the ordinary certificates of these funds (other than 'ABM–1' which is AA) have triple A ratings. A considerable number of the more recent funds involve the securitisation of a single loan. The first mortgage-loan fund is awaited, as are a number of legislative changes to permit, for example, liquidity advances, open-ended funds and the acquisition of loans with an initial duration of two years or less.

18.3 BELGIUM

Marc van der Haegen,
Liedekerke Wolters Waelbroeck & Kirkpatrick, Brussels

In practice, Belgian credit institutions seek to achieve two goals when refinancing their asset portfolios: first, the reduction of revenue or liquidity risks, (mostly as regards mortgage-backed loans since rates of interest on such loans are reviewable every five years only); and second, the improvement of their balance-sheets *vis-à-vis* the solvency ratios imposed on them by the law and the Banking and Financial Commission (see Decrees of the Belgian Banking and Financial Commission of 19 March 1991).

To achieve one or both of these goals at the same time, practitioners have already used certain exisiting legal mechanisms available to them under Belgian law. However there is no specific statute under Belgian law relating to securitisation, such as the French law relating to the *fonds commun de créance*; in the absence of such a statute, the development of securitisation in Belgium has been considerably hampered.

Under Belgian law there are several obstacles of a legal or fiscal nature to an efficient securitisation (see sections 18.3.2–4 below). Draft bills are presently under consideration (see section 18.3.7 below) in the context of the Stock Exchange reform of 4 December 1990 (see section 18.3.5 below) to facilitate securitisation. The full details of these draft bills and Royal Decrees of implementation are not yet known, so it is difficult to predict how and when securitisation will really start developing in Belgium (see section 18.3.8 below).

18.3.1 Current practice

Credit institutions currently seek to reduce revenue or liquidity risks by refinancing their loans through back-to-back loans with other credit institutions. Such refinancing does not involve any legal assignment of claims; therefore original creditor–debtor relationships are unaffected. This mechanism does not have any impact on the solvency ratios of the credit institutions which obtain the back-to-back loans.

Belgian credit institutions can achieve both goals, reduction of revenue or liquidity risks and improvement of the balance sheet, by fully assigning the loans to their customers. The formalities required to ensure the effectiveness of such transfers as against third parties are in principle fairly heavy (see section 18.3.2 below) although they can be avoided in certain circumstances. In addition, the transfer of a mortgage-backed loan attracts a registration duty of 1 per cent upon the registration of such transfer in the register of mortgages (see section 18.3.4 below).

To circumvent these difficulties, a group of notaries backed by Banque Bruxelles-Lambert (BBL), Belgium's second largest bank, initiated in 1971 an experiment of developing a secondary market in mortgage-backed loans granted by private persons to other private persons. This experiment, which did not involve the issue of new securities, did not meet much success and officially died in October 1980. However, the system that was put in place is worth describing as it might prefigure what could be done in Belgium.

The system was organised as follows. Mortgage-backed loans were embodied into titles to order (*grosses à ordre*), freely transferable by endorsement. This avoided the need to comply with the formalities of notification of the assignments of the loans to the relevant debtors and of the mention of these assignments at the register of mortgages. Furthermore, no registration duties on the assignment of the mortgage-backed loans were payable. Pursuant to the loan agreements, the borrower elected domicile at BBL and agreed to pay interest and reimburse the capital to this bank. BBL was obliged to transfer the funds to the real holder of the title. This holder could either keep the title himself or deposit it with BBL. BBL also organised a market in mortgage-backed loans, centralising offer and demand. Creditors who were willing to refinance only part of their loans were allowed to request from the notary the issuance of several titles, each of which was separately transferable.

A real estate company (Immobilière Bernheim-Outremer, a subsidiary of BBL) was charged with several ancillary tasks. First, it had to obtain a valuation of the real estate to be mortgaged. Second, it had to place a label of quality on the titles, attesting that: (1) the amount of the mortgage-backed loan and the amount of the preferred claims would not exceed 70 per cent of the current value of the real estate in the event of a forced sale; (2) the terms of the loan agreement were backed by the necessary legal opinions; and (3) a fire insurance policy was in existence, backed by a second fire insurance policy to cover the risks of a cancellation or annulment of the main fire insurance. Finally, the real estate company was responsible for the administration of the forced sale in the event of default by a borrower.

The notaries and BBL decided to put an end to this system in 1980 owing to its unsuccessful development. The technique used was considered to be too cumbersome and the system proved to be incapable of meeting the requirements of investors wanting short-term investments and tax anonymity. Except for BBL, none of the other Belgian credit institutions ever joined the market.

More recently some Belgian banks tried a securitisation experiment, which in this case involved the issue of new debt securities through special-purpose foreign-based vehicles. The Belgian Banking and Financial Commission, which is legally entrusted with the control of the solvency of banks (Article 11 of Royal Decree No. 185) commented on these experiments (1988–1989 Report, p. 41). A bank had been planning to sell a portfolio of claims to a foreign holding company, apparently based in Luxembourg, on a fiduciary basis. This holding company would have financed this acquisition by the issue of certificates and the placement of these certificates among institutional investors. The intended purpose of this transaction was to enable the bank to exclude the portfolio of claims it had sold from its capital adequacy calculations. However, after reviewing the transaction, the Banking and Financial Commission noted that the risk related to the claims was not fully and definitely transferred. It therefore decided that those claims still had to be taken into account for the weighing of the solvency of the assigning bank.

This demonstrates the Banking Commission's view that claims transferred in a securitisation process can only be taken out of the numerator of any applicable solvency ratio insofar as they are fully and definitely assigned by the assigning bank.

18.3.2 Obstacles to securitisation—publicity requirements

The main obstacles to securitisation under Belgian law are the cumbersome procedures which are required to render an assignment of claims effective as against third parties. Nonetheless, Belgian law may offer more opportunities than credit institutions are aware.

Article 1690 of the Civil Code

The assigment of a claim is valid among the parties (i.e. assignor and assignee) by their sole agreement. This assignment, however, is only effective as against third parties (including the debtor himself) when it is either notified to the debtor by service of a bailiff notice of assignment or accepted by the debtor in a notarised deed (Article 1690 of the Civil Code). This is the common law as to assignment of claims, which is applicable unless otherwise provided for by a specific statute. It is to be noted that Article 1690 is also applicable to the pledging of a claim whether civil (Article 2075 of the Civil Code) or commercial (Article 1 of the Law of 5 May 1872).

These formalities are cumbersome and expensive since they require the intervention of a bailiff or a public notary. They are also inefficient since the notification to, or the acceptance by, the debtor does not entail any real publicity but it is effective to render the assignment enforceable *vis-à-vis* all third parties.

In some respects case law and commentators have tended to render these requirements more flexible. The case law has admitted that an informal acceptance by a third party as e.g. the debtor could render the assignment enforceable *vis-à-vis* that party. But only compliance with the formalities provided for by Article 1690 make the assignment enforceable *vis-à-vis* all third parties.

Article 5 of the Law on mortgages
By complying with the formalities of Article 1690 of the Civil Code, a creditor brings the assignment only to the knowledge of the debtor. The lawmaker has been of the opinion that such publicity is not sufficient in the event of assignment of a mortgage-backed loan. Such assignment therefore is subject not only to the formalities of Article 1690, but also to those of Article 5 of the Law of 16 December 1851 on mortgages.

Pursuant to Article 5, such an assignment has to be mentioned in the margin of the inscription of the mortgage at the register of mortgages (*Conservation des Hypothèques*). The registers of mortgages are accessible to the general public.

No requirement of publicity in the event of transfer of a security
The Civil Code (Article 2279) provides that the transfer of a tangible asset is enforceable *vis-à-vis* all third parties by delivery alone. Furthermore, parties are free to embody a claim, even purely civil, into a title to bearer which, from an intangible asset, so becomes a tangible asset. The only formality required is to include a clause 'payable to bearer' in the loan agreement. The transfer of such loan would therefore be enforceable against all third parties by the sole delivery of the title and Article 1690 of the Civil Code no longer applies.

For the same reasons, the mention at the register of mortgages is not required in a case of an assignment of a mortgage-backed loan including a clause to bearer. It is generally accepted that Article 5 of the Law on Mortgages does not apply where Article 1690 is inapplicable.

The non-application of Article 1690 and Article 5 in the event of transfer of a mortgage-backed loan including a clause payable to bearer was confirmed by a recent decision of the Mons Court of Appeal (19 September 1989, *J.T.*, 1990, p. 185).

According to several authors, the same rules would apply to a loan agreement including the clause 'payable to order of . . .': in that case the loan agreement also becomes a tangible asset but its transfer is dependent, not upon the sole delivery (which is the common law for tangible assets), but upon the valid execution by the person indicated of an endorsement of the title (Van Ryn and Heenen, *Principes de droit commercial*, vol. 1, 2nd ed., no. 80; L. Raucent, 'Des créances hypothécaires à ordre ou au porteur', *Rev. prat. not.*, 1966, pp. 136–50; Genin, *Traité des Hypothèques*, no. 1243; J. De Vroe, 'Le pret hypothécaire d'Etude mobilisable', *Journal J.P.*, 1976, pp. 206–9; De page, *Traité de droit civil belge*, vol. IV, nos. 415–16 and vol. VII, no. 1114).

These principles could be a basis for the securitisation of all types of loans, even mortgage-backed, wherein it would be possible to include a clause to order or to bearer. However, the agreement of the debtor to the inclusion of such a clause will, in many cases, be difficult to obtain as this would enable the claim to circulate freely in the hands of subsequent creditors totally unknown to the debtor.

Other regimes of assignment

It may be noted that several statutes provide particular regimes of assignment of claims. Invoices, for instance, may be assigned by mere endorsement provided the assignment is notified to the assigned debtor by registered mail (Law of 25 October 1919, as amended by the Law of 31 March 1958). The same formality is also required for the transfer of consumer credits (Article 26 of Law of 9 July 1991).

18.3.3 Obstacles to securitisation—approval requirements

Mortgage-backed loans

Any enterprise which, on a regular basis, grants mortgage-backed loans to persons domiciled in Belgium has to be approved by Royal Decree and is subject to the control of *Office de Contrôle des Assurances* (i.e. the government organisation entrusted with the control of insurance and mortgage companies). In the event of an assignment of mortgage-backed loans, the assignee would also have to be approved by Royal Decree and would be subject to the same control of the *Office de Contrôle des Assurances*.

Consumer credits

In the event of an assignment of consumer credits, the assignee would have to be approved by the Minister of Economic Affairs (Article 25 of the Law of 9 July 1991).

18.3.4 Registration duties

Each assignment of a mortgage-backed loan gives rise to registration duties at a rate of 1 per cent (Article 92–2 of the Registration Duties Code) upon the registration of the assignment at the register of mortgages, which, as indicated above, is compulsory. The taxation basis is the amount of the sums guaranteed by the mortgage, excluding three years of interest (Article 93 of the Registration Duties Code).

However, such registration duties are not due on the transfer of a mortgage-backed loan including a clause to order or to bearer since a registration of a transfer of such instruments at the register of mortgages is not required.

18.3.5 The Law on Financial Transactions and Financial Markets

The Law of Financial Transactions and Financial Markets, which was adopted on 4 December 1990, and came into force on 1 January 1991, has permitted the government to authorise by Royal Decree the creation of incorporated investment companies, as well as investment funds without legal personality (*fonds commun de placement*) investing in loans exclusively (Article 122, para. 1, 7°, of the Law of 4 December 1990). Such investment companies or investment funds could serve in the future as special-purpose vehicles for the refinancing of credit institutions on the capital markets.

18.3.6 Taxation of the income of a special-purpose vehicle

The Belgian investment companies or investment funds which will be permitted to invest in mortgage-backed loans pursuant to the Law of 4 December 1990 will benefit from a regime of total tax neutrality (see Articles 143 *et seq.* of the Law of 4 December 1990).

Special-purpose vehicles which would not fall under this regime would be taxed, at a rate of 39 per cent on the spread between interest received from debtors and interest paid to bondholders, after deduction of overheads. Dividends distributed to the shareholders of the vehicle would be non-tax-deductible and would be subject to a withholding tax at a rate of 25 per cent.

18.3.7 Draft bills

A draft bill aiming at the reform of Article 1690 of the Civil Code, as well as other dependent legal provisions, is intended to be deposited by the government with the Belgian Parliament during the present session. According to the proposed draft bill, an assignment would be made enforceable *vis-à-vis* all third parties, including the debtor himself, by the sole conclusion of the assignment agreement (proposed Article 1690). However, if a debtor in good faith pays the creditor before the assignment has been brought to his knowledge, he will be validly released from his debt and will be entitled to invoke the payment *vis-à-vis* the assignee (proposed Article 1690). Article 1295 of the Civil Code, relating to set-off, as well as Article 2075 of the same Code, relating to pledges are to be modified accordingly. It is also proposed to modify the Law of 25 October 1919, as amended by the Law of 31 March 1951, with respect to the endorsing of invoices.

Another draft bill which is under consideration at the government level is designed to organise a specific institutional framework for securitisation. This would include the recognition of the concept of a 'special-purpose vehicle' to allow for the transfer of all types of claims belonging to financial or commercial organisations. The formalities of Article 5 of the Law on mortgages and the control of the *Office de Contrôle des Assurances* would be softened. Among the issues which are still heavily discussed are the question whether the special-purpose vehicle will be entitled to be financed only by shares or also by debt, and the question whether the special-purpose vehicle will be entitled to be exempt from the consolidation requirements of the promoting bank.

18.3.8 Conclusion

As they take the Cooke ratios into account, Belgian credit institutions are pressing for a modification of the law in order to allow securitisation of claims, in particular mortgage-backed claims. The Law of 4 December 1990 on Financial Transactions and Financial Markets has paved the way for the creation of investment funds in transferable loans, but there are still many obstacles which remain to be overcome before securitisation can be expected to develop in Belgium. The proposed draft bill to reform Article 1690 of the Civil Code and the related provisions will do away with certain of the formalities which presently inhibit the effective development of securitisation of loans in Belgium. But unfortunately the constraints relating to the compulsory registration of each transfer of mortgage-backed loans at the register of mortgages, and the payment of registration duties upon each such transfer are still issues to be dealt with by future legislation. Discussions are presently ongoing at government level on these various issues but no proposal has yet reached its final stages in this context.

18.4 SWITZERLAND

Patrick Hünerwadel, Lenz & Staehelin, Zurich

In the light of rapidly increasing interest rates for mortgages, securitisation of mortgage portfolios is currently discussed as a means to reduce or at least stabilise such interest rates. To date, however, the Swiss legal framework for such securitisation is very limited. There are only two main instruments that offer securitisation and pooling of mortgages. Whereas the first aims at pooling the financing and the mortgage side (*Pfandbrief-System*), the other concentrates on pooling the financing of one major mortgage (mortgage-backed bonds).

18.4.1 Pfandbrief-System

Pfandbriefe (debentures) are mortgage-backed debt securities issued by either of the two so called *Pfandbriefzentralen* in accordance with the pertaining Federal Act on debentures. The two existing *Pfandbriefzentralen* have a monopoly on the issues of such debentures. One is operated by cantonal banks (mostly state-owned banks) and the other by private banks.

The system may be briefly outlined as follows.

The proceeds of the issue of debentures by the *Pfandbriefzentrale* are used for loans to member banks of the *Pfandbriefzentrale*, which, in turn, use these funds for loans to their customers secured on Swiss real estate. The loans from the *Pfandbriefzentrale* to its member banks have to be secured by mortgages, pledges of mortgage certificates (*Schuldbrief*) or debentures. The security is perfected upon registration of these assets with the *Pfandbriefzentrale*. Accordingly, the member bank may keep the assets provided they are held separate from its other assets. The security package granted by member banks in favour of the *Pfandbriefzentrale* is in turn pledged to the debenture holders. Thus the debentures are in the last instance backed by mortgages on Swiss real estate. The obligations of the member banks towards the *Pfandbriefzentrale* and the obligations of the latter under the debentures are furthermore privileged in the event of the insolvency of any of the member banks or the *Pfandbriefzentrale*.

The debentures are issued as bearer instruments (although they could be issued as registered instruments in accordance with the law) with typical maturities of 12–15 years in denominations of SFr5,000 or SFr100,000 in the case of a public offering and in substantially higher denominations in the case of private placements. Publicly offered series of debentures are listed at the major Swiss stock exchanges. Most of these debentures are, however, kept in portfolios of institutional investors and banks as low-risk investments and liquidity reserves.

Interest on debentures is subject to Swiss withholding taxes of 35 per cent; with the exception of a possible partial refund under an applicable double tax treaty, this is a final levy for non-Swiss residents.

The practical relevance of the *Pfandbriefsystem* is, however, limited as it only accounted for the financing of some 5 per cent of the aggregate Swiss mortgage volume in 1989.

18.4.2 Bonds secured on real estate

Straight bonds may be secured on real estate in three different ways:

1. A mortgage or mortgage certificate can be created as security for the whole capital amount of the bond; a trustee is appointed to safeguard equally the interests of the bondholders, the debtor and, if different from the latter, the real estate owner.
2. A charge on real estate can be created for the whole capital amount of a loan granted by a bank or other lender and refinanced by bonds charged on the mortgage; the bonds are thus not directly secured on the real estate but on the claims of the lender against the mortgagor;
3. A mortgage can be split into a series of securities with consecutive numbers and identical terms and conditions in the form of mortgage certificates or land charge notes (so-called *Gült*), redeemable pursuant to a predetermined scheme; the securities are entered into the real estate register as one transaction specifying their number. In case these securities are not issued by the real estate owner himself, here also a trustee has to be appointed to safeguard equally the interests of the security holders, the debtor and, if different from the latter, the real estate owner.

There have been very few issues of bonds secured on real estate so far and to our knowledge all of these issues have been in the form outlined in 1 above.

For the time being, such bonds are not favoured because interest rates in the capital market are well above the actual interest rates on mortgages refinanced by other means (i.e. medium-term notes *Kassenobligationen* issued by the banks or through debentures).

Interest on bonds secured on real estate or mortgage certificates or land charge notes is subject to Swiss withholding taxes of 35 per cent; with the exception of a possible partial refund under an applicable double tax treaty, this is a final levy for non-Swiss residents. On the federal level and in some cantons the fact that a certain income is secured on Swiss real estate, Swiss mortgage certificates or land charge notes triggers federal and cantonal income taxes for investors residing in a foreign country which does not have a double tax treaty with Switzerland. Whether this should also apply in the case of interest subject to withholding taxes is presently under discussion with the respective tax authorities.

18.4.3 Conclusion

There are, to date, no working alternative methods of mortgage pooling to those described above. Although it would be possible to establish a special-purpose company that would acquire mortgages with funds granted to the special-purpose company in return for equity or debt instruments, legal and cost factors render such alternatives impossible or at least unattractive at the moment. A special-purpose company of this nature would most probably qualify as a bank and would therefore need a banking licence and be subject to costly capital adequacy requirements. Furthermore, the special-purpose company and the investor would be subject to taxes which would put the structure into a competitive disadvantage to the tax-exempt *Pfandbriefzentralen*. Finally, such investments would be restricted to domestic investors because of selling restrictions with respect to domestic real estate provided for under federal law.

Pooling on a fiduciary basis has been proposed, but here again Swiss law does not provide for an adequate vehicle to act as trustee. A contractual fiduciary solution, whereby a bank or another entity would separate a mortgage pool from its other assets and grant participations in the net cash flow of such pool to the public is perceived as bearing too many legal risks.

Finally, the present position is that mortgage pooling cannot be construed as Swiss investment funds, as mortgage certificates do not qualify as permissible investments, such investments being restricted to either negotiable securities or real estate. For the same reasons other assets have not been and are not expected to be securitised under the present legal framework in Switzerland.

18.5 AUSTRIA

Dr Otto Ortner, Ortner Pöch Foramitti, Vienna

The concept of securitisation is well established in Austria. There are two categories of securities in use for which specific assets are set aside as collateral, namely mortgage bonds and secured bank debentures. Specific legislation, summarised below, applies to each of these categories of securities.

18.5.1 Mortgage bonds

Mortgage bonds are regulated by the Statute on Mortgage Banks (*Hypothekenbankgesetz*) of 13 July 1899, [German] Imperial Legal Gazette, p. 375, introduced in Austria after the German occupation in 1938 and amended by Federal Statute no. 509 of 1974. There is also legislation of 1874 [Austrian] Imperial Legal Gazette no 48/1874, which is still applicable to banks issuing mortgage bonds under franchises issued under that legislation.

Under the Statute on Mortgage Banks, specific rules apply to banks which issue bonds secured by a pool of loans for which mortgages are inscribed on real estate located in Austria. In particular, specific governmental supervision for the entire business of such banks until their winding up is prescribed. The supervisory authority is entitled to control the records of the bank and its holdings of cash and securities. It is entitled to solicit information from the management on the conduct of the business of the bank and to sit on its board. It may veto board resolutions. The supervisory authority exercises its control by appointing a commissioner.

The activities of mortgage banks are strictly limited by statute, essentially to the acquisition and sale of and the lending on mortgages, and to lending to domestic sovereign borrowers. The term 'domestic sovereign borrowers' is a translation of *Inländische Körperschaften des öffentlichen Rechts*, which includes the Republic of Austria and its constituent provinces and the Roman Catholic Church, and also a number of entities to which this quality is conferred by law but which may be disregarded as borrowers in this context.

The designation 'mortgage bond' (*Pfandbrief*) is legally protected. Such mortgage bonds are secured up to their full nominal value by mortgages yielding at least equal interest. The law specifies other requirements for mortgages serving as collateral for mortgage bonds. They must be registered on domestic real estate as a first security and the amount secured must not exceed three-fifths the assessment value of the real estate (two-thirds on agricultural land). The law also contains rules on the valuation. The collateral mortgages are entered into a register from which they cannot be deleted without the consent of a trustee appointed by the supervisory authority. In the event of the insolvency of the mortgage bank, the holders of mortgage bonds are entitled to be preferentially paid from the assets contained in the mortgage register, which may also include sovereign bonds.

There exist provincial mortgage banks in the nine constituent provinces of the Republic of Austria. Under the charters of these provincial mortgage banks, in addition to the collateral provided in accordance with the procedures outlined above, the respective province undertakes liability in favour of the holders of mortgage bonds. Thus, the mortgage bonds are doubly secured, first by the mortgages inscribed into the register and secondly by a state guarantee, the nine constituent provinces of Austria being *Körperschaften des öffentlichen Rechts*, as described above.

18.5.2 Secured bank debentures

Secured bank debentures are issued under the Statute of 27 December 1905 relating to secured bank debentures, [Austrian] Imperial Legal Gazette, no. 213/1905. Preferential security for such debentures may be provided by entering, in a register of securities, securities for which mortgages are inscribed in a real estate record or securities issued or guaranteed by the Republic of Austria or its provinces. Safe custody of the collateral in such register is maintained by a government commissioner who also ensures that the collateral is exempt from any judicial enforcement proceedings. Set-off by a borrower of a loan which is used as collateral against liabilities of the bank to such borrower is excluded in respect of liabilities arising after notice of the entry into the collateral register has been given to the borrower. The purpose of this structure is to ensure that in the event of the insolvency of the bank, the holders of secured bank debentures are paid preferentially from the collateral kept in custody by the government commissioner in the register of collateral assets.The Statute of 24 April 1874, [Austrian] Imperial Legal Gazette no. 49, on the joint representation of bondholders, applies to both mortgage bonds and secured bank debentures. This statute provides that for the holders of each issue of bonds a joint representative is to be appointed by the court if the rights of the bondholders are in peril, in particular in the event of the insolvency of the issuer. The statute and an implementing decree regulate, in detail, the procedure in such cases.

18.5.3 Conclusion

In Austria the securing of bonds by particular pools of assets is an old-established technique for interest bearing securities in the form of mortgage bonds or secured bank debentures. Under Austrian law, the funds of minors can only be invested in investments without the risk of insolvency; mortgage bonds and secured bank debentures meet this need. S230(b) of the Austrian General Civil Code prescribes in detail the categories of securities in which funds owned by persons who are under age or under tutelage for reasons of infirmity can be invested. Such funds are labelled Wardens' Funds and, under S230(b) Wardens' Funds may be applied in the acquisition of the following securities and receivables:

1. bonds for which the Republic or one of its provinces guarantee interest and principal;
2. receivables entered into the general ledger of the federal debt;
3. mortgage bonds and municipal bonds of the domestic credit institutions admitted in accordance with the statutory regulations on the issue of such securities;
4. bank debentures issued by domestic credit institutions insofar as the credit institution is committed to satisfying in priority claims under these bank debentures and to allocating as collateral for this obligation claims of the credit institution for which the Republic is liable, securities falling with

categories 1 or 3 or 5 or cash, and this is stated explicitly on the secured bank debentures;
5. other paper stated by statutory regulations to be eligible for the investment of Wardens' Funds.

18.6 DENMARK

Thomas Federspiel, Gorrissen & Federspiel, Copenhagen

Since the latter part of the 19th century the construction and purchase of real estate in Denmark has to a very large extent been financed through loans from the Danish mortgage credit institutions. The credit institutions have in turn raised money through the issue of mortgage credit bonds (discussed below) on the Copenhagen Stock Exchange.

The present activities of credit institutions are mainly regulated by Act No. 841 of 20 December 1989 on Mortgage Credit (the 'Act') as amended, Consolidation Act No. 553 of 16 July 1991. The Act is based on two EC Directives on the Co-ordination of Laws, Regulations and Administrative Provisions relating to Credit Institutions (EC/77/780 and EEC/88/646). Under the provisions of the Act mortgage credit institutions must be approved by the Minister for Housing. At the time when the Act came into force Denmark had five approved mortgage credit institutions: three ordinary institutions (Nykredit, Kreditforeningen Danmark and BRF Kredit) and two special institutions (Industriens Realkreditfond and Dansk Landbrugs Realkreditfond).

The Act requires all new mortgage credit institutions to be formed as limited liability companies. However, the mortgage credit institutions which existed before the Act came into force as unincorporated associations can continue under their existing statutes and structure if they do not wish to transform themselves into limited companies. It is, however, expected that the majority of the existing mortgage credit institutions will transform themselves into limited companies and some have already done so.

The purpose of the mortgage credit institutions as defined in the Act is to grant loans secured by mortgage deeds registered on real estate belonging to borrowers and funded by the credit institutions' issue of mortgage credit bonds listed on a stock exchange. Mortgage credit institutions have an exclusive right to issue mortgage credit bonds. These are defined in the Act as bonds issued by an approved credit institution backed by mortgage deeds registered on real estate, provided such mortgage credit bonds are listed on a stock exchange.

The total nominal value of mortgage credit bonds listed on the Copenhagen Stock Exchange as of 31 December 1990 was DKr796,500,000,000 with a corresponding market value of DKr740,200,000,000. The total nominal value of Danish kroner bonds and other listed debt instruments was DKr1,172,400,000,000, the market value being DKr1,107,100,000,000. The total nominal value as of 31 December 1990 of all Danish shares listed on the Copenhagen Stock Exchange amounted to DKr39,953,900,000, and the market value was DKr225,600,000,000. Mortgage credit bonds do therefore play an important role in Danish public and private economy.

The bonds listed on the Copenhagen Stock Exchange and issued by mortgage credit institutions differ with respect to nominal interest, number of interest payment dates per year and the duration and amortisation terms.

Interest rates vary from 2.5 to 12 per cent per year, the lowest interest bonds being price indexed. The payment frequency with regard to interest is either once, twice or four times a year.

The bonds normally run from 10 to 35 years, the maximum being 40 years with regard to indexed bonds. Some bonds run until maturity whereas others are drawn for repayment during the term of the issue.

The international rating agencies will often rate the Danish mortgage credit institutions whereas the bonds are not rated.

Mortgage credit institutions may grant loans and issue bonds in specific series. In such cases it may be stipulated in the conditions of the series that the owners of the bonds within a specific series have claims only against such specific series or against other series which are jointly liable. The underlying loans granted by the credit institutions will also be within a specific series and the borrowers may then be liable not only for the nominal amount stipulated in the mortgage deed but also for an additional amount to cover the joint liability of the borrowers within a specific series. This additional liability cannot, however, exceed an amount equivalent to the loan. This additional liability is not a personal liability of the borrowers to the series or to the holders of the bonds, but is only secured through the obligation to pay additional amounts to the reserve fund of the series and this obligation is secured on the real estate mortgaged by the borrower.

If the system of limiting the borrowers' obligations towards a specific series does not apply the borrowers are simply liable to the credit association for the amount stipulated in the mortgage deed.

The position of the holders of mortgage credit bonds in the event of the insolvency/bankruptcy of a mortgage credit institution depends on whether a bondholder has bonds issued within a specific series under the above-mentioned specific rules or not. Holders of bonds issued within a series will have a claim against the reserve fund of that series, and in case the reserve fund does not suffice, the bondholders will have a claim against the estate of the mortgage credit institution.

Where the series system is not adopted, the position of the bondholders will be less secure in the event of the insolvency of a mortgage credit institution as the establishment of a specific reserve fund is not mandatory unless a series system with an element of joint liability is established.

Bondholders in general have preferential claims against the assets of a mortgage credit institution before ordinary creditors. However, it should be mentioned that the borrowers cannot be requested to repay their loans immediately unless otherwise agreed in the loan conditions. The bondholders do not have a direct claim against the borrowers.

In the event of the insolvency of a mortgage credit institution which has not adopted the series system the only security of the bondholders will be that their claims are preferential.

The Act contains detailed provisions with regard to the different types of loans which a credit institution may grant. These provisions specify rules applying to loans secured on different types of real estate and their valuation.

Mortgage credit institutions are not only authorised to issue mortgage credit bonds, but can also issue other kinds of securities, such as commercial paper, always provided that such bonds and securities are backed by mortgage deeds registered on real estate.

The Act provides that a mortgage credit institution established in accordance with the provisions of the Act must have a fully paid-up share capital of DKr150,000,000. Above this minimum capital requirement, the equity of a mortgage credit institution must always equal at least 8 per cent of the mortgage credit institution's assets valued in accordance with the risk attached to them and off-balance-sheet items.

The Act further provides that a mortgage credit institution must at least have listed bonds at a market value corresponding to the aggregate of 65 per cent of the institution's equity required by statute and 50 per cent of the amount by which the book value of the institution's equity exceeds the equity required by statute.

Furthermore, the Act contains other security provisions with regard to the supervision of mortgage credit institutions by public authorities, a principle of balance between payments received by the credit institutions and payment obligations of the credit institutions, and provisions dealing with the ways in which the funds of a mortgage credit institution can be invested.

As a consequence of the well established system for mortgage credit institutions, no other legal entities of any importance have been established in Denmark with a view to issuing mortgage-backed bonds on the market.

18.7 SWEDEN

Ruth Fox and Stephen Powell, Slaughter and May, London

One of the pioneers in Europe of securitisation in a form similar to that adopted in the UK was the issue in November 1990 by Osprey Mortgage Securities (No. 1) Limited ('Osprey') of notes backed by a portfolio of Swedish mortgages originated by Svensk Fastighetskredit AB 'SFK'. SFK is one of the six mortgage institutions which provide a large proportion of the finance for residential property in Sweden.

The structure of the issue was naturally dictated by the nature of mortgage lending in Sweden. Typically, Swedish homeowners finance their property by borrowing fixed-rate partially amortising loans which commonly have a term of five years. At maturity, a borrower obtains refinancing, usually through the same mortgage lender, for another five-year term at a new interest rate. When a borrower sells his property, it is usual for him and the purchaser to seek to transfer the existing loans secured on the property to the purchaser as well. By contrast to the situation in the UK, where most mortgage loans are repaid well before their contractual maturity dates, a Swedish mortgage loan is rarely prepaid: indeed, a borrower often has no right to prepay except in special circumstances.

In Sweden a security interest in land is normally created by the owner of the land pledging one or more *pantbrev*, or mortgage bonds, which are official documents issued by the official registry of real estate in Sweden upon the owner's application. Each *pantbrev* indicates the maximum principal amount which, upon the forced sale of the land, can be paid to the creditor to whom it is pledged. It is common for several *pantbrev* to be outstanding in respect of a single property, their respective priority being determined by their dates of issue and being ascertainable by an examination of the official register.

Osprey is a Jersey incorporated company wholly owned by Osprey Mortgage Securities Holdings Limited, which in turn is wholly owned by a trust company on discretionary trusts for various wildlife charities. As in UK transactions, this corporate structure is central to the treatment of the issue as off-balance-sheet for the originating group.

Osprey issued US-dollar-denominated floating-rate notes with a five-year maturity, listed on the Luxembourg Stock Exchange and having a AAA rating from Standard & Poor's. The security for the issue consists of a portfolio of fixed-rate Swedish kronor denominated loans secured on single family houses in Sweden, each having an original term of five years and due to mature between April 1994 and June 1995. The portfolio was sold to Osprey by SFK which had originated all of the loans in the course of its domestic mortgage business.

As with similar English transactions, under the terms of a management agreement SFK agreed to continue to administer the portfolio but, for technical reasons relating to the creation of valid security in Sweden, it undertook this role both on behalf of Osprey and, in some capacities, on behalf of the trustee for the noteholders.

The income of Osprey consists of the various fixed quarterly payments in kronor received from the borrowers of the mortgage loans. In order to value the loans on a comparable basis and to provide a specified single kronor interest rate which could be swapped into floating-rate US dollars to service the notes a concept of 'collateral value' was developed, reflecting as at the end of each interest period, the net present value of the anticipated cash flows (consisting of a combination of principal and interest) in respect of each mortgage in the portfolio. The collateral value concept was designed to ensure that the weighted average of the contractual interest rates generated by the individual mortgage loans would be at least equal to the yield on the portfolio required by Osprey for the swap into US dollars. The result was that the aggregate collateral value of the portfolio, when translated at a set exchange rate into US dollars, is always equal to the aggregate principal amount of the notes throughout their life. This result and the generation from kronor amounts of the US-dollar funds required to make interest payments and to redeem the notes are achieved through an interest rate and currency swap entered into with a bank counterparty, which is itself rated AAA.

As in many British securitisations, the risks of late payment or non-payment by a borrower of sums owed in respect of his loan are met by a liquidity facility and a pool policy respectively. Income is also generated for Osprey by way of interest at a guaranteed minimum rate earned on monies held on its behalf between receipt from borrowers and payment to the swap counterparty on note interest payment dates.

As is to be expected in a closed structure such as this, the noteholders are not entitled to have any payments under the notes grossed up in the event of the imposition of a withholding tax. There are provisions for the notes to be redeemed in full at Osprey's option if taxes are imposed on note payments or mandatorily if the swap is terminated without replacement and to be partially redeemed pro rata on each interest payment date mandatorily to the extent that the aggregate collateral value of the portfolio has fallen during the preceding interest period whether through the repurchase, prepayment or enforcement of any of the mortgage loans. The notes were issued in permanent global form facilitating the distribution of funds arising from these partial redemptions through the clearing systems.

As the portfolio was carefully selected broadly to match the term of the notes, and given the infrequency of early redemptions of residential mortgages in Sweden, provision for the substitution of loans or to allow Osprey to make other investments was considered unnecessary. However, in order to provide the originator with some flexibility, provision was made for it to repurchase any loan at any time in return for a cash payment equal to the collateral value of the relevant loan, triggering a corresponding partial redemption of notes.

19: Tax Issues

Fiona Ferguson, Slaughter and May, London

Tax can make the difference between whether or not the economics of a securitisation work. It therefore plays a major part in determining the structure of securitisations. The basic tax issues that arise on the securitisation of mortgages have been dealt with in other publications. This chapter aims to give only a UK overview, to draw attention to recent developments in the UK and to deal, briefly, with some of the tax considerations which arise on the securitisation of other types of assets.

The main UK tax points which have to be dealt with on UK securitisations are as follows:

- the tax position of the originator on disposal of the assets to be securitised;
- the tax treatment of the income and expenses of the purchaser;
- the establishment of a tax-efficient mechanism for passing any surplus income from the securitised assets to the originator (i.e. extraction of the 'super-profit');
- withholding tax;
- value added tax;
- stamp duty.

Tax is a complex area and one which is in a constant state of flux. It is therefore important to take professional advice on structuring particular transactions.

19.1 THE ORIGINATOR'S POSITION

Generally speaking, UK originators of securitised assets have, to date, been trading companies, such as banks or specialised mortgage companies. For them a disposal of assets at their book value to an unconnected purchaser should not generally give rise to any tax charge. Also, for a trading company expenses incurred in connection with the disposal will normally be deductible as a trading expense. The period in which a deduction is given will generally follow the originator's accounting treatment. Such expenses might include, for example, premiums for insurance policies to be used as a means of enhancing the credit standing of the securitised assets. The comparative ease with which trading companies (as opposed to investment companies) can claim tax deductions has meant that it is generally better for many of the expenses of a securitisation to be borne by the originator, rather than the purchaser, which may not be a trading company.

19.2 TAX TREATMENT OF THE PURCHASER

So far as possible matters must be arranged so that the purchaser, which will usually be a special purpose vehicle, is taxed only on its economic profit from holding the securitised assets. In principle, this may be best achieved if the purchaser is established in a tax haven, such as the Cayman Islands. However, other considerations may dictate that the purchaser is resident in the UK for tax purposes. For example, a purchaser of mortgages securing loans to UK individuals will usually need to be resident in the UK to ensure that the mortgages can remain in the MIRAS scheme. Also, where the securitised assets will require management which is to be carried out in the UK, it may be simply impractical for the purchaser to avoid being resident in the UK as a result of being centrally managed and controlled here. A purchaser of assets, such as hire purchase receivables, which require active management, would be particularly vulnerable on this point. This chapter therefore assumes that the purchaser will be resident in the UK.

(*a*) *Determining a purchaser's tax status*

A UK-resident purchaser will generally be established as a company, rather than a trust, as trusts are not entitled to interest relief on their borrowings. The purchaser's tax treatment will then depend on whether it is carrying on a trade or qualifies as an investment company for tax purposes. If it is neither, then, strictly speaking, it will remain taxable on its income but will not be entitled to a deduction for its interest or other expenses. In this connection it is important to note that the Inland Revenue take the view that a company will only qualify as an investment company if it is capable of making a profit. They also currently take the view that the profit must be commensurate with its scale of its activities, although there must be very considerable doubt as to whether this is correct.

The line between an investment and a trading activity, particularly in the financial sector, is notoriously difficult to draw. However, in practice, the activities of a purchaser will fall into one of two categories: on the one hand it may buy a portfolio of assets, such as mortgages, and hold them to maturity using the income on them to service its own debt obligations. This essentially passive role is likely to mean that the purchaser will be an investment company. At the other end of the spectrum a dynamic company which, say, buys mortgages on an ongoing basis from different originators and which originates its own mortgages should be treated as a trading company.

More recently a 'middle' category has developed in which the purchaser has basically a passive role but may buy from the originator further securitised assets at the originator's option. This option may be used by the originator in order to extend the life of bonds issued by the purchaser to finance the purchase of the assets. A purchaser in this category is likely to be treated as an investment company. In fact, recent discussions with the Inland Revenue suggest that they would not regard a mortgage securitisation vehicle as a trading company unless it originated a significant amount of mortgages itself.

(b) Tax on a purchaser's income and expenses—matching its cash flow
If the purchaser is a trading company then its tax treatment is fairly straightforward. Generally, its income from the securitised assets will be taxed on an accruals basis, and costs incurred on financing the purchase will be deductible on the same basis. The only point of doubt is that, strictly speaking, interest, other than interest payable on loans of less than one year or to certain banks recognised by the Inland Revenue, cannot be deducted as a trading expense. Such interest may, nevertheless, be deducted on a cash basis as and when paid. As a matter of practice this point is not taken by the Inland Revenue in relation to interest on debt incurred by financial trading companies in the ordinary course of their business. However, if it were to be taken the purchaser would have a potential mismatch of income and expenses—its income would be taxed on an accruals basis and its funding costs would be deductible when paid.

Other than this one slightly oddball point, trading companies are in a substantially better position than investment companies in relation to obtaining deductions for their expenses. Trading companies may deduct all expenses incurred in carrying on their trade but investment companies may only deduct 'management expenses' and certain funding costs (see below). 'Management expenses' literally means the expenses of managing the company's investments and are deductible as and when paid. Any expenses incurred in the acquisition of a company's investments may only augment the cost incurred in obtaining those investments for the purpose of computing any liability of the purchaser to tax on capital gains on disposal of the investments. A deduction in computing capital gains is nowhere near as useful a deduction as a management expense because the deduction is deferred and is given against capital and not income and therefore ultimately may not be used at all.

Turning to funding costs incurred in buying the assets, an investment company is able to deduct interest paid to certain banks with a UK banking business and also interest on loans with maturities of a year or more. It may also deduct the incidental costs of obtaining loan finance. These could include legal fees, fees paid to rating agencies and guarantee fees or insurance premiums required to be paid by rating agencies in order to obtain an appropriate rating for an issue of debt by the purchaser to finance the securitised assets.

If the investment company needs to enter into an interest rate currency swap in connection with its funding the Inland Revenue would generally treat the swap payments as taxable and deductible as and when received or paid. However, it is important to note that the basis for giving investment companies a deduction for swap payments is concessionary in nature and is currently under review by the Inland Revenue, which has recently published a further Consultative Document proposing specific legislation to deal with contracts (including swaps) which manage interest rate risk. The use of swaps as a mechanism for extracting the super-profit is considered below. Currency swaps for investment companies, which give rise to their own problems, are also dealt with below.

In addition to the restrictions on deductions investment company status also gives rise to various other inflexibilities. It is not possible, for example, for an investment company to obtain a tax deduction for issuing debt at a 'shallow' discount, that is a discount of less than the smaller of 15 per cent of the redemption price of the debt or 0.5 per cent of the redemption price for each complete year between the date of issue and redemption. Also an investment company should generally avoid purchasing accrued income (e.g. accrued interest on mortgages) because it is likely to be taxed fully on the income eventually received without a deduction for the monies paid for the accrued income.

As an investment company's income and expenses are taxable and deductible on a cash basis it is essential to match them, so far as possible, in each accounting period of the company. For example, if interest is received on the securitised assets before the end of an accounting period of the company but interest on the related debt issued by the purchaser is not paid until after the end of the same accounting period the interest expense will not be available to shelter the income.

On debt receivables matching interest streams should be quite straightforward. On hire purchase or lease receivables the purchaser will usually be taxable on the discount profit it makes as a result of buying the receivable for a price which is lower than the amount due if the receivable is ultimately paid in full. Tax will be payable on a cash basis when the receivable is discharged and the discount profit matures. Over the life of the receivables the purchaser is likely to pay interest on its funding on a regular basis. However, as each receivable matures and funds the interest expense only part of the proceeds of the receivable (representing the discount profit) will be taxable. This produces the result that there is initially an excess of deductions over taxable income. The deductions can then be carried forward to shelter discount profit in future accounting periods in which there is likely to be an excess of discount profit over interest expense.

Front-end costs, if borne by the purchaser, will usually throw up a loss which may be carried forward to offset future income. They may effectively provide a cushion against mismatches later.

(*c*) *Some common problems*

Some securitisation issues are established on the basis that in order to make the bonds issued by the purchaser to acquire the assets more attractive, there are two classes of bonds, A notes and B notes. The A notes are conventional bonds but the B notes pay a higher rate of interest and take the first exposure to any losses arising on the securitised assets. This is achieved by rolling up interest due on the B notes where the purchaser has an income deficit.

It may be argued that this exposure means that the return on the B notes is dependent on the results of the purchaser's business and that the return on the B notes therefore constitutes a distribution for tax purposes. This would mean that interest on the B notes would not be deductible in computing the purchaser's profits and would give rise to a liability for the purchaser to account for advance corporation tax. There is not complete agreement on whether this argument is correct but there is clearly a risk here especially if rolled-up interest is wiped out at the end of the securitisation to prevent an insolvent liquidation. As a matter of practice the Inland Revenue will not normally give any clearance on whether any particular payment constitutes a distribution so it is usual to work on the assumption that the argument is correct. Therefore, to avoid non-deductibility for interest on the B notes it would be normal to endeavour to ensure that the B notes are held by companies within the charge to UK corporation tax because this type of interest paid to such companies is exempted from constituting a distribution and therefore remains deductible. Subject to this point the B notes cause no difficulty for a self-standing purchaser. However, where the purchaser is expected to be a member of a UK tax group it would also be important to ensure that the B notes do not 'de-group' the purchaser from its parent company, by constituting the investors in the B notes 'equity holders' in the purchaser and thereby driving down the proportion of the 'equity' owned by the purchaser's parent below the 75 per cent necessary for it to qualify as a member of its parent's UK tax group.

To date securitisation issues in the UK have generally involved the issue of sterling bonds to purchase sterling assets. This is because the introduction of foreign currency into a UK-based transaction can give rise to difficulties unless there is very careful tax planning. The basic problem arises from the fact that for investment companies (and also for financial trading companies in certain circumstances) exchange gains and losses arising on repayment of borrowings are outside the scope of tax, but currency gains and losses on assets bought with foreign currency borrowings or arising in connection with currency swaps are taxable. The mismatch can, of course, work for or against a taxpayer but it gives rise to a situation in which, although a taxpayer may have no economic currency exposure, because its borrowings and assets are matched, it has a tax exposure. The Inland Revenue published a Consultative Document in early 1991 with proposals which may eliminate this problem in this context but they have not yet been implemented.

19.3 EXTRACTING THE SUPER-PROFIT

As a preliminary point, whether the purchaser is being established as a trading or an investment company it is advisable for it to retain at least a small margin on the securitisation. Otherwise its status as either a trading or investment company may be challenged. Subject to that, the originator will usually wish to keep any profit on the securitised assets which exceeds the purchaser's expenses.

(a) Partial assignment

The easiest way of ensuring that the originator keeps the 'super-profit' is for only part of the income stream from the securitised assets to be assigned to the purchaser in the first place. This is certainly worth considering in the context of, say, securitising hire purchase receivables or commercial mortgages; indeed, it has been used in a recent securitisation of hire purchase receivables, where a separate trust company was established to hold the proceeds of the receivables for the benefit of the originator and the purchaser.

Partial assignment would not, however, be appropriate for mortgages which are within the MIRAS scheme because the Inland Revenue are currently not prepared to have mortgages within MIRAS where the beneficial right to the interest on the mortgages is split.

(b) Dividends

If it is necessary to assign all the income on the securitised assets to the purchaser and for the originator then to extract part of it, the key tax point is to ensure that double taxation does not result from the profit extraction. One method of achieving this which has often been considered where the originator has a shareholding in the purchaser is to extract the profit by way of dividend. If the purchaser is a UK-resident company then, although any such dividend would not be deductible in computing the purchaser's profits and would give rise to a liability to account for advance corporation tax, the dividends would be received tax-free in the hands of the originator and any ACT on the dividends would be available to reduce the originator's liability to account for ACT on paying dividends to its own shareholders. Also, if the originator owns more that 50 per cent of the ordinary share capital of the purchaser and is indeed the economic owner of more than 50 per cent of the purchaser then a 'group income election' may be made so that no ACT need be accounted for by the purchaser on paying dividends to the originator.

In practice Bank of England requirements have dictated that banks disposing of assets cannot have a shareholding in the purchaser. Therefore, purchasers have often been established as 'orphans' using a discretionary trust structure and other methods of extracting profit have had to be considered.

(*c*) *Swaps*

One method much talked about particularly in the early days of securitisation was the creation of a swap between the originator and the purchaser whereby the originator would agree to pay the purchaser the interest required to service its financing costs plus a small margin and the purchaser would pay the originator an amount equal to the income arising on the related securitised assets less certain expenses of the purchaser. This sounds very straightforward but it is inadvisable to use this method for the moment because the tax treatment of swap payments is concessionary and the Inland Revenue have indicated that the concession will not be available where it would result in a more favourable tax treatment than would apply if parallel loans were used to extract the super-profit (see below).

(*d*) *Parallel loans*

A similar method for extracting profits by the use of parallel loans has been used on some securitisations. This involves the originator lending funds to the purchaser and receiving in return a rate of interest equal to the rate paid on the securitised assets less certain expenses of the purchaser. The purchaser would lend the same amount to the originator, who would pay in return the rate of interest applicable to the debt issued by the purchaser to finance the acquisition of the assets plus a small margin. The economics of this are that the rate of interest paid by the purchaser will generally be greater than that which it receives on the same amount of money. Questions therefore arise as to whether the rate paid by the purchaser exceeds the rate which a company of that type would generally expect to pay for the use of the principal amount of the loan; if so, the excess would constitute a distribution. This is a point perhaps not focused on when this method was first used but which is now being taken by the Inland Revenue. On the basis that any excess interest is treated for tax purposes as a distribution this would not be a disaster because, although the excess would be non-deductible by the purchaser, it would not be subject to UK tax in the hands of the originator. To create the right economic result it would be necessary to gross down the 'excess' interest at the corporation tax rate so that the purchaser was left with sufficient funds to pay its tax. Consideration also needs to be given to ensuring that so far as possible interest on the two parallel loans is paid gross without deduction of withholding tax. For example, where the originator and the purchaser are in the same UK tax group it would be possible to avoid withholding tax by the two companies making a group income election.

(*e*) *Fees*

One might think that the simplest method of extracting the super-profit would be to pay a fee to the originator, especially as services will often continue to be provided by the originator, for example, in relation to collecting the income stream from the assets. The VAT treatment of such a fee has tended to mean that this is not usually a viable method and problems can arise in obtaining a tax deduction depending on the purpose for which the fee is paid. A deduction will only be allowed if the fees are of such an amount as would be paid on an arm's length basis for the services rendered and are paid, by a trading company, wholly and exclusively for the purposes of its trade or, as expenses of management of an investment company.

(*f*) *Deferred consideration*

When dealing with an originator which has no shareholding in the purchaser, probably the easiest way of extracting the super-profit is for the purchaser to pay further amounts from time to time, being basically the difference between its income and expenses, by way of deferred consideration for the assets. This recognises the fact that, once initial administration has been done and credit insurance has been obtained, mortgages, for example, are worth more than the par value usually paid for them. If the assets are mortgages or hire purchase or debt receivables payments of deferred consideration should not give rise to any VAT liability. However, the deferred consideration route would only be effective if the purchaser is a trading company. Otherwise the deferred payments would not be deductible for tax purposes by the purchaser. This would lead to double taxation because the super-profit would be taxed both in the hands of the purchaser and, on receipt of the deferred consideration, in the hands of the originator.

On mortgage securitisations where it is intended that the purchaser originates some mortgages of its own, perhaps to ensure that the pool of securitised assets is not depleted too quickly as mortgages are redeemed, some transactions have been structured so that all origination of new mortgages is carried out by one company in the purchaser's group. This company, which is established as a trading company, initially buys all the mortgages to be securitised from the originator and is able to pay the super-profit by way of deferred consideration. In turn it sells on the mortgages to its various investment subsidiaries where the purchase price is funded by the issue of bonds by the respective subsidiaries. The trading company then extracts the super-profit from the subsidiaries by means of dividends (see above). This creates quite a flexible structure and perhaps enables the purchaser to have a trading entity which would not have been possible if the trading activity had been spread among a number of purchasing entities.

19.4 WITHHOLDING TAX

Withholding tax needs to be considered in two contexts: tax withheld on sums paid to the purchaser and on sums paid by the purchaser.

(a) Withholding tax on payments to the purchaser
Withholding tax is a problem which arises in relation to interest receipts and it would not apply where the purchaser's income consisted of, for example, hire purchase or lease receivables. The only other type of income which might be paid to the purchaser under deduction of UK tax would be any swap payments paid by UK payors other than recognised UK banks, recognised swap dealers or financial traders—another possible reason for avoiding entering into a swap between the purchaser and the originator.

On debt receivables, including mortgages, the purchaser will be receiving its income in the form of interest. Interest paid by UK companies on debts which may be outstanding for a year or more ('annual interest') must be paid under deduction of income tax at the basic rate. This has presented an obstacle to the securitisation of commercial mortgages and also requires consideration in relation to the securitisation of credit card receivables of corporates. There is also withholding tax at the basic rate of income tax on payments of annual interest made by a UK payer where the payee is not resident in the UK. Therefore, for example, the problem on commercial mortgages does not automatically disappear where the purchaser is located outside the UK.

One method of dealing with this withholding tax issue would be to establish the purchaser in a jurisdiction that has an appropriate double tax treaty with the UK, which would enable the purchaser to receive interest payments gross but this needs careful consideration.

Residential mortgages have their own special system of withholding tax known as Mortgage Interest Relief At Source (MIRAS). Under that system UK individuals are able to withhold tax at the basic rate from certain interest payments made to qualifying lenders. Largely by this means they secure their entitlement to tax relief on certain interest paid to purchase a principal private residence. The key point on a securitisation of residential mortgages is that the purchaser must be a qualifying lender. When securitisation originally began, the Inland Revenue used to be happy to accept that the originator would carry on with the operation at MIRAS so that it was not necessary for the purchaser to be a qualifying lender, but this is no longer the case. Except for certain approved entities, including recognised UK banks and building societies, this means being specifically prescribed as a qualifying lender by the Inland Revenue. The Inland Revenue insist that qualifying lenders are resident in the UK for tax purposes. Otherwise the only problem that arises in practice on obtaining qualifying lender status is a logistical one: there are only about two statutory instruments each year which approve qualifying lenders. It is therefore advisable to ensure that a purchaser of UK residential mortgages has applied in good time.

(b) Withholding tax on payments made by the purchaser
This arises mainly in the context of paying interest on its debt obligations. The obvious way to avoid withholding tax on debt with a maturity of a year or more is to ensure that the interest is paid on quoted eurobonds (i.e. securities issued in bearer form and quoted on a recognised stock exchange). Alternatively, interest should be paid to recognised UK banks or to non-UK residents who are able to rely on an exemption from withholding tax under an appropriate double taxation treaty.

19.5 VALUE ADDED TAX

A sale of mortgages by a UK originator will generally be an exempt supply for VAT purposes. Sales of hire purchase and lease receivables will also be exempt, assuming that the underlying assets, for example, motor vehicles, are not transferred. Securitisation is therefore likely to have an impact on the ability of the originator to reclaim VAT charged on supplies made to it. For example, VAT on legal fees incurred by the originator in connection with the securitisation may be irrecoverable because the services have been secured by the originator for the purpose of making an exempt supply.

The issue of securities by the purchaser to finance the purchase of the assets will also generally be an exempt supply. It is therefore important to minimise VAT paid by the purchaser, as it will be irrecoverable. For example, it is better not to transfer to the purchaser the underlying assets on the securitisation of hire purchase or lease receivables, on which VAT at the standard rate would need to be paid. Instead only the receivable itself is transferred—or indeed part of the receivable where the partial assignment route is being used to extract the super-profit.

The other main area where VAT planning is required relates to the extraction of the super-profit and the often interrelated topic of charging the purchaser for services rendered to it, perhaps by the originator, in managing the securitised assets. Administration services are usually subject to VAT at the standard rate, which will represent an extra cost to the purchaser. Therefore, in principle, it may be preferable not to charge the purchaser a fee for administration services. However, where services are to be provided the agencies involved in rating the purchaser's debt may insist that a fee is paid so that it may be taken into account in the purchaser's cash flows. Also, where the originator is extracting the super-profit from the purchaser and also providing services to it, it may be difficult to resist an argument by HM Customs and Excise that part of the return the originator receives is effectively payment for services rendered and is therefore subject to VAT. Where the partial assignment route is used it may be possible to minimise such fees by disposing of a part interest in a 'pre-administered' mortgage or receivable.

Extraction of the super-profit itself by way of an 'administration' fee is to be avoided because of the VAT impact unless the purchaser is a subsidiary of the originator and they are both in the same VAT group. Extraction mechanisms, where the partial assignment route is inappropriate, which do not give rise to VAT problems include dividends, swaps, parallel loans and payments made by way of deferred consideration for the receivables.

19.6 STAMP DUTY

UK securitisations can give rise to miscellaneous potential charges to stamp duty so particular care needs to be taken in this area until these charges are abolished which is expected to be sometime in 1992. In the meantime transfers of mortgages will generally be exempt from stamp duty but transfers of other debt receivables, hire purchase and lease receivables are, in principle, subject to stamp duty. This charge can be minimised by executing and keeping the transfer documentation outside the UK. Also, if it proves necessary to sue in the UK on a receivable and therefore to bring documentation into the UK, then it should be possible for a further document to be executed which would operate as a transfer of the relevant receivable in order to avoid paying stamp duty at 1 per cent on the whole portfolio of securitised assets.

20: The UK Accounting Treatment of Securitisations

Steve Almond, Touche Ross

INTRODUCTION

The accounting treatment of securitised assets is frequently of fundamental importance to a securitised transaction. One of the main objectives of a securitisation is usually to remove the securitised assets from the balance sheet of the originator, either to reduce gearing or to reduce the regulatory capital requirements of the originator. Unfortunately it can be very difficult to reconcile the differing requirements imposed on the structure to meet the accounting (and taxation) objectives, the commercial aims of the originator, and the requirement of the investors in the securitisation (and often of the rating agencies as well) to ensure a sufficiently low-risk investment.

This chapter considers:

- the accounting objectives of the originator in setting up the securitisation structure;
- the relevant requirements of the Companies Act and current and proposed accounting standards;
- the application of these requirements to the accounting problems resulting from different elements in the securitisation structure;
- the future.

We shall consider the situation of a company, referred to as 'the originator', which is transferring the assets to be securitised from its own balance sheet to a special purpose vehicle company (SPV) which will issue securities to fund the transfer. The holders of the securities have no recourse to the originator or any of its subsidiaries in the event of default by the SPV.

We do not discuss the accounting issues relating to investors in securitisations since these are relatively uncontroversial.

20.1 ACCOUNTING OBJECTIVES

The originator's objectives, from an accounting viewpoint, can be summarised as follows:

- to remove assets and funding from the originator's balance sheet; the funding so removed is thus excluded from the originator's gearing ratio calculated from the balance sheet, and thus given less significance by shareholders and analysts in their assessment of the company. The originator is then able to enter into further funding arrangements and still remain within an acceptable level of gearing;
- to exclude funding from total borrowings for the purpose of borrowing limits and covenants in the company's articles or loan agreements; the definition of borrowings for such purposes will vary from one agreement or set of articles to another, but will often not include funding through a securitisation vehicle;
- to remove assets from the originator's regulatory capital requirements. This is principally of relevance to banks and their subsidiaries. For example, under the Bank of England capital adequacy requirements, capital of approximately 4 per cent of a mortgage portfolio and 8 per cent of other commercial loans must be held;
- to avoid any loss arising in the profit and loss account as a result of charging future costs at the outset of the securitisation transaction; or alternatively, to recognise a profit by accelerating income from the assets being securitised.

To achieve these objectives, the following accounting problems must be considered:

- whether the transfer of the assets from the originator to the SPV is sufficiently complete to be accounted for as a sale;
- whether the relationship between the originator and the SPV is such as to require the consolidation of the SPV in the originator's group accounts;
- what costs arising on the securitisation, particularly those relating to credit risk and credit enhancement arrangements borne by the originator, should be charged to profit and loss account at the time of the securitisation.

These are examined in detail below, in the light of the existing and currently proposed accounting requirements.

20.2 CURRENT AND PROPOSED ACCOUNTING REQUIREMENTS

The main items relevant to securitisation issues are:

- the Companies Act 1985, as amended by the Companies Act 1989; in particular the requirements for consolidated accounts and the true and fair view;
- the draft accounting standard ED49, *Reflecting the substance of transactions in assets and liabilities*, published in May 1990. This supersedes an earlier draft standard ED42, *Accounting for special purpose transactions* and an earlier Technical Release TR603, *Off balance sheet finance and window dressing*;
- the Bank of England paper on loan transfers and securitisation issued in February 1989.

Although accounting standards, such as SSAP 14, *Group Accounts*, and SSAP 18, *Accounting for Contingencies*, are relevant, they do not specifically address the problems arising from securitisations and are not considered further here.

An exposure draft, (ED50, *Consolidated Accounts*) was published in June 1990. This deals with matters currently contained in SSAP 14, as well as those covered by SSAP 1 on associated companies, and reflects the changes introduced by the Companies Act 1989. However, the ED also represents a fundamental review of the accounting issues involved, and is not merely a restatement of the earlier standards.

The Accounting Standards Board has issued an interim statement on the interpretation of the new definitions of subsidiary undertaking introduced by the Companies Act 1989, and the consequent amendments to SSAP 14 and SSAP 1, as set out in ED50. The interim statement has the force of an accounting standard. The remaining accounting issues covered by ED50 will appear in Financial Reporting Standard form when the ASB has allowed sufficient time for comments to be made and assessed.

20.2.1 Companies Act

The financial statements of a UK originator must be drawn up in accordance with the provisions of the Companies Act 1985, as amended by the Companies Act 1989 ('the Companies Act'). Failure to do so may result in the company being required to issue amended accounts, at the directors' expense.

Although the Companies Act sets out prescribed formats and accounting rules, these are generally not relevant to the first of the accounting problems relating to securitisation outlined above. For example, although the Companies Act has a requirement for all the assets and liabilities to be shown in the balance sheet, it does not define assets and liabilities.

The Companies Act's requirements as to whether the SPV is to be included in the originator's group accounts or not are, however, much more specific. The Act requires the group accounts to be in the form of consolidated accounts and to consolidate in full all the assets, and liabilities of all the parent company's 'subsidiary undertakings'.

The consolidated accounts must, so far as possible, be drawn up as though they were the accounts of a single notional entity comprising the parent company and its subsidiary undertakings. Thus, apart from the specific exceptions discussed below, the argument for netting assets and liabilities is no stronger and no more acceptable in relation to the consolidated balance sheet than it would be in relation to the parent company's own balance sheet.

Definition of subsidiary undertaking

The definition of subsidiary undertaking in the Act is lengthy and complex. Any summary of the definition is necessarily incomplete, but the main aspects are as follows.

The definition of subsidiary undertaking has two main branches—based on *legal* control on the one hand, and based on *effective* control on the other.

Legal control is determined as holding a majority of the shareholders' voting rights, or having the right to appoint directors having a majority of votes on the board. A third possible form of legal control described in the Act is having the right to exercise a dominant influence over the financial and operating policies of the company. This third form of control can only arise from the company's memorandum and articles or under what the Act calls a 'control contract' under which the directors of the company are bound to act in accordance with the instructions of the controller, and there are doubts as to whether a UK company could lawfully enter into such a contract—at least, not without specific permission to do so in its memorandum.

Effective control arises where the holding company has a participating interest in an undertaking, and either manages it as an integrated part of its own business, or actually exercises a dominant influence over its operations—that is, that major decisions are taken in accordance with the wishes, either expressed or perceived, of the holding company. A participating interest is, broadly speaking, any long-term interest in the shares of the undertaking giving the holding company significant influence over the undertaking. A holding of 20 per cent or more is presumed to give such influence, but a smaller holding could still be a participating interest. A contingent interest, such as an option to acquire shares, can also be a participating interest.

The definition of subsidiary undertaking applies to all undertakings, including partnerships and other unincorporated associations, and not just to incorporated entities.

Conditions for exclusion from group accounts
The Act requires all subsidiary undertakings to be consolidated unless specifically excluded by the Act. Five grounds for exclusion are set out:

1. if the subsidiary undertaking is immaterial;
2. where there are severe long-term restrictions which substantially hinder the parent company's ability to exercise its rights over the subsidiary undertaking;
3. where the information needed cannot be obtained without disproportionate expense or delay;
4. where the shares are held exclusively for the purpose of resale and the subsidiary undertaking has never been included in the consolidated accounts;
5. where the activities of the subsidiary undertaking are so different from the rest of the group that their inclusion would be incompatible with a true and fair view—in this case exclusion is mandatory.

The ASB interim statement on consolidated accounts gives a narrow interpretation to these conditions—for example, it states that (3) would never be an acceptable justification for the exclusion of a subsidiary undertaking that was material to the group accounts. Similarly, (2) and (4) would be expected to apply only in the most extreme circumstances; in most cases, such situations can be more suitably dealt with by providing additional information in the notes to the accounts.

True and fair view and override
A fundamental requirement of the Act is that the financial statements must give a true and fair view of the state of affairs of the parent company and of the group at the balance sheet date, and of the profit and loss for the year. Where financial statements drawn up in accordance with the requirements of the Act are *not sufficient* to give a true and fair view, the Act requires that the necessary additional information be included in the financial statements.

The Act also provides that, if in special circumstances compliance with any of the provisions of the Act is *inconsistent* with giving a true and fair view, the directors shall depart from that provision to the extent necessary to give a true and fair view. This provision is often referred to as the 'true and fair override'. There is some dispute, however, about the extent to which the override can be applied. Certainly, it gives no authority to depart from the requirements in order merely to give a better presentation (a 'truer and fairer' view); once a true and fair view is achieved, no further override is permissible. Legal doubts have been expressed, however, on the extent to which it would allow the inclusion of assets and liabilities that did not legally belong to companies in the group.

20.2.2 ED49

ED49 was issued in May 1990 as a further step in the accounting profession's attempts to deal with a range of types of transaction where the commercial substance of the transaction, or series of linked transactions, is different from the legal form. Such transactions are not always adequately treated in financial statements in a way that enables the reader fully to understand and assess the enterprise's affairs. Many such transactions come under the general description of 'off-balance-sheet finance', whereby a company enters into obligations, and acquires assets, in a way that is commercially little different from direct legal ownership, but where, because of the legal structure of the transactions, the assets and liabilities are not shown on the company's consolidated balance sheet.

In attempting to provide a logical and comprehensive solution to the problems posed by the more extreme forms of off-balance-sheet finance, ED49 seeks to establish an accounting framework under which transactions are accounted for in accordance with the resulting commercial (not necessarily legal) rights and obligations.

Fundamental to ED49's general approach are its definitions of the concepts of the essential characteristics of assets and liabilities. These are:

- The essential characteristics of an asset are that it is a resource controlled by the enterprise as a result of past events and from which future economic benefits are expected to flow to the enterprise.
- The essential characteristics of a liability are that it is a present obligation of the enterprise arising from past events the settlement of which is expected to result in an outflow from the enterprise of resources embodying economic benefits.

ED49 addresses the accounting for the substance of transactions, rather than merely the recognition of assets and liabilities. Thus it is necessary to consider whether the transactions involved in setting up the securitisation have changed the enterprise's assets and liabilities in the sense given above; in particular whether the assets have been decreased or whether the liabilities have been increased.

ED49 also addresses a concept of a 'quasi-subsidiary'; an entity that is not a Companies Act subsidiary undertaking, but which is directly or indirectly controlled by the reporting enterprise, and is a source of benefits or risks to the enterprise which would be in substance unchanged were the entity to be a subsidiary. The existence of a quasi-subsidiary would often, in itself, constitute special circumstances justifying, and requiring, the use of the 'true and fair override' and including the entity in the consolidated accounts.

ED49 also discusses the situation where, because of the arrangements for allocation of benefits and risks arising in an entity, the question of formal control of the entity is irrelevant. Control in these circumstances should be imputed to the party receiving the principal future benefits.

It is also emphasised that the mere fact that a particular liability is to be repaid out of specific assets, with no recourse to other assets of the enterprise, is not in itself an argument justifying the netting of the liabilities against the assets.

However, ED49 also accepts the need for more detailed and specific guidance; it therefore incorporates 'application notes' covering difficult situations, including mortgage securitisation. These are not intended merely to be illustrative; under an accounting standard based on ED49, it would be a requirement to follow the application notes for transactions described therein, or for similar transactions for which the application notes provide a reasonable accounting analogy. Thus, the same principles would need to be applied to securitisation of assets other than mortgage loans but with similar characteristics; or to securitisation arrangements that are similar, but not identical, to those described in the application note.

The detailed analysis of securitisation in the application note is examined below. The application note also identifies certain specific features and conditions of mortgage securitisations that might justify the netting of securitised assets and corresponding liabilities, and the associated cash flows. The features are that the originator does not control the SPV or its assets, other than in the sense of receiving benefit from it; and that the principal function of the mortgages transferred is to generate cash rather than to be transformed into goods or services, thus distinguishing mortgage securitisation from other types of non-recourse project finance. The conditions to be met if net rather than gross accounting is acceptable are those discussed below.

20.2.3 Bank of England paper

The Bank of England paper sets out conditions under which, where the originator is a bank, securitised assets are to be excluded from the originator's risk asset calculation for capital adequacy purposes. Although not strictly related to the preparation of the originator's financial statements, in practice the accounting treatment of securitised assets almost always follows the treatment for capital adequacy purposes. The tests set out in the paper are very similar to those in ED49, which are discussed in detail below. We do not, therefore, deal with this paper further in this chapter.

20.3 ACCOUNTING PROBLEMS

We now consider the accounting problems referred to above in more detail, and examine how the accounting requirements address the issues.

20.3.1 Whether there has been a sale of the securitised assets to the SPV

There are many commercial reasons why the originator may prefer not to make a simple outright transfer of the assets to be securitised to the SPV, for example:

- there may be difficulties in legally transferring the assets, although this should not cause difficulties where there was an intention to securitise the assets before they arose;
- the originator may be reluctant for its customers (for example, its mortgage borrowers) to know that it has sold the assets to a financing vehicle;
- the originator may wish to retain a relationship with its mortgage borrowers or other customers;
- in order to establish a sufficiently high credit rating for the SPV, the originator may be required to retain some risk in the event of default by mortgage borrowers or customers;
- the originator may wish to retain control over any decisions to extend repayment terms or actions to recover funds or enforce security in the event of default, to maintain its image with its borrowers;
- the originator may wish to be able to manage the cashflow of the SPV to ensure that funds are available to make payments to holders of the securities on the due dates notwithstanding variations in the timing of cash receipts from borrowers;
- the originator may wish to be able to repurchase the assets from the SPV at some future date to enable it to refinance the assets if more favourable terms become available.

The Companies Act gives no assistance in determining what constitutes the point at which an asset should be regarded as being sold. Furthermore, there is no professional guidance in the UK that specifically addresses the topic.

It is generally accepted practice to recognise the sale of an asset as having occurred on delivery or transfer of ownership; however, case-by-case exceptions to this general rule have become established, allowing earlier recognition in certain cases (e.g. sale of property, where exchange of contracts rather than transfer of ownership is often treated as the point of sale) or deferral of recognition where substantial uncertainties remain at the time of delivery (e.g. goods sold on approval). One possible basis for establishing the time at which a sale can be recognised is set out in International Accounting Standard 18, although compliance with this is not mandatory in the UK and it does not necessarily represent generally accepted practice.

Under this standard, a sale of an asset is regarded as having been made when:

- all significant risks and rewards of ownership of the asset have been transferred from the seller to the buyer;
- the seller retains no continuing managerial involvement in, or effective control of, the asset;
- there is no significant uncertainty regarding
  - the consideration for the sale;
  - the further costs involved.

In the context of securitisation, the originator will often enter into credit-enhancement arrangements to increase the creditworthiness of the SPV, which may give rise to the retention of risk by the originator, or uncertainty as to the consideration receivable or further costs involved. Such arrangements may include:

- reimbursement in cash, or by the provision of further assets, of any losses caused by defaults;
- retention by the SPV of part of the purchase price for the assets, against which losses are charged;
- 'over-collateralisation', whereby the value of the assets transferred exceeds the securities issued by the SPV; again, the surplus is available to cover defaults;
- the use of subordinated loans or a junior/senior debt structure, whereby loans from, or debt held by, the originator are repayable only once all other securities issued by the SPV have been repaid, and thus bear losses arising from defaults;
- payments into escrow account.

The originator may alternatively arrange insurance for the assets and bear the cost of the policy itself. The payment of a straightforward insurance premium is merely an additonal cost to the originator, but often the insurance policy will have provision for the reimbursement of part of the premium if claims are small—in which case, it could still be argued that there is uncertainty as to the costs to be incurred by the originator in connection with the sale.

The extent of such recourse provisions, and in particular whether the originator's obligations under the provisions can be estimated with reasonable accuracy, are crucial in determining whether the transfer can be accounted for as a sale or not. Whether such recourse provisions are of sufficient materiality as to prevent the transfer being accounted for as a sale is a matter for individual judgement based on the precise details of the particular case.

Under ED49, the following conditions need to be met for the transfer to be accounted for as a sale:

- the transfer does not contravene the terms and conditions of the mortgages;
- the originator retains no residual beneficial interest in the principal amount of the mortgages, and there is no recourse to the originator for losses; thus many forms of credit enhancement would result in the transfer not being treated as a sale;
- the originator has no obligation to repurchase the mortgages at any time;
- the SPV, not the originator, will be party to any rescheduled or renegotiated terms for any mortgages.

20.3.2 Profit and loss account

Following on from the assumption that the transfer is accounted for as a sale, all sales proceeds and costs, including estimated future costs, should be included in the calculation of the net profit or loss on sale and taken to the originator's profit and loss account immediately.

The only exception to this general principle would be any adjustment to the sales proceeds representing an advance of future income—in this case the discounted present value of this should be deferred. Conversely, any element of sales proceeds receivable in the form of increased future income should be estimated (at its present value) and included as sales proceeds (provided it is reasonably certain to be received).

20.3.3 Whether to consolidate the SPV as a quasi-subsidiary

The question of whether the SPV should be consolidated into the group accounts of the originator must next be addressed. This can be subdivided into:

- Is the SPV a Companies Act subsidiary undertaking?
- If it is, are there grounds for omitting it from the consolidation?
- If it is not, are there any grounds for including it in the consolidation using the 'true and fair override'.

While the Companies Act 1989 introduced a much wider definition of subsidiary undertaking, it is nevertheless still possible to establish an SPV that is not a subsidiary of the originator. This can be done, for example, by having all the shares and voting rights held by a charitable trust, and by the originator taking out its share of the net income of the SPV by means of management contracts or other arrangements. Provided the originator has no interest whatsoever in the shares of the SPV, there can be no participating interest and thus questions of 'dominant influence' or 'managing on a unified basis' do not apply.

The alternative approach, of setting up the SPV as a subsidiary undertaking and excluding it from consolidation, is unlikely to be appropriate, as the arrangements for a securitisation will not usually fall within any of the provisions in the Act, referred to above, for permitting a subsidiary undertaking to be excluded from consolidation.

If the SPV is not a subsidiary undertaking, however, it is still necessary to consider whether the relationship between the originator and the SPV is such as to constitute 'special circumstances' requiring the SPV to be consolidated so as to give a true and fair view.

Some of the commercial objectives of originators that may result in a continuing close relationship with the SPV are:

- to retain the full benefit of the net income arising from the assets, after financing costs;
- to continue to perform administration services for the assets, both as a way of maintaining contact with borrowers and of controlling costs;
- to retain some discretion in setting interest rates for borrowers, both because of a continuing relationship with borrowers and so as to have control over net income;
- to provide low-cost finance from group resources and to manage the SPV within a larger group treasury operation.

All these objectives conspire against a 'clean break' between the originator and the SPV.

ED49 sets out one view of the circumstances where the relationship becomes sufficiently close for the SPV to be consolidated. It states that securitisations are often structured in a way that avoids the SPV being a subsidiary undertaking of the originator, but where the arrangements made for the allocation of benefits and risks are such that it is scarcely relevant to enquire where formal control resides. The relevance to the originator of the assets and liabilities of the SPV lies in the extent to which their associated benefits and risks flow to the originator.

ED49 states that the SPV should be regarded as a quasi-subsidiary, and consolidated in the originator's group accounts, unless all of the following tests are met:

- The originator does not bear the on-going expenses of scheme, but may make a one-off contribution at the commencement of the scheme to enhance the credit-worthiness of the SPV. However, it is not clear from the wording of ED49 whether the reference to bearing expenses prohibits the originator from bearing these costs *indirectly*, by virtue of being entitled to the net income from the scheme after deduction of all costs borne by the SPV; nor whether it would prevent the originator bearing administrative costs as part of a separate management agreement for servicing the mortgages.

- The originator does not fund the SPV and in particular does not provide temporary funding to cover delayed payments from mortgages which it services. The originator may lend on a long-term subordinated basis to the SPV provided the loan is entered into at the commencement of the scheme and is only repayable on the winding up of the scheme.
- The originator does not intentionally bear any losses resulting from the effect of interest rate changes or from normal administrative delays in implementing a change in mortgage rates for borrowers. However, the originator may enter into separate interest rate swap agreements with the SPV at market prices. This would appear to refer only to swaps on normal commercial terms, and not to arrangements in the form of a swap whereby the SPV pays the originator its net cash receipts in exchange for payments sufficient to meet the SPV's interest payments.
- The originator is under no obligation to transfer further assets to SPV, for example to make good a shortfall resulting from defaults by mortgage borrowers. This condition is relaxed for a short three-month start-up period.
- The originator has no rights under an option to repurchase mortgages or to refinance in some other way. However, there may be a provision in the agreement for the originator to repurchase the remaining mortgages when the remaining value of the portfolio has fallen below 10 per cent, provided only fully performing mortgages are repurchased. This allows arrangements to be made to permit the tidy winding up of the scheme when almost all the mortgages have been repaid; but does not allow the originator to terminate the scheme if adverse tax or regulatory changes occur.
- The originator has no liability to investors (save for negligence). Adequate arrangements for financing and servicing the mortgages must be flexible enough to permit mortgage borrowers to be treated fairly, in terms of the standards of commercial behaviour expected of the originator; and the originator must have taken all reasonable precautions to ensure that it will not feel impelled to support any losses suffered by the SPV or its investors.

Where the originator continues to service the mortgages on behalf of the SPV, particular care will be needed to ensure that the originator has no obligations to the SPV for cash flow shortages resulting from defaults, changes in interest rates and delays in implementing interest rate changes, and from any moral or commercial risk resulting from its continued association with the mortgage borrowers.

20.3.4 Disclosure in notes to the accounts

Where the conditions for off-balance-sheet treatment are met, ED49 would require sufficient disclosure in the notes to the accounts to explain the originator's interest in the SPV and the income deriving therefrom. As a minimum, ED49 would require disclosure of:

- a summary balance sheet and profit and loss account of the SPV to the same date as the originator's financial statements;
- the amount of income the originator has received from the SPV;
- an indication of the period for which the income is likely to continue to be received.

Where an originator has transferred assets to two or more SPVs, the information may be combined.

20.4 THE FUTURE

The uncertainty of whether, and in what form, ED49 will be converted into an accounting standard is, perhaps one factor in the relatively few securitisations currently being completed in the UK at present. Originators are reluctant to enter into a transaction that, while meeting the specific tests in ED49 for off-balance-sheet treatment, might fall to be treated as on-balance-sheet if the eventual standard 'moves the goal-posts' slightly. Alternatively, additional costs may result from specific features being built in to the transaction to meet specific ED49 tests that subsequently prove to be unnecessary under the standard—thus putting the originator at a competitive disadvantage. The temptation is therefore to wait and see.

It seems likely that the eventual standard will place greater emphasis on the underlying principles of asset and liability recognition, rather than on longer and longer lists of specific tests to cater for each variation in securitisation transactions. Certainly ED49 itself, despite the lengthy application notes, contains ambiguities and uncertainties and would give much scope for argument as to how particular transactions should be treated. A standard concentrating on principles rather than detailed tests would result in originators placing greater emphasis on adapting the commercial reality of the transactions, rather than the intricate details of the legal wording, to meet the new requirements. The scope for argument and debate is unlikely to reduce, however.

The full impact of the provisions of the Companies Act 1989 requiring financial statements to disclose non-compliance with accounting standards, and the possibility of companies that file defective accounts being required to reissue them in a revised form, has yet to be seen. Directors may well consider that the prospect of a well publicised court hearing on their company's compliance with particular standards, together with the costs and senior management time involved, makes venturing into the grey areas of accounting standards less enticing.

21: The Role of the Trustee in Issues of UK Mortgage-backed Securities

Julie Craik, Bankers Trustee Company Limited

In exceptional environments there are spectacular achievements and disastrous failures. For example, the installation of an oil production platform in the North Sea is a huge task. There can be an awe-inspiring moment at the start-up of production when a gun is aimed and a charge is fired to ignite a gas flare.

Everyone who has been involved in creating a securitised bond issue for a new issuer knows that it is a process which takes hours, days and months of work. The culmination is the moment when the documents are all signed and the common depository is given instructions to notify the clearing systems that the issue has closed. The issue is closed, the champagne is uncorked but for the trustee it is not the end. It is the moment when our responsibility really begins.

And what of failure? A blow-out in the North Sea is at once horrific and dramatic. This is a matter of life and death and, as such, beyond comparison with lesser tragedies. But in this context perhaps it serves to put what we do in perspective.

No one wants to contemplate the failure of a bond issue but, ultimately, that is the work of trustees. 1989 and 1990 have seen high numbers of insolvencies in the USA, Canada, Australia, the UK, France and other European countries. In the UK shares were suspended in 22 public companies in the first quarter of 1990, whereas the figure had been only 16 for the whole of 1989; insolvency practitioners have reported major increases in staff to cope with the growing levels of business.

In the US the collapse or near-collapse of the savings and loans industry may have heralded problems throughout the finance industry. Commentators have said that the property crisis for US banks may be at least as serious as the Latin American debt crisis. The US insurance business has also come in for warning reports, including one from a congressional committee; an American Express insurance subsidiary has forecast that as much as 20 per cent of major life insurance companies could go to the wall, depending on the severity of the prevailing recession.

By contrast, asset securitisation has been reported as a positive response to troubled financial times: an answer for borrowers because it may be harder for them to raise unsecured capital or they may be seeking a beneficial effect on their balance sheets; an answer for lenders and investors because their risk is tied in to a portfolio of assets, be it mortgages or car loans. Based on data of past performances, investors anticipate good future performance with low delinquency rates.

So, do we really need to worry about insolvency in this context?

Apart from the performance of the assets, the strength of a securitised issue is heavily dependent on the roles of key functions such as the servicing of the assets and the management of the vehicle company's resources, and may also have a number of credit enhancement features, such as pool insurance or a guarantee. Consequently the success of an issue relies on the care and custody of a number of different hands. We have to consider, remote though it may seem today, that tomorrow one of these could fail. In a sense, then, being a trustee is a little like guarding the guardians.

21.1 TYPICAL STRUCTURE OF MORTGAGE-BACKED SECURITIES

The structuring of mortgage- and asset-backed issues is dealt with elsewhere in this book. In order that the trustee's role and relationships with other members of a transaction can be explored, it may be useful to summarise with the aid of a diagram what we see as a typical bond structure (figure 21.1).

It is also worth noting the development of asset-backed commercial paper—an interesting dichotomy in view of the fact that this instrument was developed as a method of short-term unsecured finance.

The bond issue, as such, is created in the usual way. For example, at its launch and signing the prospectus containing the terms and conditions is released and the lead manager enters into an agreement with a group of banks to underwrite the issue. They in turn will sell or attempt to sell their respective portions on to other investors.

At the closing meeting the rating agencies confirm the ratings which they have assigned to the issue based on their prior examination of the structure and parties involved, and the insurer or guarantor formally issues its indemnity document. The issuer signs a trust deed with the trustee and an agency agreement with the paying agent. A global note representing the full amount of the debt is authenticated and released to the common depositary on behalf of the clearing systems and the issuer receives the proceeds of the issue.

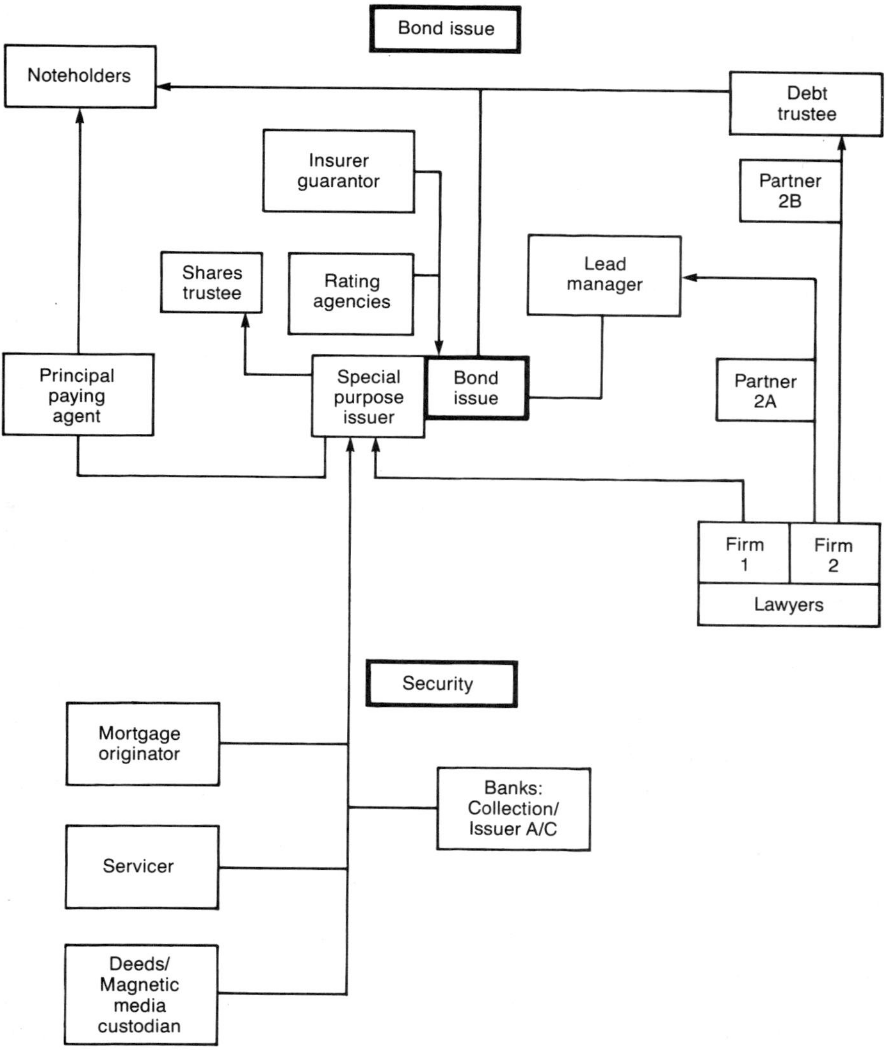

Figure 21.1. Structure of a typical bond issue.

In the actual securitisation, a portfolio of mortgages or other assets is transferred directly or indirectly by the originator to the issuing vehicle with the benefit of related insurance policies. The management of the assets continues as a result of the issuer signing a servicing ageement with the originator or specialist servicer, custody agreements for the storage of deeds and computer data, and agreements with banks to provide collection, banking and investment services. The issuer and trustee take charges over the mortgages and the trustee takes security interests over all related agreements.

21.2 AGENCY SERVICES

21.2.1 The principal paying agent

Perhaps the best paying agent is one whose activities the investors never really notice beyond the fact that they obtain their interest and principal payments efficiently and on time. The principal paying agent claims funds in respect of such payments as due from the issuer and pays out to noteholders directly or through sub-agents against presentation of notes or coupons. In performing this function the principal paying agent will routinely be the investors' single most important link with the issuer.

A fiscal agent is no different from a principal paying agent. Legally, both are representatives or agents of the issuer and in this respect, must be clearly distinguished from a trustee who, while also being appointed by the issuer, represents the interests of the noteholders.

For Eurobonds, the paying agency service is almost invariably provided by a select group of banks in London, Luxembourg and Switzerland.

A positive requirement for a local paying agent may arise due to relevant stock exchange listing rules or it may be preferable to investors if they can claim interest in a location where there will be no liability to withholding tax. The currency of the issue may dictate the need for a sub-agent in the home state of the currency.

The principal paying agent will usually be appointed by means of an agency agreement which provides the terms of appointment and sets out details and deadlines for payments by the issuer to the agent. It permits the payment of principal and interest by the principal paying agent and sub-agents in accordance with the terms and conditions of the relevant issue.

At the closing of the issue, it is now customary in London for the principal paying agent to authenticate the global note on behalf of the trustee and to arrange for authentication of definitive notes if and when printed; that is, the individual notes which evidence an investor's entitlement against the issuer.

Registered notes will also need a registrar.

21.2.2 The agent bank

A floating rate note (FRN) issue requires an agent bank to set the interest rates by adding a margin, if any, to a specified base rate. The current method is to take the average of the base rates displayed on a designated page of an on-line screen-based information service (Telerate or Reuters). In the event of the appropriate service being unavailable, the agent must revert to the traditional method, that is, telephone a panel of reference banks, usually a selection of clearing and foreign banks, and work out the rate as directed in the agreement.

21.2.3 Global and definitive notes

A global note is a single document which represents the entire debt created when an issue closes. The global note will usually be held by a common depositary bank on behalf of the clearing systems Euroclear and Cedel. Many sterling UK mortgage-backed issues are intended to remain in permanent global form. This only presents a problem for investors in the event of a default or the closure of Euroclear or Cedel for a period of time. Such events should trigger the obligatory printing of definitive notes, as global notes may not put them in a position to take direct action against an issuer. This is based on the argument that the document which conveys the benefit of the debt, the promise to pay, is not held by each investor, but by the clearing systems. Any action would have to come from the latter, although they might be reluctant to act.

The idea of permanent global notes which mean a saving for the issuer of several thousands pounds in printing costs may have been driven by the assumption that the majority of noteholders would be institutional investors and, therefore, likely to be members of the clearing systems. It is relatively small, private investors who are more likely to require definitive notes as a matter of course.

21.3 CHOOSING A TRUSTEE AND PAYING AGENT

It may seem obvious, but the best way is to interview potential candidates, and to do so as early as possible. The qualities you might look for are quite usual: experience of complex structures, integrity towards duties, a flexible and innovative attitude to solutions, strict respect for confidentiality, technical expertise and efficient working practices. It helps greatly if you actually get on with the people you meet and know who you will be dealing with down the line because it is likely to be the start of a long and, hopefully, successful relationship.

But back to the real world. Trustees are increasingly asked to quote fees on a no-names basis. We believe, however, that as it is issuers which have to live with the choice of trustee for the life of the issue, they should play a positive role in the selection process.

21.3.1 Trustees

There are around 300 trustee companies in the UK registered with the industry's 'trade association', The Association of Corporate Trustees. Within that organisation is a group dedicated to the work of debt trustees, although the range of work covered by members includes probate, unit trusts and pension funds. The Association seeks to promote an exchange of ideas and information such as current legal developments and provides a forum for lobbying the government and regulatory bodies.

Some trustees are now regulated by the Investment Management Regulatory Organisation (IMRO). A consultative paper published jointly by the Securities Investments Board (SIB) and IMRO in September 1990 stated that: 'The precise relationship between the law of trusts and the Financial Services Act is not easy to determine.' The report pointed out that the Act together with the IMRO rules was aimed at regulating investment business to the extent this was carried on by trustees. It may be said that the majority of functions performed by debt trustees do not come within the ambit of investment business as defined.

That being said, in order to clarify aspects of fundamental importance, SIB has issued a set of ten principles. It is interesting to note their similarity to the basic principles which govern the conduct of trustees under trust law. For example the first principle is that: 'A firm should observe high standards of integrity and fair dealing.' Two other principles provide for the duties to act with 'due skill, care and diligence' and to avoid conflicts of interest or if they arise, to ensure fair treatment to all customers by disclosure, the maintenance of effective Chinese walls or declining to act.

21.3.2 Reasons for appointing a trustee

There is one compelling reason to appoint a trustee for mortgage-backed issues which is, of course, the security itself. It would be impractical to convey security interests into the hands of the noteholders themselves.

For bond issues generally, the ultimate reason for the existence of the trustee, is its power or duty, in certain cases, to enforce the issue. It is not the easiest selling point, however, to tell a potential issuer that the trustee will do a wonderful job if, or when, the company is on the brink of receivership or liquidation.

Be that as it may, there are good reasons for both issuers and noteholders to have a trustee in place. Perhaps as an investment consideration, the latter have the comfort of knowing that the tasks of monitoring the issue and holding the security are being performed by a professional in that business who may also be expected to be in close touch with the issuer, more particularly at times of crisis.

Even in the face of disaster, it may be advantageous to the investors to know that if a majority decides to agree a compromise solution this will bind all the holders. In this way thay can avoid being at the mercy of a single noteholder whose actions might be against the best interests of the majority.

For issuers, trustees may provide protection against action by individual holders; possible solutions to problems which arise can be discussed in a confidential way with a company which is no stranger to them or the problems issuers face from time to time. In any case, it is the difference between a one-to-one conversation and trying to broach what may be a difficult subject with a crowd. Trustees may even be able to waive breaches or agree to amendments, although this will only be in cases where the trustee can conclude that this will not be materially prejudicial to the noteholders.

21.3.3 Potential clients

Motivations for securitising assets are discussed elsewhere in this book but it is information which trustees have to consider in assessing possible issuers. As far as UK mortgages are concerned, it is well known that companies in the mortgage business are one of four main groups: building societies, insurance companies, banks and specialist mortgage lenders. Their demand to refinance mortgage portfolios and release capital for further mortgages is driven, of course by the demand for the latter; at times of high interest rates, demand is reduced. After a fast-paced start, new mortgage-backed securities have largely been limited to repeat issues by the specialist mortgage lenders who fund themselves entirely on the wholesale capital markets and for whom securitisation is practically a *raison d'être.*

New developments have emerged elsewhere, however. At the time of writing, for example, there have been securitised eurobonds based on New Zealand and Australian mortgages (by GMBS International Nos. 1 and 3 respectively) and based on Swedish mortgages (Osprey Mortgage Securities (No.1)). In France a handful of securitised issues have appeared pursuant to a relatively recent law on securitisation ('titrisation'). The method contemplated by the law is more akin to the unit trust or mutual fund concept, but there have also been offshore securitisations of French assets.

Such developments serve to emphasise important issues for trustees. In order to perform effectively they must understand the mortgage markets which are relevant to issues in their care and the methods of operation and regulation of the entities securitising their assets. Insurance companies are regulated by the Department of Trade and Industry, banks by the Bank of England and building societies by the Building Societies Commission.

The Council of Mortgage Lenders, essentially a trade organisation, was established in 1989 and provides a forum for all types of mortgage providers and incorporates a number of specialist panels including one on securitisation. Membership tends to be co-ordinated by the trade association for each type of lender; the Council is administered by staff of the Building Societies Association. Under the Courts and Legal Services Act 1990, mortgage providers can now be regulated with regard to certain aspects of the provision and marketing of mortgages and the Council is involved in discussions on the best way of achieving the results being sought by the Act.

21.4 MORTGAGE-BACKED SECURITY AS BOND ISSUE

21.4.1 Principles of trust

As when we become adults, much of our reactions and responses are attributed to childhood conditioning, so in order to understand the motivations of trustees, and trustees for bond issues in particular, it is essential to look to their evolution:

> Thus from the settlement of the greatest wars down to the simplest inheritance on death, from the most audacious Wall Street scheme down to the protection of grandchildren, the trust can see marching before it the motley procession of the whole of human endeavour: dreams of peace, commercial imperialism, attempts to strangle competition or to reach paradise, hatred or philanthropy, love of one's family or the desire to strip it of everything after one's death, all those in the procession being dressed either in robes or in rags, and either crowned with a halo or walking with a grin. The trust is the guardian angel of the Anglo-Saxon, accompanying him everywhere, impassively from the cradle to the grave.[1]

The trust as a known legal concept is many centuries old and could be seen as one of the oldest ways of 'structuring' the use and ownership of capital, whether cash or land.

Their most notorious association is that of settlements, usually offshore and as a means of mitigating the effects of taxation in the settlor's home state. This and probate work is predominantly the world of private trusts.

Modern corporate trust developed hand in hand with the domestic and international debt markets. Paradoxically, the basic principles of trust management go far back in time. The Court of Chancery was the Court of

Equity. Heavily influenced by the Church, it represented religious mysticism made earthly law. Common law, being fairly rigid, inevitably produced harsh results. Equity was the champion of what was right and fair, albeit in the eyes of the Church; a sort of spiritual knight bearing a code of legal chivalry. Trust law and equity were born out of a need to respond to a constantly developing world which found no answers or the wrong answers in existing common law.

To recognise a trust is essentially to recognise the separation of legal from beneficial ownership. This may produce advantages for beneficiaries; their position is underwritten by the fact that assets held on trust are not available to the creditors of the trustee. Conversely, of course, they may also be subject to great power in the hands of the legal owner or trustee.

If the system was to have credibility, therefore, it needed rules to function effectively. Power and discretion on one hand had to be guided by duty on the other. By keeping the rules general and reflecting the idea of moral right, early Chancery judges created a concept of enormous flexibility and at least as significant as the eurobond itself, so many centuries later.

There are many and varied perceptions of trustees: diplomat or devil's advocate, protector or thorn in your side; good, bad, or ugly.

Professional or Corporate Trustees sell commodities which are intangible but easily recognised: these are reason and integrity. In the 1883 case of Smethurst v. Hastings, Bacon V.C. stated:

> there is one clear, homely, intelligible, but inflexible rule which has never been departed from in times ancient and modern, viz, that a trustee is bound to act in the execution of his trust as a prudent man would in dealing with his own property.[2]

In 1952, Harman J. stated in Re Waterman's Will Trusts:

> I do not forget that a paid trustee is expected to exercise a higher standard of diligence and knowledge than an unpaid trustee and that a bank which advertises itself largely in the public Press as taking charge of administrations is under a special duty.[3]

These are high ideals but how do the trustees of eurobonds really ply their trade?

The modern eurobond trust deed probably developed out of the deeds used for UK loan capital stocks. In the US the need to regulate debt issuance was considered so pressing that the Trust Indenture Act emerged in 1938 to lay down when trustees could act, when they had to decline or resign appointments and how they should perform their functions.

In Britain, while the Stock Exchange 'Yellow Book' contains provisions for the constitution of mortgage debenture stocks under a trust deed, Section 5 on eurocurrency securities states:

> The issuer must ensure that, at least in each member state in which its debt securities are listed, all the necessary facilities and information are available to

> enable holders of such securities to exercise their rights. In particular, it must inform holders of the holding of meetings which they are entitled to attend [and] enable them to exercise their right to vote, where applicable.[4]

There is a dearth of information on corporate and eurobond trust work and we must, therefore, pay tribute to the lawyers and writers who have covered the subject including Professor Hayton, Anthony Herbert, Robert Landau, James Watkins and Philip Wood.[5]

What is in a typical English law trust deed as used for sterling mortgage-backed securities?

At the top of the list must be the covenant to pay principal and interest. The debt may, in fact be directly owed to the noteholders by virtue of the promise to pay being contained in their notes. Where a trustee is used, the debt must be conveyed to the trustee for the benefit of the noteholders and this, even though the trustee provides no consideration for debt. Legally this is achieved by the trust deed.

To work in the context of a bond issue, the trust deed incorporates two more legal concepts—contract and security. Security aspects will be discussed later. As a contract, the essential terms are to be found in the so-called 'Terms and Conditions' which may be further elaborated in the body of the trust deed. These should include a summary of the issue followed by such details as:

- *The notes*—their form, denominations, procedures for exchange from bearer into registered form and information on methods and dates of interest payments and redemption;
- *The security*—type of assets and nature of security interests to be taken; in the UK the security interests, as such, would usually be conveyed through separate charging documents;
- *Covenants by issuer*—most importantly, the negative pledge, an undertaking not to charge or further charge any of its assets and not to issue debt ranking prior to or level with the current note issue;
- *Events of default and acceleration of notes.*

As a trust, the document translates the typical elements of a private trust into powers and duties more appropriate to the job of a Eurobond trustee.

We should remember that the true subject of the trust is the debt together with any associated assets or security interests, and the objects or beneficiaries are the noteholders.

21.4.2 Duties

1. *A trustee must carry out the terms of settlement.*
In the normal course of events (that is, in the absence of an event of default or breach of covenant by the issuer) the fundamental parts of the settlement are performed by the issuer. It is obvious, therefore, that the role of a bond trustee in contrast to a private trustee, is inextricably linked to that of a third party, the issuer; hence, the covenant by the issuer to perform the terms of the issue and the trust deed.

2. *The trustee must in particular observe conditions attaching to its powers.*
For example, the trustee may only agree to variations of any terms of the issue or to waive breaches provided this will not be materially prejudicial to the noteholders. In addition, it is only after an event of default that the debt trustee can take possession of any security.

3. *The trustee must take reasonable care with regard to the trust.*
Again, prior to any potential event of default, this is most clearly seen in the implied duty to monitor the issuer which arises by virtue of covenants by the issuer to keep proper accounts and supply these and other information as required to the trustee. The issuer should also confirm that there have been no events of default and conversely to notify these or non-payments.

21.4.3 Powers and rights

The trust deed should also contain rights additional to the provisions of the Trustee Act 1925, including those to seek professional or expert advice and not to incur liability unless negligent or itself in default.

There is no inherent right in English trust law for trustees to be paid. Consequently, it is imperative that the trustee should have express rights to be paid its own fees and reimbursed for costs and expenses incidental to the issue. While trustees may not profit from trust property, it should be noticed that trustees rank first in line for payment of their fees and those of receivers. Prior to default, fees will be paid by or on behalf of the issuer. After a default, the trustee would usually seek to be indemnified by the noteholders before taking action.

Bearing in mind that the trustee does not, in the main, control the actions of the issuer, the duty to monitor is counterbalanced by the right of the trustee to assume that all parties to the transaction are performing their obligations unless the trustee has actual knowledge of an event of default.

The trustee must also have the right to retire or resign its appointment. Needless to say, the trustee may also be removed.

21.4.4 Noteholders

The question of who really invests in eurobonds has long been a subject of speculation. Even if we knew who was holding what in Cedel, Euroclear or in a custody account elsewhere, this would obviously still be no indicator of the true ownership of those assets. Although paying agents in Luxembourg, Switzerland or elsewhere certainly see their share of private holders presenting coupons for payment, it appears that the majority are being held by institutional investors.

What this adds up to for the trustee is that ordinarily we do not and cannot know the identity of our beneficiaries. In any case, it is not the task of the trustee to address itself to the individual needs of noteholders but to the best interests of the group as a whole.

This can also lead to a situation which noteholders may find rather perverse, that when situations arise which provoke questions or comment, trustees may not be able to respond in detail, even in the face of definitive proof of holdings. The reason is that a trustee could be in breach of its duty to the group as a whole if it were to discuss issues with individual noteholders who made contact and so put them in an advantageous position. It could also be accused of passing on inside information.

21.4.5 Bondholder meetings

We have mentioned that,while there are circumstances in which trustees can agree to modifications of the terms of an issue or to waive breaches, the corollary is that if the trustee considers that such a decision is not within its powers, it will be necessary to call a meeting of noteholders.

The trust deed should contain conditions under which meetings may be called by the issuer or the trustee or requisitioned by a proportion of noteholders. It has become traditional for more detailed conditions applicable to meetings to be included in a schedule to the trust deed. There are four underlying principles for meetings: reasonable advance notice, clarity with respect to the issues to be raised, adequate opportunities to vote whether in person or by proxy and recognition that certain matters (such as deferment of interest) are so fundamental that for resolutions to be passed, both the quorum and the voting pass-mark are set at specially high levels.

So why the need for a trustee if questions of major importance have to be agreed with the noteholders in any case?

Rather than viewing noteholder meetings as a burdensome necessity, they should be viewed as a valuable facility. The issuer has a predetermined means of meeting with investors at times of change or crisis.

The economic importance of the eurobond markets has been widely acknowledged, not least by the European Community, which itself has also upheld the principle of bondholder representation in directives of admission to listing. Without such representation issuers are open to attack by individual holders, even for minor defaults, which may also have an adverse effect on the interests of the majority of holders.

In the case of trust deeds governed by English law, as a noteholder representative is not entrenched in law, it is only through the use of trustees that this can be achieved. In other European countries, such as Luxembourg and Switzerland, there are, embodied within their civil law codes, variations on the theme of bondholder representatives although the English trustee concept has no direct equivalent.

Nevertheless, one question remains. Whichever governing law or method is selected, there can be no guarantee of mutual recognition as between states. As this runs to the heart of who will be deemed to be beneficially entitled to assets, if a trust is not held effective, this could have a serious and adverse impact on the basic structure of a securitised issue.

While it is likely that trusts and similar devices will be mutually upheld between common law countries, the current position as between European countries including member states of the EC is uncertain. It is interesting to note that, pursuant to the Convention on Mutual Recognition of Trusts, France, traditionally an opponent to the trust system, has introduced a draft trust law.

In relation to EC member states it is not entirely clear whether trust or investor representation services are included within the ambit of the EC Banking and Investment Services Directive (in draft form at the time of writing). The inclusion of such services would certainly facilitate the provision and mutual recognition of the different systems throughout the EC and so assist in removing any existing doubts.

21.5 THE TRUSTEE AS NEGOTIATOR

21.5.1 Lead managers

Asset securitisation is a huge subject and the first debt issue by any company is likely to be difficult and expensive. Repeat issues are, at least in theory, cheaper and easier. If there is one over-riding principle we have learned, however, it is this: Try to plan the process like a military operation. Determine a strategy and keep each group to it.

And whose task is this? Generally, the lead manager or arranging bank will act as campaign manager. It is helpful if the approach of each group is agreed early in the process, preferably in a face-to-face meeting. Progress should be reviewed at regular intervals to ensure that the amount and type of work equates with original expectations. This will also provide the opportunity to adapt the strategy where unforeseen problems and changes in the structure of the deal demand this.

This is all about time and money. The best management is no guarantee of success but it should at least help to avoid greater than planned uses of both of these commodities.

Hitherto it has not been widely expected that trustees may actually want to negotiate aspects of the deal itself. Attempts to do so might be treated with surprise and extreme caution. We may hear the argument that investors who buy the deal do so on a take-it-or-leave-it basis and would not be able to complain to the trustee if, having taken it, some of the terms emerge as not to their liking.

We agree that there are many aspects of a transaction which the trustee is not in a position to negotiate. However, two main issues must be of concern to the trustee. First, if it is apparent that practically or logistically, the deal will not work in some way. It is in the issuer's interest that the trustee should point this out and, if possible, suggest an alternative approach. If not, the flaw is likely to lead to a request to the trustee to approve amendments after the deal has closed—more on this later. Second, aspects of the structure may run counter to the way the trustee perceives its duty in accordance with the basic principles, two of which are particularly relevant.

The duty to ensure that the trustee does not put itself in a position where it will be compromised between different interests is discussed further below.

The duty to take reasonable care arguably extends back to the negotiation stage of an issue in that certain types of information may require to be specially disclosed or highlighted in the terms and conditions or offering circular. This could be, for example, legal or practical restrictions affecting special noteholder rights, or particular aspects relating to the status of the issuer. In these circumstances, if such special mention is not forthcoming, it may be incumbent on the trustee to insist on their inclusion.

21.5.2 Lawyers

The relationship between trustees and their lawyers for securitised issues is an interesting one. While the paying agent will usually be advised by the lead manager's lawyer, the trustee must have independent advice. However, it has become quite usual with respect to eurobonds for the trustee to instruct the same firm as that advising the lead manager, but a different partner. The trustee should never instruct the firm advising the issuer.

In London, as might be expected, the leading law firms have emerged as experts in the field of Eurobonds and securitisation. Generally, these firms have groups experienced in advising lead managers and may also have specialist trust partners.

In addition, it will usually be necessary to involve legal advisers with respect to the security, whether this is property or other assets, in the location of those assets to ensure that valid security interests are obtained and potential enforcement problems identified.

If the assets are overseas, the need for full co-ordination between the lawyers advising the trustee cannot be over-emphasised.

The working relationship which trustees establish with their lawyers is a crucial element in bringing a securitised issue to a successful conclusion. Trustees should ensure that their lawyers are briefed on points of principle which the trustee will have an interest in negotiating in respect of its own or the noteholders' rights. The problem is that there is often a fine line between these areas and aspects which the trustee must accept as part of the deal.

The sheer number of participants in a deal can also give rise to another problem. In the face of pressures to make visible progress in constructing an issue, it is nevertheless vital to allow sufficient time for comments to be made on draft documents, assuming, for their part, that commenting lawyers and their clients also return comments in a timely way. We do not underestimate the difficulty of co-ordinating this task, again it is probably a case of an ideal world versus the practical reality.

The trustee's need to take advice from lawyers, not to mention other experts, may not end when an issue, particularly a securitised issue has closed. The more work that is done before launching an issue based around the question 'Does this actually work in practice?', then generally speaking, the less a trustee will have to take advice and use up the SPV's precious profits in paying for it.

21.6 CONFLICT OF INTEREST

Before even accepting a trust it is imperative that the potential trustee considers the existence of any conflicts of interest. In the same way that lawyers may not advise opposing sides—and still claim that they acted in the best interests of each client—so debt trustees must not allow circumstances to interfere with their overriding duty to the noteholders or lenders.

Two aspects of a structure may be relevant here, the special purpose vehicle itself, and the credit enhancement technique whereby the issue is created as a senior/subordinated note issue.

21.6.1 The special purpose vehicle

The trustee shareholder acts as the owner of the special purpose vehicle (SPV) and may also provide some or all of its directors. It should not, in our view, be the same as the debt trustee.

Still, certain trustees may agree to take on both roles. The argument may be that as the issuer is only a shell company, the debt trustee is being put in a position of greater control in actually owning the SPV.

At this point, it may be useful to refer to the Report of the Committee on Company Law Amendment of 1946 (also known as the Cohen report):

> It has further been suggested to us that no person should be eligible to act as trustee for debenture-holders who has interests liable to conflict with those of the debenture-holders. For example, directors of companies are sometimes trustees for the debenture-holders. Though a director may himself be the principal holder of the debentures and is likely to have a better understanding of the finances of the company than anyone else, his duty to the company may be to dissuade debenture-holders as far as possible from exercising any rights in a manner inconvenient to the company though in the interests of the debenture holders.[6]

It would clearly be very difficult for the trustee itself to wear both hats and yet effectively discharge its obligations to each group. The position would only be exacerbated if the trustee had also supplied directors of the SPV. If the debt trustee is in a position of conflict, when the time comes to enforce an issue, or take action against the directors he may be liable to severe criticism.

The fact that the SPV issuer is only a shell company does not affect this view for it is not just the activities of the mortgage servicer which would jeopardise the future of the SPV.

Management of the SPV

The manager may be appointed under a contract constituting the latter as an agent of the SPV. Typically, cash may be received from the mortgage servicer and the manager will invest it or apply it to payment of interest and redemption of notes. The servicer should account for funds remitted to the SPV and the SPV's manager should account for what it does with those funds.

Mismanagement or loss of that cash in any way should become apparent at the next point when it becomes necessary to fund interest payments or redemptions. Failure to pay on the due date or within any grace period would, of course, constitute an event of default.

The trustee must ensure that it has a clear understanding of the methods which will be applied to dealing with available cash including long-term investments. The money should either be invested with or guaranteed by a good quality credit institution independent of the issuer or related group companies. At the same time, care should be taken to avoid qualifications impossible of achievement. This will only be a rod for the trustee's back if it is ever asked to consider alternatives for the debt trustee may have to make a virtual credit assessment of the proposed alternative.

Before creating an SPV it is essential to consider what you are going to need from it. Primarily, it may be the vehicle through which profits are taken out by the securitising entity. It is also essential, however, to consider the tax and regulatory position which is required or which will result. In fact, as far as UK mortgages are concerned, the SPV has to be approved by the Inland Revenue for MIRAS purposes, in order that mortgagors within the SPV's portfolio can continue to pay their interest net of basic rate tax. This in turn may depend on the nationality of the company and the shares trustee and consequently determine the likely candidates for the job.

Depending on the location chosen, the shares trustee should be able to assist with information related to the administration of the SPV: incorporation and other up-front or annual costs, registered offices and administration, annual reports or returns, local legal advice, accounting and financial reporting not to mention providers of these services.

In order to seal its appointment, the shares trustee will usually execute a declaration of trust in respect of the shares. It may also be given a floating charge over the assets of the vehicle and consequently, should be asked to confirm periodically that this has not crystallised; in other words, that there has not been an event which has caused the transformation of the floating charge into a fixed charge attaching to specific assets.

As mentioned above, the shares trustee may also be asked to provide one or more directors of the SPV. In addition to paying the fees of those directors, it may be necessary to provide insurance cover for their liability as directors.

21.6.2 Senior/subordinated structures

Securitisation can be an expensive process. Partly in an effort to find more cost-effective methods, issues have evolved incorporating both senior and subordinated debt where, in the event of a shortfall of funds and usually in return for a higher return on the investment, the subordinated level bears the loss in priority to the senior level.

On the face of it, this must fly in the face of the general rule that, in theory, trustees should not act for different levels of debt. However, by developing techniques to avoid (as far as possible) compromising the rights of note-holders at each level, the market practice is for the trustee to do just this. Certainly, special attention must be given to disclosure and protective language in the documents. Despite everyone's best intentions and efforts, however, it may not be possible to avoid the political or moral fall-out if one of these issues goes wrong, particularly where the subordinated issue has not been retained by a company 'related' to the issuer.

At a conference in 1989, Bruce Carnegie-Brown stated:

> If B-Bond investors once suffer a delay in payment of interest on the due date, it is likely that the perceived risk-return equation will change dramatically, rendering further B-bond issues uneconomic.[7]

21.7 THE TRUSTEE AS MONITOR OF THE ISSUE

Trustees have at least an implied duty to monitor issues as part of their duty of care. Generally, the trustee cannot control the business activities of issuers provided they do not impact on the terms of any trust deeds in which the trustee has an interest. By tradition, therefore, trust deeds contain exculpatory language to limit the circumstances in which the trustee is expected to know about or take action in the event of default by the issuer. It is acknowledged, however, that it would be difficult for trustees to claim immunity in circumstances where, clearly, they should have been but were not aware of problems or where the response had been less than diligent.

What standard of knowledge and understanding should be expected? Again, traditionally trustees have not claimed to offer expert financial monitoring as their own resources and fees for standard eurobond trustees would not be commensurate with that type of service.

For a number of reasons, trustees have had to review the way they do their business.

First, trustees now work on a wider range of corporate finance and capital markets products including securitised bond issues than ever before. It is simply not possible to work on such products effectively without a thorough understanding of each transaction.

Second, trustees have come in for a variety of criticisms during the last two years. For example, in the US, according to reports, trustees of bonds which may have been sold in breach of tax laws are being sued in respect of their alleged failure to scrutinise the terms of the bonds prior to their being issued. This is not the only outstanding case of this kind. In Australia, the trustees of certain unit trusts were reported to be facing potential legal action following the failure of the unit trust and appear subsequently to have decided to go into voluntary receivership. In the euromarkets, trustees have received criticism for apparent failure to call issues following an event of default.

It must be said that much of what is published reflects a certain lack of understanding of the role of the trustee. Suggestions have been made that given the number of appointments which individual trustees are supposed to monitor, there should be some sort of co-operation with the credit analysis departments of major banks or that fees (to be reimbursed by the issuer) should be paid to the rating agencies to reconfirm their initial ratings on an annual basis.

The problem with the first of these suggestions is the potential for conflicts of interest since the credit analysis department of a bank will invariably be advising the corporate finance arm of that bank. The rating agencies idea does have merit and the relationship with rating agencies is discussed further below. It is understood that with regard to securitised issues, the rating agencies maintain a high level of surveillance in any case.

Trustees have had to step up to the challenge of monitoring complex issues and performing more functions than ever before, but like everyone else, corporate trustees are in business to make a profit. Assuming there is a way round the conflict problem identified above, if trustees are either to provide ever more sophisticated monitoring or insist on suitable arrangements being made, it needs to become more readily accepted that trustees are justified in making such demands and must expect to be paid appropriately.

21.7.1 Rating agencies

In the past the identity of the trustee for bond issues was not necessarily a matter of concern to the rating agencies (essentially Standard & Poor's and Moody's). Mortgage-backed securities have produced a noticeable shift in this attitude for the very reason that, due to the complexity of such issues, they considered it important to satisfy themselves that there were trustees with the necessary capability.

It has become apparent that both trustees and rating agencies are likely to have similar interests with respect to issues and standards to be maintained by participants. Consequently, it is both essential and mutually beneficial to establish contact and maintain good lines of communication. While each group owes a duty of confidentiality to its clients, there are often provisions in issue documents whereby trustees must inform the rating agencies of events or information where they could have an adverse effect on the rating.

Of course, the rating agencies are also concerned with credit assessment, including the initial and periodic examination of projected cash flows compared with actual performance and the reassessment of economic and other risk factors which may affect the performance of the issue. Their methods for reviewing and assessing parties such as the mortgage servicer provide an informative guide for trustees.

21.8 THE TRUSTEE AS PROTECTOR OF THE SECURITY

21.8.1 The trustee's security interests

It is a fundamental responsibility of the trustee for mortgage-backed securities to ensure that valid security interests are perfected and maintained. As a general rule, the methods for taking valid and enforceable security interests depend on their situation. Legal advice must be taken in the location of the assets.

In England the trustee should take a floating charge over all the assets of the issuer. The effect of doing so for the trustee are reviewed below in relation to enforcement of the issue.

Apart from the floating charge, the trustee must acquire rights by way of security to or assignments of all relevant and related assets, including the underlying mortgages (preferably first, fixed legal or equitable charges), insurance policies (pool policies and those related to the individual mortgages), bank accounts and future receipts from the Inland Revenue.

Typically, the issuer will have acquired the mortgages from the originator pursuant to a sale agreement and may also have taken the legal benefit of the mortgages.

It is more likely that, pursuant to a deed of charge, the issuer will grant to the trustee equitable rather than legal charges and the trustee should recognise the consequences which may flow from this.

An equitable charge is basically an enforceable interest that has not been perfected or completed as a security interest by means of registration at the Land Registries. An added complication is that not all English land has been brought within the registered as opposed to unregistered system to date. In time the former will be the only system in operation but until then, possession of title deeds in respect of unregistered land continues to be sufficient.

There are two consequences. First, the trustee must be ready to take action to transform its equitable charges into legal charges within a very short time-frame, should this ever become necessary. Until it has done so, it may not be able to take direct action in relation to the underlying mortgages. The registration process can take many weeks for a single mortgage and the trustee might be completing these formalities for up to 2,000 mortgages or more. Second, an equitable charge carries the risk that security interests other than those of the trustee could acquire prior ranking.

In contrast, legal charges obviously carry the advantage that registration formalities are complete but they do mean that the trustee will have at least minimal involvement in the servicing process. The servicer will usually have been granted a power of attorney but this should be strictly for the purpose of facilitating routine processing. As legal charges mean that the trustee appears in the Land Charges Register (and consequently the trustees interest is revealed in the course of title searches), any dealings in the property which affect the mortgage, such as redemptions or further advances, may be referred to the trustee, who should ensure that such enquiries are passed on to the servicer without delay.

Another possible area of concern for our purposes is the risk of fraud or mistake, perhaps by an individual employee of the servicer, or on the part of any solicitors or valuers involved with the mortgage pool. Most servicing companies, and for that matter, participants in MBS, are highly aware of this risk and carry some level of employee fidelity and negligence insurance, although this may not be a complete answer to the problem. Solicitors should be covered under the Law Society professional indemnity scheme and valuers are also likely to carry professional indemnity insurance. It is also possible to insure against mortgagors granting a second charge over the property prior to obtaining a further advance from the originator. The benefit of this should be extended to the issuer to provide cover for events prior to the closing of the issue. This will be all the more relevant where there is provision for further advances in relation to mortgages which will return to the issuer's pool or substitution of mortgages into the pool.

21.8.2 Credit enhancements

Apart from senior/subordinated structures, the other major form of credit enhancement is insurance and guarantees. Based on past structures the selection of one or another has meant very different emphasis on the role of the trustee.

Insurance

Pool insurance arrangements are likely to cover three main risks: shortfalls in receipts as a result of delinquent mortgagors, shortfalls as a result of a failure to set a sufficiently high mortgage rate compared to the rate on the notes and shortfall in sale proceeds following enforcement of mortgages.

The trustee must satisfy itself as to what insurance cover is available and who is providing it. It must receive full reports on any claims made and if the issuer asks the trustee to consider changes, it is vital that insurance cover can be confirmed in the light of such changes if approved. An event of default should be triggered if the insurer fails to pay.

There may be a catch to pool insurance. In relation to enforcement proceeds from individual mortgages, it is usually designed to pay out when a loss can be quantified. This will only be possible when the underlying property has been sold. At times of high interest rates, experience has shown that it becomes much harder to sell properties. Unless the parent company of the issuer has an obligation to repurchase defaulted mortgages, the sale process could take a very long time.

The trustee should check that repossessed, vacant properties are being properly managed and that suitable efforts are being made to achieve sales, including dropping the price within reasonable margins.

Guarantees

Issues guaranteed by large American monoline insurance companies have become a feature of the euromarkets. The nature of such guarantees may give rise to highly detailed examinations of all aspects of the issues and potential risks, and to a high level of surveillance by the guarantor for the life of the issue. These issues tend to be structured so that there is always a defined controlling party or beneficiary, and this will invariably be the guarantor unless it defaults on its obligations.

It is also a typical feature of this form of guarantee that if circumstances, such as a default by the issuer, give rise to claims on the guarantor, the issue is not necessarily accelerated, the guarantee being for scheduled payments of interest and principal. It is as if the trustee is, in effect, answerable to one noteholder, for the guarantor will inherit the relevant coupons or bonds and thus stand in the shoes of the holders *vis-à-vis* the issuer with respect to any payments made pursuant to the guarantee. It is consequently essential to maintain a high level of communication with such guarantors as they may maintain a specific interest in the performance of the trustee. Trustees must ensure that any proposed changes to the structure of an issue will not affect the validity of such guarantees.

21.8.3 Servicing the security

The three main functions involved with servicing mortgages are: the servicing itself or administration, the custody of title and other property documents and the provision of banking services (collection, processing and disbursement of funds).

One of the first tasks of the trustee, therefore, is to find out who will be performing these functions and establish contact, certainly with the servicer and the deeds custodian.

The next stage is to take the earliest possible opportunity to make the first of what should be periodic visits to their operational units. Even though the lawyers and the lead manager will probably carry out due diligence investigations, the trustee must gain its own understanding of the methods which will be used by each of these parties.

Depending on the location of assets, it may be necessary for the trustee to appoint a collateral agent to maintain on-the-spot supervision of the servicer and other functions. This should not relieve the trustee of the necessity to make its own checks during due diligence visits.

The servicer

The servicer is likely to be the same company which originated the mortgages either for its own account or as a service to an external mortgage funder. While the servicer will be appointed by the issuer under contract, the profile of administrative duties will probably remain unchanged and should include:

- routine duties such as setting the mortgage rates, monitoring collection of mortgage and insurance payments and processing storage of documents and retrieval from solicitors if necessary;
- special duties such as dealing with arrears according to specified procedures, taking enforcement action if necessary and making claims on the pool insurer.

To this end it is appropriate to carry out a reasonably detailed review very similar to many aspects covered by the rating agencies to obtain a profile of each servicer; aspects such as the adminstrative hierarchy, computer systems, loan origination and credit approval process, qualifications and training of underwriting and arrears staff and auditing procedures.

It is particularly important to be vigilant if there is ever a system upgrade or replacement to ensure that the integrity of the data is maintained. Trustees may consider that they need the power to step in and set a mortgage rate where it has otherwise been set at too low a level.

Generally, the vast majority of reports received by the trustee will be generated by the servicer. Clearly the most important aspects are the level of arrears and the action being taken and sources and application of funds.

Trustees should be given power to remove the servicer in the event that it is unable to perform its duties efficiently.

As the computer systems are likely to be central to the servicing function, there must be a positive duty on the servicer to maintain its software licences and the trustee should try to ensure that it will have a direct right to assume the contracts with the software company. Spare sets of computer data tapes must be stored off-site in appropriate facilities for magnetic media and the tapes should be updated and rotated on a daily basis.

Stand-by servicer

The ideal situation is to have a contract in place from the outset with a servicer who will step in on short notice either to retrieve and service the mortgage portfolio or potentially takeover and run the facilities of the original servicer until a more permanent solution is worked out. Fees for such an arrangement would be paid by the issuer.

Whether or not issues are made with the benefit of such arrangements, trustees should maintain close touch with the servicing industry and may find it helpful to make contingency arrangements with specific servicers. To this end, resources are probably more important than specific compatibility of systems.

In our view, it is not a trustee function to accept the ultimate obligation to service mortgages. The obligation should rather be that they will use their best efforts, if need be, to appoint a replacement servicer.

The custodian

The concept in the UK of registered title of land has lessened the value which must be placed on the possession of title deeds relating to a property covered by the system. Even though the vast majority of mortgages in a securitised portfolio are likely to be in respect of registered land, it remains appropriate to hold the certificate of title, the title deeds and other documents in safe custody. The deeds store must physically conform to high specifications in terms of size, shelving, fire and security precautions. Procedures for acceptance and release of documents and record-keeping in the deeds store should also be of a high standard.

It is not obligatory in every case, but may be advisable for the custodian to be a separate company, independent of the originator and servicer. Theories behind this include the minimisation of the risk of fraudulent or possible negligent removal of deeds packets and the need to facilitate retrieval of the deeds by the trustee or prevent their retrieval by the servicer following its removal or an event of default.

Trustees should be provided with details of procedures applied as between the servicer and the custodian and the portfolio deeds should be physically stored together and separately from other deeds stored at the same location.

Periodic deeds location reports will put the trustee in a position to locate deeds if necessary but routinely, exception reports are more useful in highlighting deeds not currently held by the custodian together with their location, period of time at that location, and action being taken to secure return if overdue.

The trustee should, of course, be able to remove the custodian for inadequate service but it may be of rather more concern that the custodian's own resignation, becomes effective after a specified period of notice. If this happened it could be the responsibility of the trustee to take immediate steps to find and assess an alternative.

The trustee will, in any case, have to assess both new premises and procedures if deeds are ever relocated, and should seek confirmation of adequate transportation and insurance arrangements.

Bank accounts

In the UK the flow of funds in relation to a mortgage-backed security is likely to be along the following lines. Individual monthly mortgage payments are claimed from the bank accounts of each mortgagor using the direct debit system and, provided claims are honoured, funds will be transferred to the collection account of the mortgage servicer. Funds in respect of the issuer's mortgages are then identified, probably manually, and transferred to the issuer's account, which may be at the same or a different bank. Principal repayments, where mortgages have been redeemed, are also credited to the collection account and thence to the issuer's account.

The manager of the issuer's funds will arrange for their investment, ensuring that sufficient interest monies are available for each interest payment date and that redemption monies are applied, if necessary, to redemption of notes. This is always remembering that there should be a funding mechanism in place to provide for shortfalls in monthly receipts or principal payments. First, from the trustee's perspective, the direct debiting of the issuer's funds straight into its own account would cut out a potential source of mistakes, difficulty in identification of funds, misapplication of funds, or even fraud, all of which may contribute to delay in receipt or non-receipt of funds by the issuer. Second, while the trustee should be entitled to receive copies of bank statements for both sets of accounts, it is realistic to expect the trustee to monitor receipts and flows of funds on a current basis using these alone.

In order that noteholders receive their money on each interest payment date, what is required is that:

- all funds collected from mortgagors reach the issuer promptly;
- the servicer efficiently identifies funds not received, makes insurance claims accordingly and the insurance payments reach the issuer's account promptly.

It may be preferable for the trustee to be provided with monthly schedules of anticipated payments together with information on funds not received for previous months clearly related to insurance claims made in respect of such funds. Bank statements should confirm the figures in respect of funds credited.

21.9 THE TRUSTEE AS ENFORCER

Baudelaire said a trust was a financial speculation. This is about as far from the English legal definition as it is possible to go but in looking at the question of enforcement we now have to go some way down the path, at least of speculation.

The various forms of credit enhancement with which most English law mortgage-backed securities have been endowed should go a long way to avoiding losses being incurred by noteholders. It should be emphasised that the trustee's response would be completely dependent on the actual events at the time and assuming the trustee was aware of them, these would be closely and continuously reviewed with the benefit of legal, financial or other advice, as appropriate.

Let us first look at the contractual basis for action. Events of default will be found in the terms and conditions of the issue and should include:

- failure by the issuer to pay interest or principal;
- the issuer or insurer/guarantor stopping payment, ceasing business or being wound-up;
- the issuer, servicer or manager of the issuer SPV failing to perform their contractual obligations.

In the case of the contractual obligations mentioned, the trustee may have to give time for the situation to be rectified, say one month.

In all cases except the issuer's failure to pay, the trustee may have to certify that the event is materially prejudicial and then separately make a decision to 'call' the issue; that is, in the usual official language, declare the notes immediately due and repayable. Additionally, the trustee may have to call the issue if requested by the holders of fixed percentage of the outstanding notes (perhaps 20 to 25 per cent) or directed by an extraordinary resolution. Such events, or the charged property being considered otherwise in jeopardy, may prompt the trustee to perfect any equitable security interests into legal interests.

Remedies available to the trustee should include:

- the appointment of a receiver;
- an action for the debt or the sale of the security;
- taking possession of the charged property.

A disadvantage associated with the last of these is that responsibility for the mortgages would then fall to the trustee which is unlikely to possess the operational systems to manage them.

Additionally, if the trustee holds a floating charge over the assets of the issuer, it will be notified of any application to appoint an administrator and have the opportunity to appoint an administrative receiver. Both procedures are contained in the Insolvency Act 1986. Administration is often likened to 'Chapter 11' in the US, which permits companies to file for a court order which effectively gives them protection against creditors and a breathing space to allow reorganisation. In view of this impact, the trustee might be well advised to appoint an administrative receiver. However, given that we are dealing with an issuer which is a vehicle company and has as its sole purpose the issue of the notes and the ownership of the underlying assets, it may be considered unlikely that the issuer would find itself in this position or that the issue would be in default as a result of problems isolated to it alone.

Perhaps one of the biggest risks is a failure by the servicer. If the servicer was failing to perform adequately (for instance, not pursuing arrears diligently), the most appropriate course of action might be to move the servicing function of the issuer's mortgages to another company as quickly as possible. On top of this, however, an audit of the pool at this time might reveal incomplete records which would have to be reconstructed, perhaps using bank statements or even information provided by each mortgagor. Further, it might also be clear that many mortgages were seriously in arrears or in default.

It is also possible that an administrator might be appointed to the servicer by one of its creditors, other than the issuer.

All in all, careful judgement would need to be applied in assessing whether at one end of the scale, a replacement servicer was sufficient to cure the problem or, at the other, that it had become necessary to call the notes and appoint a receiver.

Apart from the effect of the general economic climate at the time, it could well prove difficult to sell a portfolio of mortgages with incomplete servicing records, not to mention a high proportion of delinquencies. We should not, of course, forget that it might be necessary to enforce the defaulted, underlying mortgages.

This brings us back to our starting point, that as trustees, while we earnestly hope for the success of each issue, we must also be prepared for failure. Yet even in failure, a trustee should provide a flexible response to problems, whatever they may be, in looking for a solution in the best interests of the noteholders.

1 Lepaulle, Pierre. *Traite theorique et pratique des trusts en droit interne, en droit fiscal et en droit international*, Paris 1932, p. 113, cited in *Laws of Trusts*, Professor D. Hayton. Sweet and Maxwell: London, 1989.

2 (1885) 30 Ch.D 490.

3 (1952) 2 All ER 1054. Butterworths.

4 The above extract from the Admission of Securities to Listing as amended at April 1991 is reproduced by kind permission of the London Stock Exchange.

5 Goodall, Charles. Eurobonds issued with the benefit of Trust Deeds. *IFLR* 19, February 1983.

Hayton, Professor D. Developing the law of trusts for the 21st century. Inaugural lecture, 5 May 1989.

Herbert, Anthony. Why have a trustee for a eurobond issue? (1987) I JI BL 48.

Landau, Robert I. *Corporate Trust Administration and Management*. Columbia University Press: 1985.

Smart, A. M. H. Fiscal Agency or Trust Deed? *IFLR* 18, December 1982.

Watkins, James. How to reschedule a bond issue. *Euromoney*, January 1983, p. 103.

Wood, Philip R. *The Law and Practice of International Finance*. Sweet & Maxwell: London, 1980.

The Law of Subordinated Debt, Sweet & Maxwell: London, 1990.

6 HMSO.

7 Carnegie-Brown, Bruce. Cost-effective Structures and Markets. Speech at conference on Mortgage Funding and Securitisation, Institute for International Research, 26 January 1989.

Index

The following titles in the *Finance and Capital Markets* Series are also published by The Macmillan Press Limited:

Off Balance Sheet Finance ISBN 0-333-56041-8

Written in the light of the Accounting Standards Board, this book discusses the various financing practices which have grown up over recent years and explains how they will be affected by the new accounting standard being developed by the ASB. It will provide an expert analysis of the accounting rules which will govern the treatment of off balance sheet finance when the standard comes into force.

March 1992 £95

International Securities Lending December 1991 £75 ISBN 0-333-55922-3

Risk Management with Derivatives March 1992 £75 ISBN 0-333-55924-X

Options Explained December 1991 £75 ISBN 0-333-56911-3

Bund Options December 1991 £75 ISBN 0-333-56910-5

Bunds and Bund Futures November 1991 £75 ISBN 0-333-56987-3

For fuller information on these and other titles in the *Finance and Capital Markets* Series, or to order copies, please call **0256 29242** or write to **Carla Jones, Globe Book Services Ltd, Macmillan, Houndmills, Basingstoke, Hampshire RG21 2XS.**